Language and Nationality

Language and Nationality

Social inferences, cultural differences,
and linguistic misconceptions

Pietro Bortone

BLOOMSBURY ACADEMIC
LONDON • NEW YORK • OXFORD • NEW DELHI • SYDNEY

BLOOMSBURY ACADEMIC
Bloomsbury Publishing Plc
50 Bedford Square, London, WC1B 3DP, UK
1385 Broadway, New York, NY 10018, USA
29 Earlsfort Terrace, Dublin 2, Ireland

BLOOMSBURY, BLOOMSBURY ACADEMIC and the Diana logo
are trademarks of Bloomsbury Publishing Plc

First published in Great Britain 2022
Paperback edition published in 2023

Cover photograph by Pietro Bortone

A catalogue record for this book is available from the British Library.

A catalog record for this book is available from the Library of Congress.

ISBN: HB: 978-1-3500-7163-6
        PB: 978-1-3500-7164-3
      ePDF: 978-1-3500-7166-7
     eBook: 978-1-3500-7165-0

Typeset by Integra Software Services Pvt. Ltd.

To find out more about our authors and books visit www.bloomsbury.com
and sign up for our newsletters.

Contents

Contents vii

Preface

This book looks at the links commonly presumed to exist between language and nationality. The inspiration for the book came to me while I was doing fieldwork in Asia among a linguistic community whose identification with its country was questioned by its fellow citizens on account of its use of the language of a neighbouring country. There were groundless assertions that such community's retention of another tongue indicated that it was harbouring, seditiously, a different national identity, a different religion, and a secret loyalty to a different state. That particular case, however, is not what I will treat here. In this volume, instead of focusing on one particular linguistic minority, or nation, or historical incident, I want to present a bigger picture, and help those interested in the whole topic of language and nationality see why people tend to think about these matters the way they do.

The following pages therefore explore how people draw a host of value-laden inferences from the way we speak (or write) – often accurately, but by no means always; how their stance towards different languages and linguistic styles varies sharply and why; how language is regarded and used as a group marker – though not necessarily; and how languages differ significantly among themselves and may subtly reflect social and cultural differences, and yet do not inescapably dictate our worldview. The latter part of the book highlights and critiques the widespread, if implicit, perception that nationalities are partitions merely inherent in humankind; it therefore retraces the creation of national states, and the development and promotion of national 'identities', noting the role given to languages in that process. It then analyses the creation of standardized and national forms for languages, and the effect that it has had on our perceptions of languages, of nations, and of individual speakers. Finally, the book discusses the way in which languages and nationalities are frequently equated in public discourse, and assesses the twin assumptions that the use of a language indicates a given nationality or national identity, and that, conversely, having a given nationality or national identity entails, or should entail, having a given language.

It is clear that, by using language, we do put labels on ourselves in manifold ways. Some of those ways are explicit and willful: we introduce ourselves, refer to ourselves, and describe ourselves, using language. Some other ways are indirect or covert, but just as consequential: from the particular language we speak and from the way we speak (and write) it, people feel able to build a rich biographical, physical, social, psychological, dispositional, political, and moral picture of us, regardless of whether we are aware of this or not, we want them to do so, and we agree with their conclusions. The book therefore starts, in Chapter 1, by reviewing one use of language that is assumed to be fortuitous and insignificant but from which others draw essential information about somebody: personal names. Names and surnames are usually unchosen by their bearer and semantically opaque; as a result, although they are recognized as important means of identification, they have been described by several scholars as being devoid of real meaning. But, upon close observation, we can see that they are not, and that they are not even really considered to be so: strangers who hear or see our names and surnames read a lot into them. And, as we discuss in Chapter 2, even aspects of our use of language that explicitly and deliberately convey information about us, such as our ordinary conversations or writings – when we report our own thoughts, feelings, opinions, activities, and experiences – provide or suggest, covertly and unwittingly, also additional information about us. How we speak or write is assumed to signal or reveal our class, ethnicity, age, gender, character, and more besides. And this raises another question that we shall consider, since it is relevant to the issue of language and nationality but also to any language-based 'identity': how much of a person's linguistic quirks are innate, and how much they are, instead, cultural conventions that we learn. Even more relevant to our concerns here is the fact, which we shall likewise analyse, that others *judge* the language, dialect, style, or accent that we use and, consequentially, judge us too: they have views about language which reflect not only their linguistic and aesthetic dislikes but also their social and political antipathies. Their views have concrete repercussions in the way they see us and treat us. It is generally the case, as we review in Chapter 3, that language is employed as a social border to divide 'us' from 'them' – another fact important for the question of nationality. However, in truth, our use of language, and the image of ourselves that we choose to project through our language use, do not stay the same across different situations. On this point, as we shall see, much can be learnt from bilinguals, and from language learners. Their experience brings into relief also the question, which we consider in Chapter 4, of whether languages can really be considered merely different codes through which one can say the same thing. Many academics have been eager to affirm that which language one speaks matters little because languages are equivalent, of equal complexity and, deep down, similar; but all this, though politically well-intentioned, can be questioned. Languages display very different grammatical features and many untranslatable words. And, as we observe in Chapter 5, they also have some words and concepts that reflect, and arguably teach, a particular culture. Furthermore, the use of each language is governed by specific social conventions which one learns together with the language, and those too reflect and promote a certain outlook. Such facts may raise the understandable concern that communities who adopt the language of a politically and economically stronger country unconsciously and uncritically adopt also the culture of that country. We shall, therefore, also appraise, in Chapter 6, the popular theory that our language (assuming that we have only one) lays down the limits of our thinking. That theory was, for a long time, automatically assumed to be true, and then assumed to be nonsense, and we review pertinent evidence. This is relevant to the question of nationality also because, if language does dictate people's thinking style, and if nationality comes with a particular language, different nationalities should be expected to be unable of seeing eye to eye.

In the second part of the book, the focus moves onto the second topic: nationality. There is a widespread perception that nations correspond to natural divisions of the human race, that they are each inherently imbued with their own distinct 'national character', and therefore that a distinct collective national identity, of which language is a key part, arises naturally. It is worth considering, then, what makes a nation, and the role played by language in the making of a nation – especially by the recognized national language that many a country has. Having explored all of this, at the end of the book, we shall be able to see better how and why languages and nationalities are often equated, and whether or not they should be. So, in Chapter 7, we start by looking at the concept of *nation*, and briefly observe the history that led to the 'Age of Nationalism'; we trace the development of nation-based states, and of the ideology that makes states of that kind normative; and we consider the consequences of the spread both of the nation state model, and of the view that nationalities are natural, inevitable groupings. We also note, in Chapter 8, that a national identity is actively taught, and we consider how language contributes to this: we look at the performative power of declaring that a nation exists, at the importance of writing, and at the use of literature and of historiography. A national language, as we discuss in Chapter 9, has often been developed in tandem with a nation state, promoted prescriptively through schools, media, and officialdom. Given that the variety of language selected as the national tongue has usually been the variety spoken by a particular class and region, we also observe that its selection is both an effect and a cause of class division within the nation. That said, one must, as we do in the rest of that chapter, acknowledge the benefits and advantages of having a standard common language. However, as we argue in Chapter 10, one needs also to be aware of the prejudicial effects of having a language with that kind of status. One such effect – not pointed out frequently enough – is that our very perception of what languages are, and of what they are like individually, gets distorted, because the diffusion, the orthography, the lexicon, and the grammatical features of languages have often been artificially changed in order to affirm a distinct and homogeneous national identity. Furthermore, the promotion of a standardized national language has typically resulted in a diminished respect and tolerance for linguistic minorities and for regional variations. For these and several other reasons, it is therefore proper to ask, as we do in Chapter 11, to what extent the common equation between language and nationality holds and should hold. We must become aware of how that conceptual equation developed and, above all, of the impact that it has had. We should, again, also recognize its justifications and merits, but nonetheless come to see – much more than is commonly done – how it prejudices our perceptions and descriptions of languages, of countries, and of people.

Language and nationality are two immense topic areas, and what can be covered in a single work about them and about their links is necessarily a selection. While this book can be used as a critical introduction to the whole subject area, it is far from being a general survey book. Nor is it a summary of the current consensus in a field. It draws from disciplines other than linguistics – from classics to social sciences – and, above all, it incidentally questions a few tenets that are almost articles of faith for some linguists.

This is an academic book; however, in writing it, I have felt that I have a duty of clarity towards the readers. I have therefore often added incidental explanations, out of fear that, through the effort to be concise, as Horace warned, an author can become obscure.[1] I have also endeavoured to minimize the use of unnecessary jargon and, above all, I have refrained from making up new terms, either to describe concepts or to postulate novel subdivisions of the area of inquiry, which is an academic territory-marking exercise that is of little help to readers. I have also focused on the subject matter rather than detailing the history of the academic debates on the subject. From the scholarly literature, I have selected only *some* of the works that seemed valuable for the discussion at hand, and I have mostly passed over, rather than attacked, what seemed misguided. I have translated into English the classical and foreign works that I have quoted, though I have provided the original texts in footnotes, which the uninterested reader can just ignore. With those footnotes, however, I have made those texts readily available to other scholars, and made it possible for them to verify the claims or interpretations that I have put forth – and to check the translations supplied in the main text, which are all my own. I have also indicated the page numbers, not just the years, of all the academic works cited, so that scholars looking them up can find the relevant passages at once.

This book was written in tandem with other books. It is a pleasure for me to thank the Berlin's Institute for Advanced Study (Wissenschaftskolleg), the Swedish Collegium for Advanced Study at Uppsala University (SCAS), and Rhodes University of South Africa, for the fellowships awarded to me, during which I did some of the research and writing for this book.

---

[1] Hor. Ad Pis. 25–6: 'breuis esse laboro, obscurus fio'.

1

Language labelling us explicitly

Is it true that the language you use, the way you use it, and the way you present yourself linguistically establish, even against your will, what your nationality or national identity is? And does it matter? In this chapter, we begin our journey towards addressing those questions by looking at what is perhaps the most explicit and obvious 'identity' label that language attaches onto us: our names. Names and surnames are relevant to those questions not just because they are words we use for telling others who we are, but because – while, at first blush, they seem accidental and often meaningless as words – they do say, even if perhaps unbeknownst to us or falsely, a lot about us.

Names

As the ancient classics proclaimed – before modern anthropologists confirmed it – names are virtually universal:

> For indeed not one among humans is wholly nameless,
> neither the vile or the noble, as soon as he is born;
> but to all do parents assign [a name], when they beget [children][1]
>
> (Homer, Od. 8.552–4)

A name is a term used to summon or mention someone. However, its perceived functions, and therefore its importance, do not end there. Giving a name to a baby socially individualizes it, and attributes to it the status of *person*. The concepts of 'persons' and of 'names' (in the plural) are sometimes conflated also lexically: 'names' is a word used to mean, generically, 'persons, people'. In the New Testament, we see phrases like 'seven thousand names died in the earthquake', or 'there was a throng of names', meaning 'there was a throng of people' – a usage that reflects the wording in the original Greek.[2] Many anthropologists distinguish biological birth from 'social

---

[1] 'οὐ μὲν γάρ τις πάμπαν ἀνώνυμός ἐστ᾽ ἀνθρώπων, οὐ κακὸς οὐδὲ μὲν ἐσθλός, ἐπὴν τὰ πρῶτα γένηται, ἀλλ᾽ ἐπὶ πᾶσι τίθενται, ἐπεί κε τέκωσι, τοκῆες᾽.

[2] Rev. 11:13: 'ἀπεκτάνθησαν ἐν τῷ σεισμῷ ὀνόματα ἀνθρώπων χιλιάδες ἑπτά᾽, and Acts 1.1.5: 'ἦν τε ὄχλος ὀνομάτων᾽. So also Rev. 3:4: 'ὀλίγα ὀνόματα ἐν Σάρδεσιν ἃ οὐκ ἐμόλυναν τὰ ἱμάτια αὐτῶν᾽. Cf. the regional Modern Greek νομάτοι 'individuals, people᾽.

birth', because the latter, in many societies, takes place days or weeks after the former, when the baby is introduced to the community and receives a name. In a variety of cultures, the act of bestowing a name is accompanied by a ritual or some solemn ceremony. Among several populations, for example the Inuit of both north America and Greenland (Searles 2008: 242), assigning a name to a child is thought to be also how the child acquires a soul. For the Ainu too, the name is the person's soul (Hoerr Charles 1951: 34–5). According to the Japanese, there exists a 'word soul' (言霊), and people are affected when their name is uttered. And in Jewish mysticism, the name of all individual beings is thought to contain their life force. Examples of such beliefs could easily be multiplied. More generally, names are widely believed not to be adventitious and arbitrary but to have an intimate connection with what they name. There is a mistaken but widespread idea, discussed already in Plato, that the names of all beings are inherent and in the nature of their referents.[3]

Ancient Greek philosophy appears not to have distinguished, initially, objects from words. In Biblical Hebrew too, the term *davar* (דָּבָר) can mean – or, at any rate, is traditionally translated, in different parts of the Bible, as – 'word' or 'thing'. Child psychologists, starting at least with Piaget ([1926] 1947: 48), have long noted that young children think that 'the name is part of the essence of the thing' and that 'the essence of the thing is not a concept: it is the thing itself … not like a label glued to a thing, but its invisible character'.[4] A name thus not only identifies but *is identified with* the individual that it names: the two are often conceptually conflated – a relationship of identity not just in the psychosociological but in the logical sense of the term. This is why, for instance, stating someone's name is considered equivalent to stating simply who someone is, and those who go by a name unrelated to their natal name are seen by some as being untruthful. Our daily use of English makes it clear that names are not perceived as accidental, arbitrary tags, but as coinciding with the person: in English, you may describe safeguarding what others think of *you* as 'defending your name', and the word 'name' means 'reputation' in many languages. And this is not just a matter of how *others* see you: research has established that there is a correlation between liking one's name and self-esteem (Joubert 1991: 822) or self-acceptance (Strunk 1958: 66).

One of the primary purposes of uttering a name is to attract that person's attention or to prompt such person to come to us. As a result, according to many belief systems, pronouncing names can magically conjure up those named; uttering people's name is thus a statement of familiarity with them, and even of control over them. For these reasons, there are prohibitions against uttering certain names, such as the secret names that many cultures assign to their members, and the name of deities. Religious Jews have ceased to utter the name of their God at least since the destruction of the Second Temple, and restrictions were in place already earlier. The taboo was not confined to

---

[3] Crat. 383a, 390d-e, 391a: 'ὀνόματος ὀρθότητα εἶναι ἑκάστῳ τῶν ὄντων φύσει πεφυκυῖαν … ἑκάστῳ φύσει πεφυκὸς ὄνομα … φύσει τὰ ὀνόματα εἶναι τοῖς πράγμασι … φύσει τέ τινα ὀρθότητα ἔχον εἶναι τὸ ὄνομα' etc.

[4] 'le nom fait partie de l'essence de la chose … Mais il faut ajouter aussitôt que, pour ces enfants, l'essence de la chose ce n'est pas un concept, c'est la chose elle-même … Le nom est donc dans l'objet, non à titre d'étiquette collée contre l'objet, mais à titre de caractère invisible'.

the spoken word: the written use of God's name also came to be avoided: Hebrew (like Greek, Armenian, and other languages) could use letters also as numerical signs, and the number 15 should ordinarily have been written in Hebrew as יה (literally 10+5); but since that combination of numbers, if read as letters, is a name of God, an alternative, non-decimal, combination was resorted to (usually טו, lit. 9+6). The name of the Devil is, likewise, unmentionable in many languages, because it is felt to constitute a summoning or a dangerous expression of intimacy, and is replaced by circumlocutions: in Romanian, *nefârtatul* 'the enemy'; in Modern Greek, ο εξαποδώ 'the [stay-]out-of-here'; in Serbian/Croatian, *nečastivi* '[the] dishonorable [one]'; and so on. In some languages, dreaded animals were, in a similar way, not named directly but called by some descriptive term. In Slavic languages, the bear is called 'honey eater', e.g. Russian медбедь, Czech *medvěd*, and in Finnish *mesikämmen*, lit. 'honey palm'.

Does your name, apart from naming you, say something about you, true or false as that may be? Among philosophers of the modern era, a view frequently expressed about personal names is that, although names are individuative (they single out someone) and deictic (they point to such person), they are not descriptive (they add nothing *about* such person). The claim, in other words, is that names refer to someone but mean nothing. John Stuart Mill (1843: 40), for example, asserted that 'Proper names are not connotative: they denote the individuals who are called by them; but they do not indicate or imply any attributes as belonging to those individuals', and he concluded that 'A proper name is but an unmeaning mark' (ibid. 43). In the past, linguists of various language backgrounds echoed this idea (cf. e.g. Gombocz [1926] 1997: 156–7).[5] A number of modern theoreticians have professed a similar belief: Bourdieu (1986: 70b) argued that a name cannot describe any properties and does not convey any information about what it names.[6] Kripke too (1980: 26ff.), who has written extensively about naming, has broadly concurred, stressing that reference to someone (denotation) is not an abbreviation of meaning (connotation). The argument, in short, is that while a noun like *dog* applies to any entity whose nature and appearance satisfies certain set criteria, a name like *Fido*, applied to your own specific dog, picks out a referent without describing it. Similarly, the name 'Albert Einstein' (the famous physicist, not some homonymous other) merely denotes a specific individual. To us, it may also mean the author of the theory of relativity, and much besides; but that information is not contained in the name. The discoverer of relativity, in different historical circumstances, could have been someone else, whereas the name 'Einstein' (for that physicist) would always have referred to that one person, unless he had never been born. Kripke has therefore described names as 'rigid designators' (ibid. 48–9), arguing that they would denote the same object in any possible state of the world. In this line of thinking, even a place name – say, *Oxford* – merely refers to a referent, points to a particular city, but asserts nothing about it: although the name *Oxford* has a

---

[5] 'A tulajdonnevekhez nem fűződik semmiféle értelem … egyetlen célja az identifikáció'.

[6] 'le nom propre ne puisse pas décrire des propriétés et … il ne véhicule aucune information sur ce qu'il nomme'.

literal etymological meaning (a ford for oxen), if I point out of my window and say 'this is Oxford', in the absence of a ford for oxen, my statement is still true.

Nonetheless, there is more to people's names than this. A name, besides referring to somebody, has also the ability to present that person in a given light, and to suggest something about him or her. Borrowing a distinction made by Frege (1892: 25–6), we may say that a name can express meaning (*Sinn*) besides reference (*Bedeutung*). Frege used the term 'name' extremely broadly, applying it also to the nouns and even phrases that identify something descriptively, like 'triangle' or 'my next-door neighbour'; it is therefore easy to see why he argued that 'names' present their referents to us in a way that contains 'real knowledge' and provides additional information about them.[7] To apply this argument to personal names may seem a stretch, because any additional information that names may convey is not always clear or accurate. Yet names often do communicate more than reference. For a start, as in the case of the name *Oxford* cited above, a name may have an etymological meaning with descriptive value, and can adumbrate certain traits in other ways. Even the name *Fido* does so: it means 'trusty', and tells you that the referent is a dog. Similar, and indeed richer, observations can be made about the names of people.

In many languages, the etymological meaning of a person's name is often immediately transparent, because that word may be still in use in its original function as noun, adjective, or verb. It is unlikely that the speakers of that language who choose such word as a name for their child do so regardless of its meaning. The choice of some names presupposes, at least originally, not only the ability to understand a language, but even literacy in that language: the Turkish female name *Elif*, for example, is the name of the Arabic and Ottoman letter '*alif*, whose shape (‌ا) is felt to suggest the image of someone tall, slightly curvy, light, elegant, and above all slender (those choosing that name for their baby daughter are presumably unaware that the original Semitic meaning of the letter's name '*alif* was 'ox').

Parents conclude that a particular name suits their child for a reason. For example, in many cultures, names reflect the circumstances of birth: in Japanese and in Akan (Ghana), names can indicate the order in which children were born. They can also indicate the day or the season of delivery: the Twi names *Kofi* (M) and *Afua* (F) are derived from the word for 'Friday', whereas *Bótwe* means 'eighth-born'. Several African names refer to some event surrounding the birth. While it is true that most European names are semantically bleached in terms of any original lexical meaning, the etymologizing of names is extremely popular, especially among parents who are trying to decide what to call their offspring. Most parents do some thinking, searching, and discussing before deciding on a name for their baby. Even when the etymological meaning of a name is unknown to parents, that name may be selected because, by being or having been the name of a relative, acquaintance, or celebrity, it is felt to carry that person's characteristics as part of its meaning. In those cases – and all the more when the name is a pre-existing word of well-known meaning – names therefore may

---

[7] 'deuten zugleich auf die Art des Gegebenseins, und daher ist in dem Satze eine wirkliche Erkenntnis enthalten'.

reveal what the person was brought up to be. They may implicitly claim to describe the person, even if mistakenly; and they may aim to confer certain characteristics. Granted, a woman called *Sophia* may lack wisdom (though 'wisdom' is the Greek meaning of the word σοφία), one called *Pia* may be an atheist (though the term *pia* in Latin means 'devout woman'), and one called *Grace* may have none; a man called *Ernest* may be not at all serious, *Aziz* (عزيز) may be not powerful, *Yŏng* (勇) may be not brave, and *Athanasios* (Ἀθανάσιος) is certainly not immortal, despite these being the meanings; but that is not the point. Names are often chosen in the belief or, at least, the hope that they will bring a particular fate. Such nominative determinism was a common belief already in antiquity: the name is thought to be a predictor or signal, *nomen atque omen* (Pl. Per. 4.4). This is the reason for modern names like, for example, *Victor* (Latin for 'winner'), *Bella* (Italian for 'beautiful'), *Bernhard* (Germanic for 'bear-strong'), *Sa'īd* (سعيد, Arabic for 'happy'), *Zdravko* (Serbian/Croatian and Bulgarian for 'healthy'), *Mutlu* (Turkish for 'happy') *Kamran* (كامران, Persian for 'successful'), *Toivo* (Finnish for 'hope'), *Isaac* (יִצְחָק, Hebrew for 'he will laugh'), *Saoirse* (Irish for 'freedom'), *Jié* (傑, Chinese for 'hero'), *Thabo* (Sotho for 'happiness'), or *Irene* (εἰρήνη, Greek for 'peace'). The same can be said of English female names such as *Joy* and *Felicity* – not to mention more disconcerting ones like *Fidelity* and *Chastity*. In literature too, characters are frequently given names that hint at what the author has in mind for them. Already in Greek tragedy, characters destined to come to harm may have foreboding names – for example, the name of the doomed king Pentheus (Πενθεύς) derives from *pénthos* (πένθος) 'grief', and the link was even ominously remarked upon in the play itself.[8] In the Bible too, we find that ill-fated or negative characters may have names that describe them as being so, like Nabal (נָבָל), and again the parallel between name and personality is even remarked upon in the text.[9] One may object that, in several cultures, from eastern Europe to Africa to southeast Asia, it is not entirely unusual to give effacing or outright negative names also to one's beloved children. In those cases too, however, just like when parents choose positive and flattering names like those we cited earlier, the literal sense is significant and wishful. Negative monikers are apotropaic: they are appellations assigned in the belief that they will avert and direct elsewhere malevolent or envious forces or will make the child less attractive for demons. This is how we can understand names such as the Mongolian Хэнбиш 'Not (a) person' or Энэбиш 'Not this (one)'. In the European cultures that have or have had such names, these are often explicitly called 'protective names' (e.g. Hungarian *óvónevek*, or Serbian заштитна имена).

The parents' wish to determine their children's future is shown, all the more clearly, by names reflecting the parents' own identity, especially their religion, with names like *Christian*, *Yehudi* ('Jew'), *Abdullah* ('servant of Allah'), and *Krishna*, or with names stating the parents' ethnic identification, like *Hrvatin* ('Croat'), *Öztürk* ('pure Turk'), *Italo* ('Italian'), *Illyriana* ('Illyrian', for 'Albanian'), *Erin* ('Ireland'), or *France* (a girl's name popular among the French during wartimes). At birth, parents give a name

---

[8] Eur. Ba. 508: '- οὐκ οἶσθ᾽ .... ὅστις εἶ. / - Πενθεύς ... / - ἐνδυστυχῆσαι τοὔνομ᾽ ἐπιτήδειος εἶ.'

[9] 1 Sam 25:25: כִּי כִשְׁמוֹ כֶּן־הוּא--נָבָל שְׁמוֹ, וּנְבָלָה עִמּוֹ

to their child that expresses their own expectations, values, feelings, and mentality, not – to state the obvious – the child's viewpoint. This is even better exemplified by the old Chinese names once given to daughters whose birth was considered a let-down because they were not sons. Such names, expressing only the hope that the next child would be male, include:

pàn-dì (盼弟) 'hope for + young brother'
lái-dì (來弟) 'come/next + young brother'
zhāo-dì (招弟) 'beckon/recruit + young brother'
qiú-dì (求弟) 'seek/request + young brother'
xiang-dì (想弟) 'want/miss + young brother'
lǐng-dì (领弟) 'lead + young brother'

The importance of the meaning of names is even recognized officially. The laws of a number of countries prohibit certain first names, typically foreign or unconventional ones. This, unsurprisingly, was the case, for example, in Italy under Fascism and under the ensuing Christian-Democrat governments; but names deemed bizarre are prohibited also in liberal and multi-cultural Sweden today, where there is a 'Name Law' prescribing that no name shall be accepted if it 'can cause offence, or can be supposed to lead to discomfort for the person who shall bear it, or [is a] name that, for some other reason, is obviously not suitable as a first name'.[10] Similar laws exist also in Denmark and elsewhere. Before we decry this as restrictive, we must consider that such laws are often meant to avoid children becoming victims of taunting or bullying on account of the names given to them. In 2014, in the city of Sonora, in the Mexican state of Hermosillo, a law was passed (article 46 of the Law of the Civil Registry) with this expressed aim, and the registry, on that occasion, published a list of names that would no longer be accepted. These included *Facebook*, *Yahoo*, *Harry Potter*, *Robocop*, *Escroto* ('scrotum'), and *Hitler* – names that, previously, before the legislators' intervention, apparently had been chosen by some parents (Samuel Butler's quip that 'parents are the last people on earth who ought to have children' comes to mind). All this highlights two things. The first, and most relevant to us here, is that both those who choose those names and those who forbid them, evidently, do so because the names do have certain meanings or connotations. The second is that not everyone can assign a name: a special power is required. Several religious texts and traditions of magic narrate that someone, endowed with the appropriate power, created the elements of reality by naming them. Many historical instances underscore how naming is an exercise in power. However, naming would not be an important exercise in power, if it did not also impose a *meaning*. Black slaves in southern US states were given distinct new names by their owners, an act that both erased their past and marked them as different. In Nazi Germany, a law (RGBl I, 1044 of 17 August 1938, coming into force in 1939) required that all Jews should add to the their name also a mandatory appellation (*Zwangsname*)

---

[10] Namlagen 1982: §34: 'Som förnamn får inte godkännas namn som kan väcka anstöt eller kan antas leda till obehag för den som skall bära det eller namn som av någon annan anledning uppenbarligen inte är lämpligt som förnamn'.

that marked them as Jews: *Israel* for men, and *Sara* for women (a name then not used by non-Jews; now it is one of the most common names for German girls). It was also decided that 'Aryan' Germans should have only German or Germanized names. Many other nationalist governments, instead of striving to distinguish ethnic minorities, have sought to assimilate them by force, and therefore have passed laws imposing names and surnames in the national language. For example, in Turkey, Kurds are not allowed to give conspicuously Kurdish names to their children, and Catalan names were not allowed in Spain under Franco.

Among social theorists, there is a line of thinking, worth mentioning here, that regards all names as an imposition that forcibly shapes us into something; as Derrida (1967: 164–5) maintained, the first name that we are given (the one that most people consider our 'real' name) is a *première violence*. Some thinkers argue, as Lacan did, that the whole of language – any language that we are brought up with (we do not get to choose which one) – is 'Other', is an alien cognitive framework that constrains our thinking, our self-conceptualization, and our self-expression. They also argue – as Foucault too explicitly contended (1982: 227),[11] followed by other theorists (e.g. Butler 1997: 2ff) – that the social, political, and legal powers above us, through that imposed and limiting language (which is used to describe us, and which we too learn to use for talking and thinking about ourselves), shape each of us into a self, into a subject, into an 'I'. Personal names, as we mentioned, attribute to us personhood; they do so also in juridical terms, and contribute to establish each of us as an entity accountable for what he or she has done at other times. Just as a noun like *river* is separative (diacritic, as Socrates says[12]) because it gives the impression that the entity named is something separate from the rest of reality, that it constitutes a single cohesive thing that remains itself across situations, so (all the more) does a name distinguish each individual from the rest, suggesting that each of us is a distinct person, is a single centre of consciousness and agency, and is the same person over a lifetime. This is also the implicit philosophical view that most people have of what a person is like: a discrete, unified, and perduring unit. Adopting, with the aid of names, that view of people strengthens each person's sense of self and the perception that one's life is a single, coherent, individual story. However, philosophers of many traditions have contested the accuracy of that view of people. Indian philosophies such as the Advaita Vedānta school of Hinduism (cf. Deutsch 1966: 6) warn that approaching someone by name is misleading, because names and labels wrongly suggest that the individual is something real and self-standing. In Taoism too, authorities such as Chuāng-Tzǔ contend that an 'accomplished human being' (至人) has no name, and is attached to no self (Fêng 1952: 243). Among Western philosophers, there is a long line of thinkers, from Plato to Locke to Parfit, who have questioned the notion that we are fully the same person over time. Even in popular literature, it is often noted that the names that perhaps fitted us

---

[11] 'C'est une forme de pouvoir qui transforme les individus en sujets. Il y a deux sens au mot «sujet»: sujet soumis à l'autre par le contrôle et la dépendance, et sujet attaché à sa propre identité par la conscience ou la connaissance de soi. Dans les deux cas, ce mot suggère une forme de pouvoir qui subjugue et assujettit.'

[12] Pl. Crat. (388b-c): 'ὄνομα ἄρα … ἐστιν … διακριτικὸν τῆς οὐσίας'.

in the early stages of our life may become increasingly inappropriate later because we change. As Kosztolányi wrote in his classic novel *Skylark* ([1924] 1985: 10), 'the name sticks to someone, threadbare like outgrown children's clothes'.[13]

However, while it is true that names tend to present each of us as an unchanging entity, it is important to note that name changes, in specific conditions, are considered possible and are even the cultural and legal norm. Interestingly, such changes are meant to acknowledge (or perhaps performatively to impose) transformations in the person or in the person's circumstances. In Western countries, women traditionally change surname upon marriage. Some populations – such as the Balinese, the Sirionó people of Bolivia, and the Penan nomads of northwest Borneo (Needham 1954: 416) – have teknonyms: new denominations assumed by people after they become parents. Other cultures refer to people by a different name after their puberty; some apply a new name to those who have died. In many religions (Hinduism, Islam, Judaism, and sometimes Christianity), one changes name upon converting and embracing a particular god. Anthropologists report that populations who believe that people receive new souls in the course of their lives also assign new names (Hoerr Charles 1951: 11). The fact that we are not exactly the same person over time or cross-situationally is also nominally acknowledged, in Western cultures, through the interplay of forenames, surnames, titles, and nicknames: *Little Bill* grows into *Mr Smith*, and *Commander Smith* is to his underlings someone rather different than he is, as *William*, to his drinking friends at the weekend. Even deities, in several religions – Islam, Judaism, and Hinduism, for example – have multiple names, thought to express their many functions and facets.

Name changes are sometimes effected by the name bearers themselves, in replacement of the name assigned to them at birth. They may have decided, even without political or philosophical readings, that their natal name is an externally imposed convention that does not fit them. After all, the names put on us at birth were not chosen by us, were applied to us by people who did not know us, and may later feel to us like a misrepresentation of our personality or circumstances – another demonstration that names are not just pointers but, implicitly, descriptors. This is not new: in the Bible, Naomi, whose name is probably from a root meaning 'pleasantness', asks to be no longer called that way but, on the contrary, Marah, a name she relates to a root meaning 'bitter', explaining that God has been bitter towards her.[14] Many people who change name choose for themselves new denominations that project a different image: they take a name that is grander or more common; some give themselves a name suggesting a different class, or a different nationality, or a different sex, or a different faith or worldview from those implied by their previous name. Essentially, they adopt a name that, in their opinion, can express better their individual character, values, or lifestyle. And they therefore argue that it is disrespectful to call or refer to them by their rejected name (the rather telling slang verb used by transgender people is 'to deadname' someone). Those who insist on calling them by their earlier name do

---

[13] 'Azóta a név rajta ragadt, és viselte, mint kinőtt gyermekruhát'.
[14] Ruth 1.20: וַתֹּאמֶר אֲלֵיהֶן אַל־תִּקְרֶאנָה לִי נָעֳמִי קְרֶאןָ לִי מָרָא, כִּי־הֵמַר שַׁדַּי לִי מְאֹד.

so – again – for reasons of meaning: they dispute the implications of the new name, such as that the person is truly of the class, or sex, or ethnicity, or native language that the new name suggests.

The adoption of a new name that suggests a different class or (especially) ethnicity is also contested by some who say that it is a cowardly capitulation to societal prejudice. This accusation is frequently levelled at those who assume a name that is locally more mainstream instead of insisting on the 'ethnic' name they received at birth. Many people who have moved into a community of a different language take on a name in the language of the latter: either a different name altogether (say, *Andrew* for *Wang*), or the local form of their birth name (*Andrew* for *Andreas*), or at least a modified pronunciation of the birth name (*André* pronounced [ændɹej] rather than [ɑ̃dʁe]). This is sometimes decried as a psychologically coerced and damaging decision that only reinforces the notion that being of foreign background is a fault to be concealed. It can be: many people who change their foreign forename to a local one do so because they fear – not unrealistically – that their birth name will, at least in some contexts, mark them as outsiders and bring them social rejection, and feel that asking everybody to pronounce correctly and memorize a 'difficult' name is an awkward social introduction. Some studies do indicate, sadly, that names that are deemed easier to pronounce *and their bearers* are better liked and trusted (Laham, Koval, and Alter 2012: 755; Newman et al. 2014: 3). There is a well-established, if deplorable, correlation between familiarity and liking, including in terms of letters and sounds (cf. Zajonc 1968: 12, 23); in general, people tend to be more wary of things whose names are harder to process: experiments have shown, for example, that people rated ostensible food additives as more harmful if their names were difficult to pronounce (Song and Schwarz 2009: 136). The decision to change one's foreign forename, however, may also be encouraged by other considerations. Many locals may never get the name quite right, or get it wrong in ways that are misrepresentative of the bearer and therefore feel offensive – such as using a form of that name which attributes to the person the wrong ethnicity, or the wrong religious background, or some unfavourable characteristic. For example, they may pronounce your Swedish name as if it was German (e.g. *Sten* made to sound like 'shten'), or use the Hebrew version of your Arabic name (e.g. *Yakob* for *Ya'qub*, يَعْقُوب), or call you *Harry* in the belief that your name *Ari* (by coincidence, a name existing in Arabic, Greek, Albanian, Hebrew, Armenian, Hindi, and Finnish) is your 'low-class' or 'ignorant' pronunciation of *Harry*. If they are in a higher position in society or in employment, you might not dare to correct them. Besides, while some people would regard adopting a different name as a denial of their true self, others regard their new name as an unproblematic and expedient equivalent of their birth name, or see it as a playful change, or as a positive way to extend their repertoire of social personas. Others yet may feel that each of their two names, the 'ethnic' and the 'local', on its own, obscures part of, and therefore misrepresents, their personal history, cultural references, personality, and self-image, and that a single name is not enough. The new name, after all, does not have to replace the earlier one altogether but can be used alongside it: in Western countries, many people with immigrant parents have an 'indoor name' and an 'outdoor name'. Most importantly, some children of immigrants are more at home in the wider community and in the local mainstream culture than in the culture of their parents, and feel that their new name expresses better who they are. The view that adopting a local name can only mean 'selling out' and, above all, that someone's true and appropriate name is necessarily the 'ethnic' one, though it is a view now widespread in liberal-thinking circles, is therefore hardly a liberal one: it refuses to distinguish individuals from their official ethnicity, and looks at them as lacking agency. There are dangers in seeing minorities as merely unaware passive victims (cf. Haraway 1988: 592). Those who champion the retention of 'ethnic' names assigned at birth are absolutely right in arguing that someone of foreign ancestry should not have to worry about being penalized for being different, and that changing one's foreign name may appear to endorse a social demand to conform; and yet, this is not always the whole story. The opposite can also be true: those who do wish to adopt a new name sometimes refrain from doing so in an effort to avoid being guilt-tripped, mocked, or cold-shouldered at home: they fear being chastised for not being sufficiently like their elders and more obedient siblings, and even to be told that they are betraying their roots and insulting their background. That is how meaningful a name can be. The retention of one's birth name too, therefore, like the adoption of a local moniker, can at times be subtly coercive, and stem from a pressure to conform.

All this highlights what the main issue about the meaning of a name is: it is not the name's literal meaning, but its social meaning. A name denotes an individual, yes, but also connotes social features, and is often chosen or avoided by parents for that reason. In the United States, almost half of the names given by black parents to their children are names never used by white parents (Levitt and Dubner 2005: 181–2); conversely, for black parents, giving their child an 'ethnic' or 'black' name may have covert prestige at community level, while choosing a 'white' name may be disapproved of and seen as turning one's back on the community. Many northern Italians would not dream of giving their children names typical of southern Italy, like *Calogero, Gennaro, Salvatore*, or *Concetta, Immacolata*, and *Assunta*. Many upper-class English parents would not dream of calling their children *Dwayne* or *Tyler, Sharon* or *Tracy*; conversely, self-identified British working-class parents would steer clear of names like *Rupert* or *Hugo, Henrietta* or *Melissa*, deeming them too posh. In July 2013, right-wing British commentator Katie Hopkins caused a storm by affirming insistently in an interview on ITV's *This Morning* that she would not even let her children socialize with children with names such as *Tyler* or *Charmaine, Chantelle*, or *Chardonnay*, arguing that such names enable her to gauge quickly the children's class, behaviour, and even likelihood that they have done their homework. Worrisome as Hopkins' opinion may be, it is certainly not rare. A similar uproar had already erupted in September 2005 when it was noticed that on the website of the *Times Educational Supplement* a number of teachers had gleefully admitted to forming strong views about their pupils, before ever meeting them, just by reading their names on the register. They openly stated, only in part for levity, that on the basis of their experience they knew that certain names 'spell trouble' – presumably because they usually belong to children of certain social backgrounds. Some teachers even listed the names that were, in their view, typical of either problematic or, on the contrary, of charming children. They reported that their heart sank learning that they will have in class a *Wayne, Liam, Charmaine*, or *Kyle*, and reported that they expected aggravation from pupils with hyphenated first names like

Bobbi-Jo, or with ordinary names spelt oddly, such as *Jordon, Kristopher, Jayne*, or *Kloe*. On the other hand, teachers said that they would look forward to teaching children called *Alice, Asam, Ben, Charlotte, Daniel, Gregory, Imran, Isobel, Jamie, Joseph, Kate, Lucy, Sam*, or *Sean*.

Entirely comparable information comes from other Western countries. As reported by the German press in 2009, a survey was carried out by Astrid Kaiser and Julia Kube, who submitted a roll call of imaginary pupils to primary school teachers.[15] Five hundred teachers answered a questionnaire about names and pupils. They indicated that they expected girls named *Marie, Charlotte, Sophie, Nele*, or *Hannah*, and boys named *Leon, Simon, Alexander, Maximilian, Lukas*, or *Jakob* to be friendly, pleasant, and unobtrusive pupils. They expected, on the other hand, insolence, misbehaviour, and poor performance if a girl was called *Vanessa, Angelina, Chantal*, or *Mandy*, or if a boy was called *Justin, Marvin, Cedric*, or *Kevin*. Names like *Angelina, Justin*, or *Kevin*, in Germany, are not routine or random: they became known to many Germans mainly as names of American celebrities; and most teachers reported having negative expectations about German children with such names because they are considered derived from trash culture. One teacher stated bluntly that '*Kevin* is not a name; it's a diagnosis'. No less than 64 per cent of the teachers, when asked what names they would *not* give to their own child under any circumstances, put *Kevin* at the top of the list (the German press was quick to talk of *Kevinism*).

We should be very concerned that such *a priori* assumptions can lead teachers to treat pupils unfairly, and that this will affect those children's future. Names are *interpellations* in the Althusserian sense: they are labels assigning to us a social position, a position that often then comes to be felt as inevitable, natural, intrinsic; names can become a self-fulfilling prophesy. It is nonetheless not meaningless that the teachers argued that their responses were based on their previous experience. This should not, of course, allow them to prejudge future pupils, but does show a fuzzy *statistical* correlation between names and family background – the social meaning of names. Names are, as we noted before, a reflection of the cultural horizon and aspirational values of the parents who choose them. A name may not say much about the baby who is given it, but it may say something about the outlook of parents who regard such name as attractive or glamorous. The attitude, behaviour, and abilities displayed by children at school are also largely the product of parental input, and often tell us what is provided, what is allowed, and what is prized in their milieu. In the same way, the teachers who regard those names as 'trashy' do so owing to their own educational background, social circles, and ensuing values, prejudices, tastes, and lifestyle; and these too will be reflected in the upbringing – and in the names – that they will choose for their own children.

In the United States, academic studies highlighting the existence of name-based stereotyping and bias in teachers go back decades. They report, again, a dislike for unusual names, especially in boys, which affects also the teachers' evaluation of the pupil's work (cf. Harari and McDavid 1973: 223–5). It has, moreover, been found (Levitt

---

[15] For example, *Der Tagesspiegel*, 18 September 2009.

and Dubner 2005: 192–8) that first names correlate with parents' level of education and income. Research in the United States has also identified (Kalist and Lee 2009: 47) a correlation between unpopular first names and juvenile delinquency. There are two main explanations for this, and they are not mutually exclusive. On the one hand, such names are believed to be prevalent in very low-income family units with limited ability to look after, guide, and educate their children, a situation thought to be linked with a higher chance of later delinquency; on the other hand, name-based discrimination on the part of potential employers and others can certainly hinder a person's access to good jobs, housing, and even romantic dates. Several experiments (consisting usually of sending two identical CVs differing only in the name) have demonstrated that, for example, job applicants with the same qualifications but an 'ethnic minority', 'black', or 'immigrant' name are far less likely to get called for an interview. This was shown to be the case in the United States (Bertrand and Mullainathan 2004: 997–1006) as well as in a number of European countries (cf. Riach and Rich 2002: F495).

First names can become synonyms of some social category even to the point of becoming regular nouns for that whole category. Examples of this abound. The name *guy* has long become an American English term for 'man' or even 'person (of either sex)'; *sheila* has become an Australian English term for 'woman'; *jack* or *johnny* are dated terms for any unknown man; *karl* is a Swedish colloquialism for 'man'; *titius*, originally a Latin first name, became a medieval juridical term for any unknown man; *pali* in Hungarian is a diminutive of *Paul* but has become a general term for 'bloke, guy'; and *meri*, derived from the English *Mary*, is a Tok Pisin word for 'woman'. Some meanings are more specific: the term *nanny* is originally a form of the name *Annie*; *tommy* is a dated term for 'British soldier'; *john* is English slang for a prostitute's client; *paddy* a derogatory colloquialism for 'Irishman'; *taffy* a derogatory colloquialism for 'Welshman'; *becky* is American slang for a 'racially insensitive white woman'; *karen* is a similar term for a 'self-entitled middle-aged white woman'; *maca*, originally a diminutive of *Maria*, is a Hungarian sexist term equivalent to 'tart'; *mehmetçik*, a diminutive of the male name *Mehmet*, is a Turkish colloquialism for 'Turkish soldier'; and *katina*, originally a diminutive of *Katerina*, in Modern Greek is a term for 'ignorant and gossipy woman'.

We mentioned that the use of someone's forename usually implies a certain familiarity. It should also be noted that the forename applied to a given person can have also variants indicating different degrees of familiarity and informality, such as diminutives, including diminutives of diminutives: *James > Jim > Jimmy*. In many languages, these can be very numerous. So Modern Greek *Maria > Marió, Máro, Marighó, Marousó, Maroúsa, Maroúla*, and *Maráki*, among others. Russian *Mariya > Maška, Maša, Mashen'ka, Mašunya, Mašečka, Mašunečka, Manya, Marusya*, etc. The important point is, again, meaning: native speakers know that each form conveys a different nuance (Gladkova 2015: 35). By using one variant rather than another, the person addressing you can express a particular stance towards you, or reflect the current type of interaction that there is between you two, or signal what particular response is being sought. A lot of people introduce themselves, at least in certain circumstances, with a diminutive form of their name; while their reasons may include mere habit or fondness of someone who used to call them that way, it is, not uncommonly, the wish to present themselves in a certain light.

People do read much into names, and feel that they provide real knowledge about someone – according to the Kabbalah, one gets to know even God by studying his name. As we saw, personal names are very commonly perceived to communicate nationality, ethnicity, religion of upbringing, language, and social class. They are also felt to mark someone's age, since the names given to children can follow fashions (they clearly do in Western countries), and therefore roughly pinpoint the period of birth. Furthermore, names often mark someone's sex, as in Spanish *Paco* (M)/*Paca* (F), or Greek *Panayótis* (M)/*Panayióta* (F). One might object that, in English, names are not morphologically marked for sex, and that only by observing empirically, over time, to whom each name is applied do we learn which names in English are for men and which are for women. But English names are not quite so random. Even though most native speakers do not consciously realize this, the names used in English-speaking countries have, in the main, structural characteristics that mark them as likely male or likely female names; they contain phonological cues to gender (Slater and Feinman 1985: 437–8, Barry and Harper 1995: 812). These include, for women's names, being accented on the second or later syllable (*Elizabeth, Nicole*) and ending in a vowel, notably a schwa (*Samantha, Amanda*) or a sonorant consonant (*Susan, Megan*), and for male names, being accented on the first syllable and ending in a plosive consonant (*Derek, Richard*), or just being short (*Eric, John*). In experiments, when children and adults were provided with lists of made-up names constructed according to these rules, they applied them to dolls of the gender that one expected (Cassidy, Kelly, and Sharoni 1999: 364). This shows, again, that members of a language community are, even subconsciously, aware and attentive to implicit descriptive cues that names may provide – and that names do provide them.

Surnames

Similar considerations can be made about surnames. Surnames do differ from forenames in certain ways – for example, they are often hereditary, and are not universal (very many cultures have no surnames at all). Nevertheless, they too can have literal and, more importantly, social meanings.

Of course, surnames are frequently preceded by appellations (e.g. Doctor, Brother, Baroness, Reverend, Count, Senator, Lady, President, Chancellor, Judge, Colonel, etc.) that indicate social role, nobility rank, hierarchical position, or professional title. And such appellations suggest also additional information about the person in question: someone called *Doctor* Smith is probably not a child, *Reverend* Smith is probably not an atheist, *Miss* Smith is probably not a man, and *Senator* Smith is probably not British. However, a lot of information may be supplied by the surnames themselves.

In English-speaking countries, as in many other parts of the world, your surname marks your descent from a particular parent, usually your father, and thereby your membership of a particular family. Surnames, or second names, inherited from one's mother also exist – particularly in the Philippines, in parts of India, and at times in

Europe – but are far less common globally. In many cultures, the *forename* of the father (the patronymic) is used, in some form, as identifier for their children; in Ethiopia, for instance, a father's first name is applied to his offspring similarly to a surname: if a man is called *Admasu Zenawi*, his father's forename must have been *Zenawi*; if *Admasu* has a daughter called *Beza*, her full name will be *Beza Admasu*. This means that the surname (if it can be so described) will change at each generation. A similar system (though placing the father's name first) is standard among the Tamils. In several cultures, the father's forename is made into an adjective that becomes a byname for the son or daughter – this is a system already attested in Ancient Greece: Homer frequently refers to Achilles, whose father was called Peleus, simply as *Pēleídēs*, meaning something like 'Peleian', i.e. son of Peleus. In many languages, the full expression 'son of/daughter of' is incorporated into the surname. In Icelandic, if a man whose first name is, for example, *Kristján* sires a son called *Jón*, the surname of the latter will be *Kristján-s-son*, and the surname of Jón's children will be *Jón-s-son* for his sons, and *Jón-s-dóttir* for his daughters. In most European cultures, surnames are now fossilized forms that remain constant across generations, but 'son-of x' is the original meaning of surnames such as the English *William-son*, the Swedish *Sven-s-son*, the Danish *Niel-sen*, the Norwegian *Ib-sen*, the Scots *Mac-Donald*, the Spanish *Martín-ez*, the Slavic *Alexandr-ovich*, the Romanian *Anton-escu*, the Hungarian *Pál-fi*, the Armenian *Iosif-yan*, the Georgian *Giorga-dze*, or the Turkish *Ahmet-oğlu*. In languages such as Russian, Bulgarian, or Gujarati, although people now have an inherited surname that, along the father's line, does not change, they have also a patronymic which is part of their legal name and is used a bit like an English middle name, for example *Sergei Vasilyevich* (= son of Vasiliy) *Rachmaninoff*. Arab names can have an equivalent structure: *Mohammed bin Rashid Al Maktoum* means Mohammed son of Rashid of the Maktoum family. In Somalia, as among many Arabs, it is common for a person's full name to consist of a first name followed not only by the father's name but also by that of the paternal grandfather, thereby identifying a whole stock. In several parts of the Balkans, of South Africa, and of southeast Asia, clan names have also been or are part of a person's name.

Not only in Icelandic, as we saw above, but also in other European languages such as Latvian, Modern Greek, and many Slavic languages, the surname of a woman marks also her sex, with a specific ending. In Greece, a daughter is traditionally assigned the surname of her father, as a son would also be, but in the genitive case: while the surname of the son of Mr *Mitrópoulos* will usually also be *Mitrópoulos*, the daughter will usually be *Mitropoúlou*, in the genitive, and this indirectly marks her as female. In several countries, a man's surname is often extended – though far less automatically nowadays – also to the woman he married, to signal that she is his wife. This is the (now waning) traditional way among Europeans, but also among the Thai, the Pashtu, or the Yoruba. When women adopt their husband's surname, they signal publicly the family they married into – and proclaim their change in marital status to those who knew them before under another surname. Sometimes, the husband's surname is only added to the 'maiden' surname, not used in replacement of it, and this marks even more clearly a woman's status as married. In Lithuanian, a single surname marks not only a woman's sex but communicates her marital status also to those who did not know her before, because the surname of married women has a special ending: while a man can have a surname like *Kazlauskas* without variations according to marital status, the corresponding forms of this surname for a woman is *Kazlauskaitė* if she is unmarried and *Kazlauskienė* if she is married. In Modern Greece, as we just said, women at birth commonly acquire their fathers' surname in the genitive; upon marriage, they traditionally acquire the surname of their husbands in the genitive case (although this is no longer obligatory since 1983); the use of the genitive not only marks their sex but, being the grammatical case that indicates possession, also marks them as somehow *belonging* first to their fathers and then to their husbands – a disagreeable nuance that was not lost on Greek feminists. In numerous Western countries, many women nowadays no longer assume their husbands' surname. Since women in those countries now usually have a choice, their choice is likely to be not a default but the result of a conscious decision (Laskowski 2010: 81–2). Some sources (Etaugh et al. 1999: 821) note that one of the consequences of this is that the women who do change their surname to take on that of their husband are not only thereby simply understood to be married but, precisely because the change of surname has become optional, are also perceived (correctly or incorrectly) as less independent and self-determined. Even if the surname they take on is semantically opaque and accidental; therefore, it is felt to say something important about the person bearing it.

For babies who were abandoned and are brought up entirely in institutions, since the parents' surname was unknown, a new one had to be invented. Traditionally, foundlings received distinct surnames that indirectly marked their history and therefore social status. Quite common were surnames marking the time or circumstances of the foundlings' arrival – in this case not of their birth, about which not much was known, but of their appearance at the baby 'wheel' of a convent or at a hospital. Their surname could therefore be, for example, that day of the week. In several countries, foundlings were often given more descriptive surnames, many of which still exist as regularly inherited surnames: in France, *Trouvé* or *Trouvat* (lit. 'found'); in Poland, *Znaleźny* (cf. *znaleźne* 'finder's reward'); in the Nederlands or Belgium, *Vondeling* ('foundling'), *Verloren* ('lost'), or even *Ongemack* ('inconvenience'); in Romania, *Lepădat* and *Lepădătescu* ('rejected, thrown away'); in Italy too, *Proietti* ('cast off') or *Abbandonati* ('abandoned'), although the clergy frequently conferred to foundlings surnames with wishful meanings, such as *Diotallevi*, lit. 'may God bring you up', or *Diotaiuti* lit. 'may God help you' – another example of the widespread belief in the performative power of names.

Several surnames are, in origin, descriptive; it is likely that common English surnames like *Short*, or *Armstrong*, or *Whitehead* are to be explained that way. Many other surnames originally indicated someone's profession. That was, of course, the sense of widespread English surnames like *Smith, Taylor, Baker, Thatcher, Butler, Carter, Shephard, Clark, Weaver, Cook, Porter, Cooper, Tanner, Glover, Potter, Hunter, Miller, Fowler, Page, Spencer,* and countless others. This is not just English usage; for example, the surname *Smith* corresponds exactly to the French surname *Lefebvre*, the German *Schmidt*, the Italian *Fabbri*, the Czech/Croatian/Slovene *Kovač*, the Estonian *Sepp*, the Russian Кузнец, the Lithuanian *Kalvis*, the Arabic حداد. The English surname *Taylor* corresponds to the German *Schneider*, the Italian *Sarti*, the Turkish *Terzi*, the Hungarian *Szabó*, the Estonian *Rätsep*, the Russian Портной, the Arabic خياط, and so forth. Other surnames indicate the place of origin (or of contact) of the family. Many surnames are names of cities or nationalities; many Jewish surnames belong to this type: *Berlin, Tehrani, Amsterdam, Warshaw, Lichtenstein, Moscowitz, Verona, Espinosa, Dantzig, Ginzburg, Unger, Galitz, Pollack, Litvak, Deutscher*, and so forth.

Surnames, like forenames, can also be a class marker. Many English and European surnames, as we just saw, indicated profession, and therefore also indicated, originally, a person's place in the community. In countries such as Tunisia, surnames prefixed with *Atig* (from أعتق 'to emancipate, set free') or like *Abid* (عبد 'slave') can mark descent from slaves, suggesting that the bearer is black, and may have class implications. In India, surnames could indicate to which caste someone belonged. The socio-economic position of someone could affect the surname in other ways too. In 1787, Emperor Joseph II of Austria issued an imperial command requiring Jews to adopt a German surname; there is a contested story that officials in Western Galicia, now Poland, would assign flattering or derogatory names depending on the bribes they received (Franzos 2012 [1880]: 132–6; Rottenberg 1977: 50) and that families therefore ended up with surnames that reflected their financial means. This reportedly explains the difference between local surnames such as *Reichmann* (wealthy man), *Weisheitsborn* (wisdom spring), *Goldreich* (rich in gold), *Ehrlich* (earnest), *Biedermann* (honest man), *Perlmutter* (mother-of-pearls), or *Freud* (joy) – and disconcerting surnames such as *Stinker* (stinker), *Galgenstrick* (rogue), *Taschengreifer* (bags-grabber), *Todtschläger* (murderer), *Wucherer* (usurer), *Geier* (vulture), or *Woismeingeld* (wheresmymoney).

One may object that surnames, after a while, became hereditary, and their literal meaning came to be ignored. There is, nonetheless, evidence that people have often remained very aware of the literal meaning of surnames, even when these had become fossilized. For example, many of those who emigrated into a different language community often have not simply changed but translated their surname: in English-speaking countries, several people called *Stein* became *Stone* (and *Feuerstein* became *Firestone*), *Neustadt* became *Newstead*, *Jung* became *Young*, *Weber* became *Weaver*, and *König* became *King*. Some Italian Jews called *Cohen* (כֹּהֵן, Hebrew for 'priest') adopted *Sacerdoti* ('priests') as surname, while some called *Blumberg* (literally 'mountain of flowers') became *Montefiori*. In Hungary too (cf. Farkas 2012: 9), when foreign (usually Germanic and Jewish) surnames were changed into Hungarian ones, if they originally had a clear meaning, this often was, at least partly, retained in the Hungarian surname adopted: *Weiss* (German and Yiddish for 'white') could become *Fehér* (Hungarian for 'white'), *Stern* (lit. 'star') became the Hungarian *Csillag*, of the same meaning; in a like manner, the surname *Gross* (lit. 'big') became *Nagy* (Hungarian for 'big'), *Klein* (lit. 'small') became *Kis* (Hungarian for 'small'), *Schwarz* sometimes became *Fekete* ('black'), and *Fischer* became *Halász* ('fisher').[16] In German-speaking lands, the Yiddish surname *Sholem* (< Hebrew שָׁלוֹם 'peace') could become *Fried*, of the same meaning; among Spanish-speakers, *Chaim*

[16] Often, in the Hungarian surname, the original noun phrase becomes an adjective (Farkas 2003: 153): *Kleinhaus* (lit. 'small house') > *Kisházi* (< *kis+ház*); *Schönberg* (lit. 'beautiful mountain') > *Széphegyi* (< *szép+hegy*); *Spiegel* (lit. 'mirror') > *Tüköri* (< *tükör*); *Fried* (lit. 'peace') > *Békés* 'peaceful', or *Békési, Bekesi* (< *béke*).

(Hebrew חַיִּים 'life') could become *Vidal*. Conversely, when European Jews emigrated to Israel, and were urged to adopt new Hebrew names, they often translated their surname into Hebrew; thus sometimes *Mendelssohn* became *Ben-Menachem* (בֶּן־מְנַחֵם 'son of Mendel'), *Fischer* became *Dayag* (דַּיָּג 'angler'), *Goldberg* became *Harpaz* (הַר־פָּז 'mountain of gold'), *Lampel* became *Lapid* (לַפִּיד 'torch'), and *Wolfson* became *Ben-Ze'ev* (בֶּן־זְאֵב 'son of the wolf').

Surnames' translations have occurred also under coerced assimilation. In Fascist Italy, for example, in the north-east of the country, families with the Slavic surname *Vodopivec* ('Water drinker') were forcibly renamed *Bevilacqua* ('Drink water', a preexisting Italian surname), and some called *Mladossich* (< *mlad(os)*- 'young') had to become *Giovanetti* (same meaning). Similarly, families who had Germanic surnames such as *Mittempergher* (< *Mittemberger* 'mid-mountain') became *Mezzomonti* (of the same meaning), and many similar changes to many other surnames were proposed: *Frei* to *Liberi*, *Berger* to *Montani*, *Altmann* to *Vecchi*, *Schäfer* to *Pastori*, *Fröhlich* to *Allegri*, *Hell(mann)* to *Chiari*, *Müller* to *Molinari*, and so forth. Italians in the United States, on the other hand, often translated the meaning of their Italian surnames into English: *Molinari* became *Miller*, and *Casalegno* became *Woodhouse*. Translating one's surname into a language regarded as having wider currency, of course, is an old phaenomenon: several of the medieval European scholars (especially sixteenth-century Germans) who wrote in Latin and gave themselves Latin or Ancient Greek names translated the literal meaning of their surname, if one was identifiable. Jakob *Berg* (surname literally meaning 'mountain') used the Latinized name Jacob *Montanus* (a Latin adjective meaning 'mountain'); Johannes *Fischer* used the Latinized name Johannes *Piscator* (Latin for 'fisherman'); Johann *Goldschmidt* (lit. 'gold smith') used the Latinized name Johann *Aurifaber* (Latin compound meaning the same); Georg *Bauer* (lit. 'farmer') used the Latinized name Georgius *Agricola* (Latin for the same); Franz *Friedlieb* (lit. 'peace lover') used the Greek name Franciscus *Irenicus* (Greek εἰρηνικός 'peaceful'); Hieronymus *Bock* (lit. 'ram') used the Greek name Hieronymus *Tragos* (Ancient Greek τράγος 'ram'); and Philipp *Schwarzerdt* (lit. 'black earth'), wrote his works as Philippus Melanchthon (Greek μελάγχθων 'black earth'). All this makes it clear that, as we saw also with forenames, although the link between referent and word is generally arbitrary (the basic answer to Plato's *Cratylus* question, which we mentioned earlier[17]), the link is not random.

People seek to change their surnames also nowadays, as they can do with their first names. In Britain, while some people change their surname in order to simplify the spelling (e.g. *Phillips* to *Philips*), or to stress their connection to a different branch of their family, or to carry the surname of someone they love, a quick look at the official public records makes it clear that others do it so as to drop a surname likely to elicit mockery because of its meaning or, arguably, to avoid the disadvantages associated with its ethnicity. Studies in the United States too reported, already in the 1950s (Broom, Beem, and Harris 1955: 39), that many people changed their surname owing

---

[17] Exceptions are marginal components of a language vocabulary that are somehow imitative of the referent, usually imitative of its sound. Cf. onomatopoeic terms (e.g. English *boom* or *fizz*) and phonaesthemes (e.g. English *sn-* in *snout, sniff, snort, snore, snarl, sneeze*, etc.).

to 'ethnic considerations', and regarded name changing 'a mechanism to achieve desired statuses, roles, and participation otherwise impeded'. There is evidence also from recent years, and even from countries such as Sweden, that, for immigrants, changing one's surname to a local one statistically increases earnings (Arai and Skogman Thoursie 2009: 141–5).

From all of this it is clear that people's surnames could – though not always and not systematically – signal or attribute kinship, language, ethnicity/nationality, sex, marital status, profession, and social class, with substantial consequences.

In sum, names and surnames, elements of language that are central to our self-presentation but that some postulate to be random and uninformative, in truth, can say, or can appear to say, a lot about our background, personal characteristics, collective memberships, social attributes, and 'identity'. As we see next, people read a lot also into other elements of our use of language – again, with considerable consequences.

2

Ways of speaking

In the last chapter, we analysed the names and surnames that are assigned to us and we showed, among other things, that even an element of language that refer to us in the most explicit way often convey also covert information – though at times misleadingly. Now we can focus on the larger part of language use that communicates – or is believed to communicate – a lot about us, and that prompts others to put labels on us. It is constituted, of course, by what we ourselves say. In that part too there is, on the one hand, a component that is explicitly informative about us, which is the *content* of what we say (we talk about ourselves, we express opinions, we tell stories from our lives, and so forth) and, on the other hand, a component that implicitly, almost subliminally, provides personal data about us that get us labelled, which is *the manner* in which we say it. When we use language, we do not just communicate referential meanings. How we use language is usually sufficient for others to categorize us in a particular fashion and to decide how they want to respond to us. Even upon hearing a single word like 'hello', people are often able to assign the speaker to a particular ethnicity or race (Purnell, Idsardi, and Baugh 1999: 22). If they briefly hear a stranger talking on the phone or on the radio about a neutral topic, without seeing or knowing this person, they usually gauge – often correctly – this person's age, gender, class, native language, region of origin, extent of education, degree of friendliness, state of health, mood, and grade of fatigue or intoxication. They quickly form opinions also about the speaker's level of intelligence, type of profession, political leanings, sexual orientation, degree of sincerity, and morality. They even build a picture of his or her appearance. And all this strikes us as normal. Already in the fifth century BC, Socrates, pressingly questioned by Meno, replied:

- Even blindfolded one would know, o Meno, by how you converse, that you are good-looking and you still have men coming after you.
- Why so?
- Because you [do] nothing [but] command in your talking, as those living a lifestyle of luxury and wantonness do, just as they are despotic as long as they are in the flush of youth.[1]

---

[1] Pl. Men. 76b-c: 'ΣΩ. κἂν κατακεκαλυμμένος τις γνοίη, ὦ Μένων, διαλεγομένου σου, ὅτι καλὸς εἶ καὶ ἐρασταί σοι ἔτι εἰσίν. ΜΕΝ. τί δή; ΣΩ. ὅτι οὐδὲν ἀλλ᾽ ἢ ἐπιτάττεις ἐν τοῖς λόγοις, ὅπερ ποιοῦσιν οἱ τρυφῶντες, ἅτε τυραννεύοντες ἕως ἂν ἐν ὥρᾳ ὦσιν'.

Nurture and nature in linguistic peculiarities: gender

If our manner of talking reflects the kind of person we are, we should ask whether, or to what extent, the linguistic traits that reveal that we are someone of this or that category may be biologically innate or may be learnt from the surrounding culture. The answer can be considerably different depending upon which social category we are considering, and upon which corresponding linguistic feature we are examining. We should be wary of both the old assumption that our traits are all preordained by our 'nature', and of the doctrine, popular in recent decades, that everything is a cultural convention. Socialization is what plays the chief role in our communication style. Biology, however, plays a part too: some aspects of our linguistic output, starting with our voice, are clearly rooted in our anatomy. It is anyway misleading to think of self-expression, and of communication in general, as being nothing but a learnt code, consciously implemented, and unconnected to our biology; humans, like other animals, communicate also through means other than language – for instance, with chemical signals – of which they have little control and often limited awareness.

A clamorous debate as to whether linguistic peculiarities are socially conditioned or biologically predetermined is most likely to arise when the topic is linguistic differences between the sexes. Some of these differences are clearly highly conventional: many languages, like Arabic or Spanish, have structural gender-marking differences, such as mandatory gender-contrastive endings in verbs or adjectives; as a result, in Spanish, in order to say, for example, 'I am tired' a man must say *estoy cansado* but a woman must say *estoy cansada*. Other languages have verb forms that depend on – and therefore express – the gender of the speaker. In these, by making a simple statement like 'I speak', you are also, mandatorily, putting a gender label to yourself. In Modern Hebrew 'I speak', said by a male, is *ani medaber* (אני מדבר) but, said by a female, is *ani medaberet* (אני מדברת), something that may appear exotic to speakers of European languages, but it is less so than it may seem.[2] In Russian, the first person simple past has gender-specific forms: a man says *ya priyehal* (я приехал) 'I arrived', a woman says *ya priyehala* (я приехала). The use of such grammatical forms suggesting the sex or gender of the people involved is obligatory and pervasive: when one speaks in Spanish or Russian, one cannot avoid them. And this is one of several ways in which language enables speakers – but also teaches them normatively – to classify themselves constantly by sex. A number of other languages have, or at least encourage, more markedly different speaking styles depending on sex; in Japanese, the style for women (女性語), besides entailing more honorifics and a higher register, and therefore what is perceived as an altogether gentler tone, includes specific sentence-ending particles. In Ubang, a language of south Nigeria, gender-dependent linguistic differences are such that men and women are said to speak different languages. A few languages also have distinct pronunciations or sounds, depending on the gender of the speaker. For example, in Atsina, an Algonquian language spoken in the US state of Montana, men reportedly

---

[2] The 'present tense' of Modern Hebrew, so labelled after the categories of European languages, consists of the gender-marked participial forms of Classical Hebrew, with the copular verb ellipsed (as if, for example in Classical Greek, instead of the gender-unspecific λέγω one said ἐγὼ λέγων and ἐγὼ λέγουσα).

pronounce as affricates (e.g. /ʧ/, like English *ch*) some sounds that women pronounce as velar stops (e.g. /k/), although the distinction is influenced also by other factors like age of the interlocutor and social status (Taylor 1982: 301–5), which shows that those gender-based features are both obligatory and negotiable.

However, there are also subtle *non-structural* differences in the way men and women usually talk – including in English. From the end of the 1960s, linguists have been striving to pin down and account for such differences. Research in this area has come up against several problems, which are in themselves rather enlightening. The main one is that there is vast variation in usage among women (and among men), as well as in the usage displayed by the same woman (or man) in different circumstances. Gender-related linguistic peculiarities may become prominent or subside according to the situation: they are not just steadily and uniformly signalled whenever someone speaks. In other words, any feature widely perceived as female is not displayed by all women, is displayed also by some men, and the women who do display it may not display it consistently.

Nevertheless, there tend to be, *statistically speaking*, fine stylistic dissimilarities between women's and men's usage. As regards English, early studies reported that, by and large, women's speaking manner is less curt and more polite and focused on the interlocutor; and that, in group conversations, male speakers tend to talk longer and to interrupt more than women, also when men talk to other men (Kramer 1974: 16). All this fits a general picture of gendered behaviour, because there are also other ways, unrelated to language, in which men, statistically, tend to be more assertive than women. These differences may even originally stem, in part, from biological factors. However, there is also a social stigma attached to women's talk; as many adages attest, there has traditionally been a belief that silence is the appropriate thing for women.[3] Indeed, women were complaining about this already in antiquity. To regard speaking as a *proprium* of men, as a male thing ill-suited for women, is not only unfair but flies in the face of developmental evidence: as a rule-of-thumb, girls start speaking sooner than boys, expand their lexicon quicker than boys, and in their school years tend to outshine boys in language-related tasks. So, if some women are less verbally forthcoming, this cannot be assumed to be simply an innate trait exhaustively explained by biology. Besides, silence can also be a form of forceful resistance or protest (Gal 1995: 171). Even granting that some differences in the use of language by men and women may have their ultimate origins in genetically determined dissimilarities in the brain, it is clear that such differences reflect (and ultimately reproduce), within a conversation, differences in upbringing, behavioural models, social status, and level of power. The earliest studies of 'women's speech' (e.g. Lakoff 1973: 49–57) spotlighted, as distinctive of women's use of English, features such as frequent tag-questions ('isn't it?'), over-the-top adjectives ('divine!'), milder expletives ('oh, dear'), and detailed colour terms ('mauve', 'aquamarine'). Such features fit a certain stereotype of femininity: unassertive, excitable, aesthetically punctilious. To these features we

---

[3] Soph. Aj. 292–3: 'ὁ δ᾽ εἶπε πρός με βαί᾽, ἀεὶ δ᾽ ὑμνούμενα·/ γύναι, γυναιξὶ κόσμον ἡ σιγὴ φέρει', a passage quoted also by Aristotle (Pol. 1.1260a). Injunctions to teach women to keep silent are then found also in the Christian tradition, e.g. 1 Tim. 2.12: 'διδάσκειν δὲ γυναικὶ οὐκ ἐπιτρέπω οὐδὲ αὐθεντεῖν ἀνδρός, ἀλλ᾽ εἶναι ἐν ἡσυχίᾳ'.

can add general characteristics that are said, quite reasonably, to be statistically more frequent in (Western) women's than in men's speech – e.g. a tone that is supportive and intimate rather than independent and confrontational, a focus on bonding rather than instructing, on asking rather than stating, and on listening rather than talking. Men's narratives (Coates 2003: 137), more often than women's, communicate acts of defiance or bravado, contest, and success; they are a bit more about action and less about feelings, more about individual enterprise and less about relationships, and include fewer admissions of vulnerability. However, these too are also part of a stereotype of the genders. We can therefore ask whether a woman is more likely to speak in a given way because she is biologically female, or because she identifies as a woman and she uses language in the way she has learnt through her socialization as a woman. Even if some features are proven to be more prevalent in the speaking style of one sex, this does not automatically prove that each difference is genetically predetermined; either way, there is often room for choice and agency. For example, just as, since the beginning of Western philosophy, language has been considered a fundamental feature that distinguishes human beings from animals, so swearwords have been traditionally regarded as a typical feature of men, in contrast to women: as unladylike, as inappropriate in mixed company, and as an intrinsic and natural part of men's aggressiveness, roughness, high sex drive, and verbal posturing to signal dominance (Stapleton 2010: 292; Vingerhoets, Bylsma, and De Vlam 2013: 297–8). Swearwords have been considered something bound to come out of your mouth if you have a male anatomy and mind. In Bulgakov's story 'Heart of a dog' (2012 [1925]: 195), the dog who has been implanted the testicles and pituitary gland of a man (admittedly, of a boozing criminal) then promptly 'utters all the swearwords that only exist in the Russian lexicon'.[4] Research on English has indeed confirmed that the genders differ considerably in the use – and the choice – of swearwords (McEnery 2006: 35). As social mores have evolved, however, many women have come to feel able to swear liberally (de Klerk 1992: 278), while there are a few men who do not swear much at all. Therefore, if swearing is statistically more of a male thing, and even if it is fuelled (let us hypothesize) by biological factors, it is clear that cultural inputs are a key cause of it. There is also a causal loop: if swearing is regarded as masculine and as expressing traits considered masculine, such as dominance or sexual prowess, since masculinity in men is prized in most cultures, men have an incentive to swear more. So, while a tendency to swear more may have some remote connection to men's innate differences and often different experience of sex, it is also connected with the fact that, for a man, to come across as sexually assertive and unconcerned with politeness conventions is traditionally considered status-enhancing. More generally, many studies report that men are often far less loath than women to use language in a fashion that violates the rules of the long-established norms of language (cf. Wells 1982: 19–20), or that is considered sub-standard, rough, and uncultivated, rather than well-enunciated and gentle; and this is a tendency already noted by Cicero in 55 BC.[5] If this is true, it can

---

[4] 'Он произносит … все бранные слова, какие только существуют в русском лексиконе.'

[5] De Orat. 3.12: 'facilius enim mulieres incorruptam antiquitatem conservant … non aspere ut ille, quem dixi, non vaste, non rustice, non hiulce, sed presse et aequabiliter et leniter'.

be explained, to a degree, by the fact that talking in ways perceived as unpolished and defiant of prescriptive rules is considered masculine and, in a man, is appreciated (cf. Trudgill 1974: 94). Standard English, for many English speakers, is only the poncey form of English imposed by schools and by formal settings; a man may therefore feel that flouting its rules makes him look more self-assertive, tough, and untamed; in the right setting, it may well enhance his manly image.

For a different example of linguistic difference between the sexes, one that does seem purely biologically determined, we can consider a very physical aspect of people's voice: the pitch. The fundamental frequency used by men and women usually differs: women, on average, have a higher pitch than men, and this is connected with the testosterone-induced development of the larynx in men – there is, in other words, a biologically driven statistical difference between the sexes. However, there are, evidently, also huge individual and contextual variations: the pitch *range* used by (English-speaking) women is often broader than men's, and women use more fall-rise tones than men, a distinguishing trait that cannot be caused by anatomy. There is also evidence that, when women want to be taken seriously, they avoid high pitches. In Britain, it is common knowledge that Margaret Thatcher, in her fateful rise to power, received voice training to lower her pitch, reportedly dropping it by as much as 60 Hz (Henton 1992: 46). Much research indicates that a deeper or huskier voice is commonly taken to signal dominance and therefore authority, self-assurance, and competence; and it has also been established that voters, both male and female, tend to pick deeper-voiced candidates (Klofstad, Anderson, and Peters 2012: 2700–2). In explaining linguistic differences between men and women, we should therefore be sceptical of both those who dismiss any evolutionary, biological factors, and those who dismiss cultural, social factors.

We also need to be aware that, conversely, our idea of what being a woman or a man amounts to is shaped also by these differences. Another question that therefore arises is whether we may sometimes read such characteristics into a person's speaking style because we are aware of that person's sex. In the same way, the perception of any given social group affects public perceptions of its language, so that, for instance, the speaking style of the upper classes is said to 'sound posh'. Particular linguistic forms are treated not only as indices of social categories (e.g. southerners, women, the upper-class, etc.) but as self-evident examples of the characteristics attributed to that group (e.g. uncouthness, daintiness, elegance, and so on). So, with an empty tautology, women's use of language, in England as in Japan or elsewhere, is often described as feminine. If one assumes that women are, for example, gentler than men, then a linguistic feature more prevalent amongst women may get labelled gentle because it is used by women. This circular reasoning can then be used also in reverse: the prevalence of features thus defined as gentle is then invoked as evidence of women's gentleness. Even if such reasoning were correct, it still would not rule out the possibility that those features are mainly used by women because women learn that they are expected to sound dainty as compared with men. Women may also realize that such speaking style, in many environments, helps them to be accepted as 'part of the club' among women, and that many men consider that style attractive in a woman.

As we noted above, men may make a point, even unconsciously, of speaking in a way that defies a norm; but they are, at the same time, striving to adhere to a different, unstated norm – concerning masculinity. This is confirmed by the fact that men not only tend to use more linguistic forms widely considered sub-standard, but they even claim that they use them when they don't (Trudgill 1972: 187–8). Men thus may make a show of rejecting official notions of prestige, but anxiously seek covert prestige of another kind. The way in which most of us speak often contains also a wilful affirmation of one's gender – understanding the term 'gender' as not meaning biological sex, but the image package as man or woman. Indeed, if we accept gender theorists' contention that gender, in that sense, is not something you inherently have, but something you recreate behaviourally moment by moment, claiming it, defending it, and seeking its recognition in interactions, we can see that a particular use of language does not only signal gender, but is part of what constitutes it.

It is not difficult to detect the ongoing negotiation of one's image that underlies most conversations. A fundamental goal of conversation is usually that of presenting oneself in a light that will allow one to preserve face, gain acceptance, and secure status. Asserting a particular gender may well be part of that goal, all the more in the case of men, since masculinity is in itself a status enhancer. Listening carefully to people's conversations – or reading carefully transcripts of them, proves the point. Coates (2003: 2) transcribed a casual dialogue that well exemplifies such gender-affirming 'identity work': young men reporting with satisfaction to a friend that they played football in their underwear outdoors at night, noisily, with protests from a Welsh neighbour. Throughout their brief chat, the speakers strive to demonstrate implicitly that they are the *approved* kind of men (boisterous, fun-loving, defiant), as do their interlocutors with their concurring noises and well-placed swearwords; they validate each other's image as 'proper' men, and they thus bond as the in-group. One can spot that the youngsters narrating their exploits, while eager to declare their rebelliousness to social conventions (being noisy at night, shedding clothes in public, being confrontational with those who complain), at the same time also demonstrate their keen *conformism* to social norms on gender: they indirectly affirm their adherence to a status-enhancing stereotype of rowdy masculinity, incidentally stress their deference to its taboos (they clarify that, once they got together, they shed their clothes but only within limits), and eagerly claim their membership of the in-group through their disparagement (essentially, the 'othering') of their protesting neighbour by mocking his Welsh accent. Even if we cannot see the people involved in the dialogue nor hear their voices, just by reading their first words, as Coates notes (ibid. 34–5), we are immediately, unmistakeably sure that the speakers are young males.

Expressed linguistic dislikes

It is common to hear someone describe point-blank a way of speaking, or just an accent, as graceful, boorish, smooth, stupid, sophisticated, lovely, warm, irritating, sexy, endearing, melodious, weird, or normal. And we treat this as unremarkable. People may like, approve of, and indeed admire the way we speak (or write); but many a time they do not. As Bernard Shaw, over a century ago, remarked in the preface to his *Pygmalion*

(1916: 99): 'it is impossible for an Englishman to open his mouth without making some other Englishman hate or despise him'. Even when the difference between our usage and that of our listeners or readers is not such as to affect comprehension, and nothing of what we say, in terms of content, is deemed objectionable, our use of a language can be the subject of vehement disapproval, and even be the cause of contempt or hostility towards us. This is caused by several factors, which we shall now review.

One of them is the language variety that the person hearing us or reading us has previously internalized. A different pronunciation or grammar may sincerely, if irrationally, strike one as odd, as misinformed, or as unnatural. Hearing one's own language with an unexpected accent or grammar may sound like a familiar music piece being played on a piano out of tune, a feeling that is not easy for everyone to outgrow. The phonological characteristics of the language variety that one has learnt natively are often felt to be also aesthetically pleasing and proper: grammar books have routinely explained sound rules as being due to *euphony*; language instructors often make the same assumption and treat it as intuitive and self-evident. A native teacher of Welsh, when I asked how to predict the mutations of consonants in Welsh, replied, 'you change them to the letter that sounds better'. An English teacher, surprised by a mistake made by one of her first-year pupils, asked her, in my presence: 'can't you hear that it sounds horrible?'. Aesthetic comments used to be considered appropriate in philological treatises: for example, Jacob Grimm (1822: 836), in his monumental grammar, introduced the German past tense indicated by a change in the stem vowel (found also in English: *fall > fell*) by explaining that this 'must be regarded as the foremost beauty of our language'.[6] That would appear odd today, but Grimm's description of the verbs that follow this pattern as 'strong', and of those that, instead, form the past tense by the addition of an ending (like English *call > call-ed*) as 'weak' is still current terminology.

A second powerful factor fuelling linguistic disapproval is a normative view of language use. At school, one may have been taught the standard language (the one variety said to be 'correct') in prescriptive terms, with non-standard usage being dismissed as wrong, unintelligent, even wicked (after all, pupils' mistakes are *punished* by lowering their grades). One may therefore have learnt to despise those who appear to violate the official standard, and feel a vicarious sense of embarrassment when observing how such people speak or write. Upbringing, and personality in a broader sense, also plays a part: someone more tolerant and easy-going is likely to be more unruffled by linguistic usage that in many quarters would be considered sub-standard, or by mistakes such as misspellings. However, while linguistic disapproval is mostly reserved for usage that veers from the prescribed official standard, the perception that the dialect or accent that one has internalized is inherently and self-evidently the normal and uncontrived one is found also among non-standard speakers. Linguistic prejudices and misconceptions are, in other words, expressed also against the language variety widely deemed standard and prestigious – not only against the varieties that many consider ungrammatical or of low social standing. School prescriptivism has a powerful influence, but linguistic prejudices exist in all quarters.

---

[6] 'Das *starke praet.* muß als hauptschönheit unserer sprache … betrachtet werden'.

A few speakers of a recognized and prestigious language variety, for instance of standard English with an RP accent (i.e. 'received pronunciation', what used to be referred to as 'Queen's English' or 'Oxford English' or 'public school English'), argue that many other pronunciations, or syntactic constructions, or lexical uses, are factually wrong, and report that these feel to them like the screech of fingernails on a chalkboard. However, there can be no doubt that non-standard usage, though different and usually not highly regarded, is not wrong in absolute terms, nor objectively cacophonous. The arguments with which those standard speakers buttress their objections to other types of usage betray a perception that the standard language is *the* (English, French, Japanese, etc.) language, the only form of that language that is ontologically real, and whose rules are objectively and forever right. Many also cite conventional orthography as the ultimate true form of words, as a timeless Platonic ideal of which pronunciation is only a shadow; they may, for example, claim that, because the word like *city* is spelled with a *t*, it is wrong to 'drop the *t*' (i.e. to replace the /t/ with a glottal stop /ʔ/, as in Cockney or Scottish), or to 'pronounce it like a *d*' (i.e. to turn it into a flap /ɾ/, as ordinarily in the United States, and sometimes in Australia and New Zealand). In truth, the word *city* came to English, via French, from the Latin stem *civitat-*, so the pronunciation /sɪtɪ/ too, in that line of thinking, should be considered the result of a 'slack' pronunciation of an older form once sanctioned in writing. In the same way, not pronouncing initial *h-*, as is done in many British dialects, is neither a sign of stupidity nor cause of intolerable confusion; speakers of standard British English may argue that it is inconvenient to lose the distinction between *art* and *heart*, or *eat* and *heat*, if you are used to having it, and they have a point; but even the 'poshest' speakers do not distinguish *our* from *hour*, or *air* from *heir*, and have no communication problems. Similarly, it is jarring, for those unused to it, to hear English pronounced with no distinction between *writing* and *riding* or between *ant* and *aunt*, as in American English; but standard British English has lost, without any disastrous consequences, the distinction between, say, *court* and *caught*, or between *pawn* and *porn*, a distinction still audible in most regions and sociolects of the United States, and in many regional forms of British English.

Some standard speakers also object to semantic innovations in the lexicon: they may assert, for example, that the meaning of *aggravate* is 'make worse' and should not be extended to 'annoy' – a 'notorious vulgarism … best avoided', according to classic handbooks of English (cf. Fowler and Fowler [1930] 1962: 68). In response, one can retort not just that the original Latin verb, *aggravare*, already had both those meanings but, more importantly, that if the meaning of words could not be extended, the verb *arrive* would have to be used only with reference to ships but not to buses, because it literally means 'to come ashore' (cf. French *à rive* 'to (the) shore'); similarly, the verb *embark* (and *disembark*) should only be used when one talks about boarding (and alighting) boats, not airplanes, as this is the etymological meaning (cf. Late Latin *barca* 'small boat'). In the same fashion, if we disallowed semantic shifts, a *passport* should be only the document used for entering a country by arriving at a harbour (to *pass* the *port*) and not, by extension, if crossing a border by train, car, or on foot. In a comparable way, the word *journal* should not be used of a monthly, semestral, or yearly magazine because it etymologically means 'daily' (Latin *dĭurnālis*, cf. English *diurnal*) and its application was later extended to any periodical publication. Conversely, the application of many other words gets restricted over time; if we disallowed this, all vegetarian dishes should be still classified as *meat*, because the word *meat* used to mean 'food' in general; such broad meaning was narrowed to the sense of 'animal flesh' only in the thirteenth century but, in Old and Middle English, *mete* was any kind of edible material (the English saying *one man's meat is another man's poison*, still heard today, preserves the old broad sense of *meat* as generic nourishment; in related languages, like modern Norwegian and Swedish, the cognate word *mat* is still the general word for 'food'). By the same token, the word *egregious* should not be employed to say 'shockingly bad' but 'outstandingly good', as this is the original meaning that it not only had in Latin (*ēgregius* 'excellent, uncommonly good', lit. 'away from the herd') but, until relatively recently, that it had in English too. A plethora of other examples could be added, because a vast part of standard English lexical usage – as in any language – is the result of semantic shifts.

The objections that prescriptivists raise also against non-standard *syntax* are, likewise, accompanied by rationalizations that do not hold water. Many people invoke logic in order to contest utterances such as 'I didn't buy nothing' (in the sense of 'I did not buy anything' or 'I bought nothing'), arguing that such sentence can only mean, on the contrary, 'I bought something', because two negations logically cancel each other out. But one can instead, as many languages do, embrace the 'logic' that repeating something is an effective way to emphasize it: double negatives are standard in most languages, from Persian to Japanese to Afrikaans. In fact, one can have also three, four, five negatives with no ambiguity. In many European languages it would be perfectly standard to word a phrase like 'nobody has ever said anything to anyone' as 'nobody hasn't never said nothing to no-one':

French	*personne n'a jamais rien dit à personne*
Serbian/Croatian	*niko nikada nikome nije ništa rekao*
Italian	*nessuno non ha mai detto niente a nessuno*
Hungarian	*senki sem mondott senkinek soha semmit*
Modern Greek	κανείς δεν έχει πει ποτέ τίποτα σε κανέναν
	[ka'nis ðɛn 'ɛçi pi po'tɛ 'tipota sɛ ka'nɛnan]

Clearly, the perception of what is linguistically right or wrong is guided by each person's own mental grammar and vocabulary. A good demonstration that we perceive other people's use of our mother tongue, and even of other languages, largely from the perspective of our own is provided by the way we perceive pidgins based on our language. Consider Tok Pisin, a creole based on English that is spoken in Papua New Guinea, where it has the status of national language. In Tok Pisin, even in its written, formal, and technical use, words and phrases like the following are standard:

toktok 'conversation' (from the English *talk talk*)
bikpela God 'the Lord God' (from *big fellow God*)

maus gras 'moustache' (from *mouth grass*)
gras bilong ai 'eyelash' (from *grass belong eye*)
bagarap 'car accident' (from *bugger up*)

Many, if not most, English speakers would feel that all this sounds funny or even silly. However, in a sense, the joke is on them. The meaning and the stylistic register of all words is not inherent but always in flux, and the lexicon of communities who speak differently from us is therefore not distorted. The impression that we form when we hear or read their usage is, on the other hand, distorted – by the lexicon that *we* have internalized. It is natural but also misguided to feel that the meaning and connotations of a familiar word are intrinsic and real, and that a divergent usage of the same word is therefore wrong, ignorant, comical, or stupid.

Having noted all this, it must be stressed that non-standard speakers too often have unfounded prejudices. Just as a few speakers of standard English perceive certain other accents (e.g. Brummie, Scouse, Cockney, or Glaswegian, but also Indian or Caribbean) as uneducated, incorrect, or dumb, speakers with regional or with reputedly low-class accents often describe a standard RP accent as pompous, affected, or pretentious, and see their own accent as more natural and neutral. Their perception is, at least in part, a projection: since they are native speakers of a very different accent, they could speak in RP only by faking it or in pretence. Such accent would indeed be affected, pompous, and pretentious if *they* used it; but to those for whom a conservative RP accent is native, such accent is the most neutral and clearest, and unfamiliar deviations from it may seem jarring. Of course, an RP accent *can* be an affectation: some individuals, consciously or subconsciously, veer towards RP and disguise the accent that would come more natural to them in order to appear higher-class; but the reverse also can occur: some RP speakers may temporarily adopt non-RP features in order to 'pass' in a different environment.

Some non-standard speakers misperceive as affectations also the grammar and vocabulary used by standard speakers. Those who speak and write English in its standard form are not all sticklers or pedants who consciously adhere to outdated rules taken from prescriptive textbooks. To them, those rules are not an artificial prescription but an accurate description of the usage that comes natural to them. If they take exception, for example, to double negatives, they are not quoting a rulebook but are reacting on the basis of their own internal grammar, in which a certain rule applies, and a sentence like 'you didn't buy nothing' does only mean 'you did buy something'. In the same way, they may object to a sentence like 'she was literally on cloud nine' because, in their own mental lexicon, 'literally' (despite occasional precedents in good literature) still only means 'concretely, not figuratively', and that sentence to them says something absurd. Similarly, those for whom the pronoun 'they' has really only a plural meaning are bound to find its use as a generic singular jarring: if, for example, they see a newspaper article[7] which asks 'do you tell your partner you appreciate them?', they will wonder how many partners one is expected to have.

---

[7] *The Guardian*, 6 November 2016.

Underlying social dislikes

While influential factors in our assessment of other speakers' usage certainly include, as we said, the pronunciation, grammar, and lexicon that we have learnt and internalized, and the prescriptive schooling that we have received, the main reason for linguistic disapproval and disdain is, nonetheless, another. It is our *social* dislikes. Language attitudes reflect the wider sociocultural system in which they arise. It is easy to show that opinions on language use are shaped decisively by the image that one has of the speakers, especially in relation to oneself. Judgments on other people's use of language are seldom merely linguistic; they are interpersonal self-positionings and carry ideological implications which make implicit reference to social hierarchies. As such, they also have political ramifications. After all, we often judge *positively* certain people who speak in a way that diverges from ours. We are likely to feel that those who speak differently from us because they belong to a different class, social group, or nationality *that we like or admire* sound sophisticated and authoritative, or cute and endearing, or gritty and rough but in a 'cool' and sexy way. When others speak differently from us because they belong to a nationality, class, or other social category that we dislike or look down on, we are more likely to feel that their usage sounds daft, crass, or laughable.

It is easy to see how all this can happen. We grow up learning, if wrongly, that different speech styles are intrinsically and exclusively connected to certain sources, and that this is the natural order of things (think of how some horror films, when aiming to depict a world suddenly turned frighteningly weird and unpredictable, feature children talking like adults, women having deep male voices, or toys suddenly speaking). We come to regard each speaking style as an inherent and distinctive mark of a particular type of people. Already in ancient texts one finds it stated as an axiom that our use of language indicates the kind of person we are. To quote just a few: Menander averred that 'the character of a man can be recognized by his speech';[8] Cicero stated that 'such as the person himself may be, so is his speaking style';[9] and Publilius Syrus asserted that 'speech is a likeness of the soul: such is the man, so is the talking'.[10] Speaking styles are, after all, shared within groups, so they are perceived as indicating, expressing, and buttressing particular social networks and cultural milieus. It is not strange or irrational that they may have immediate, well-known, and powerful associations in our minds:

> Language varieties and forms have indexical properties which allow them to 'stand for' communities, metonymically. Language is often, therefore, more than just 'a characteristic of' or 'a quality of' a community. It is able to enshrine what is distinctive in that community, or, we might even say, constitutes that community
> (Garrett, Coupland, and Williams 2003: 12).

---

[8] Arr. Fr. 72 / VIII 4,91: 'ἀνδρὸς χαρακτὴρ ἐκ λόγου γνωρίζεται'.
[9] Tusc. 5.47: 'Qualis autem homo ipse esset, talem esse eius orationem'.
[10] 'Imago animi sermo est: qualis vir, talis oratio'.

The use of language has indeed sociolinguistic variables (Labov 1972: 237), i.e. traits that signal, either inadvertenly or deliberately, the speakers' membership of various social categories, causing listeners to assign the persons they hear to certain categories, and to build a mental picture of them. Matched-guise tests (Lambert et al. 1960: 44; cf. Giles et al. 1992: 501), in which the same actor, without being seen, spoke twice on a neutral topic saying roughly the same thing, or reading the same text, but with two different accents, have shown that the listeners, interviewed afterwards, described what they believed were two separate speakers confidently attributing to them very different personalities, looks, lifestyles, attitudes, and abilities. Nor should this surprise us: it is a general rule that language and identity are two topics about which the uninformed public can be relied upon to hold strong opinions and be ready to express them with minimal prompting.

We often make unhesitating, though possibly unwarranted, guesses about other people's social affiliations based on their pronunciation, morphology, and syntax, as well as on several other linguistic variables. Voice quality, pitch, and speech rate are among them. Language register also plays a role, because formal language (Levin, Giles, and Garrett 1994: 265) makes one appear more competent, intelligent, and able – though, on occasion, also overly distant or deferential – whereas informal language makes someone look more relaxed and more approachable. The richness of someone's vocabulary also matters, as it has been shown to convey an impression of higher ability and higher status (Bradac, Bowers, and Courtright 1979: 263). And the particular words one uses can mean much more than their lexical meaning. Some English words, for example, are perceived as class shibboleths: in Britain, many feel that whether you normally say *sofa* or *settee*, *napkin* or *serviette*, *vegetables* or *greens*, *toilet* or *loo*, and whether you call your evening meal *dinner*, *supper*, or (*high*) *tea*, pinpoints your social class. This is not only an English phaenomenon: in India, the Tamil spoken by the Brahmins (the highest caste) distinctly differed in vocabulary, as well as in grammar and phonology, from that of the lower castes. In England, some terms can clearly mark also your age: nobody below a certain age would now say *wireless* for *radio*, or *looking-glass* for *mirror*. The use of apposite jargons too, as we shall see, can affect decisively the way in which a person is assessed and categorized. Furthermore, vastly different assumptions are made about someone depending on which *language* he or she speaks natively – a key issue that we will discuss when we look at the title topic of this book: the links between language and nationality.

Examples: vocabulary, accent, syntax, whole languages

Let us zoom in on accents, because in England they have an exceeding social significance due to their notoriously close connection to class. While the upper-class accent is, to a considerable degree, supra-regional and without much local inflection, the accents of those born and raised further down on the socioeconomic scale were, and to a significant extent are, marked by regional peculiarities. It is not an accident that accents are central to most stereotypes. The correlation between certain features of British pronunciation and social class is well documented by sociolinguists, but also empirically well-known to the general public. A 1980s survey across Britain (quoted in Wells 1982: 15) asking what distinguishes upper-class people found that 'the amount of money they have' was only the seventh most frequent factor indicated, after what job they have, where they live, or what social circle they are in. The top answer was 'the way they speak'! Conversely, people from the opposite end of the socioeconomic spectrum have usually been said to have an accent that marks them as low-class or 'common'. From all this we can see that accent does not just signal class, but also *constitutes* it. Accent in Britain can then have further associations. Until some years ago, the accent of British politicians was enough to signal to which of the two main political parties they belonged: RP meant Conservative, and regional accents meant Labour Party. In recent decades, the class structure of Britain has become less rigid; and yet, when one hears different British English mother-tongue speakers, by their accent one can often – though by no means always – infer their social class of origin.

A readiness to draw some inferences from an accent is therefore not just a prejudice, and cannot surprise; but it has somewhat worrisome aspects. Many people, having their own ideas about social classes and regional character, treat accents as personality tests and as IQ diagnostics. Several studies have confirmed (Giles and Powesland 1975: 68) that non-standard speakers are inferred to be less intelligent, less educated, and less industrious, though also warmer, more honest, and more good-natured. Market research has investigated to which accents people in Britain would respond most favourably in a commercial phone call; it has found that while many judge a voice with a northern English accent to belong to someone unsophisticated or insufficiently competent and reliable, they also picture that person as artless, trustworthy, and warm. In 2017 – one example among many – Carpeo, an estate planning firm, announced its decision to open in south Wales its new funeral call centre, and to recruit locally, stating that a Welsh accent is 'sympathetic and consoling' and therefore best suited to greet callers enquiring about arranging a funeral.[11] A voice with a standard or prestigious accent, on the other hand, is thought to belong to someone more knowledgeable, more professional, and more up to the job (cf. e.g. Giles et al. 1992: 501) but also unfriendly, and perhaps patronizing and self-interested. RP is often said to be elegant and authoritative, but is also sometimes perceived as cold and snooty. It retains a special glow because it was, and to a good extent still is, the cross-regional marker of upper-class membership; it has become associated in people's minds, therefore, with 'breed', education, sophistication, and power – even though, at times, it is taken to betoken pompousness, arrogance, and a limited experience of life outside of a privileged bubble. Research in more recent years has found that RP is still recognized as attractive and prestigious, but that the awe it used to command is hugely diminished among the young, while regional accents have gained much more acceptance; RP is nonetheless still favoured over urban vernaculars, which are looked down on, except for the interviewee's own vernacular (Coupland and Bishop 2007: 81–5). Internationally too, perhaps owing

---

[11] *BBC News*, 10 May 2017

to a *Downton Abbey* image of England, there is a fairly widespread predilection for a standard British English accent: it is perceived by most European speakers of other languages as 'nicer' or more 'elegant' than an American accent. In the United States itself, English visitors who speak with an accent even only slightly close to RP are frequently told 'Jee, I love your accent' – something that Brits are not likely to say to Americans. The American perception that a standard British accent sounds intelligent is deep-seated enough to have long been the stuff of comedy: in the classic TV series *Cheers* (season 1, episode 12) the waitress says warmly to a British visitor: 'say, you from England, eh? Because you sound smart even when you say stupid things'.

Perceptions of accents, dialects, or languages are strongly influenced by the perception that one has of those who typically speak in such accents, dialects, or languages. This is borne out by certain correspondences. We often hear the accents associated with poorer strata of society being described as 'vulgar', and the accents of the higher classes as 'stuck up'. The stereotypes that many have of foreigners and of their way of speaking also match (Lambert et al. 1960: 44). As internet fora also attest, many people judge German to be exact, austere, and peremptory; Italian to be musical, stylish, and emotional; French to be romantic, elegant, and supercilious; and so on.

The opinion that people form about you is thus extended to the way you speak. It has been shown that if people like a person, they find also the accent appealing (Nisbett and Wilson 1977: 252–4); if they dislike someone's behaviour, they also, sincerely, find that person's appearance and accent irritating. Conversely, if they think someone's accent is 'ugly', they are more likely to suppose that so also is that person's behaviour. In England, experiments with voice actors have shown (Dixon, Mahoney, and Cocks 2002: 165) that one is more likely to be deemed guilty of a crime if one has a Birmingham accent than if one has a standard English (RP) accent. In the United States, experiments found that when hearing statements delivered by someone with a foreign accent, people perceived the statements as less likely to be true (Lev-Ari and Keysar 2010: 1095). All this, appalling as it is, from a purely cognitive angle is not astonishing: it is generally the case that our opinion about one feature of a person affects our judgment of other aspects of that person, with various consequences. For example, American studies have shown that juries give lighter prison sentences to good-looking defendants (Leventhal and Krate 1977: 316–18) and that good-looks, for either sex, appear to result in a wage premium in all professions, whereas having an unprepossessing appearance has a marked earnings penalty (Hamermesh and Biddle 1994: 1181–7).

Although there can be a link between the perception that people have of certain linguistic styles and the perception they have of certain social groups, this does not validate the conclusion that certain linguistic sounds or grammatical constructions are, objectively and inherently, either slovenly, uncouth, stupid, and ugly, or elegant, proper, beautiful, and refined. A few examples can demonstrate this. Some English speakers feel that there is something intrinsically and self-evidently unclassy, sub-standard, or dialectal in the intervocalic or word-final glottal stop ('dropping one's Ts', e.g. pronouncing *better* as /bɛʔɐ/ and *pot* as /pɒʔ/). English voice coaches (e.g. Rodenburg 2002: 130) still advise actors that the glottal stop 'can damage the voice' and 'produce vocal abuse'. However, in many related languages, for instance Danish, a similar articulation is a feature of the formal standard language: *mord* 'murder' is pronounced /moːʔɐ/ (in contrast with *mor* /moːɐ/ 'mother') and *hund* 'dog' is pronounced /hunʔ/ (in contrast with *hun* /hun/ 'she').[12] A glottal stop in such position would be deemed appropriate for the most formal speeches of the Queen of Denmark, although in England it would be considered the opposite of the Queen's English. The perceived 'low' social connotations or social associations of a particular usage are therefore not universal. Another simple English example is the pronouncing of R in all positions in a word, instead of not pronouncing it unless it is followed by a vowel. In England, *not* pronouncing non-prevocalic R (i.e. pronouncing *never* and *park* as /nevə/ and /pɑːk/, as if spelled *nevva* and *paak*) has come to be regarded as an essential feature of the standard, higher-class, 'proper' pronunciation, and pronouncing the R in such positions is deemed regional and perhaps lower-class. But in New York (cf. Labov 1972: 48–50), it is virtually the reverse: the higher the class of the speaker, the more consistently the R is pronounced in non-prevocalic position (saying something like /nevəɹ/ and /pɑɹk/); in the United States, after the Second World War, this has become the standard.

In many cases, there is also language-internal evidence that the perception of certain features as objectively bad is mistaken. In broad Cockney, the RP diphthong [aɪ] is pronounced [ɒɪ] (e.g. the word *right* sounds approximately as if it were spelled *royt*); and the RP sound [eɪ] is pronounced [aɪ] (e.g. the word *name* sounds approximately as if it were spelled *nime*). Some speakers of standard English argue that there is something self-evidently unpleasant and vulgar in the use of such sounds. However, the Cockney pronunciation of words like *line, tile, sigh, bile* almost as if they were spelled *loyn, toyl, soy, boyl* cannot be an inherently ugly or coarse sound, even from an RP perspective, because that is similar to the RP pronunciation of the words *loin, toil, soy*, and *boil*. In the same way, to dismiss as ugly the Cockney pronunciation of *lane, tale, say*, and *bail/bale* as *lyne, tyle, sy*, and *byle* is unjustifiable in terms of sounds or aesthetics, because it roughly matches the RP pronunciation of *line, tile, sigh*, and *bile*.

We can dismantle with analogous arguments the assertion that non-standard *grammar* is objectively defective or vulgar. For example, the copula deletion, i.e. the omission of the verb *to be* in the present tense ('he tired', 'she nice'), which is characteristic of many forms of Black English, and has often been stigmatized, is not only rule-governed, but is also completely standard in Russian, Turkish, Hungarian, Japanese, Bengali, Malay, Kannada, and in languages of 'classical' status like Ancient Greek, Classical Latin, Sanskrit, Qur'anic Arabic, and Biblical Hebrew.

Similarly, the perception of entire languages as prestigious or low-level is affected by culture-specific and context-specific considerations. Speakers of native languages of South America may add Spanish elements to their speech for added prestige; Spanish speakers from the same countries may, however, add English elements to their Spanish

---

[12] In Danish, this is a suprasegmental element (the *stød*) whose articulation – rather variable across speakers and regions – is often a laryngealization rather than a stop, though it still sounds like a glottal stop to untrained ears. The distinction need not detain us here.

for added prestige. And the cachet and status of languages also change over time. In Sweden, before the First World War, German was the foreign language taught in schools (previously it had been French), and was deemed the illustrious conduit of a model high culture; however (Östling 2008: 207–13), in the 1930s and especially after the Second World War, the Swedes' wish to distance themselves from Nazism contributed to a forceful veer towards English: in 1946, English replaced German in Swedish schools, an emblematic shift in line with Sweden's general cultural re-orientation from Germany to the United States, which continues to this day. In 1948, Denmark too introduced some orthographical changes, such as the abolition of the capitalized initial for all nouns, in a move understood to be an effort to make Danish look less like German.

Well into the twentieth century, even eminent linguists were making judgmental pronouncements on whole languages. Just to take one example: Jespersen (1912: 2–11), described the English language as 'grown-up', 'masculine', 'possessing male energy but not brutal force', and as having a word order that manifests 'business-like, virile qualities' – also because, he wrote, 'women as a rule are not such economizers of speech'. He contrasted English with Hawaiian, which he thought sounded 'child-like and effeminate', such that 'You do not expect much vigour or energy from people speaking such language'. He stated that since Russian, Dutch, Italian, and Hungarian have many diminutives, this 'cannot but produce the impression that the speakers are innocent, childish, genial beings with no great business capacities or seriousness in life'. Today, linguists feel committed to bias-free descriptivism and scientific objectivity; many, however, may privately admit to baulking at certain usages or to disliking certain accents. The assertions – which nowadays linguists make a matter of principle – that all languages, and all variants and usages of any language, are equal and uncriticizable is also, in a sense, somewhat dogmatic and disingenuous. After all, most linguists would probably believe that a book is, stylistically, either well or badly written; they may have their favourite words, admire certain languages because of their unusual features, and, when quoting someone else, they may distance themselves from usage that they do not like for ideological or anyway extra-linguistic reasons: they may, for example, signal their disapproval of the use of *he* as a universal pronoun by adding *[sic]* after it.

Real repercussions of linguistic attitudes

Attitudes towards the language use of others are not inert opinions, but emotionally charged evaluations which lead to overt responses. This is not a recent discovery: people have long realized that their speaking style may ill-dispose listeners. Socrates, at his trial in 339 BC, started his defence by asking the jurors that, as a point of fairness, they should disregard his manner of talking, and that they should, instead, consider and focus on whether what he said was just or not.[13] Nevertheless, while modern scholarship has long been clear that social interaction affects a person's use of language, only in recent decades has it come to appreciate also how much, conversely, peculiarities

---

[13] Pl. Ap. 18a: ʽτοῦτο ὑμῶν δέομαι δίκαιον, ὥς γέ μοι δοκῶ, τὸν μὲν τρόπον τῆς λέξεως ἐᾶν ... αὐτὸ δὲ τοῦτο σκοπεῖν καὶ τούτῳ τὸν νοῦν προσέχειν, εἰ δίκαια λέγω ἢ μή'.

in language use affect social interaction. Research on this has gathered momentum surprisingly late. Linguistics, for a long time, dismissed people's attitudes to language usage as an irrational fallacy of little relevance to the discipline; but language attitudes affect the linguistic phenomena that linguists aspire to understand and describe, such as language change and death. Above all, they have serious social impact (cf. Hutton 1992: 254–5). They have repercussions in various social, educational, legal, and employment contexts. A plethora of studies across countries has ascertained that a non-standard accent may bar access to prestigious jobs or job-training positions (there is now talk of 'accentism') – though, conversely, a standard accent may lead decision makers to reject applicants for low-class job training (Giles and Billings 2004: 194). The deference that the traditional upper-class in Britain was afforded has been diminishing, and people from different backgrounds have attained much more space in education and the media (in some quarters there has even been a concerted pushback against RP); nevertheless, job advertisements may still state that applicants ought to be 'well-spoken', and assume that you will know what that means; some firms may tacitly equate classy accents with the 'good communication' and 'polish' that they explicitly seek in job candidates. One may counterargue that employers may understandably prefer an applicant with the kind of accent that was traditionally associated with an expensive and exclusive private school education because they trust that such schools have more stringent standards and deliver a better education thanks to their small class sizes, larger libraries, better laboratories, more hours of instruction, or personalized attention to students. But even if such argument were plausible, what is noteworthy is that it assumes that the accent alone, in absence of any other evidence, is a sufficient indication of a first-rate education: a linguistic trait is again used as a diagnostic of a non-linguistic one.

Speakers of the standard form of a language tend to believe that what they speak is not a dialect, and that they have no accent; and they take for granted their own social advantage (just consider the advantage in school: they are the native speakers of the language variety everybody is learning). The prejudice against non-standard language varieties and accents, conversely, not only conditions the attitude of those who have a prestigious style and pronunciation, but potentially also of those who do not. The assertion that the standard variant of a language is the only correct and reputable one is often accepted and internalized by speakers of other variants, who learn to regard their own usage as ugly or defective, and even say that it is. When I mention to native speakers with limited education that I am a linguist, many promptly apologize to me for their grammar. Speakers of languages that I speak only to some degree – but the little I know is in the standard form – tell me, rather absurdly, that I speak their language better than most of their compatriots. Whole dialects and languages are often deemed to be second-rate, or less beautiful, or to be not a language at all, by the speakers themselves. Speakers of Canadian French have argued with me that the French of France is objectively better their own. Speakers of Yiddish and Pontic have argued with me that their mother tongue does not constitute a language. Such feelings are still common even though at least since the time of Franz Boas linguists have been saying that there are no intrinsically inferior languages, dialects, or accents.

Although, as social psychologists stress, humans have also a tendency to see the traits of their own in-group in an unrealistically positive way, they may be unable to do so if the image of their group in the wider society is pervasively unfavourable. Members of social categories considered inferior or deviant tend to internalize a negative view of themselves, and to feel that their low status is justified. They may, in the same way, also espouse the prejudice against their own linguistic style expressed by the dominant community. The status of that community, and of its language usage, as 'better' comes to be accepted as objective and self-evident, and its superior position as logical, legitimate, and inevitable. This is hegemony in the Gramscian sense: the dominant community achieves and maintains power and control over the other groups by inducing them to adopt its view and to come to see their own subordinated position as warranted and natural. Speakers of non-standard (i.e. reputedly sub-standard) varieties of a language are likely to see someone's native use of the standard language or accent as showing higher ability, intelligence, competence, and finesse, instead of seeing how socioeconomic power has created such an impression (a *méconnaissance* in Bourdieu's sense). The mechanism is circular: the continued ascendancy of the standard language presupposes the acceptance of its alleged superiority also by those disadvantaged by it.

Internalized linguistic prejudice has also other consequences, important for linguists. One is that self-reported usage becomes unreliable. As much behavioural research confirms, there is a general human tendency to misperceive one's conduct as being virtuously in line with received standards. As a result, while some non-standard speakers are self-deprecatory about their own speaking style, others affirm proudly (but mistakenly) that they would never use non-standard features. People have an unreal, idealized view of their own usage, and it is not rare for them to endorse publicly, in total sincerity, prescriptive rules that, in practice, they do not follow (Milroy and Milroy 2012: 15–16). Many interviewees in sociolinguistic studies, when specifically asked, proclaim their disapproval of certain pronunciations, words, registers, or syntactic constructions, and assert, in good faith, that they do not use them – only to go on to use them later in the conversation: all the researcher needs to do is to distract them by switching to an exciting topic and keep the recorder on. An acquaintance of mine, while chatting to me recently, turned to respond to a request from her little son, and criticized his speech saying sternly: 'we pronounce our Ts in this house'; and then resumed her conversation with me, in which she proceeded to drop her Ts systematically. You may be familiar with the old joke about the prim school teacher complaining to the mother of a pupil; the joke is predictable and very rude (you are warned), but there is some truth to it:

– Madam, we have a concern I need to raise with you. We are aghast with little
   Trevor's use of coarse language in class.
– I know. It's terrible. He picks it up from his mates. It's their fault. We keep f***ing
   tellin' him to stay away from those c***s, but he doesn't f***ing listen to a single
   word we say.

People can have an unrealistic perception even of which *language* they tend to use: the Belgians who are pro-French but use Flemish most of the time, claim sincerely to speak mostly French (Vandermeeren 1996: 168).

Another consequence of internalized linguistic prejudice is the deliberate alteration of one's speaking style. Those at the receiving end of negative language-based assessments are often aware that their use of language is looked down on and that this can have concrete repercussions. While we all, consciously or subconsciously, slightly modulate our use of language according to the situation and the image we wish to project, some of us go further. In England, it is not rare for someone to take elocution classes to iron out a regional or working-class accent – although nowadays a politician whose native accent si considered posh may, conversely, improvise a more 'common' pronunciation in order to be seen as 'a man of the people'. Both may get criticized and mocked, because speaking in a style that is not your native one is considered disingenuous, and because producing a consistently accurate rendering of another accent requires some skill. It should not be thought, however, that prejudices about accent, parodies of them, and efforts to disguise them in society are a peculiarly British or even modern phaenomenon. In ancient texts we see disparagement of accents, and reports of people exerting themselves to project a favourable social image through a particular pronunciation style. We even find derision of the socially self-conscious *parvenues* who, when trying to speak posh, produce wrong hypercorrected forms because they lack the necessary education. For instance, the mocking of English speakers who, having the tendency to 'drop their aitches' (to delete voiceless glottal fricatives), then misapply them in overcompensation – as in *My Fair Lady*'s 'urricanes ardly hever appen' – has a first century BC antecedent. In Catullus' eighty-fourth poem, a man is lampooned for prefixing aitches even to words that did not have one in the belief that he had thus spoken beautifully. After his departure, according to Catullus's pitiless assessment, finally 'everyone's ears rested' from the ordeal.[14]

Writing and its consequences

In the next chapter, we will look more extensively at the ways in which people alter their use of language in order to claim (or reject) membership of a group, and the ramifications of this. Before that, we need to consider the effect of language attitudes when you use language in writing rather than in speech. Even then, your usage is still clearly subject to judgments on the part of others, and to adjustments on your part – but with a few subtle differences. When you write, you have much more control over what your style expresses. In a publication, many cues that you inadvertently give off when you are present in person are hidden. In writing, you may modulate more effectively the image you project, and be less easily pigeonholed. Some social theorists have realized and acknowledged that writing books enables one to speak while becoming, in a sense, invisible; in this way, one does not have to disclose an identity as much as one does when speaking, nor therefore to abide by one consistently. Foucault (1969: 28) candidly declared:

---

[14] 'Chommoda dicebat, si quando commoda vellet/dicere, et insidias Arrius hinsidias, / et tum mirifice sperabat se esse locutum, / cum quantum poterat dixerat hinsidias ... / Hoc misso in Syriam requierant omnibus aures: / audibant eadem haec leniter et leviter ...'.

several – like me, no doubt – *write so as to no longer have a face.* Do not ask me who I am, and do not tell me to remain the same.[15]

However, even if you write without discussing any personal or sociopolitical issues (unlike Foucault), your writing style can have strong social connotations, just as your accent can. The way you write, even on a neutral topic, can lead others to draw inferences about the kind of person you are, and to make decisions about how to respond to you. As in the case of speaking, one of the factors that usually determines the image that others form of you is whether your writing does or does not conform to a received standard. Writing, like speech, has a grammar and a vocabulary; it has no accent but, unlike speech, it has spelling. And here too, people's prescriptive schooling plays a considerable role in their perceptions. But their inferences about you may also be guided by other considerations that are not necessarily groundless, though at times are unjust. Set standards such as orthography are, admittedly, fairly arbitrary and transient conventions, but if you demonstrate unfamiliarity with standard spelling, you may give the impression that you do not read much, or were not well educated; at a minimum, that you are being slovenly or unconcerned. This may be an accurate inference in many cases, but is unfair, for example, to those suffering from dyslexia, who are often bright, hardworking, and skilled even above the average. Moreover, incorrect spellings are often treated – unjust as this is – as indications that the writer ranks low not only in education, social class, and perhaps IQ, but also in professional reliability and even in morality (Horobin 2013: 2). All this, obviously, makes a difference, for example, when one seeks an employer or customers: career experts state that experiments they have conducted indicate that one spelling mistake on a CV can reduce someone's chance of getting a job by 50 per cent.[16] Misspellings may also suggest, or reveal, that one is not a native speaker, triggering prejudices in the reader. To take a light-hearted example: Italians, who tend to be rather picky and normative about food, are wary of eating in 'Italian' restaurants in foreign countries, because they find the food there to be often too unlike the genuine article; many therefore use the orthography on the menu displayed outside the restaurant as a shibboleth: if the menu has misspellings, they infer that the restaurant is not run by real Italians, and that it is therefore best given a wide berth.

It should also be noted that the way one writes, even when it does conform perfectly to a standard and has a neutral content, can still betray – or deliberately signal – the writer's stance on other issues. For Modern Greeks in the mid-twentieth century, writing in *dimotikí* (the vernacular standard of Greek) was a signal that one was a leftist; to write in *katharévousa* instead (the archaizing variety of Greek) signalled that one was a conservative. In contemporary English usage, the adoption of terms recommended for political correctness or religious orthodoxy tends to indicate endorsement of the view behind them. Even mere spellings can convey that information: writing the word *women* as *wimmin* (to avoid including

---

[15] 'Plus d'un, comme moi sans doute, *écrivent pour n'avoir plus de visage.* Ne me demandez pas qui je suis et ne me dites pas de rester le même'.

[16] *The Independent*, 21 June 2017.

the letter-sequence *men* in the word), or spelling the word *God* as *G-d* (to avoid 'taking the name of the Lord in vain') clearly suggests something about the writer's beliefs. Computer-based analyses of word occurrences in texts have identified some correlation with personality traits (cf. e.g. Pennebaker and King 1999: 1307; Fast and Funder 2008: 335, 342–3). It is common for a person's writing style to be individually distinctive, to constitute an idiolect as much as a speech style can. Classicists, for centuries, have been trained to write compositions in the manner of this or that Greek or Latin author; such practice was based on impressionistic assessments of what each author's style consisted of, but those assessments have, in recent decades, been corroborated by rigorous quantitative studies (Moerk 1970: 228–9): individual classical authors are objectively recognizable by their use of language. After all, as Pennebaker and King (ibid. 1296) note, academics often can work out the identity of their students when reading nameless exam papers, or of their peer reviewers when receiving anonymized feedback on their manuscripts. Once again, language usage, as this and the previous chapter have expounded, reveals more than we think.

In the next chapter, we continue to gather elements that may ultimately help clarify the link perceived to exist between speaking a given (variety of a) language and being a member of a collectivity like a nation. We shall therefore look at how linguistic usage, and languages altogether, act as affirmations of social similarity or difference, as distinctive markers of social groups, and become, or are made to become, principles for social inclusion and exclusion – including self-inclusion and self-exclusion.

3

Preference for the linguistically similar

The language one speaks and the way one speaks it, as we saw, act as markers of social categories; they thus create a feeling of either commonality or disconnection, and – as we are going to discuss in this chapter – become principles for social inclusion and exclusion. Because of this, most of us at times modify, even subconsciously, the language or style that we are using: doing so helps us to feel and assert either that we belong or that we are different; for the same reason, using a second language (as bilinguals and language learners discover) can alter a person's public image and self-perception.

Languages and dialects that constitute the internal code of a community are perceived by their speakers to be cosier, or more expressive, more colourful, more flavoursome (cf. Silverstein 2003: 539), and as having unparalleled immediacy and emotional charge. There is a common wisdom that talking to people in their native language naturally engenders empathy, or trust, or a positive bias. Nelson Mandela is widely reported to have said that 'if you talk to a man in a language he understands, that goes to his head; if you talk to him in his own language, that goes to his heart'. The evidence supports this. Experiments in the United States and in France (Kinzler, Dupoux, and Spelke, 2007: 12578–9) found that infants looked longer at, and accepted toys more readily from, an unfamiliar adult who had previously spoken to them in the language normally used in their environment, as compared with an adult who had spoken in a foreign language. Infants showed also a social preference for an adult who had spoken in the same accent of the people in their environment, as compared with an adult who had spoken the same language but with a foreign accent. And five-year-old children who had been shown images of children while hearing a voice, alternatively, with or without a foreign accent, when asked which child they would rather have as a friend, tended to pick a child without a foreign accent. Experiments conducted in Africa (Kinzler et al. 2012: 221–6) gave comparable results: children from an isiXhosa-speaking environment, overall, chose isiXhosa speakers over French speakers and over speakers of Sesotho (an African language less unfamiliar to them than French). A more playful example of bias in favour of those linguistically akin to oneself is provided by seemingly benign competitions such as the annual Eurovision Song Contest, a high-profile kitchfest in which many countries enter a song, and viewers in each country can vote for any songs they like except the one from their own country. Although, with rare exceptions, performers increasingly look and sound alike (i.e. American – including the British), there are detectable national voting preferences, which are hard to attribute to the quality of the songs. If we look at the assignment of the highest score in a random year, we see that, for instance, in 2011, Cyprus voted for Greece, the UK voted for Ireland, Belgium voted for France, Germany voted for Austria, Turkey voted for Azerbaijan, Iceland voted for Denmark, Serbia voted for Bosnia-Herzegovina, San Marino voted for Italy, Romania voted for Moldova (and vice versa), and so forth.

There is also abundant evidence that humans are well aware that linguistic similarity tends to generate feelings of personal or collective affinity and increases the odds of a favourable reception. People are eager and quick to reproduce the linguistic peculiarities of those whose support and acceptance they need. They usually acquire their first language (their 'mother tongue') from their parents, upon whom, initially, they entirely depend, and they later modify it through contact with their peers. Adolescence is notorious as a formative stage in which choosing and fashioning one's public persona and self-image becomes a central and conscious task, to be carried out under the judging gaze of parents, of other adults such as teachers, but – above all – of other adolescents. Peers set new values and attitudes, and indicate what is required to gain acceptance and status outside of the family, including among possible romantic partners. Language usage in adolescence is usually marked by the quick adoption of an ever-shifting argot or slang, and this shows clearly young people's eagerness to signal their membership (or at least their eligibility for membership) of their new social entourage. While adolescents are thought to be more likely to experiment with roles, lifestyles, and the associated 'identities' than their less dynamic elders, they are also, as a rule, more afraid of peer exclusion and rejection than adults are. But adults too can display similar behaviour, and we will look at instances of this: when people want to become established in a new community, or in a new job, or in a new social circle, so as to signal that they rightfully belong there, they rapidly pick up and use the relevant specialized lingo; and, even in brief social meetings, they tend to mirror, often unwittingly, the usage of those they want to be liked by. People's use of language is therefore not simply an unmanaged expression of what they happen to be, let alone a continuous and invariable display of one preset 'identity'. It is, in part, an ongoing negotiation of their public image. The image of oneself that one projects through language thus varies; in fact, that image can even be untrue: it can be sheer wishful thinking, or an outright conscious deception. Many ancient sources, as we saw, opined that human speech reveals the speaker's character; but among them there were others who warned that this is not the whole story: 'Dionysius' Cato was adding the obvious qualification that 'human speech equally conceals and reveals human character'.[1]

Language as a social border

Within the same language community, subtle linguistic differences can persist because of social divisions. For example, working-class white and black people in the UK, as

---

[1] Dion. Cato 4.20: 'prospicito tecum tacitus quid quisque loquatur / sermo hominum mores et celat et indicat idem'.

also in the United States (Joseph 2004: 170), may have the same nationality, same gender, same regional provenance, same current location, same education level, same job, same class, same sexual orientation, same political leanings, same position on religion, same hobbies – and yet may have recognizably different use of language. This tells us something, alas, about community boundaries. But differences in language usage are not only the *result* of the membership of a different community; in some circumstances, they can also be, in part, the *cause* of it – and people know this, and often try to modulate their use of language depending on where they would like to belong.

Adopting a speaking style or a jargon is a key strategy for self-positioning, for claiming to belong in whatever restricted circle one covets membership of. Jargons, whether of students, professionals, or gangs, are a social border: they are used, and constantly updated, not only to imply specialized knowledge or to claim the power to innovate, but to distinguish insiders from outsiders. As academics, we have a good example of this under our noses. Academics are nowadays quick to deconstruct and denounce political incidents in which language has been used as a tool to exclude or to bamboozle part of the population. And yet, many of them routinely do, in a sense, something very similar, even in the very lectures or articles in which they proclaim their disapproval of any exclusionary or obfuscatory use of language. The use of a deliberately abstruse form of one's language is not hard to find among academics. Their use of unexplained arcane terms and obscure acronyms stems also, we must grant, from an effort to be conceptually precise and stylistically concise; but it is difficult to shake off the suspicion that, often, an additional goal is to mark off the 'in' crowd, proclaiming one's position as insiders, and to make the banal look more esoteric, profound, and technical, to the untrained – after all, our colleagues in fields such as physics or computer science do, by necessity, talk with terms unintelligible to outsiders. In the humanities, some of the terms definitely have specific meaning and justified applications, but their use can also mark fashions and cliques. Graduate students often rush to learn and employ the currently trendy terminology and concepts, because they are keen to establish their credentials for membership of academia (their essays now rarely lack terms such as *discourse, metanarrative, aporia, interpellation, interstitial, trope, liminality, hegemonies, interrogate, sites, spaces, gesturing, paradigm, doxa,* etc.). And many such terms often come from (translations of) the personal usage of particular academics: e.g. *discourse* from Foucault, *metanarrative* from Lyotard, *aporia* from Derrida, *doxa* (despite its long history) from Bourdieu, *interpellation* from Althusser, *interstitial* from Bhabha, and so forth. Many academics continue to make up (1) new juxtapositions of common terms, (2) new acronyms, (3) new meanings for ordinary terms, or (3) new terms coined, often ineptly, from Latin and Greek, in the hope of sounding impressive, of being quoted as the source of innovative concepts, and of seeing their usage catch on among the *cognoscenti* – as we saw earlier, assigning names to things is a claim to a power. The trick is periodically successful, also thanks to an 'emperor's new clothes' effect: those who denounce the vacuity of some jargon risk appearing philistines or not *au fait* with the latest discovery; whereas if they adopt the jargon (and collude in the trick) they may appear privy to a secret understanding from which the uninitiated and the unworthy are excluded. Audiences seriously trained in linguistics and in classical languages may find it easier to see through the use of many of these terms, but in ordinary English-language conversation, as research has found, using more words of Latin origin, rather than of Germanic origin, while making you appear less approachable and friendly, makes you appear more intelligent, competent, and of higher status (cf. Levin, Giles, and Garrett 1994: 267–8).

Since language reflects *and reproduces* social inclusions and exclusions, speaking a particular language, rather than another, is also, as we shall discuss more extensively in later chapters, a *politically* significant boundary marker. Many modern nationalists identified language as an effective tool for blocking out undesired 'Others'. The nineteenth-century Irish nationalist Thomas O. Davis (1846: 174–5) observed: 'A nation should guard its language more than its territories – 'tis a surer barrier, and more important frontier'. This is the view from both sides: in Baltic states such as Latvia and Estonia, where a large Russian population settled in the Soviet era and now makes up about a quarter of the inhabitants, knowledge of Estonian or Latvian, after the collapse of the Soviet Union, was made a prerequisite for citizenship, and this was felt by some Russians to be a way to delegitimize and discourage their presence.

In all sections of society, linguistic choices – i.e. decisions to use a particular language, dialect, or words – are made not only on the basis of whom one wants to reach, but also of whom one wants to exclude. Children too have often devised simple 'secret' codes involving patterned changes to the language they are growing up with; examples include English *Pig Latin*, Spanish *jeringonza*, Italian *farfallino*, and Swedish *allspråket*. Their goal of excluding outsiders (other children or the grown-ups) is usually explicit. The children's parents too can resort to some simple encodement of their shared language in order to speak in the children's presence without being understood. An example of this is *fe-ki-boli* (ف کی بولی) in Urdu, in which an /f/ is inserted before the vowel of each syllable. Among English-speakers, one hears many parents, or other family elders, occasionally talk to each other replacing the word they don't want their preschool offspring to understand with its spelling, e.g. 'is there any *see-ey-kay-ee*?'. Parents conversant in a foreign language unknown to their children, often use that in the family, as a cryptolect (my grandmother spoke German to my father when we children were not supposed to understand, and my parents spoke French to each other for the same purpose; and in multilingual families this is not uncommon). In England there have been, besides many jargons, slangs, and argots, also many historical forms of cryptolalia: encoded speech that clearly had exclusionary goals. For example, Cockney rhymes, mostly created in the mid-nineteenth century, were once a cryptolect: saying 'plates' meaning 'feet', 'bacons' meaning 'legs', and 'Germans' meaning 'hands', was intelligible only if one knew the intermediate phrases 'plates of meat', 'bacon and eggs', and 'German bands', in which the second component, the key clue, rhymes with the intended word. In present-day England, one still occasionally hears phrases like 'he's me best *China*' ('China plate' > 'mate'), 'I'll get me *Barnet* cut' ('Barnet Fair' > 'hair'), 'use your *loaf*' ('loaf of bread' > 'head'), 'I've not heard a *dicky bird* from him' ('dicky bird' > 'word'). A few terms thus created have entered mainstream British colloquial use; the common verb 'to rabbit (on)', meaning 'to chatter', comes from 'rabbit and pork' > 'talk'; and few people using today the term *berk* 'fool, idiot' realize that it was originally a much stronger insult, as it is the first component of 'Berkeley *Hunt*'. In early-twentieth-century England, there was also a comparable, though more cryptic, use of *Polari*, a restricted English gay slang largely developed – at a time when being gay was entirely illegal – from the argot of criminals, with elements also from Romany (the language of the 'Gypsies'), and from varieties of Romance. Once relationships between men in England became legal in 1967 and then increasingly mainstream, Polari mostly died out, and the occasional word from it (such as *naff* 'lacking in taste') even became part of general colloquial British English. Before, Polari constituted coded communication not only in the sense that the content of what was being said was intelligible only to those already clued in, but also in the sense that, in more public contexts, interposing just one Polari word or two – something easily overlooked by casual listeners not in the know – was a veiled way to identify oneself selectively as gay to possible initiated others, without risks that the information would be registered by the mainstream population or by the police.

In many social contexts, the use or interjection of just a few words or phrases in a particular language can be an effective social diacritic: those words are separative markers that affirm, in a subtle but well-targeted way, somebody's membership of a group. The differences in the way we use language are seen as 'acts of identity' (Le Page and Tabouret-Keller 1985: 2). And full knowledge of the relevant language, let us note, is not necessary. I noticed in my fieldwork among Romeyka speakers in the early 2000s that Turks of Romeyka-speaking background, if not at all fluent in Romeyka, when visiting their villages of origin, used a few words of Romeyka just to assert their status as non-outsiders. In Greece too, Greeks of Pontic descent who do not speak Pontic fluently but wish to claim membership of the community may throw in a few Pontic words as an identity signal. Some Irish speakers may sprinkle some Irish terminology into their English for the same reason. Members of many ethnic minorities do something analogous to this, especially in greetings and conversation openings, or may interject incidental phrases from their ancestral language such as traditional sayings, proverbs, or songlines. In Latin inscriptions we sometimes find some incidental expression in Oscan, or in another locally near-extinct language; these are, again, 'a claim to a certain type of regional identity' despite a language shift (Adams 2003b: 271–2, 752). Jews in the Ancient Greek or Roman world who knew only Greek or Latin often made inscriptions that included one or two basic Hebrew words in a similar vein. Today, some monolingual English-speaking Jews, when among other Jews, may use a few Yiddish or Hebrew expression to signal their membership of the group. After all, some Jews even keep Shabbas though they do not believe in God; they are sometimes criticized by both the religious and the anti-religious for this, but their practice serves its purpose: it identifies them as Jews, because non-Jews would not keep Shabbas. As the Ancient Greeks thought, what matters, in order to belong, is the public observance of the prescribed practice, more than the prescribed dogmas: the orthopraxy rather than the orthodoxy (Parker 2001: 313).

The linguistic choices made by a person or group are guided by the cultural meaning that each option carries, and a particular language can be used not only in the company of members of the community characterized by that language, but also when addressing outsiders, in a gesture that is all the more symbolic. One may even choose to use a language that is entirely unknown to one's listeners, purely so as to be seen as speaking it. One may do so, for example, for social prestige, to show off one's knowledge or one's connection to a community deemed of higher social level; alternatively, to assert a difference between oneself and one's listeners; or, conversely, to assert one's membership of more than one community. In the same way, people can choose to speak, even briefly, a language that is not their own, as a political statement of bridge-building and inclusion. In all these scenarios, the content of what one says is secondary at best. As Joshua Fishman (1972: 4), was arguing half a century ago, 'the medium is (at least partly) the message'; and accommodating to someone else's linguistic preferences is an important interpersonal and social message. Many organizations, from governments to commercial companies, choose to use a particular language to send out a token signal; for example, they may address their audience in several languages not only to ensure cross-linguistic communication, but to appear to give equal and distinct space to everyone. This is perhaps why, even when a word is extremely similar or identical in the two or more languages to be used on plaques, signs, or packagings, it is still printed multiple times. It is also perhaps one of the reasons why, sometimes, translations in minority languages are utterly careless, as if the mere gesture was what really counted, and just going through the motion sufficed. At the memorial ceremony for Nelson Mandela in December 2013, the African interpreter for the deaf seen translating the speeches of world leaders into sign language, in truth, made only random gesticulations, flapping his hands with no meaning. When this became widely known, there was understandable indignation that deaf viewers had not been properly provided for. However, one can cynically opine, as Slavoj Žižek did,[2] that the signing still had meaning, as it had made the ceremony appear right-on, inclusive, and egalitarian; and it had catered well for the larger hearing public, as it had enhanced the self-congratulatory feeling of the majority who could listen to the speeches and knew no sign language. The value of the (apparent) signing was not in the content of what was being said, but in being seen as saying it in a particular language or linguistic style.

Linguistic accommodation

Language is described as the most pervasive and flexible of the symbolic resources available to humans for the production of their 'identity' (Bucholtz and Hall 2004: 369). Speakers indeed adjust their language style depending on the situation, on the topic, and on the goal of their speaking – but also on the image that they wish to project. Managing one's image through linguistic choices entails fine on-the-fly adjustments that depend on one's audience, on the feedback that the audience provides, and on the preferences that such audience displays through its own usage. As Howard Giles highlighted in his Accommodation Theory, in a conversation, if you want your

---

[2] *The Guardian*, 16 December 2013.

interlocutors to be at ease with you, to feel pleased with you, and to include you, or to perceive your respect or solidarity, you are very likely to alter subconsciously your speech pattern and make it more similar to theirs (Giles, Taylor, and Bourhis 1973: 183), reflecting their choices of language, or their accent, or their style register, or their distinctive expressions, or their speaking tempo, or pitch, or volume. Such convergence, of course, is not limited to verbal features, but can extend to your body language, and may pervade other aspects of your self-presentation. Labov (1972: 45), studying the different pronunciation used in top, medium, and low price department stores in New York, found that the sales personnel, when interacting with potential customers and therefore eager to please them, unwittingly adopted their pronunciation. Instead of using invariably the pronunciation that they used out of the store with their friends and families, at work they used an accent that matched the class of the store and of its clientèle. Mirroring someone's use of language in order to be liked presupposes that people have a preference for those who speak (and who therefore, in some sense, *are*) like them. This, as we noted at the start of the chapter, is generally borne out by the evidence. Speakers, unless perceived as parodying, or as intruding, or as overreaching, are usually well-received by those towards whom they are linguistically converging (Giles and Ogay 2007: 297–8). Experiments have shown that even when interacting with a fictional character on a computer, people subconsciously warm up to it more if it speaks to them in a voice that mimics their voice prosody (Suzuki et al. 2003: 569).

Social networks typically impose norms, including linguistic norms; if you need to be accepted as one of the established members, you will be inclined to conform, though you may or may not do it well. We noted earlier that those aspiring to 'move up' often adopt, and even undergo training to acquire, the usage distinctive of those higher up the socio-economic scale by whom they wish to be recognized as peers. While making your speaking style converge with that of your interlocutors is not entirely a one-way process (a tacit negotiation of relative positions may occur for both sides, while both sides endeavour also to save face), a proclivity to attune to (and perhaps, more broadly, to imitate) one's interlocutors is, unsurprisingly, more marked in those in a weaker social position. It is more frequently done by those who usually speak a language, dialect, or accent of low social standing. Adjustments in language use are typically towards those more socially dominant. This was first noted in job interviews: candidates realign their speech style, including accent, with that of their potential employers (Giles, Coupland, and Coupland 1991: 5), rather than the other way round. Some speakers, at least in certain contexts, do not accommodate to their interlocutors.

There are also many who do alter their speech, but in the direction of what is less standard or less prestigious. However, this too is – again – in pursuit of social acceptance: telling examples include the linguistic shifts that can be observed in urbanites moving to an atmospheric but poorer rural village, or in teenagers from middle-class families seeking inclusion in a rougher group that has its own slang. Someone keen to gain membership of a local community may adopt its non-standard linguistic features – which are sneered at elsewhere, yes, but are well-received locally, and therefore have covert prestige: amongst speakers of a certain dialect or cant, high proficiency in the local speech style confers high internal status, even if it may give lower status in mainstream society. People often make linguistic choices that, in a wider social context, are not convenient, economical, or prestigious – choices that, in the dominant community, or upper class, or in elevated contexts, are viewed negatively. A lowly language, dialect, or accent may, however, provide a valuable interpersonal connection and group membership, though it may be stigmatized elsewhere. Many people indeed preserve their native way of speaking that, although widely frowned upon, allows them to preserve their affiliation to their background. We know that even speakers of a socially despised accent or dialect or language may retain it in order to signal their continuing loyalty to the (perhaps now absent, but psychologically internalized) members of their community. They are satisfied that their usage, though non-standard or not highly regarded, matches that of those who matter to them. Some people of working-class origin would have the ability to mimic effectively and effortlessly a prestigious accent, but choose not to do so, because they too associate accents with specific social strata, communities, lifestyles, and outlooks, and would regard adopting another accent as misrepresenting who they are and as a repudiation of their background.

There are also a few situations in which one may obtain more appreciation by *not* converging towards one's interlocutors, and even by noticeably diverging from them. Wherever someone has reasons to expect to be liked better if his or her speaking style signals membership of a *different* social category than that of the interlocutor, accommodation does not take place and, indeed, the opposite phaenomenon usually occurs. Giles, Coupland, and Coupland (1991: 33–4) cite the scenario of a romantic date between a traditional man and a traditional woman who want to appeal to each other and therefore stress, respectively, their masculinity and femininity through their voice and speaking style. Although the man and the woman are not converging in their use of language, they are still accommodating to the (presumed) preferences of their potential partner in the hope of finding favour and acceptance.

Linguistic divergence

In most situations, nonetheless, linguistic divergence occurs – whether consciously or subconsciously – when you do not particularly like your interlocutors, or do not wish to get closer to them: when you do not want to be seen as equal, or as deferential, or as keen to build bridges; or when you wish to signal your disagreement in other areas, or to justify the fact that you are different in other respects. Language, like dress, is a way to fit in or to stand out. Our linguistic choices not only associate us with certain social categories but also disassociate us from others: they can intimate that we do *not* (want to) belong to a given class, age group, ethnicity, nationality, gender, and so forth. What makes us assume such position does not have to be overt hostility; it can be just a quiet (if at times questionable or smug) satisfaction in being something else. People who value their distinctiveness stiffen their group boundaries also linguistically. In the famous case of the revival of dialectal pronunciation in the isle of Martha's Vineyard (Labov 1972: 36–8), the young locals, whose pronunciation had been gradually veering towards the standard, were found to unconsciously intensify the local features of their pronunciation once their island started receiving hordes of summer visitors from the mainland. Of course, linguistic divergence can also reveal abominable attitudes. An experiment in which researchers (Lawson-Sako and Sachdev 1996: 74–5) asked for directions in the street of a popular resort in Tunisia, where both Arabic and French are in common use, found that, although the response to everybody was polite and helpful, passers-by, as a rule, replied in the language in which they had been addressed (i.e. displayed linguistic convergence) when the person asking was Tunisian or European, but replied in the other language (linguistic divergence, affirming a distinct self-image by disassociation, a distancing strategy) when the person asking for direction was a Black African.

Refusal to accommodate, moreover, occurs not only in the active production of a language (speaking or writing) but also in the reported comprehension of someone else's language (listening or reading). Intelligibility is often either asserted or denied according to whether a difference between a group of speakers needs to be emphasized or downplayed: some Danes have claimed to me that they cannot understand any Swedish, although (or perhaps because) it is a language extremely similar to their own; a few Greeks, conversely, have asserted to me that, even without training, they can understand Ancient Greek (a language of great cultural cachet) and even described it as being 'the same language' as their mother tongue.

For the same reasons of social positioning, it is possible also to diverge linguistically from one's own linguistic background or to allege linguistic difficulties with it. Sometimes one hears first-time-abroad travellers who, returning from a few months in another country, act as if, or claim, they have partly forgotten their native language – the alleged evidence usually is a few unidiomatic phrases, calqued from their language of study, which they caught themselves using in their native tongue. Actor Dolph Lundgren, having achieved international stardom in the United States, where he had filmed for a few months, when he returned temporarily to his native Sweden and was interviewed on Swedish TV, reportedly requested to be interviewed in English claiming that he had forgotten his Swedish. Here too, the social meaning and social associations of different languages arguably play a role, and divergence expresses a conscious wish to be seen in a new, more glamourous and flattering light: to be seen as moving in a wide social circle, leading a more interesting life, belonging in a more exciting locality or more prestigious culture.

Linguistic divergence, being an assertion of difference, is also a common strategy among generations. For adolescents, the use of slang and of taboo expressions (i.e. words that adults deem obscene, blasphemous, or in other ways transgressive) is an obvious way to distance themselves from the rules of linguistic and social authorities such as parents and teachers, and to affirm their own autonomy. Children of immigrants sometimes understate or undercommunicate their knowledge of their ancestral language, pretending they know it less than they do, so as to assert implicitly that they are rightful members of their country of residence and of its society, and that they are different individuals from their parents. A parallel development can occasionally be seen in the youth of the dominant, non-immigrant community. In a number of western countries, some white adolescents assume, if partly or intermittently, the speech pattern of local ethnic minorities, essentially adopting an ethnolect as a transgressive and 'cool' sociolect (which their elders deem foreign or even contemptible). For example, some American white suburban teenagers adopt features of African-American speech associating it with hip hop culture; some British working-class teenagers in ethnically mixed contexts choose to adopt features of Afro-Caribbean Creole or of Asian English; some inner-city young ethnic Germans consciously adopt prosodic, phraseological, and syntactic elements from the German spoken by their Turkish classmates (such as zero copula in present-tense sentences, the omission of articles, or the lack of V2 word order); features of the speaking style of Persian, Arabic, and Balkan immigrants to Sweden are also consciously adopted by some Swedish teenagers living in urban districts with a high immigrant presence. This, even though it is not at all meant as a mockery, could be experienced by those of immigrant background as 'cultural theft' or commodification; but it can also be, and is at times accepted by them, as a positive overture, inviting them to the development of a new 'us'. The young generation of native local teenagers can, in this way, make a quiet bid for acceptance by their peers (through linguistic convergence) and affirm independence from their parents (through linguistic divergence). Many other young people use other stigmatized speaking-styles in order to cultivate a gritty, rebellious image, or to make a political point. The linguistic behaviour of their parents is often the reverse, and is another form of divergence. Parents may deliberately adhere to speaking styles and linguistic behaviour that they know to be old-fashioned, and do so with a quiet pride that, in their conservative view, they are neither foreigners nor young pipsqueaks with 'poor grammar'.

One final point about linguistic divergence should be made. If accommodating to a socially higher-rated speech style wins you more approval in some quarters, it can also get you into trouble in others. While the adoption of standard languages and accents may confer prestige and aid success, it may also occasion loss of belonging and of solidariety in your community of origin, notably if you move from a background considered low on a social scale (by locality, or class, or also by ethnicity) to a social circle considered higher. It may elicit resentment and animosity from your background – we saw this when we talked about name changes. Starting to speak in a more standard, more widespread, and more influential language or dialect or accent can get viciously rebuked as a betrayal ('selling out'), as fraudulence ('passing'), and as getting above yourself (as the French graphically put it, 'vouloir péter plus haut que son cul'). Those who strive to integrate into a different speech community are often told, depending on whether they succeed or not, that they are either failed wannabes, or a distortion of what they truly are. In post-war England, Hungarian-born British humorist George Mikes, in his phenomenally popular book *How to be an Alien* ([1946] 1952: 8), advised other immigrants: 'imitate the English. There can be only one result: if you don't succeed in imitating them you become ridiculous; if you do, you become *even more ridiculous*'. The truth is much more nuanced: most people's public image and self-image can have several genuine facets – including multiple languages, or dialects, or accents, which they can use flexibly because they are appropriate in different contexts. Although not many people can switch between several different languages, even among monolinguals there are no single-style speakers. There can be significantly different registers in a single language, which are used for different occasions (Ferguson 1994: 16) and are indeed determined by them (Biber 1994: 51). In other words, everybody has a linguistic repertoire consisting of distinct linguistic codes selected according to the audience, the setting, the tone of the occasion, and the purpose – in sum, depending on the role one has to play in that context. The same person can be, for example, a daughter, a mother, a girlfriend, a consoler, a protester, an employee, a public figure, and so forth, and the salience of each of her various roles and affiliations keeps shifting in her daily interactions; different facets of her personality thus come to the fore, and may lead her to speak in different ways.

Bilingualism

The linguistic codes that an individual uses can differ among themselves less or more – they can be just different accents, or different levels of formality, but also mutually unintelligible languages linked with considerably different cultures. For those cases, a question arises: if, having been brought up multilingual, you think, express yourself, and interact in more than one language, switching perhaps from English to Arabic and then maybe to Chinese, does that switch change you? Popular wisdom thinks so. Quintus Ennius (second–first c. BC) claimed that, since he knew Greek, Latin, and Oscan, he had three hearts;[3] Ottoman Turks would say: one language, one person; two languages, two persons;[4] in Eastern Europe, even more open-endedly, they say 'as many languages you know, so many persons you are'.[5] There is evidence that this belief, although worded in a hyperbolic form, has some justification. Many eastern Asians recognize (and onlookers who know them confirm this) that they are verbally more assertive when speaking American English. Already in the 1960s it was noticed (Ervin-Tripp 1964: 96) that Japanese 'war brides' who lived in the United States expressed much more forthright and individualistic views when speaking English. A study of bilingual Chinese Canadians (Ross, Xun, and Wilson 2002: 1047) found that they expressed more thoughts in line with Chinese cultural norms when completing experimental materials in Chinese, but exhibited Western thought patterns when completing the same materials in English: writing in Chinese, they made more 'collectivist' self-statements, and expressed more agreement with Chinese cultural views; when using English, they included more favorable than unfavorable statements about themselves, reported more positive than negative moods, expressed higher self-esteem. When using English, they were similar to native Canadians, despite their different birthplace, different upbringing, different exposure to Western outlooks, and different fluency in English. They were not quite aware of this, so it was not just an issue of public display, but of cultural frameworks.

---

[3] Cf. Gel. NA 17.17: 'tria corda sese habere dicebat, quod loqui Graece et Osce et Latine sciret'.

[4] بر لسان بر إنسان ايكى لسان ايكى انسان 'bir lisan, bir insan; iki lisan, iki insan'.

[5] This saying is popular, for instance, in Czech: 'kolik jazyků znáš, tolikrát jsi člověkem', as also in Hungarian: 'ahány nyelvet tudsz, annyi ember vagy', etc.

Speaking in one language rather than another can affect also extra-linguistic behaviour. Experiments have shown subconscious changes in the physical comportment of the same person depending on the language used. It seems that a language comes with a behavioural package. Venezuelan bilinguals in Spanish and American English were observed to sit significantly farther apart when speaking English than when speaking Spanish (Sussman and Rosenfeld 1982: 71–2): when using Spanish they sat closer than Americans, when using English they sat farther apart than Americans. Some English speakers realize (and onlookers who know them also confirm this) that they are more effusive when speaking Italian or Portuguese or Greek, even if they learnt these languages as foreign languages. Since individual languages tend to be associated with a specific set of cultural conventions, multilingual people are able to play different roles or public facets of their personality through different languages (cf. Burck 2005: 80–5). Such behavioural differences can also be exploited knowingly by the speaker: multiple varieties of a language or multiple languages can be used to modulate deliberately one's own public image.

But this is not all. Through language (and body language), people project, consciously or unconsciously, an image of themselves not only to others but also *to themselves*, and this affects also their own perception and opinion of themselves. Native bilinguals frequently have different images of themselves that cohere around each of their languages, because each of their self-images was developed in the context of acquiring a particular language as children. After all, in our minds, events are often tied to a particular language, and vice versa (cf. Aragno and Schlachet 1996: 31–4). Two languages can be experienced as being segregated in one's head, especially if the life domains in which they are used are separate. As we noted, the self-appraisals reported by bilinguals have been shown to vary dramatically according to the language they use; this extends also to their sense of ethnic or national belonging. Many bilinguals from ethnic minorities report feeling more of a particular ethnicity when speaking that ethnicity's language (Pao, Wong, and Teuben-Rowe 1997: 626). There is also evidence that speaking a language, even temporarily, can make you feel a member of a particular linguistic community, and stimulate ingroup preference for it: French-Arabic bilingual Moroccans exhibited much stronger pro-Moroccan attitudes when assessed in Arabic than in French, and bilinguals in (south American) Spanish-English showed a stronger pro-Hispanic stance when assessed in Spanish (Ogunnaike, Dunham, and Banaji 2010: 1001).

Second language learning

If those brought up bilingual can perform and experience themselves differently depending on the language that they are speaking, and if switching languages can cause in them a culture switch, it behoves us to ask what all this can mean for adults who learn a foreign language to full proficiency. What are the effects – whether positive or negative – of adopting another language? In general terms, the positive effect are plenty. Some research has found that even in countries with one very dominant language, like the United States, those who are completely bilingual earn much more, at the start of their career, than monolinguals with comparable cognitive skills, educational achievements, and parental social class (Agirdag 2014: 458). But the advantages of multilingualism are not just material. In reading, writing, speaking, and studying a new language there can be a profound aesthetic pleasure. Such feeling may not be very scientific, but it is well known to those who have worked extensively at mastering other tongues. You may have heard them enthusing about the precision of German nouns, the abundance of the Finnish cases, the gracefulness of Arabic calligraphy, the romanticism of the Slovenian dual, the Lego-like neatness of Turkish suffixes, the musicality of Italian pronunciation, the ingenuity of Chinese characters, the archaism of Lithuanian declensions, the fun of Xhosa clicks. You may also have heard them reporting that learning languages is a unique mental workout – a notion that does have a well-established scientific basis: learning a new language improves general cognitive function, notably memory and attention, and delays the onset of dementia by several years (cf. e.g. Bialystok 2007: 215–20; Schroeder and Marian 2012: 597–99). The structure of the brain undergoes positive alteration if a second language is acquired: learning another language increases the density of grey matter in the left inferior parietal cortex, especially in those who become really proficient, and who learn the new language early (Mechelli et al. 2004: 757). Indeed, such results are even better if one learns more than two languages (Bak et al. 2014: 961–2). And many intellectual benefits are experienced by the learner consciously. Another language can provide a different way of ordering and expressing your thoughts, of breaking reality into concepts, of commenting implicitly on what is being said. And there is a wisdom that can come from this. Studying a second language can make you truly aware of your first language – Goethe (1833: 44) was not completely off the mark when he claimed that 'those who do not know foreign languages know nothing about their own';[6] all the more right were old teachers who insisted that studying Latin and Ancient Greek was good mental exercise. Learning a second language not only makes you notice the grammatical rules of your first, but makes you aware that your native language has no inherent natural connection to its referents, that it has expressive limitations, and that it carries debatable ideological assumptions. Those who have taken the trouble to learn foreign languages to high proficiency, and not simply dabbled in them, discover that learning a foreign language is a cultural eye-opener also in other ways: it gives you access to a different community, to its outlook, to its literature, to its cinema, to its media, to its songs, to its humour, to its customs, and much besides. Furthermore, high proficiency in an additional language does not only make you come across as more learned or more brainy; it makes you come across differently, and integrates you in a new social circle; it allows you to participate in previously inaccessible exchanges, and to become, marginally or even fully, a member of a new community of practice (Lave 1991: 64–5). And the process is circular: the more you become accepted as a member of the community, the better you learn the language and therefore feel at home in it.

---

[6] 'Wer fremde Sprachen nicht kennt, weiß nichts von seiner eigenen'.

And if this happens, your lifestyle, your public image, and your own self-perception may change. Ultimately, a new language can be a door to slightly different way of being, and becoming completely fluent in it constitutes a form of self-development and self-expansion. When your linguistic knowledge is not passive, and a foreign language is not only an external object that you look upon, but something that flows out of you, it is a new part of you. A number of adult second-language learners report earnestly that the full adoption of a new language has made them feel different or that it plainly changed them. As we saw before, linguistic choices of all kinds are, not infrequently, about being *the kind of person* that speaks in a particular way.

There's also the rub. Some may regard such an outcome as negative. They may therefore resist learning another language to native level, and remain ambivalent about using it extensively. There was, for a long time, little understanding that learning a second language (an L2) is a process that can result in a significant shift in a person's public persona and self-image. Second-language teachers then became more aware that the investment that one makes in learning a second language is linked to one's investments in one's social identity (Norton 1997: 411); and this may also explain a reluctance to learn too well. Conversely, immigrants who have a negative perception of their native language (L1) often allow their knowledge of it to deteriorate over time. Theoretical studies of motivation in L2 learners (Dörnyei 2009: 29–39) now recognize that the amount of success one has in learning a second language is related also to one's 'ideal self', to the person one ideally would like – or not like – to become. There are, of course, several reasons why some people never learn a foreign language well. Having (or not having) assets such as a good ear, willpower, free time, training, or help makes a huge difference; but some studies on the attainment of native-like proficiency in second-language learning have reported that age of first exposure to the L2 is slightly less important than it has been made out to be, and that motivation is a vital but underestimated factor (Piller 2002: 201).

For example, immigrant parents and their children often prefer to use different languages, even when talking to each other; the reason is often not only the difference in their objective proficiency, but also the different self-image they wish to protect and project. If the parents show limited success in mastering the culture and the language of the new country (to the embarrassment of their children), this is not necessarily just a matter of deficient learning or laziness. It may be an unconscious strategy to safeguard and to actively communicate their different national, ethnic, cultural identity – another case of language divergence. And this phaenomenon is neither limited to spoken usage nor to modern times. Lucullus, an eminent Roman politician, wrote his histories in Greek rather than Latin, but apparently stated that he had interspersed certain 'barbarisms and solecisms' to ensure that the text would easily show that it was written by a Roman, not a Greek.[7]

Of all the people who learn a new language, adult migrants are indeed among those who experience most vividly the change in one's sense of self that can come

---

[7]   Cic. Att. 1.19.10: 'Lucullus de suis historiis dixerat se quo facilius illas probaret Romani hominis esse idcirco barbara quaedam et σόλοικα dispersisse'.

with a shift of language (cf. Block 2009: 75). They may have moved to a new country – and therefore to a new culture and *Sprachraum* – out of necessity, even against their will, and with the illusion that this was temporary, only later realizing that it was for good. The new setting, new customs, and new language may undermine their sense of continuity in their life, break the linear narrative of their personal history, and make the complete preservation of the same identity very difficult for them. The fear of losing such identity may lead immigrants to retain an accent in the dominant language, or to learn that language less well, even consciously (Marx 2002: 275). Research on language teaching has wised up to this:

> Remember that the attainment of native proficiency in English not only demands strenuous efforts, but it may also lead to a loss of native identity in one's L1 – a price many would find far too dear to pay
>
> (Medgyes 2001: 431).

For those who settle in a new country – but also for language students – progress in learning a new language can be constrained by an attachment to a particular self-image, by a feeling that their authentic self is being effaced, by a fear of betraying their ethnic background, or by the belief that they are being asked to express themselves in a way that, in their original culture, is deemed inappropriate: too outspoken or too servile, too pretentious or too low-class, too deferential or too confrontational, or whatever connotations the new language has in their minds. Some immigrants or expats just do not bother to learn the local language well, nor make major efforts to integrate. They may, perhaps subconsciously, reject the language because they reject the culture (the values, ideology, practices) and the image associated with it. They may also strive to preserve their early identity through their offspring: many want their children to go to special schools, places of worship, and clubs that will pass on to the children key features of the parents' identity: language, religion, knowledge of the ancestral country, and so forth. And given that, in their country of current residence, they may be disfavoured or looked down on because of their nationality of origin, appearance, and class, they may not want to engage with the locals more than necessary, because in those interactions they feel forced to adopt and accept the subordinate and contemptible position to which they are assigned. In a rather circular way, since their limited comprehension and command of the local language may create the unjust perception that they have limited opinions, limited skills, limited humor, even limited intelligence, they avoid situations where they have to use that language extensively – and because of that, they do not become more proficient in it.

   Not all those who are plunged into a new language feel this way, however. Assuming that your skills, dedication, and opportunities make it possible for you to learn a new language to the point where your native one takes a back seat, you may view that situation with dismay but also with relish. Being out of your element can be discomfiting but also stimulating, or both. This dual aspect is captured well by the French term *dépaysé* 'disoriented' (etymologically, 'out of one's country') because of its double meaning: (1) feeling disconcerted, lost, like a fish out of water; (2) feeling refreshed and invigorated by a change of scenery, by the end of the routine.[8] Learning a new language is a process that can take you from an earlier stage of tedious and frustrating self-translation to a satisfying feeling of mastery – not only of a language, but of the 'identity' that you can don with it, and therefore of the (perhaps hitherto unexplored or inaccessible) opportunities for self-expressions which that new language, by positioning you in another culture, affords you. An additional language – even when the second language is acquired late and through effort – may give you the chance to break out of a set role, to step out of a limiting self-image, and to escape definitions. For example, for many second-generation immigrants to western countries, women in particular, becoming proficient in another language, even by necessity, can feel ultimately empowering – although it must be noted that such re-acculturation brings them also under the influence of another set of normative social conventions, expectations, and limitations.

While people can go to notoriously extreme lengths to preserve their social labels, we should not forget that many are, on the contrary, prepared or even anxious to change them. Some are eager to learn another language precisely in order to modify their public image or professed 'identity'. Those who do not feel protective of their 'identity' have an advantage when they try to learn a new language. Many language learners do well because they aspire not only to better jobs or nice holidays abroad, but to the persona, social entourage, status, and lifestyle that they can acquire in and through that language. In the same way in which one may be incentivated to work not simply by the aspiration, for example, to buy a certain apartment, but by the aspiration to become, and be seen as, the kind of person who has that sort of apartment, so in language learning one can be motivated by mental representations of one's future self attaining a certain social image.

It may be objected that the new 'identity' label that one may receive with a new language is not authentic. But the reality is not as straightforward. Some foreign language learners, when they speak their second (or third) language, feel that they are finally able to express a pre-existing part of themselves, or a mode of being that suits them but that could not be conveyed effectively in the other language owing to its cultural associations. Besides, someone's linguistic behaviour, like other parts of a person's behaviour, does not simply express who an individual is, but gradually shapes it – after all, the same happens at a collective level: language usage not only reflects a community and its culture but fashions them and maintains them. Burck (2005: 177) reported the following about her research participants, who had been (in some cases, reluctantly) learning a second language:

> Individuals often conflate authenticity with what is usual. Doing something new becomes constructed as inauthentic because it does not fit with ideas about the self or other. It appears that individuals learning to live in a new language are forced, through the necessity to communicate, to stay with their 'performance' despite its disruption of their sense of authenticity. These reiterative performances in the new language became constitutive of the speaker, who becomes a different kind of speaker from the first language speaker.

---

[8] In the next chapter, we shall, among other things, talk more about useful words of other languages that are not fully translatable into English.

What is initially enacted consciously can later become largely subconscious and automatic: this is true of walking a regular route, playing the piano, or driving a car. Many theoreticians argue that a certain way of styling oneself can be performed often enough that the actors themselves identify with it, and it becomes second nature to them. Bourdieu's notion of *habitus* is akin to this idea, and so is Butler's contention (1991: 18) that the repetition of the acts with which a certain identity is associated is what not only makes such identity durable, but leads one to internalize it and to believe in it. By dint of practice, self-perceptions may change. After all, behaviour, even when self-consciously altered, modifies feelings and self-perceptions, as we know from experiments in other areas. For example, through their posture and comportment, people evidently (although, as a rule, involuntarily) project an image to others, who then develop an impression and an opinion of them; some studies indicate that if people force themselves to adopt a different body posture (though this posture may be or feel fake), they eventually come to feel differently about themselves. After holding postures signalling powerfulness (Carney, Cuddy, and Yap 2010: 1366–7), participants reported feeling more powerful and showed increased testosterone and decreased cortisol levels, as one finds in people high in dominance and competitiveness; exactly the reverse effects were observed in those who were asked to hold submissive, self-effacing postures: the feigned body language did not, therefore, just send an effective message to outsiders, but induced real psychological and physiological changes in the subjects. People often experience interacting in a new language as a self-conscious and even tiresome, if amusing, act that does not, at least initially, fully match their sense of who they are; but those who, either by choice or out of need, persist often come to sincerely identify, at least to a degree, with this new practice, and with this new image of themselves. As happens to native bilinguals, their languages can become also 'identities' sincerely claimed.

The skepticism towards the professed 'identities' that are based on learning a foreign language stems from an essentialized and biologized idea of what a person's language is. Cultural traits of the parents are often treated as if they were part of the DNA of the children (consider how reputable media outlets such as the BBC casually use terms such as 'Muslim babies'); similarly, the language of your parents and ancestors is often considered your only authentic and natural one. I recall a Greek lady living in London who insisted on sending her young son to Greek classes despite his vehement protestations, and explained to me her refusal to relent by saying that it was unthinkable that the child should 'not know his language'.[9] I tried to impress upon her that, while in my view Greek is a language certainly worth learning, the fact that the little boy (fluent in English) did not know much Greek showed that Greek was, by definition, not his language, even if it was hers – but she would hear none of it. This essentialist view is very common: adults who set out to study the language of their immigrant parents or grandparents, of which they have only minimal knowledge, are described, even in serious linguistic literature, following the American example, as 'heritage speakers', a term that is as pompous as it is misleading. Above all, if they eventually achieve high

---

[9] 'δεν είναι δυνατόν το παιδί να μην ξέρει τη γλώσσα του'.

proficiency and learn to interact fluently with native speakers, they are unlikely to be accused of faking an identity, although both their linguistic proficiency and their new social persona are clearly a willful and belated construction.

Learning and using a new language to native level is a cultural eye-opener also in another way. In first-language acquisition, especially in an entirely monolingual community, a child may be unaware that other language-based 'identities' are possible. But, in the conscious and deliberate process of acquiring a second language as an adult, the feeling that one is becoming qualified for membership of a new social network, and the realization that one is seen by others differently depending on the language spoken make one realize that there is a link between linguistic choices and social labels. One notices that speaking a different language can entail projecting a different image, and that it can trigger a different social response. This new self-awareness makes the learners simultaneously actors and onlookers of their linguistic performance, and enables them to deliver it with a hint of detachment and perhaps irony – in both the serious (Rortyan, if you will) sense of the term, and in the ordinary playful sense. They become more aware that speaking any language is a performance and, to take a phrase from Butler (1990: 137–8), 'part of the pleasure, the giddiness of the performance is in the recognition of a radical contingency'. Many people who become totally fluent in two cultures and languages are better able to spot that in all language-based 'identities' (notably in ethnic and national ones) there is therefore an element of acting. Burck (ibid.) observed also the following in her research participants who had learnt a new language and were now using it ordinarily among native speakers (emphasis added):

> Some research participants retained a sense of themselves as performers, of themselves 'doing a linguistic identity'; *several had this sense of themselves in all of their languages.* For others, their performance became experienced over time as natural

Through their L2, they come to realize that there was something accidental, contextual, and constructed also in their use of their first language, and in the 'identity' associated with it. This is another realization that makes some people feel threatened and lost, but others free and fortified.

We saw that several cultures claim that having multiple languages is like having multiple personalities, that the behaviour and self-appraisal (including the feeling of attunement to a nationality) of bilinguals can vary according to language, and that many successful L2 learners exhibit a cultural shift (and report an 'identity' shift) following their acquisition of a new language. The next questions that we must ask, therefore, are: how do languages differ among themselves?, do they somehow embed different cultural understandings?, and does having a particular native language make you perceive the world differently from those who have another mother tongue? We shall tackle these three questions in the next three chapters. Once we have done so, we can move on to the question of nationality and, finally, on to the role of language in it.

4

Linguistic diversity

The different features of other languages

If differences in language mark and reflect differences in nationality or national identity, it is important to have some awareness of the dissimilarities that exist between languages. This may help us understand which connections exist – and which do not – between languages and the populations that speak them natively. It is often stated in linguistics textbooks of various schools (and repeated in academic books of other fields) that 'human languages are surprisingly similar' and that 'all known languages are at a similar level of complexity and detail' (Akmajian et al. 2017: 9); indeed, that '[a] central finding of linguistics has been that all languages, both ancient and modern, spoken by both "primitive" and "advanced" societies, are equally complex in their structure' (Forston 2010: 4). Already in the 1950s, it was standard to say that 'impressionistically … the total grammatical complexity of any language, counting both morphology and syntax, is about the same as that of any other' (Hockett 1958: 180). These statements can be questioned. Different languages are not merely alternative collections of words with which one can say the same thing. And they can be dramatically unlike one another not only in their vocabulary but also in their structures; parts of the vocabulary and structure of one may even have no equivalent in the other. Moreover, as we shall see, such lexical and grammatical idiosyncrasies serve certain useful functions, and can be linked to social and cultural particularities of each linguistic community. The fact that a language may have a word for something that another language lacks, or that it may have the ability to express particular conceptual distinctions through its grammatical forms which other languages cannot, is not only useful for its speakers but also instructive for everyone else. The comparative study of languages shows that many concepts that one may imagine to be universal are not so, and that words or expressions that are assumed to be equivalent across languages (and therefore to be good translations) may also not be so: a real equivalent may be lacking, and near-equivalents may have different connotations that tell us something about the culture, the society, and the history of the speakers. In our own language too (whichever that be), words that we presume to be neutral can carry cultural and ideological assumptions, and we shall look at examples of this. There is also much variation in how languages are used in practice. Each community may have different notions of what is appropriate and normal: different speaking styles, tones of voice, paces of conversation, ways of articulating statements, requests, orders, wishes, and compliments, or of indicating disagreement, assent, gratitude, annoyance, solidarity, and much besides. All this also contributes to the way different nationalities and ethnicities perceive, and indeed stereotype, one another. As we will see in Chapter 5, the etymology of words specific to each language can also embed and reveal a lot about the history, geography, and outlook of the speakers. And since languages can differ in their default ways of describing reality and of framing issues, it is fair to ask whether being a (monolingual) speaker of a particular language constrains or dictates the way one thinks; the belief that it does was the standard opinion in the nineteenth and early twentieth centuries, and then came to be denied as patent nonsense; there is, however, some evidence that, in very small ways, it may be true – as we shall discuss in Chapter 6. And we shall discuss whether this should be a concern, given that languages are often imposed on other people, obliterating their original languages – and given that, ultimately, we all grow up with a language that was developed and shaped by others, and that through that language we learn to understand and to express ourselves.

Studying other languages makes one aware that some languages have features that others do not have, both formally and semantically. Let us review a few examples. Hungarian verb forms, unlike English ones, can include marking of the subject and the object, e.g. *kereslek* 'I am looking for you'. Latin verbs have forms that can convey the sense of a gradual (inchoative), repeated (iterative), or tentative (conative) action, e.g. *nosco* 'to (try to) get to know'. Turkish verbs can be conjugated to mark impossibility of an action: *vazgeçemem* 'I will not be able to give up' (one word for eight English ones). Hungarian verbs, like Turkish ones, can be conjugated to indicate possibility, causativity, and even both: *zongoráztathatnak* 'they may get someone to play the piano'. Standard Arabic verbs often mark the sex of their referents: 'they write' is *yaktubuun* if referring to males, *yaktubna* if to females. Slovenian is one of several languages that have the dual – a specific form, in nouns as well as verbs, that indicates that what is being talked about is not one entity (singular) or many (plural), but two:

knjiga   'book'
knjigi   '[two] books'
knjige   '[three or more] books'

delam   'I do'
delava   'we [two] do'
delamo   'we [three or more] do'

One might retort that, since many languages (even languages closely related to Slovenian) do *not* have this feature, and yet they appear to function well, such a feature is perfectly dispensable. However, it is far from superfluous: among other things, it may disambiguate between groups of subjects in a narrative; it also conveys the sense that the two entities mentioned constitute somehow a unit or share some connection or intimacy – what Germans would describe as *Zweisamkeit*, lit. 'two-some-ness' (further on, we will talk also about useful words of one language that are lacking, or difficult to render, in another). Having a dual is convenient and effective when one talks, for example, about a person's eyes or hands, or about two lovers. There are also languages that have dual forms with additional features. Hawaiian has not only dual pronouns distinct from plural ones, but also alternative forms of them to mark clusivity, i.e. to indicate whether the addressee is included or not:

kāua   I and you (you being one person)
māua   I and one other person other than you
kākou   I and other (multiple) individuals including you
mākou I and other (multiple) individuals excluding you

These four Hawaiian forms, given the distinctions they make, are arguably very handy; if one translates them with English pronouns, however, one can only say 'we' in all four instances. Other languages have multiple words even for the singular pronoun 'I', the choice depending on who the speaker is, as well as on the context, and on who the interlocutor is. For example, in Japanese, when one refers explicitly to oneself, the term that one can use can be 私 (/ɯᵝataɕi/, わたし) which has a polite or business tone; or /ɯᵝatakɯɕi/, which is a more formal-sounding variant; or /ataɕi/, which is informal and used by women; or 僕 (/bokɯ/, ぼく) which is down-to-earth and somewhat humble, and used almost only by males; or 俺 (/oɾe/, おれ) which is used by men wanting a rougher or assertive tone; and yet more options exist. In the course of a conversation, a Japanese speaker can also shift between these terms, thereby modifying the image projected, and adjusting the mutual position of the speakers in the exchange.

Many languages indicate, in the form of their verbs, distinctions not marked in English. In the Iliad (22: 361–5), when Achilles kills Hector, he triumphantly exclaims 'téthnathi' (τέθναθι), a verbal form that a number of published English translations render with 'die!'. Looking also at German, French, Swedish, Italian, Russian, Danish, Hungarian, or Modern Greek translations of the Iliad, we find that these too render *téthnathi* with the present-tense imperative of the verb 'to die' of their respective languages ('Stirb!', 'Meurs!', 'Dö blott du!', 'Muori!', 'Умирай!', 'Døe kun du!', 'Halj meg!', 'Πέθανε εσύ!'). However, such translations are not correct, and also make little sense in the context of what is being described. The original text makes it clear that, at the moment of Achilles' utterance, Hector has already been killed.[1] What Achilles is doing is therefore gloating at something that has by then happened, and his exclamation is indeed grammatically very precise: *téthnathi* is the perfect-tense imperative of the verb 'to die'. The reason for the mistranslation into English and the other languages is that these cannot conjugate a verb as Ancient Greek could: they have no past tense imperatives. The translation 'have died!', though accurate, would not be English.

Modern Greek has no past-tense imperatives, but is one of several languages that, unlike English, indicate aspectual distinctions in its future tense forms. Compare the following sentences, and their identical translations in English:

---

[1] '... τέλος θανάτοιο κάλυψε, / ψυχὴ δ' ἐκ ῥεθέων πταμένη Ἄϊδος δὲ βεβήκει ... / τὸν καὶ τεθνηῶτα προσηύδα δῖος Ἀχιλλεύς·/ τέθναθι.'

tha sou grápso (θα σου γράψω) 'I'll write to you'
tha sou gráfo (θα σου γράφω) 'I'll write to you'

The English translation 'I'll write to you' is correct for both sentences insofar as this is what native English speakers are likely to say in contexts in which native Modern Greek speakers would utter one or the other of the Greek sentences listed above. However, in Greek, the second form has a sense of iteration or of extension over time that the first has not. Greeks would use the first form when, for example, promising you an email later on in the day; and they would use the latter form when reassuring a departing friend that they will be in regular contact by correspondence. The difference is aspectual: perfective vs imperfective. Now observe the two Turkish sentences:

dün akşam Yusuf geldi 'last night Yusuf came'
dün akşam Yusuf gelmiş 'last night Yusuf came'

Again, the English translations, despite the difference in the Turkish, are both correct insofar as native English speakers could use identical English sentences in contexts where a native Turkish speaker would make the distinction indicated. The difference between the two Turkish verbal forms is first-hand vs second-hand knowledge: the form *geldi* implies that the speaker was present at the event, and saw Yusuf come; the form *gelmiş* says that the subject learnt from someone else that Yusuf came or has deduced it from other factors, like spotting Yusuf's car. Again, it would be a mistake to assume that verbal forms that mark this distinction are superfluous: native speakers of languages that have it report that they keenly miss it when speaking English; even native English speakers who have become extremely fluent in languages that make such distinction report that they miss it when they return to their English-speaking homeland (Friedman 2003: 210).

Equal complexity but not quite

These few examples, to which a profusion of others could be added, suggest not only that languages differ in the convenient features they provide to speakers, but also that we can question the tenet that all languages are equally complex. Linguistic complexity, it must be granted, is a notion that can be understood in various ways, and that is anyway arduous to measure; but, for our present purposes, it can be roughly conceptualized as the length that an exhaustive account of a language's structure would have, or as the amount of rules (and the exceptions thereto) needed to predict a language's grammatical forms and sentences. Features that increase linguistic complexity in the morphology of a language may include, for example, uncommon specifications such as the Slovenian duals and Turkish evidentials cited above, as well as the degree to which forms and meanings are in a one-to-one correspondence – a variable that we shall consider shortly.

The perception that a structurally more complex language is a sign of, or leads to, cultural superiority was common in the nineteenth century. In all probability, such a notion was empirically (though mistakenly) grounded in the observation that languages that were the medium of great intellectual traditions such as Ancient Greek, Latin, or Sanskrit have a highly complex grammar. Many reputedly 'exotic' languages with which Westerners came into superficial contact, on the other hand, appeared to have very little morphology and a relatively linear syntax. This was thought to reflect the perceived lack of sophistication of the speakers – another instance of what we discussed in the previous chapter: the image or stereotype of the speakers and that of their language affecting each other. Scholars who studied those languages in depth, however, came to realize that the impression of simplicity was often highly deceptive. M.B. Lewis (1917: xiii), who published a grammar of Malay, started it by writing:

> Malay is an easy language. Bafflingly easy. At the end of ten weeks you feel that you know all that there is to be known. At the end of ten years, you know that you never will.

The equicomplexity tenet has been championed in order to contrast the once-common assertion that there are primitive languages and evolved languages, and that the latter ones are the western European ones. That assertion undoubtedly expressed an ethnocentric prejudice. But it can also be misleading to say – as it later became the orthodoxy to affirm – that all languages are equally complex. There is an element of well-meaning but misleading political correctness in such a claim. We can take the first example that is likely to come to the mind of English speakers who have grappled with a foreign language in school: many languages attribute a grammatical 'gender' to sexless referents. In German, *Apfel* 'apple' is masculine, *Birne* 'pear' is feminine, *Obst* 'fruit' is neuter, and this must be reflected in the articles and adjectives applied to such nouns. In modern English there are no such complications (though, in Old English, *æppel* 'apple' was indeed masculine, *peru* 'pear' was feminine, and *ofett* 'fruit; legume' was neuter). Many of the foreign languages most commonly taught at school in Britain have also 'agreement', i.e. the marking of features such as gender or number on co-referential items. For an example, compare English with Spanish, below. If one describes, for instance, one or more children in some way (e.g. as quiet, relaxed, and happy), the adjectives in Spanish must take different forms depending on the sex and number of the child(ren) being referred to:

Table 4.1 Example of agreement for gender and number

one boy (male, singular)	chico tranquilo, relajado y contento
one girl (female, singular)	chica tranquila, relajada y contenta
multiple boys (male, plural)	chicos tranquilos, relajados y contentos
multiple girls (female, plural)	chicas tranquilas, relajadas y contentas

We should note that, when one talks about complexity of languages, the concept of *complex* should not be confused with that of *difficult*. The latter describes the subjective experience of a learner, not the inherent constitution of the language, and depends on personal factors such as which languages one knows already: for instance, learning English is relatively easy for Dutch speakers, more taxing for French speakers, and quite hard for Chinese speakers. Objective complexity, on the other hand, is an additional mnemonic burden not only for foreign students but also for mother-tongue children. Consider the way in which languages such as Turkish construct their equivalent of European relative clauses. This consists in the creation of a single verbal noun (with up to sixteen phonologically dictated variants), to which one has to attach person-marking possessive endings, after (typically verbal) features such as tense markers and (typically nominal) features such as case endings. Compare an English sentence with its Turkish translation:

English   *see [the things that I will do]*
Turkish   *gör [yapacaklarımı]*

The Turkish sentence starts off like the English one, with the imperative of the verb 'to see' (*gör* 'see'), but condenses the rest in *yapacaklarımı*, a word which is constituted by the root of the Turkish verb for 'to do' (*yap*), with a future marker (*acak*), a plural marker (*lar*), a first-person singular possessive marker (*ım*), and a definite object marker (*ı*). This is a bit more laborious and time-consuming to learn – and not only for speakers of western European languages. Children who grow up speaking Turkish apparently take much longer (Slobin 1977: 191) to master this construction than children who have to learn to construct English-style relative clauses ('the things *that I will do*'), even in highly inflected languages like, say, Serbian/Croatian ('stvari *koje ću raditi*'). If this is so, the impression that the English and Serbian/Croatian construction is simpler than the Turkish is not a Eurocentric prejudice. After all, we are able to see clearly that, in other areas of its grammar, Turkish is, on the contrary, much simpler that European languages. For example, the declension pattern of Indo-European languages (not only of ancient ones like Greek, Latin, or Old English, but also of modern ones like Serbian/Croatian or Lithuanian) entails a gamut of variations due to features such as gender and number, and of allomorphs that depend on the sound in which the stem of the word ends. The declension pattern of Turkish, on the other hand, is a single one, and entails a readily identifiable single set of endings in two variants (the choice of which is rule-governed and entirely predictable) with no distinctions of gender or number in themselves:

Table 4.2 Example of different complexity in noun declensions

	Serbian/Croatian		Turkish	
case	'woman'	'women'	'woman'	'women'
Nom.	žen-a	žen-e	kadın-	kadın-lar-
Gen.	žen-e	žen-a	kadın-ın	kadın-lar-ın
Dat.	žen-i	žen-ama	kadın-a	kadın-lar-a
Acc.	žen-u	žen-e	kadın-ı	kadın-lar-ı
Loc.	žen-i	žen-ama	kadın-da	kadın-lar-da
Instr.	žen-om	žen-ama	kadın-la	kadın-lar-la
Voc.	žen-o	žen-e	kadın-	kadın-lar-

Turkish, as shown in the rightmost column, in order to talk of women rather than one woman, inserts an invariable segment (the morpheme *lar* that we met previously) to indicate that the noun is now plural, and then uses the same case endings that it uses also in the singular, each ending having its own function, in a one-to-one correspondence. The result of this simplicity is not merely that foreign students can learn Turkish declension with ease and speed, but that mother-tongue children do so too. The Serbian/Croatian table on the left, besides being more complex because its plural forms are unrelated to the singular ones, shows only one of a dozen declension patterns (i.e. set of endings) that exist in Serbian/Croatian, unlike in Turkish. Furthermore, the spelling of the Serbian/Croatian forms listed in the table conceals (because so does standard orthography) important fluctuations in pitch and vowel length that are marked in pronunciation; for example, the nominative singular is actually *žèna* whereas the genitive plural is *žénā*. And a further complication is that adjectives referring to a Serbian/Croatian noun like this will also receive endings (unlike adjectives in Turkish), and those endings will not always be the same ones that appear on the noun. All these differences have consequences. The declension system of Serbian/Croatian is not taxing and laborious only for foreign students; children learning Serbian/Croatian natively master their declensions much later than Turkish-speaking children master theirs (Slobin, ibid.). The difference in complexity is therefore, at least in part, objective. And it is easy to come up with other examples of inherent complexity in very different areas of a language. For instance, the names of numbers in Dutch (as in German or Slovenian) sometimes entail reading the figures from left to right and sometimes right to left: a number like fifty-seven, though written in figures as 57, it reads out as seven-and-fifty (*zevenenvijftig*). This is not only somewhat inconvenient for English-speaking learners, but appears to require more cognitive steps for native speakers, with the result that Dutch-speaking kindergarteners lag behind English-speaking children in symbolic approximate addition (Xenidou-Dervou et al. 2015: 487).

Besides, languages can also have complexities that are not structurally inherent but conventional, and these have the same effect. Turkish, to continue with the same example, used to be written in a form of the Arabic alphabet until 1928, when a form of the Latin alphabet was adopted instead. Turkish children have since learned to write much faster than they did previously. The view that alphabets such as that of Arabic (for all its beauty) are more difficult and time-consuming than the Latin is therefore not just a Western impression. Similarly, the spelling of Spanish or Finnish is more phonemic (i.e. close to having a one-to-one relationship between letters and fundamental sounds) than that of English or French, and is therefore objectively easier, both for those learning the language natively as children and for those learning it as adults.

Features such as grammatical gender, or agreement in case, gender, and number, are not simply gratuitous and useless – we should make this clear, since learners often grumble about them. Although they are usually described under the heading of 'redundancy' by many linguists (usually and tellingly, by English-speaking linguists, who do not have those features in their own native language), grammatical gender and agreement are not superfluous: they allow syntactic flexibility and greater ease of processing. Thus, in Polish, a sentence like 'the mother saw the daughter' can be translated as *matka widziała córkę* (lit. 'mother saw daughter') but also with those words in another order, for instance *córkę widziała matka*. In English, rearranging 'mother saw daughter' as 'daughter saw mother', which is what we have just done in Polish, would change radically the meaning of the sentence; in Polish, however, the two nouns are marked for grammatical case, and therefore make clear who is doing the seeing (the subject) and who is being seen (the object). If it were the daughter who is seeing the mother, the marking (the endings) would be reversed: *córka widziała matkę* (again, with words in variable order: it can be also *matkę widziała córka*, etc.). The verb *widziała* here also indicates, in its form, that the person doing the seeing is a woman; if the sentence had been 'the mother sees the son', the verb too (whatever the word order) would have contributed to clarifying that the subject is the mother and not the son. This syntactic flexibility and co-ordinated marking has its advantages. Consider the opening verse of the Greek national anthem:

Σε γνωρίζω	από την κόψη	του σπαθιού	την τρομερή
[se ɣnorizo]	[[apo] [**tin** gopsi]]	[**tu** spaθçu]	[**tin** dromeri]
'I recognise you	by the sharpness	of the sword,	the fearsome [one]'

The literal English translation cannot make clear whether the constituent *the fearsome* refers to *the sword* or to *the sharpness*; but in Greek, both the article and the noun in the constituent *the fearsome* are marked with feminine gender and accusative case, and it is therefore immediately clear to Greek speakers that *the fearsome* refers to *the sharpness*, as that is a noun of feminine gender in the accusative case (and marked as being so by the ending *-i* and the article *tin*). In this verse, *the fearsome* cannot be referring to *the sword*, which is a noun of masculine gender and in the genitive case (and marked as being so by the ending *-u* and the article *tu*). If the referent of *the fearsome* had been *the sword*, although the sequence of the words could have remained the same, the marking for gender and case agreement of *the fearsome* would have been different:

Σε γνωρίζω	από την κόψη	του σπαθιού	του τρομερού
[se ɣnorizo]	[[apo] [**tin** gopsi]]	[**tu** spaθçu]	[**tu** tromeru]

That is, both words in the sequence *the fearsome* would have also been masculine and genitive, since so is *the sword* in the Greek. Thanks to case marking and gender marking on nouns there is no ambiguity, and the intended meaning is likely to be received correctly. Indeed, 'redundancy' is a pervasive feature of our mental computation also of other external inputs, such as visual ones (Jackendoff 2011: 590). In vision too, redundancy makes the system more efficient and adaptable: if cues are in surplus, they reinforce one another, and incoming information is processed better; the overall input, if redundant, is more robust; and when the input is, in some other aspects, weaker, the multiplicity of cues maximizes the chances that the information will be still received correctly.

Let us go back to the equicomplexity tenet. The fact that there is a variable degree of complexity in languages is confirmed also by the changes that can be seen *diachronically*, i.e. observing the structure of a single language over time. There are clear instances of either loss or accretion of complexity. Many languages, including English in the course of its past history, have shed complicating features, such as nominal declensions and verbal conjugations with person-specific marking. If we compare the forms of verbs in Middle and Modern English, we see that English divested itself of several morphological distinctions – which are still retained by German, for example – whereas Swedish has shed more than English and therefore uses the same ending for all persons; Afrikaans has gone furthest, having cast off all endings:

Table 4.3 Example of variable complexity in verb conjugations

English	Middle English	German	Swedish	Afrikaans
(I) sing-	sing-e	sing-e	sjung-er	sing-
(you) sing-	sing-est	sing-st	sjung-er	sing-
((s)he) sing-s	sing-eþ	sing-t	sjung-er	sing-
(we) sing-	sing-en	sing-en	sjung-er	sing-

Furthermore, when we study the historical evolution of languages, we see the importance of their social and demographic context. Loss of linguistic complexity has often happened when a language has come to be adopted by a larger population and to be used for a larger variety of purposes. For example, the notoriously complex grammar of Ancient Greek discarded many irregular forms and allomorphs, and thus became slightly simpler, when, in the Hellenistic era, Greek became for the first time the language of an immense community. There are robust theories that link the degree of complexity – and therefore particular language typologies – to particular types and size of societies or of social networks (cf. Nichols 2009: 120; Trudgill 2009: 98; Nettle 2012: 1831–2; for a dissenting view, Campbell 2015: 211). The point for which there is firmest evidence is that smaller, more isolated, tightly knit communities tend to have more complex languages. This is one more way in which a language and the population that speaks it characterize each other. The causes of this are uncertain, but it is likely that a small community preserves rules (in language as in few other areas of life) longer than a more anonymous, atomistic, diverse population does.

The tenet that all languages are equal in complexity and detail is largely due to two factors. One, as we mentioned, is egalitarian angst: since there is a popular notion that each language sets, through its structure and vocabulary, the limits of its speakers' ability to think (a notion that we shall discuss in more detail in Chapter 6), any admission that the complexity of languages can vary may seem tantamount to describing the speakers of certain (simpler) languages as intellectually inferior. The concern that linguistic simplicity might be used to justify prejudice is understandable: foreign languages that are in some respects simpler than English have indeed been often mocked as a result – for example, for lacking articles, for having no verbal endings, for not using present-tense copular verbs. Many nineteenth-century German philologists, including Humboldt and Schlegel, assumed that rich inflections were the mark of superior languages. However, linguistic complexity too has been used as an excuse for denigrating foreign languages: relative intricacies like nominal cases and gender marking have regularly been cited by English speakers in diatribes against other languages – a well-known example being Mark Twain's (1880: 264, 271) tongue-in-cheek but also petulant (and inaccurate) piece *The Awful German Language*.

A second factor that has motivated affirmations of universal equicomplexity in languages has been the belief, prevalent in linguistics from the 1960s onwards, that underneath limited superficial variations, all languages have the same fundamental structure – a belief that has been blindly embraced by the linguists who like to talk about 'language' in general while knowing well only one. The Chomskyan approach to language analysis has focused on a putative 'language faculty' innate in the brain of everyone, and sought to identify universal features (such as 'all languages have pronouns'). However, the search for linguistic universals has not been quite so fruitful as it was expected to be. Besides, some of the traits that do tend to recur across languages need not be innate, but could be due to the shape of the environment we all share. Meanwhile, the structural variations that are discovered by the linguists who take the trouble to study languages continue to surprise us. This does not mean that the naturally occurring possibilities are infinite; it would be absurd to suggest that there is no end to linguistic variation. It is true that all languages are subject to some inherent universal constraints – no natural language will, for example, have no vowels at all, or form questions by swapping mandatorily the third word in any sentence with the fifth. But variations are considerable.

If the equicomplexity tenet is approached empirically, it becomes clear that it is weak at best. Some languages have about a tenth of the phonemes of others, some have no inflections and no tenses, some virtually no numbers, some perhaps not even the distinction between nouns and verbs (Levinson 2003: 29–31). Other languages, on the other hand, exhibit multiple basic word orders, tones, noun classes, cases, a vast panoply of moods, and many paradigmatic variants (allomorphs) to any of these. This differential in complexity can be recognized without fear, because, of course, it does not mean that those who imagined the languages of the aboriginals of Australia, or of isolated tribes of Africa, or of the original natives of America to be unsophisticated and simple, and their speakers to be primitive and witless, were right – such ethnocentric assumptions, rife in nineteenth-century anthropology, have been entirely disproven over a century ago by Franz Boas and his followers. Indeed, exceptionally complex features are found precisely in the languages of populations once regarded by Westerners as inferior: for example, noun incorporation is found in Iroquoian and Algonquian languages, and polysynthesis is found in West Greenlandic and in native languages of Australia and America. During world wars, the US military used speakers of native languages such as Navajo as 'code talkers' to transmit secret messages, counting on the very complexity of their language as a secure form of encoding.

Differences in lexical semantics

Variations in vocabulary are also remarkable. It is not uncommon for multilingual individuals to be asked (by students, language learners, tourists, and suchlike) what, in another language, is the word for something; the question is usually posed with the confident assumptions that such a word must exist. But this need not be the case. Contrary to popular perceptions, words are not like stickers applied to pre-existing universal concepts. Even concrete things that exist in all societies and cultures are not all conceptualized and lexicalized (i.e. identified by a specific word) in all languages. For example, although a word for *body* is a likely universal, *toe* is not, even if we all have toes. While English, like Germanic languages in general, makes a lexical distinction between *fingers* and *toes*, very many languages do not, and use the same word for both (if disambiguation is needed, these languages can refer to toes as 'foot fingers' or something similar):

Table 4.4 Cross-linguistically common lack of lexical distinctions made in English

English	Spanish	Hungar.	M.Greek	Turkish	Hindi	Welsh	Japan.
fingers	*dedos*	*ujjak*	δάχτυλα	*parmaklar*	उँगलियाँ	*bysedd*	指
toes	*dedos*	*ujjak*	δάχτυλα	*parmaklar*	उँगलियाँ	*bysedd*	指

Czech	Persian	Malay	Arabic	Vietnam.	Georgian	Hebrew	Swahili
prsty	انگشتان	*jari*	أصابع	*ngón*	თითები	אֶצְבָּעוֹת	*vidole*
prsty	انگشتان	*jari*	أصابع	*ngón*	თითები	אֶצְבָּעוֹת	*vidole*

Conversely, English is one of several languages that use the same word to indicate body hair and hair on someone's head:

Table 4.5 Cross-linguistically common lack of lexical distinctions lacking also in English

English	Swedish	Polish	Romanian	Arabic	Hebrew
(body) hair	*hår*	*włosy*	*păr*	شعر	שֵׂעָר
(head) hair	*hår*	*włosy*	*păr*	شعر	שֵׂעָר

But many other languages do have distinct words:

Table 4.6 Cross-linguistically common lexical distinctions lacking in English

English	Spanish	Turkish	Hungarian	Finnish	M.Greek	Japanese	Thai
(body) hair	*pelos*	*kıllar*	*szőr*	*karvat*	τρίχες	毛	ขน
(head) hair	*cabellos*	*saçlar*	*haj*	*hiukset*	μαλλιά	髪	ผม

Baffling discoveries can be made when we seek words that one might suppose to be universal because they refer to things that are under everyone's nose; as Oscar Wilde remarked (1890: 16) on a serious note, the true mystery of the world is the visible, not the invisible. For example, an extensively researched area of semantics is that of colours and their names. It may seem fair to assume that, with the exception of those who are blind or colour-blind, we all identify the same colours regardless of cultural factors. It has been argued (Berlin and Kay 1969: 5–7) that, despite some variation in inventory size and in borderline distinctions, colour terms exhibit, across languages, an above-chance degree of consistency, and that there is agreement, cross-linguistically, on what hue constitutes the prototype of a colour (for instance, on which is the 'reddest' red, the most classic or best example of red). However, the notion that there is a universally shared, innate set of divisions of the colour spectrum is looking increasingly problematic: information about the colour terminology of previously untested, remote cultures has been accruing, and it undermines the idea of a universal set of basic colours (Roberson and Hanley 2007: 605) as well as the idea that the foci of colour categories are cross-linguistically set. The human eye can detect millions of fine differences in hue, saturation, and brightness, though the basic colour terms found in a language are very much fewer. There are, it must be conceded, robust universal tendencies in the partitioning (and naming) of colours. But that is not quite the whole story. For a start, colour terms, across languages, are not a fixed number, but are known to range between two to more than a dozen, which means that a colour considered to be a self-standing and self-evident thing in one language is subsumed by another colour in a different language: mental categories that many populations take for granted are not recognized by others. Some languages, for example, do not distinguish lexically what to us are *black* and *blue*; several do not distinguish *green* and *yellow*: Korean does have *green* (*choruksek*, 초록색) but has also what to English speakers would be a *yellow/green* (*yondusek*, 연두색). Chinese *qīng*, Japanese *ao*, and Vietnamese *xanh* /saɲ/ (all three written as 青) can cover both *green* and *blue*, and the same can be found in many native languages of America. On the other hand, the English word *blue* covers what speakers of many languages, including Russian, Modern Greek, Lithuanian, Italian, Albanian, and modern Hebrew, given the lexical distinctions in their languages, regard as two basic different colours:

Table 4.7 Example of a common lexical colour distinction not found in English

English	Italian	Lithuan.	Russian	M.Greek	Alban.	M.Hebr.
(dark) blue	blu	mélyna	синий	μπλε	blu	תְּכֵלֶת
(light) blue	azzurro	žydra	голубой	γαλάζιο	kaltër	כָּחֹל

To translate the two one-word colour terms of these languages into English as 'dark blue' and 'light blue', respectively, is a reasonably accurate description of the colours being referred to, but misses entirely the point that those other languages, by labelling those colours as they do, describe them as two separate and independent colours that cannot be subsumed under another. The labels 'dark blue' and 'light blue' express the English perception that this is the same one colour in two different degrees of saturation. Similarly, what English speakers – like Russian, Modern Greek, Italian, or Lithuanian speakers – classify as *red*, in darker or lighter variants, Hungarians see as either *vörös* and *piros*, which they conceive as two different basic colours. To Hungarian speakers, neither of these two colours can subsume the other – unlike the English *scarlet* and *crimson*, which are merely types (hyponyms) of *red*. Hungarian *piros* and *vörös* are thus not fully translated by 'red' and, ultimately not even by 'bright red' and 'dark red', because such translations would fail to convey the neat categorial distinction that Hungarian makes: *piros* and *vörös* are conceived as two *unrelated* colours. Indeed, *piros* and *vörös* have each also distinct connotations, associations, and metaphorical uses, as basic colour terms typically have (think of the figurative meanings of the adjectives *red, black, white,* or *blue* in English), with differences across cultures. Even terms that, in the same language, refer to the very same colour, such as the two Turkish terms for black (*kara* and *siyah*), or the two Modern Greek terms for white (άσπρος and λευκός) have different connotations and ranges of applicability, unconnected to colour as such.

The problem of unmatching colour categories also exists – and is worse, because we have no native speakers to interrogate – with ancient languages. William Gladstone (1858: 3: 458–83), a nineteenth-century scholar of Ancient Greek (and British Prime Minister) produced a lengthy essay on Homer's use of what we call colour terms; though he himself admitted that his musings were not 'scientific', Gladstone puzzled over the fact that Homer pays little attention to colour and uses a disconcertingly meagre 'colour' vocabulary, noting mostly black and white. Above all, Homer employs the same term to describe entities whose colours appear to us to be strikingly different; conversely, in order to describe the same referent, he uses colour terms that to us are mutually exclusive. Indeed, in the long texts attributed to him, Homer never uses a word for 'colour' itself. And this, we can add, is despite Homer's remarkable aesthetic perceptiveness, poetic skill, rich imagery, emphasis on beauty, and use of a vast range of verbs meaning 'seeing' or 'looking'. Gladstone's bold conclusion (1858: 3: 488) was that 'the organ of colour and its impressions were but partially developed among the Greeks of the heroic age'. He thus thought the cause to be physiological, not cultural. It is, however, unlikely that the organs of perception of the Ancient Greeks were underdeveloped. There is anyway a difference between visually perceiving and mentally attending to; one can do the former without the latter – although the English verb *to see* is rather ambiguous on this. One might see a colour as anyone else does but without understanding it in the same chromatic terms. Besides, Homer's meagre colour vocabulary is unlikely to be due to a lack of attention to colours among the Ancient Greeks: their frescos and, originally, their statues were variously, garishly coloured. From contemporary languages, we know that speakers of languages that use the same colour term for what English classifies as green and blue, or the same colour term for what English classifies as green and yellow, can *see* the difference, but just think of those as two shades of the same colour. Many languages in the world, furthermore, have terms that pay attention to moistness, granularity, and shine in different ways and degrees, rather than to a palette of well-identified hues. It is conceivable that Homer's attention was less concentrated on hue and more on contrast and brightness, on other features such as texture and pattern, and on connotations such as freshness or ripeness.

The English concept of 'colour' conflates several visually perceptible features. What we hastily dub a 'colour term' of other languages, which may seem to us to cover unrelated colours, presumably spotlights some common element that we, as speakers of another language, do not readily understand. Languages may distil into a distinct single concept and into a single word other optical attributes of an object, such as what in English we call saturation, brightness, sheen, gloss, texture and, more ambiguously, shade or tone. Several unrelated non-Western languages have no terms expressing hue alone (Wierzbicka 2005: 220); nor do they have a word that means 'colour' as such. It is therefore not entirely preposterous to ask whether some languages have 'colours' at all, at least in the way we mean that term. Perhaps we should not believe in colour too much – *nimium ne crede colori*, to put a different spin on Virgil's phrase (E. 2.17).

We should note that languages differ not only in their inventory of content words such as adjectives (of colour or otherwise), nouns, and verbs, but also in their repertoire of function words like adpositions and conjunctions. For instance, English uses the adversative particle *but* both in sentences like 'I wanted to go to the party *but* I was ill' and in sentences that correct the information they just cited and denied, like 'she is coming not today *but* tomorrow'. In many other European languages, a different particle must or can be used in this second case:

Table 4.8 Semantic distinction marked by two different conjunctions in many languages but not in English

English	German	Italian	Serb/Cr.	Hungarian	Spanish	Swedish	Romanian
(1) *but*	*aber*	*ma*	*ali*	*de*	*pero*	*men*	*dar*
(2) *but*	*sonder*	*bensì*	*već/nego*	*hanem*	*sino*	*utan*	*ci*

Similarly, modern English uses the same particle to give an affirmative answer to a positive question (e.g. 'did you go? – yes, I did') and to contradict a negative question (e.g. 'you did *not* go? – yes, I did'); several languages, in the second case, use a different word:

Table 4.9 Semantic distinction marked by two different particles in many languages but not in English

English	German	French	Swedish/Danish	Hungarian	Icelandic	Arabic
(1) *yes*	*ja*	*oui*	*ja*	*igen*	*já*	نَعَم
(2) *yes*	*doch*	*si*	*jo*	*de*	*jú*	بَلَى

There are basic meanings for which all, or nearly all, languages have a word, like *want, see, hear, think, say, do, move, be, can, die, this, I/me, you, mine, same, before, after, much/many, more/very, good, bad, far, big, small, near, here, body, if, not, like/as, because* (cf. Wierzbicka 2006: 18; Goddard 2010: 462; Goddard and Wierzbicka 2013: 12); but ultimately, semantic universals are now thought not to be very many.

The position of multilinguals

Those conversant in more than one language are particularly aware of the expressive limits of each of their languages. They periodically find themselves groping for a word that may convey a meaning expressed exactly by some word they know in another language. They can think of a spot-on word in one language that has no exact equivalent in the others. When addressing another multilingual or highly educated interlocutor, they may interject such foreign word as it is, for conceptual precision and brevity. After all, one of the main reasons why languages often permanently adopt some words from another language (loanwords) or create new words with their own native elements but on the model of a foreign language (calques) is the fact that speakers need to express a concept or nuance that is lacking in their mother tongue but available in another.

There are now several informal books and internet sites that list cute foreign words and idioms with no direct equivalent in English. It may be rightly objected that some of those untranslatable foreign words are in fact borrowings, or that they are mistranslated, or that they are even made up: some websites quote an allegedly Russian word, 'razbliuto' (*разблюто), supposed to mean 'feeling you have for someone you previously loved but no longer do'; but there is no such word in Russian. Nevertheless, it is true that most people who have learnt other languages besides English, either acquiring them natively or by becoming proficient to near-native level, can reel off their own examples of words that they miss in English. Some of those words may have a meaning that can be conveyed in English far less felicitously but fairly adequately, with two or three words instead of one; but others have more complex, or subtle, or elusive meanings. I often switch between conversations in different languages, I travel quite a bit and thereby find myself acting informally as my friends' interpreter, and I frequently work on texts written in ancient languages; so it is not rare for me to look for translational equivalents and realize that they do not exist. Having come to this topic in the writing of this chapter, in the last few days, whenever I noticed, while chatting or working on another text, that there was no simple English equivalent for a term or expression that I needed to translate, I made a note of that. And below is part of my list, provided as a virtually random set of examples (my glosses are not literal translations, and do not always convey all possible meanings; they report the sense, or combination of senses, for which I was seeking an English equivalent):

- German *ausschlafen*, a verb meaning 'to sleep as much as one needed, to have one's fill of sleep, waking then up only spontaneously' (as opposed to the plain verb *schlafen* 'to sleep, to have some sleep');
- Italian *coda di paglia*, lit. 'hay tail', idiom meaning 'being secretly aware of being at fault or of having something to hide, and being therefore defensive and touchy, prone to interpret innocent comments as covert references to the issue';
- Swedish *tjuvträna* or *smygöva* 'to practice or exercise (so as to develop) one's abilities or those of a pupil in secrecy (especially ahead of an occasion when one's higher skill will be revealed to the surprise of others)'.
- French *mignon* 'small – but said in a positive sense, with an admiring, not belittling tone, implying that the person or the object that is being so described is therefore lovely and attractive';
- Modern Greek χαβαλές 'hours-long, relaxed, aimless, occasionally rowdy, humour-filled light conversation with one's group of friends (usually at a bar or at the home of one of them), with little activity other than chatting and bantering';
- Turkish *estağfurullah* (from Arabic أستغفر الله), exclamation used to say 'you (almost) embarrass me with your excessive compliments, praises or thanks – or, conversely, with your excessively self-berating, self-deprecating comments';
- Romanian *vrednic*, an old adjective that combines the following meanings: 1) hard-working (diligent, industrious); 2) skilled (capable, competent); 3) dignified (respectable, decorous); (4) worthy (deserving, meritorious);

- Latin *relata refero*, an apologetic and/or defensive disclaimer, meaning, in practice '(don't take it out on me), I am only reporting directly what I have been told (which can be true or false, just or injust, but that is not my fault)';
- German *Besserwisserei* 'tactless instruction, correction, or criticism for not following rules or methodologies that one considers universally right and purports to follow unfailingly, thereby implying one's cultural and ethical superiority';
- Italian *sfizioso* (adj.) 'that satisfies a little whim or a particular and exacting desire; pleasing and enjoyable because not banal, more original, more refined, more interesting than the usual';
- Swedish *orkar* (verb mostly used with negation) 'to have enough physical energy or strength left to manage to do something; given one's tiredness, to still feel like, or be still able to do something';
- Swiss Italian *biluxare* 'to flash the headlights of one's car, or briefly alternate high and low lights, not to aid one's own vision and driving, but to catch the attention of another driver or of a passer-by and signal something';
- Ancient Greek φθορά (term used also in Modern Greek) 'gradual but inexorable and irreparable deterioration and dissolution due to the natural impermanence inherent in everything, esp. human aging and passing out of existence';
- Turkish *kolay gelsin*, lit. 'may it come easy', an expression of sympathy used to greet people who are working, e.g. when entering a shop or office, walking past workers, or parting company with someone who is off to work;
- Latin *tertium non datur*, expression meaning, in practice, 'it must be either of these two options or interpretations, because no third possibility exists' (phrase originally expressing the 'law of the excluded middle' of traditional logic);
- German *fremdschämen* 'to cringe and feel embarrassed or ashamed on behalf of someone else (not because of any shared responsibility or involvement in the embarrassing action, but vicariously, by witnessing it)';
- Italian *merenda* 'late afternoon substantial snack, smaller than a meal, taken a few hours before dinner, often consisting of bread with some topping (jam, honey, nutella, cheese, ham) or a cake, and a (non-alcoholic) drink';
- Swedish *bottna* 'to (be able to) touch the bottom of a water mass (i.e. a lake, sea, swimming pool, etc.) with one's feet while one's head is above the water (and so being still able to breath meanwhile)';
- French *démerdard(e)* 'someone who is very resourceful and highly skilled at handling (and wriggling his or her way out of) all difficult, dangerous, or embarrassing situations by himself/herself';
- Modern Greek μικροδείχνω 'to look and come across as younger than one is, naturally' (cf. the verb νεάζω, which means mostly 'to pretend to be, or actively strive to act or seem, young', and can be disapproving);
- Turkish *üşenmek* 'not to feel motivated enough to do something; not to do owing to insufficient interest or desire or stimulus; to be too slothful or lazy to take the trouble to do; not to be able to be bothered to do';
- Romanian *sluj* (a rare term, mostly referring to four-legged animals like dogs which normally walk on all fours) 'standing up vertically resting only on one's hind legs (in an uncomfortable, servile position, eager to obtain something)';

- German *Angstlust* 'mix of dread and pleasure; enjoyment of one's fear, or probably of one's successful coping with, and surviving, a seemingly scary experience (cf. those who like horror films, bungee-jumping, etc.)';
- Italian *stillicidio* 'an exausting, seemingly never-ending series of unpleasant incidents of the same kind; the harrowing unfolding, in staggered parts, of a distressing event';
- Swedish *dygn* 'the whole day, understood to include also the night, i.e. the twenty-four hour sequence that is considered to be part of the same day, from midnight to midnight';
- French *attentisme* 'policy of inaction or of deferred action, in the belief that it is strategically best to hold on or be on stand-by until further developments or information; wait-and-see attitude and its resulting practice';
- Ancient Greek ἀνέκαθεν (a word still used in Modern Greek, though borrowed from archaic usage) 'forever, but looking backwards in time rather than forwards; i.e. during all the time in the past up to the present moment'.

Conversely, when I am chatting in other languages, I miss the equivalents of many English words whose meaning can only be conveyed in some of those languages either vaguely or with a circumlocution. A few such words are technical academic terms like *tutor* or *fellowship*, but most are everyday verbs, nouns, and adjectives that have particular nuances. Many languages other than English have a word for *boil* but not a specific single word for *simmer*, a specific word for *response* but not for *feedback*, for *model* but not for *pattern*, for *responsible* but not for *accountable*, for *critical* but not for *judgmental*, for *secure* but not for *safe*, for *embarrassing* but not for *awkward*, for *discussing* but not for *brainstorming*, for *manipulate* but not for *gaslight*, for *tiredness* but not for *jet-lag*. And I miss also grammatical forms: in German, I somewhat miss the distinction that English makes between *I have done* and *I have been doing*; in Modern Greek, I occasionally miss the distinction between *I was*, *I used to be*, and *I had been*. The list could go on.

Monolingual speakers too intermittently feel the deficiencies of their mother tongues: they can think of useful concepts they have no word for, and often complain that words that come to their mind do not exactly fit an idea that they are trying to express. They can also point to common items for which they know no term. Both eloquent and inarticulate speakers are likely to name certain objects promptly, specifically, and consistently, but not other objects, which have low codability into words. Even speakers very familiar with those objects refer to them by different words, often tentatively, and with qualifying phrases like 'a sort of'. For those who work with language, from philologists to poets, coming up against the limitations of a language, though frustrating, is an instructive and potentially fruitful experience. Many writers have described their struggle with the imperfect correlation between their lived experience and the words they had to use to express it. As a result, new words and, above all, additional meanings for pre-existing words and phrases have been invented, sometimes very felicitously. As Ezra Pound (1931: 21) observed, 'great literature is simply language charged with meaning to the utmost possible degree'.

New words are coined or adopted

Many terms and concepts that we now take for granted did not previously exist in our own language. Languages regularly create or acquire new words to express new concepts. In Classical Greek, the existence of a rich, subtle, detailed intellectual vocabulary cannot be simply attributed to an inherent plasticity of the Greek language: in the history of Greek, such vocabulary was a development, not something that Greek speakers possessed from the start – nor something that all Greek speakers possessed even when it had become current in Greek intellectual circles. All the more telling is the case of Latin: in the Middle Ages in particular, Latin was a language of philosophical discourse, but its philosophical vocabulary (much of which has entered English) was derived largely from Greek. In many instances, it was taken from Greek directly, for example:

Table 4.10 Greek philosophical terms adopted by Latin and thence by English

Greek	literal meaning of the Greek	Latin borrowing	English
φιλοσοφία	'love/pursuit of knowledge'	*philosophia*	philosophy
ἀναλογία	'proportion, correspondence'	*analogia*	analogy
διαλεκτική	'discussion, questioning'	*dialectica*	dialectics
κατηγορία	'predication, attribution'	*categoria*	category

And, in many other cases, the Latin terminology was calqued, i.e. translated morph-by-morph, from Greek:

Table 4.11 Greek philosophical terms literally translated by Latin and thence adopted by English

Greek	Greek transliteration & meaning	Latin calque	English
ὑπόθεσις	*hypó-thesis* lit. 'under-placing'	*sup-positio*	supposition
ποιότης	*poiótēs* lit. 'of-what-sort – ness'	*qual-itas*	quality
ὑποκείμενον	*hypo-keímenon* lit. 'under-laid'	*sub-iectum*	subject
ὑπόστασις	*hypó-stasis* lit. 'under-stance'	*sub-stantia*	substance

This was the result of a conscious effort to endow Latin with something it previously lacked. Similar considerations can be made for the Latin grammatical vocabulary, upon which the English grammatical vocabulary is also based. The English word *grammar* itself came from Latin but ultimately from Greek (γραμματική); most other English linguistic terms come from Latin, but the Latin words are usually morph-by-morph calques on Greek.[2] For example:

[2] Much of this terminology was either adopted or calqued also in other languages. E.g. grammatical case, which Greek called πτῶσις, lit. 'fall', is called *Fall* in German and Icelandic, *eset* in Hungarian (< *esik* 'to fall'), *padež* 'fall' in multiple Slavic languages, *tuiseal* in Scots Gaelic (< *tuisle* 'fall'), etc.

Table 4.12 Greek grammatical terms literally translated by Latin and thence adopted by English

Greek	Greek transliteration & meaning	Latin calque	English
σύμφωνα	*sýmphōna* lit. 'together-sounding'	*consonantes*	consonants
πτώσεις	*ptṓseis* lit. 'falls'	*casus*	cases
μετοχή	*metokhḗ* lit. 'partaking'	*participium*	participle
αἰτιατική	*aitiatikḗ* (cf. *aitiáomai* 'to accuse')	*accusativus*	accusative
πρόθεσις	*próthesis* lit. 'fore-placement'	*praepositio*	preposition
ἐπίρρημα	*epírrēma* lit. 'at-verb'	*adverbium*	adverb

The direction of lexical borrowing (i.e. which language provides words, and which language takes them) tells us something also about the advances of a population in a given field, and about the comparative prestige and clout of its culture. Despite the intense intellectual contacts between Greeks and Romans, the adoption of technical loanwords between Classical Greek and Classical Latin was almost unidirectional. This can, in many ways, be compared to the adoption (or the literal translation) of English terms by many contemporary languages, especially in fields of technology such as computing: it is not accidental that the English word *computer* is now found in Japanese, Dutch, Russian, Albanian, Lithuanian, Polish, Azerbaijani, Thai, Romanian, Bengali, Indonesian, Amharic, Bulgarian, Maltese, Burmese, Uzbek, Malay, Pashto, and in more languages besides.

The interplay between Ancient Greek and Latin shows also something else. There is nothing new in the realization that translating can be difficult, that languages can benefit from calques and borrowings, and that the vocabulary of a given language can, in some respects, be poorer than that of another. In the first century BC, the Roman poet Lucretius, who was determined to make the philosophy of Epicurus, originally written in Greek, available to the Latin-speaking public, stated in the first chapter of his didactic treatise:

> It does not escape me, in my mind, that it is difficult to elucidate
> in Latin verses the recondite discoveries of the Greeks,
> especially since many will have to be treated with new words,
> given the poverty of [our] language, and the novelty of the subject[3]

This also suggests that words, and other features of a language and of its use, can also sometime presuppose a given culture – the issue to which we now turn.

---

[3] Lucr. 1.136–40: 'Nec me animi fallit Graiorum obscura reperta / difficile inlustrare Latinis versibus esse, / multa novis verbis praesertim cum sit agendum / propter egestatem linguae et rerum novitatem.'

5

Culture hidden in the language

Culture in the etymology

Having looked at some peculiarities of individual languages, we must consider whether languages can implicitly presuppose a given outlook. We shall start, again, with words. Having been created within a speech community, words may reflect the perceptions, the beliefs, the circumstances, and the material reality that gave rise to their original use. This is clear in the etymological meaning of untold numbers of them – and examples can easily be thrown up. The Turkish term *başvurmak* means 'to resort to, turn to, or appeal to; to apply for (jobs, funds, etc.)', but it literally means 'to bang head', which requires little comment. The Hungarian *útlevél* 'passport' and the Icelandic *vegabréf* 'passport' literally mean 'road letter', which obviously describes the original format and use of such a document. The Sanskrit term बहुव्रीहि (*bahúvrīhi*) means 'rich', but literally means '[having] much rice', a reflection of what wealth meant in a particular cultural context. Similarly, in Latin, the word *pĕcūnĭa* 'money; wealth' is a derivative of *pĕcus* 'cattle; sheep', and indicates that cattle was once treated as exchangeable wealth and that minted money was conceptualized as equivalent to that. The international term *influenza* literally means 'influence' (of the stars), and as such exemplifies the mystical pseudo-explanations that were once commonly given for illnesses (even terms suggesting a concrete cause for a particular illness were often misguided: *malaria* literally means 'bad air'). In Norwegian and other continental Scandinavian languages, the word for 'married' is *gift* (which also means 'poison') and, like the English word *gift*, etymologically means 'given', because marriages used to be arranged by families, and the spouse was therefore given to someone in marriage. The late Greek verb ὑπανδρεύομαι 'to get married', which is now applied to both sexes but used to be said only of women, literally meant 'to get placed under (the power of) a man', which was, alas, what getting a husband entailed. In a number of languages, the word for 'married' literally means 'who has a house', e.g. Spanish *casado* 'married' (< *casa* 'house'), Turkish *evli* (< *ev* 'house'), Hungarian *házas* (< *ház* 'house'), Kazakh үйленген (< үй 'house'); this is not accidental, but reflects the fact that, traditionally, new generations acquired a family and/or a separate habitation only upon getting married. The Greek verb γαμῶ is the 'f-word' of Modern Greek but in Ancient Greek meant 'to marry'; the reason why the same word first meant 'to marry' and then 'to have sex' is arguably the fact that, in older times, one act required, first, the other: couples were not allowed to have sex unless they had got married; only once they had got married was sex permissible, and was considered an obligation (cf. 1. Cor. 7.3). The German term for 'pubic hair' is *Schamhaar*, lit. 'shame hair', and the area of the body between a person's legs in German is traditionally termed *Schamgegend* 'shame region' (a word that mirrors the Latin term for genitals, *pudenda*, lit. 'things to be abashed about'); the attitude may have changed, but those terms clearly attest certain cultural roots: an antisexual outlook that taught shame about the body. The Italian colloquial term *sfiga* 'bad luck' etymologically means 'lack of p***y', and reflects the male view according to which obtaining sexual access to vaginas is the definition of good luck and success. The sexist, racist, and classist culture in which words may have been created or selected is also fossilized in the etymology of many terms, including terms used today in English. Many, strangely, have escaped the recent drive to replace prejudiced terms in modern Western languages. For example, the term *vagina* considers the organ it names as merely instrumental to the male: in Latin, *vagina* means 'sheath, scubbard'. The strong generic insult *bastard* originally meant 'born out of wedlock', and thence 'cross-bred', 'spurious', 'illegitimate', 'inferior'; it thus epitomized the abhorrence of unwedded relationships, and the stigma once placed on children whose parents were either not married to each other or were considered members of other categories that should not interbreed, such as different 'races'. The English term *Ethiopian*, which was used as a generic term for someone black, not necessarily from Ethiopia, comes from the Greek Aἰθίοψ which probably means 'burnt looking' and therefore expresses a perspective that takes being white as the norm. The country name *Sudan*, similarly, comes from the Arabic word *sūdān* (سُودان) meaning 'blacks'. The negative term *vulgar* 'tasteless, socially unacceptable, obscene' etymologically means 'of ordinary people' and its semantic history encapsulates the contempt felt for the lower classes. Such etymologies may be opaque to the average user; they therefore synchronically do not affect our thinking, nor need to be brought out in a translation – but they are evidence of a certain cultural history.

We should note that even the function words of a language, such as prepositions, can reflect the culture and the material life of the speakers. Many languages have developed prepositions or postpositions from nouns indicating parts of the human body, so that, for instance, the word for 'on' is based on the word for 'head'. In some pastoral societies, on the other hand, the parts of the body from which such terms have been created are those of cattle, so that the word for 'on' is based on the word for 'back' (cf. Bortone 2010: 101–2).

We talked previously about differences in the colours that each language has words for; those differences reflect also peculiarities in the natural environment and intercultural history of the speakers (Lucy 1997: 340–1), because languages develop in places with dissimilar animals, vegetation, and minerals. Many colour terms derive from locally available natural dyes, i.e. from local plants/fruits, local fauna, local inorganic substances, and culture-specific items. For example, Modern Greek (a considerably different language and culture from that of Homer, which we discussed before) has a set of basic colour terms that is very much in line with the average European language; but the etymology of the terms still reflects the materials that happened to be locally available:

Table 5.1 Some Modern Greek colour terms and their origin

English	Modern Greek	Greek etymon and meaning
'yellow'	κίτρινο *kítrino*	< *kítron* 'citron(fruit)'
'green'	πράσινο *prásino*	< *práson* 'leek'
'orange'	πορτοκάλι *portokáli*	< *portokáli* 'orange(fruit)'
'brown'	καφέ *kafé*	< *kafé* 'coffee'
'light brown'	καστανό *kastanó*	< *kástano* 'chestnut'
'red'	κόκκινο *kókkino*	< *kókkos* 'kermes (a scale insect)'
'purple'	πορφυρός *porfirós*	< *porfíra* 'murex sea snail'

English is not that different. Plants, fruits, flowers, seeds, roots, animals, metals, and their derivatives known to English speakers have generated many English colour terms, such as *orange, lilac, fuchsia, rose, ginger, peach, mustard, lime, apricot, crimson, amaranth, cream, ebony, coffee, maroon, hazel, indigo, mahogany, ash, silver, gold, chocolate*, and *champagne*. And not only the material culture and geographical position, but also the sociocultural history of the speakers of a language is thus reflected in its colour terminology. To continue with the example of Modern Greek: France had huge influence on Greece in areas like high-end fashion, cosmetics, and design, and Greek colour terms now include many loanwords from French (Mackridge 1985: 314): *roz* 'pink' (ροζ, from French *rose*), *ble* 'blue' (μπλε, from French *bleu*), *mov* 'pale purple' (μωβ, from French *mauve*), *bez* 'beige' (μπεζ, from French *beige*), *lilá* 'lilac' (λιλά, from French *lilas*), *gri* 'grey' (γκρι, from French *gris*).

Presumed translations

Despite the many untranslatable terms that we discussed in the last chapter, there is still, as we noted, a common presumption that all the words that one knows in one's own language must have an equivalent in other languages, and that, conversely, one can understand what a word or phrase in another language exactly means by thinking of a word in one's own language. Many monolinguals believe that translating is straightforward: you say *the same thing* in a different language. In truth, translations are not always and entirely possible. As we are reminded by Dorian (2010: 96), translators who have seriously tried to produce a book translation completely equivalent to the original know that this is a laborious and ultimately doomed endeavour. We could say that translation efforts are asymptotic: a translation may be brought ever closer to its original, but it will never coincide with it. Even two words that, in different languages, refer to concepts that are cross-linguistically common, or pairs of terms that are widely accepted as correct translations of one another, often do not cover exactly the same semantic range, and therefore do not have quite the same situational applicability. For example, the English *guts* indicates a body part but also courage; in most languages, the literal translation of *guts* does not have the secondary sense of 'courage', though another body part may have it: French *estomac* 'stomach > courage'; Italian *fegato* 'liver > courage'; Modern Greek κότσια 'hocks, ankles > courage'; Georgian გუ̂ლ3ი 'arse > courage'. Even nouns that share the same etymology and refer to concrete entities may conjure up different images, associations, and feelings in different cultures. An English word like *forest* appears to have an equivalent – and, etymologically, a cognate – in Spanish *foresta*, but it is nonetheless likely to bring to mind a very different image to someone who has always lived in England rather than in South America.

Furthermore, the subtle difference between two words of different languages that are wrongly thought to be the correct translation of each other may be culturally significant. And this is not just an academic issue. For example, I have repeatedly heard Americans who live in different parts of Europe express disappointment that locals who have known them for years, though only superficially, still do not refer to them as 'a friend of mine' – but only as 'a good acquaintance of mine'. The latter expression, interestingly, does not even exist in English, but is common in other European languages: German *ein guter Bekannter von mir*, Hungarian *egy jó ismerősöm*, Italian *un mio buon conoscente*, Polish *mój dobry znajomy*, Spanish *un buen conocido mío*, Serbian један мој добар познаник, etc. Describing someone in such terms, from a European viewpoint, is not dismissive; it is descriptively accurate. The American use of the term *friend* covers also such casual 'good acquaintances', but the semantics of the German word *Freund* (as also of Hungarian *barát*, Russian друг, or Romanian *prieten*, among others) does not. These words suggest something more serious, with more depth, attachment, and commitment. At a dinner I once attended in the United States, a young American stated incidentally that every time he had moved to a different city he had dropped forever any contact with all his previous 'friends', and had simply formed a new social circle in his new location; another American nodded and said that he had done the same, and both were puzzled that two Europeans who were present were shocked.

Analogous considerations can be made also for verbs or adjectives. Many books and websites tell you how to say 'I love you' in many languages, listing short phrases in each language as equivalents. However, the Italian *ti amo* expresses specifically a strong romantic-sexual feeling (being in love and desiring someone physically), and so would not be said to a platonic friend, or to a pet, or to a sibling. It does not, therefore, cover the same broad semantic area as the English phrase *I love you*, or of the German *ich liebe dich*, the Serbian/Croatian *volim te*, the Hungarian *szeretlek*, the Russian я люблю тебя, the Greek σ'αγαπάω, the Polish *kocham cię*, or the Turkish *seni seviyorum*. In many contexts, it would be a seriously incorrect (and socially awkward) translation of them. Similarly, language learners are usually misled about the translation of the English verb *to like*: they are told that a generic phrase such as *I like her* corresponds to Spanish *ella me gusta*, Modern Greek μ'αρέσει, Russian она мне нравится, Italian *mi piace*, Latvian *man viņa patīk*. But those phrases tend to mean 'I find her physically attractive'. A neutral comment like 'I think she likes me' may therefore not be well translated by Spanish *creo que le gusto*, Greek νομίζω ότι της αρέσω, Russian думаю я ей нравлюсь, Italian *credo di piacerle*, Latvian *man šķiet, ka es viņai patīku*, etc. as these mostly mean 'I think she fancies me'. In a comparable way, the English verb *enjoy* is not translated well by the French *jouir*, the Italian *godere*, or the Portuguese *gozar*, as these mostly denote a much stronger and often sexual pleasure. It is difficult to translate feelings, and it is also too easy to presume – mistakenly – that they are universal concepts and therefore have lexical equivalents. The English adjective *happy* (cf. Wierzbicka 2004: 35–6), contrary to what language learners are routinely taught, is not correctly translated by the Italian *felice*, the Swedish *lycklig*, the Modern Greek ευτυχισμένος, or the Hungarian *boldog*, to name but a few, all of which refer to a more pervasive, complete, almost ecstatic joy. *Happy* is a much weaker and fuzzier term. Websites ask you 'are you happy to accept cookies', giving you the option to click 'Yes, I am happy', which only means you are prepared not to raise objections. While in American English 'the pursuit of happiness' indicates a reasonable search with a realistic goal, the translations of such phrase into those languages (Italian *la ricerca della felicità*, Swedish *strävan efter lycka*, Modern Greek η επιδίωξη της ευτυχίας, Hungarian *a boldogság keresése*) sound more like a chimaerical quest for a lasting state of total bliss, and therefore an empty chase. This semantic difference means also that surveys emphasizing that Americans are happier than Europeans – i.e. that more Americans than Europeans answered yes to the question 'are you happy?' put to them in their language – are fundamentally flawed. Besides, they ignore that, in some cultures, to declare that you are normally happy would seem shallow and selfish, while in the United States it is considered image-enhancing. The assumption that English (or any other medium) is a universal metalanguage with which one can approach objectively other cultures, and that its words are neutral analytical tools, can lead to social *faux pas* and occasionally to skewed research. It is surprising that only few academics notice how the words of a language, including their own native tongue, can be culturally loaded.

Implicit connotations and culture references

These variations in meaning bring in the issue of cultural differences; some theoreticians even talk of 'ethno-semantics'. In many cases, words have connotations and connections that are known to native speakers but are not obvious outside of that culture; they may have elusive overtones and associations that simple translations cannot render, and that language learners cannot even imagine. Many examples of this can easily be produced. In Turkish, the term *bereket* is not simply 'abundance, plenty' as pocket dictionaries may gloss it, but contains the implication of a divine grace; it comes from the Arabic بَرَكَة 'blessing, benefaction, boon, abundance', and suggests a gift bestowed by Allah, and therefore also tends to imply a sense of gratitude. No English one-word translation could convey this. The French verb *tutoyer* has no English equivalent, and the translation 'to address someone in the second person singular', though basically correct, does not convey any of the social rules that govern that practice nor its emotional connotation. Even in the other languages that have the same custom of addressing a person either in the second person singular or, more formally, in the second person plural, and that even have a verb like

French *tutoyer* (e.g. German *duzen*, Spanish *tutear*, Finnish *sinutella*, Swedish *dua*, Lithuanian *tujinti*, Russian тыкать, Hungarian *tegezni*, Slovenian *tikati*), the usage of the two forms of address does not necessarily have exactly the same connotations and social conventions. The Modern Hebrew *aliyah* (עֲלִיָּה, literally 'ascent'), means 'Jewish immigration to Israel' and, besides lacking a monolectic equivalent in English, is not politically neutral: it suggests spiritual elevation and communion, though originally perhaps a movement northwards. Conversely, emigration out of Israel is sometimes referred to as *yerida* (יְרִידָה) 'going-down' and, like the related term *yordim* (יוֹרְדִים) 'Israelis who have moved to other countries', has often connotations of reproach. Another term connected to emigration, the Modern Greek *ksenitiá* (ξενιτιά) means '(living) abroad', but would not be used of someone living it up in a better place: it has connotations of isolation and longing. The related Ancient Greek word *ksénos* (ξένος) meant, as in Modern Greek, 'stranger, foreigner, refugee'; in antiquity, however, because of the Ancient Greeks' religious beliefs and hospitality rules, it meant also 'someone you (must) host', 'a guest', 'a friend visiting' – connotations very different from the English 'stranger' or 'refugee'. The German term *Sitzpinkler* means 'man who habitually urinates sitting down on the toilet (as women do) instead of standing before it'; this term – another one with no equivalent in English or in most languages – not only presupposes cultural knowledge of how Western toilets are shaped and of how they are traditionally used by the two sexes but, as a result of these factors, has additional, value-laden connotations: it can be a laudatory term suggesting that a particular man (as compared to the average bloke who urinates standing up) is more considerate, cleaner, more receptive to women's recommendations, and less hung-up about gender conventions; but *Sitzpinkler* is also used as an insult, to suggest that a man is over-domesticated, yielding, and unmanly.

There are different layers of meaning in a word, and therefore different levels of translation – to the extent that a translation is possible. A translation can range from a literal gloss of the original term to the (literally different) expression that speakers of the target language would use in the same situation in order to convey a roughly comparable thought. However, this still fails to convey the host of cultural associations implied by the original word and the world view that gives rise to it. Take, for example, the Arabic expression *mashallah* (ما شاء الله, used also in Persian, Turkish, Urdu, Bengali, Indonesian-Malay, and elsewhere). Put generically, it is an appreciative and polite exclamation in response to something positive or beautiful, expressing admiration and surprise. If it is necessary for the English translation to be brief, in terms either of time (e.g. when interpreting a live speech) or of space (e.g. when composing a film subtitle), you might go by analogy, and translate *mashallah* simply with something like 'splendid!' or even with just 'wow!', given that this is what one may spontaneously say in English in a comparable context. Such translations, though, tell one nothing about the literal meaning of *mashallah*, which may be what someone asking you the meaning of *mashallah* wants to know. That meaning is 'what Allah has/had willed'. However, to most English speakers this translation would not communicate any of the non-literal sense – what the person saying *mashallah* means by saying it, or the reason why such sentence is uttered in that context. For example, if someone looks at a baby and says *mashallah*, the English translation 'what Allah has willed' would mean very little, and would not convey at all the thoughts and attitude it expresses. But even a translation like 'what a lovely baby', though that is part of the spirit of the utterance *mashallah* in this context, would be woefully inadequate. Any translation of *mashallah* that fully related what the phrase can mean to an Arabic speaker would have to go into a digression about the culture that has produced that phrase. At least in origin, *mashallah* presupposes implicitly (1) the belief in a God; (2) the belief that such God is the God described by Islam; (3) the belief that the reality we see stems from such God and embodies his will; (4) the belief that one should praise him upon seeing beautiful things; and (5) the belief, intimated by the past tense embedded in the phrase *mashallah*, that everything is preordained. And even with such lengthy explanation, nothing yet has been said about the pragmatics, about what uttering *mashallah* is supposed to achieve: crucially – but unimaginably for those unfamiliar with the culture, no matter how good their literal understanding of Arabic is – the act of saying *mashallah* (6) seeks to prevent the evil eye from jinxing what is being appreciated; to those who understand the culture and not only the language, that expression *says* all of this. In the light of that, we can also see why, if we need, conversely, to translate into Arabic the admiring 'wow!' uttered by an American (or by an American film), *mashallah* would be an incongruous rendering, given its cultural (religious, superstitious, etc.) background, and its ethnic associations. Of course, with time, these associations can also fade, as all words can change in meaning: in the Slavic languages of ex-Ottoman lands such as Serbia, Croatia, Bosnia, Montenegro, Bulgaria, and North Macedonia, the word *mashallah* (spelt *mašala* or маша́ла) is indeed now used also by non-Muslims in the neutral, generic sense of 'great! well done!'. However, such semantic shift obviously cannot be arbitrarily produced on the spot by someone tasked with translating into Arabic an American 'wow!' (or a German 'geil!', or similar colloquial exclamations in other Western languages).

Even words whose meaning may seem to be culturally universal and to have straightforward translational equivalents everywhere may have applications that are culturally specific and revealing. An example is the Korean use of *uri* (우리) 'we; our' in contexts in which Western languages would say 'my', as in *uri nampjang* 'our husband' (우리 남편), which a woman can say when talking about her husband to a friend. This is a routine way to underline social connectedness and establish rapport with one's interlocutor, and is thought to stem from the collectivist, interdependent, self-effacing orientation of Korean culture.

In so many respects, therefore, translation can only be approximate, with subtleties being inevitably lost or inevitably added. The case of German reminds us also that, as was clear to thinkers such as Bakhtin, words and phrases are often employed by native speakers with some awareness of the *history* of their usage – and with the awareness that their interlocutors too may be alert to that history and will respond accordingly. In German, to this day, words such as *Pflicht* 'duty' and *Volk* 'people', and above all words like *völkish* 'ethnic' and *Sonderbehandlung* 'special treatment' make Germans very uneasy because of their previous employment in Nazi discourse, and their use is constrained by this.

Cultural nuances in cognates

Some words exist in more than one language, with the same root and same basic meaning; and yet, even then, their connotations differ, and can do so in a way that reflects a cultural difference. For example, someone eager to advance professionally and socially is termed *ambitious* in American English and *ambizioso* in Italian. The two words are not 'false friends' in the way that, for example, English *brave* (i.e 'courageous') and Italian *bravo* (i.e. 'skilled') are: *ambitious* and *ambizioso* are adjectives that will be applied to the same person, in reference to the same attitude that such a person displays. But the view that the two cultures take of that attitude is different, and so are the implications of the words. In the United States, the view, and the meaning, of *ambitious* is usually that someone is an enterprising, hard-working, forward-thinking, focused, admirable achiever. In Italian, the view, and the traditional meaning of the term, is often that someone is a power-hungry, self-interested, status-seeking, narcissistic, unscrupulous go-getter. Only in recent years, following the cultural model of the United States, has *ambizioso* started being used in a laudatory sense. The same, in essence, is true of the French term *ambitieux*, of the Spanish *ambicioso*, of the Romanian *ambiţios*, and even of cognates in some non-Romance languages, such as the Lithuanian *ambicingas*. The connotations of the original Latin word *ambitiosus*, from which all of these ultimately derive, were mostly negative: it indicated someone lobbying and fawning over others so as to move up socially or politically; somebody vain and obstentatious, scheming and self-interested, lusting for status and power. And it was thought that *ambitio* is unwise because it entails being constantly at the mercy of the judgment of others.[1] The English word *ambition* too, originally, had a disapproving sense. The semantic evolution of *ambitious* in American English is somewhat comparable to the trajectory of words such as *fanatisch* in German: with the advent of Nazism, *fanatisch* underwent a shift from being a berating to being a commending description (Klemperer 1947: 62–7). As studies have shown, in Europe there is far less frequently 'a focus on self-interest or a desire to get ahead' (Vignoles et al. 2018: 880). A Hungarian saying teaches: 'happiness begins there, where ambition ends'.[2] Very broadly speaking, in Europe, unlike in the United States, there has been strong disapproval of those who appear highly competitive, ambitious, overweening, and self-entitled; only since the 1980s, largely through US influence, has this started to change. European cultural traditions, from the beginning, appear to have preached self-limitation, modesty, self-effacement, recognition of one's shortcomings, and coyness about wealth. Among the Ancient Greeks, in line with the old Delphic precept 'nothing in excess' (μηδὲν ἄγαν), which was widely thought to be right,[3] much of the extant literature teaches that the most shameful and disastrous personality trait is *hybris* (ὕβρις): overconfidence, excessive pride, wild aspirations, and overestimation of

---

[1] Cf. Seneca, Brev. Vitae 1.1: 'ex alienis iudiciis suspensa semper ambitio'.
[2] 'A boldogság ott kezdődik, ahol a nagyravágyás végződik'.
[3] Plato, Men. 247b: 'Πάλαι γὰρ δὴ τὸ μηδὲν ἄγαν λεγόμενον καλῶς δοκεῖ λέγεσθαι· τῷ γὰρ ὄντι εὖ λέγεται'.

one's worth and abilities. Periander, one of the Seven Sages, taught that financial gain is shameful (κέρδος αἰσχρόν); Aristotle, reaffirming the ideal of moderation, (μέσον),[4] argued that those who seek to attain more honours, money, or other gratifications than others get are selfish, get reproached, and rightly so.[5] Among the Romans too, in the Classical period, *mediocritas* was affirmed to be 'golden' (Hor. C. 2, 10, 5) and to strive after honours, though common, was often decried.[6] One of the main philosophical schools of the post-Classical period, the Epicureans – with eminent followers among both the Greeks and the Romans – preached that we should spend our life in obscurity (λάθε βιώσας), theorizing this as the way to happiness. It recommended keeping a low profile, living quietly and modestly, limiting one's desires and aspirations, and avoiding confrontations and intense emotions. The term considered the Modern Greek translation of 'ambitious', φιλόδοξος, was used disparagingly already in antiquity.[7] And, of course, in the Judeo-Christian tradition, pride was the mother of all sins, 'hateful to God and men'.[8] In the north of Europe too, the traditional social rule was that one should not aim too high, nor think of oneself as more intelligent, more popular, or more important than others – Scandinavians call this *the law of Jante*, and is in keeping with the Swedish principle of aiming for *lagom* ('not more than what suffices'). In Britain too, despite a common language with the United States, what used to be socially encouraged was self-effacement, self-deprecation, understatement, and reserve. All this is virtually the opposite of mainstream modern American culture, which teaches individual self-assertion, extroversion, unlimited confidence and aspiration, and urges one to seek the limelight and adventure, to push oneself to the front and to dare to take risks in order to live life to the max. It seems fair to suppose that the different connotations that the word 'ambitious' has, or used to have, in Europe in comparison with the United States cannot be unconnected to all this.

Cultural explanations for lexical gaps

However, we should ask whether we are justified in explaining semantic differences with cultural ones. How we can demonstrate a link between culture and vocabulary (Enfield 2002: 14)? Or does it become just a matter of hermeneutics and, as such, not one that can be settled with definitive proof? To answer that question, we must make

---

[4] Aristot. Nic. Eth. 1106b: 'μέσον τε καὶ ἄριστον, ὅπερ ἐστὶ τῆς ἀρετῆς. ὁμοίως δὲ καὶ περὶ τὰς πράξεις ἔστιν ὑπερβολὴ καὶ ἔλλειψις καὶ τὸ μέσον. ἡ δ᾽ ἀρετὴ περὶ πάθη καὶ πράξεις ἐστίν, ἐν οἷς ἡ μὲν ὑπερβολὴ ἁμαρτάνεται καὶ ψέγεται καὶ ἡ ἔλλειψις, τὸ δὲ μέσον ἐπαινεῖται καὶ κατορθοῦται· ταῦτα δ᾽ ἄμφω τῆς ἀρετῆς. μεσότης τις ἄρα ἐστὶν ἡ ἀρετή, στοχαστική γε οὖσα τοῦ μέσου'. From the Medieval period on, the principle that *in medio stat virtus* became a common motto.

[5] Aristot. Nic. Eth. 1168b: 'φιλαύτους καλοῦσι τοὺς ἑαυτοῖς ἀπονέμοντας τὸ πλεῖον ἐν χρήμασι καὶ τιμαῖς καὶ ἡδοναῖς ταῖς σωματικαῖς· τούτων γὰρ οἱ πολλοὶ ὀρέγονται, καὶ ἐσπουδάκασι περὶ αὐτὰ ὡς ἄριστα ὄντα, διὸ καὶ περιμάχητά ἐστιν ... δικαίως δὴ τοῖς οὕτω φιλαύτοις ὀνειδίζεται'.

[6] E.g. Cic. Off. 1.87: 'Miserrima omnino est ambitio honorumque contentio', etc.

[7] Cf. e.g. Diogenes, Ep. 28: 'φιλόδοξοι καὶ ἄλογοι καὶ ἀχρήστως τρεφόμενοί ἐστε'.

[8] Cf. e.g. Sirach 10.7: שנואה לאדון ואנשים גאוה (LXX: μισητὴ ἔναντι Κυρίου καὶ ἀνθρώπων ὑπερηφανία).

first a number of broader observations. Many words expressing concepts important to
a given civilization may be entirely absent in another language: distinctive household
objects, sources of livelihood, environmental features, types of dress or habitation,
institutions, symbolic practices, and social roles and norms concerning interpersonal
relationships. A culture will not have the word for a technological instrument, or a
dish, or a festivity, if it does not have the thing that the word names. If many languages
of the world, beyond English, do not have terms like *pubcrawl*, this is not an accidental
lacuna in their vocabulary, but a conceptual, cultural, and practical one; even the
analogous French *tournée des bars* is not completely equivalent, if nothing else because
English pubs and French bars, though similar, traditionally differ in architecture
and design, in the types of drinks and snacks they offer, and in their procedures for
ordering, serving, and tipping. One problem with all this is that many terms exist
in one language and not in another *even though the referent does exist in both*. How
are we to explain this? Let us look at the terminology of interpersonal roles, which is
particularly informative. English and several European languages do not have specific
terms (or, in some cases, any terms at all) for several kinship positions indicated by
special words in other languages. We can consider, for a start, some Serbian/Croatian
terms. There is, of course, a little bit of variation between Serbian and Croatian usage as
well as among Serbs and among Croats; nevertheless, it can be said that many speakers
use the following terms with these meanings:

> *šurnjaja* / шурњаја (mostly Serbian) = wife of your wife's brother
> *šurjakinja* / шурјакиња (mostly Croatian) = wife of your wife's brother
> *jetrva* / јетрва = wife of your husband's brother
> *zaova* / заова = your husband's sister
> *svastika* / свастика = your wife's sister
> *snaha* or *snaja* / снаха or снаја = your brother's wife (for some, your son's wife, as
> in Slovenian)

What is noteworthy is that these concepts would all be translated in English simply as
sister-in-law, just like they would all be translated as *belle-sœur* in French, as *cognata* in
Italian, and as *svägerska* in Swedish. One may suppose that this reflects the more limited
importance or specificity attributed in western Europe to such kin positions in a family,
or rather the lack of a distinct role for the women occupying such positions. If that is
correct, what we are looking at is not merely a lexical difference, and is not accidental – the
difference is cultural, and that is what causes the lexical difference. Indeed, as traditional
extended families with many members living permanently in proximity have become less
common, some of the Serbian/Croatian terms have become also less common: less used
or less known. This might be compared to the way in which the names of many plants are
becoming unknown to generations of language users who live nearly exclusively in cities,
or the way the names of tools of many obsolescent manual professions are no longer
widely known. Besides, some more evidence that culture is the explanation for kinship
terms can be found if we look at languages with an even more complicated lexicon
of family relations. Mandarin has not only distinct terms, for example, for someone's
brother's wife, like Croatian *snaha* above, but has further subdistinctions according to

birth-order position (though the Chinese one-child policy, in partial force especially since the end of the 1970s, is making such distinctions obsolete):

dàsǎo (大嫂) = *oldest* brother's wife
sǎo (嫂) or *sǎozi* (嫂子) = *older* brother's wife
dìmèi (弟妹) or, in other regions, *dìfù* (弟婦) = *younger* brother's wife
or, conversely:
xiǎo gū zi (小姑子) = husband's *younger* sister
dàgū zi (大姑子) = husband's *older* sister

And, albeit not frequently (and less unambiguously, as the terms can denote also your female cousins on your mother's side), one can also distinguish:

yíjiě (姨姐) = wife's *older* sister
yímèi (姨妹) = wife's *younger* sister

Again, being the wife of your oldest, or older, or younger brother are roles that English, French, Italian, or Swedish would express with the same one term. Distinct birth-order appellations are not common in European languages. Is it plausible to suggest that the lack of terms equivalent to the Chinese words listed above in languages like, say, Swedish is due to the fact that, in Sweden, extended families are not as tight-knit and hierarchical? In China, birth order is much noted. Besides, addressing by name relatives who are senior to oneself is very uncommon and considered rude. The custom is to refer always to all family members just by their kin position in relation to the speaker. So their kin titles need to be different from those of others in order to avoid confusion, and they are constantly stated. Above all, those titles reflect also a social hierarchy and power relations within the traditional family: the clout of your oldest brother's wife, in China (unlike in Sweden), is superior to that of your younger brother's wife, for example. In other words, the difference is not only lexical, and people may have good reason to remind others of their status. And if you think that this is overemphasizing the importance of culture, and that the application of kinship labels is merely a matter of naming objective biological links, just reflect on this: a person who, to Europeans or Americans, is a grandfather on the mother's side will not even classify as kin in the eyes of cultures with only patrilineal kinship. We might have considered a label (and a kinship position) like *grandfather* to be just objective and universally clear, because it is usually biologically defined; and yet, it turns out to be, in a certain sense, arbitrary and culturally determined.

Consider now what Swedish does have: in Swedish there is, for example, a rich vocabulary to indicate long-term romantic/sexual partners that are not formally wedded spouses. This includes: *sambo* 'partner not married to you who lives together with you full-time'; *delsbo* 'partner not married to you who lives together with you part of the time'; *särbo* 'partner not married to you but in a long-distance relationship with you'; *närbo* 'partner not married to you, who does not live with you, but lives in your vicinity', and so forth. If the languages of traditional and conservative cultures lack such terms, this is unlikely to be an accidental gap in their lexicon. It would be difficult to claim that the Swedish terminology above is not related to the relative openness of Swedish culture and society, and to the fact that Swedes feel that these options (which other cultures may abhor or forbid) are available to them. In social circles that are even more sexually open, one finds other concepts and words entirely unknown outside of them. In polyamorous networks, in which multiple sexual partners are allowed, the term *compersion* is used to indicate the empathetic joy that some people feel at their partner's delight in a new romantic or sexual liaison with somebody else. The term *compersion* obviously reflects a certain subculture, and the lack of such term in other cultures is unlikely to be just a lexical gap: in mainstream society, the concept or the experience of 'compersion' is not known, or anyway not commonly recognized (some members of traditional couples may sometimes confess that they find the thought of their spouse or partner in intimacy with someone else a turn-on, but this is not admitted frequently and publicly enough to establish a word for such a feeling).

At the same time, when reading cultural and practical implications into the dissimilarities that exist in the lexicon of different languages, one must exercise caution. Consider, for example, how several languages can use the same word for pairs of concepts that English distinguishes as a matter of course:

Table 5.2 Words overlooking distinctions considered essential in English

English	Lithuanian	Russian	Swahili	Mod. Greek
hand	*ranka*	рука	*mkono*	χέρι
arm	*ranka*	рука	*mkono*	χέρι
English	**Lithuanian**	**Russian**	**Swahili**	**Mod. Greek**
foot	*koja*	нога	*mguu*	πόδι
leg	*koja*	нога	*mguu*	πόδι

Obviously, we would not argue that this demonstrate a lack of distinct use of those limbs on the part of the speakers of those languages.

Another category of words that, though rare, is culturally informative and therefore of relevance here, is words that fuse two referents into one – what philologists, following Sanskrit grammar, call a dvandva compound (द्वन्द्व समास). Terms of this sort are often indicative because they reveal the cultural perception that two particular entities naturally go together. In Modern Greek, for example, there are several such words, like *maheropírouno* (μαχαιροπήρουνο), a compound based on the roots of the words for 'knife' and 'fork' merged into a single concept, equivalent to the English 'cutlery', or like *andróyino* (αντρόγυνο), a compound based on the roots of the words for 'man' and 'woman', meaning 'couple'. More interesting, and with no equivalent in English, is *yinekópetho* (γυναικόπαιδο), a compound based on the roots of the words for 'woman' and 'children' which presents a woman and children as belonging together and as forming an unindividualized unit. The noun occurs mostly in the plural, which makes each woman or child even less distinct; and it has strong connotations of vulnerability and helplessness (it is used typically with reference to situations of war). And as this case shows, parallel words that do *not* exist are also telling: a similar Greek compound fusing 'man' and 'children', *andrópetho* (αντρόπαιδο) does not exist, except as a rare improvised term meaning 'childish man', 'man who has failed to grow up'; there is no term meaning 'man+children unit'. It is not unreasonable to submit that the existence of *yinekópetho*, and the inexistence of *andrópetho* in that sense, reflect a given social reality and cultural outlook.

It is important to note that culture-specific conceptual categories are also cognitive frames: they lead one to interpret situations in particular ways, and they therefore trigger particular responses which, in that culture, will be perceived as logical (Sharifian 2017: 11–12). Consider how, in the following examples, a particular concept (italicized in the sentence) that other cultures do not have or may understand in a different way, is used as a self-evident explanation, as a frame for justifying and understanding the event reported by each sentence:

- he said nothing just because he is *shy*
- she will speak first because she is the *Vice-Provost*
- they are fasting because it is *Lent*
- we closed the window at once because there was a *draught*[9]

Some words that are unique to a language are often said *by the speakers themselves* to embody the values, the social rules, the fundamental and immanent features of the culture of the community. A case loved by the media is the untranslatable Danish term *hygge* (which is both a noun and a verb, with many derivatives and compounds). It indicates a warm, homey feeling (or atmosphere, or place, or time) characterized by cosiness, well-being, relaxation, safety, sociability, intimacy, authentic human contact, belonging, non-competitiveness, and quiet, simple contentment. Many Danes describe *hygge* as a pervasive local value, a symbol of the Danish message that society should be an environment that is familiar, trusted, and where one feels at ease. According to them, the championing and defence of *hygge* is a pillar of a counterculture that rejects market-driven values, inegalitarian relationships, status obsession, corporate mentality, and display of wealth (Linnet 2011: 27–9). Visitors and Danes alike readily identify *hygge* as quintessentially Danish also in the normative sense that immigrants to Denmark, in order not to remain outsiders, are expected to learn it (Levinsen 2012: 80–1, 102). It establishes, we can say, what is 'inside' also in the sense of Japanese *uchi* (うち): what is domestic, what is distinctly 'our', what identifies 'us' (and, in this light, it is therefore a concept that can also mark some other people as outsiders).

English words reflecting English concepts

Just as other languages have culturally significant words that have no equivalents in English, English has very many terms and expressions that have no equivalents in

---

[9]   In several cultures, notably in south-eastern Europe, an air draught in a room (Croatian *propuh*, Serbian промаја, Hungarian *huzat*, Bosnian *promaha*, Bulgarian течение, Romanian *curent*, Russian сквозняк) is believed to be very dangerous to health.

other languages and that carry culture-specific assumptions, beliefs, and values. Take *privacy*, a word long established in English. It has been in use in its modern sense since the nineteenth century: already then there was talk of the 'right to privacy'. *Privacy* has no correspondent in many languages. Even in other European languages, a word for it is often lacking, except as a recent loanword or calque from English. The fact that *privacy* is a specifically English word is arguably not accidental. The word bespeaks a cultural emphasis, which is typically Western and especially Anglosaxon, on individual agency, and on *personal space*, another concept missing in many other cultures. Indian, Chinese, and Greek friends have pointed out to me, at times with unconcealed pride, that in their languages there was no native word for *privacy* (the nearest terms available connote secretiveness, isolation, or at most discretion). They presented this to me as evidence that their culture is more sociable, direct, and sharing.

Several common English nouns that describe people are not universal. An example is *teenager*. It is a word based on the English names of numbers (13–19), and it refers not only to the defining biological aspects of that phase of human life, but also to the behaviour and psychology displayed by people of that age *in a specific social set-up*. That set-up includes a particular family structure, school system, gender scripts, class conventions, media models, habitation layout, and so forth. The meaning of *teenager*, therefore, is not exactly a universal concept, and to say 'he behaves that way because he is a teenager' can be a misleading biologization of a partly cultural phaenomenon. In a comparable way, while all populations have children, who need looking after, and in many cultures children are temporarily looked after by someone other than the parents, the concept of, and therefore the term, *babysitter* is culture-specific, and is the product of given historical, social, political, and economic developments. In the United States, in the early twentieth century, it became the accepted norm for parents to seek to spend a short time away from home and children, for mothers to want and have an outside job, for other adult members of the family to be no longer numerous enough nor living close enough to provide all needed childcare, for very young unmarried women to spend time (including perhaps nights) at other people's homes, and to seek to earn some money on their own. Thus the figure of 'the babysitter' – archetypally, a very young woman – came into existence. The word *babysitter* is, indeed, American and first attested in 1937. Many cultures, to this day, do not have a term truly equivalent to a *babysitter*, and to ask what the word for *babysitter* is in certain languages therefore constitutes a myopic and ethnocentric question. All this can be said, all the more, for later terms like *catsitter* (first attested in the United States around 1948), which presupposes, among other things, that it is normal to keep cats in one's home full time, that it is common to have planned absences from one's residence lasting many days, and that everybody understands that providing cats with regular food, cleaning, and company is a moral duty for those who keep those cats in their home.

The whole fabric of English embeds specific cultural references, assumptions, and values (cf. Parker 2004: 24–9). English metaphors, for example, are sometimes revealing: in English-speaking cultures, time is often conceptualized as money (Sharifian 2017: 17). Time is therefore not just *passed* or *lost*, as in French, but it is *spent* or *saved*. Wierzbicka (2006: 61–167, 202–3, 305–9), has argued that there is a culture-specific worldview not only behind the tacit pragmatic rules of English (e.g. how to address people, or how to formulate requests, or when to talk or be silent), but also in the grammar of English (which, she says, exhibits an unusual focus on degrees of free will and on individual agency) and – especially – in the English vocabulary. Wierzbicka's key examples include the words *alleged, fair, reasonable, impartial, bias, sibling, commitment, compromise, efficiency, deadline, pros-and-cons, presumably,* and *arguably.* English is thus not merely an inventory of universally shared concepts, but sometimes reflects an appreciation for specific thinking styles, validates particular social attitudes, and presumes certain ethical postulates. We mentioned before that one reason why learning several languages is, in itself, a cultural eye-opener is that, by providing a contrast, those languages highlight the peculiarities of your own language and its cultural underpinnings. The English terms and concepts that scholars like Wierzbicka highlight as culture-specific will strike many monolingual speakers of English as ordinary, as common sense, as inevitable – but that is precisely the issue. Monolingual speakers of other languages too tend to feel the same way about the vocabulary of their language. They are all like the proverbial fish that is unaware of water.

However, the *new* terms and speaking styles that are spreading in English (or in another language), and that initially strike speakers as strange, do sometimes enable a speaker to notice that words and styles can contain certain unstated assumptions and suggestions, and that they therefore tacitly foster a particular outlook. In Britain, for example, a certain use of language has become increasingly common, especially in work-related communications; those who are not young and grew up with a different style were struck by its arrival and by the frame of mind it implicitly promotes. Below is the text of a short email that I recently received from a British academic, unknown to me, who is the head of a British academic institution. Until a few years ago, this tone in Britain would have been surprising, and would have been regarded as purely American. In just a few lines, it well exemplifies a particular style and the presupposition that a certain culture is now universally shared. *The real test is how ordinary this text does or does not appear to you.* I have italicized relevant terms and redacted a few words to maintain discretion:

Dear *Peter,*

Today I am *delighted* to share with you the 10-year *strategy* for [this institution], a new *vision* and *direction* for [it] which aims to keep our inspiring … institution … *relevant* to students of the *future* … [Our] … core *goals* are to *promote* the *advancement* of university education … Yet today we face uncertainty … and other … *challenges.* In light of these *challenges,* this *strategy* aims to ensure that we take [this institution] *forward* and remain a *vibrant* and *resilient* institution in the *coming decades* … The *strategy* sets out … areas of *priority* and our *vision* for them: … *excellen[ce]* … *inclusivity,* equality, and *diversity* … *celebrated* across the *community* … students reaching their *full potential* … a *plurality* of cultural activities within a *positive* working environment … *financially robust* and with [an] operating budget focused primarily on the core *object* … Thanks to [donors'] generosity … [we have] been able to progress many *important* projects. As we enter this *new era* I hope you will continue to offer your *support.*

If you are able to step out of the culture that generated such use of language, or can remember when such style was unheard-of, you will notice some distinguishing features: the fake camaraderie; the empty emotional hyperboles; the strictly goal-orientated outlook; the subtle metaphors of battle; the metanarrative that life is about constant upgrading; the relentless optimism and 'positivity'; the obligatory hyper-excitement; the self-praise and self-celebration; the underlying theme of winning and, if ever beaten, of bouncing back; the fear of becoming *passé*; the ranking of everything by priority; the presentation of one's ambitiousness as admirable; the lip service to a generic notion of community despite the pervasive competitive tone; the grandiose description of one's activities; the implicit emphasis on money; and the explicit dependence on private financial support. Regardless of whether one likes or dislikes the style and mindset of this email, it is difficult to deny that it expresses, presents as normal, and reinforces a particular culture. And that jubilant and grandiose style is now common: another UK university has recently advertized a job (in linguistics) describing it as 'exciting', and explaining: 'The appointee will exercise leadership, demonstrate vision, and empower others in order to deliver the agreed departmental strategy'.

Some American terms and usages, when imported into Britain are felt by older Brits as having connotations that reflect a distinctly American mindset, and as promoting a different mentality. An effective example of this are various forms of management-speak or corporate jargon that have become widespread in recent years, and are increasingly being applied to ordinary interactions. These include not only expressions such as *to touch base* (from American baseball), *to have the bandwidth*, *to be at capacity*, and *foodchain*, but a rich jargon that describes all human exchanges as a market transactions: people and events unrelated to finance are described with terms such as *buy-in*, *stakeholder*, *leveraging*, *benchmarking*, *value add*, *rate of return*, or *cost-effective*. It would be naïve to counterargue that those expressions are just metaphors that do not colour our thinking: as shown by Lakoff and Johnson (1980: 239, 247), we do perceive things in terms of the metaphors used, and we respond accordingly; and 'the people who get to impose their metaphors on the culture get to define what we consider to be true'.

To communities that speak another language altogether, the culture-specific and value-laden nature of such American usage is initially all the more evident, because those words need to be either adopted as foreign loanwords or translated; an equivalent term in the local language may not exist, or its occurrence in that new sense may sound bizarre at first. For example, boardroom speeches or adverts that talk emphatically of *empowerment*, *pushing the limit*, *deserving the best*, or *taking control*, if presented or translated to people not already imbued with a certain culture, sound overblown, narcissistic, self-entitled, macho, and discernibly vacuous. The view, indeed self-view, that they propose is domineering, self-important, unjustifiedly confident, and power focused. A random example: I am looking to order a new laptop, and the webpage of the company describes the characteristics of the new model by stating:

> Designed for those who defy limits and change the world, the new [product's name] is by far the most powerful ... Boundaries are meant to be pushed ... This [product's name] is a game-changer ... This is an amazing amount of power to carry around ... powerful ... bigger ... better ... The most powerful ... ever .... The power of [brand's name] taken further ... powerful

A related buzzword that is particularly common and worth zooming in on is *challenge*; its history is telling, because *challenge*, in English, originally indicated something only undesirable – which is not surprising, since it comes ultimately from Latin *calumnia*, meaning a 'malicious false accusation' from which one must defend oneself. The meaning of *challenge* appears to have received its unexpectedly positive spin in the late twentieth–century, in the United States. The conceptualization of a *challenge* as something to be always welcomed and actively sought is arguably part of – and reinforces – a competitive culture that urges constant vying (to *raise the bar*), that believes in unlimited growth, that expects striving without end, and that teaches one to seek notoriety and *visibility*. The message is that one injects meaning into one's life by putting oneself continually to the test, i.e. that one has to continually *prove oneself* – another expression that, interestingly, innumerable languages, even European ones, have no translation for – and that, by declaring to be eager to do that, one wins public approval. This is all regarded as healthy. The idea that *challenges* can only do you good also rests on, and in turn promotes, the doctrine (which shapes also the basic plot of countless US films, biographies, documentaries, interviews, and news stories) that if one deserves success and works for it, one is bound to succeed – a doctrine rooted also in a religious faith that all merits are destined to be eventually rewarded. The social obligation to constantly profess belief in that doctrine, and the psychological imperative to safeguard it from the overwhelming counterevidence, requires a constant whitewashing of the negative, and therefore vastly affects the use of language and makes it distinctive. It also fosters a relentlessly and unrealistically upbeat tone. Accordingly, on an average day, you do not say 'I am well', but 'I am *wonderful*'; sellers do not write to you simply that your order has been processed, but that they are *super-excited* to tell you so; individuals aware that their success is not guaranteed are not described as clear-sighted, but as *lacking in confidence*; the suggestion that some things are impossible is not dubbed healthy honesty but toxic *negativity*; workers sacked for expediency are not said to be wronged, but to be given the *opportunity* to pursue new goals; Jesus, as a young American once told me, died on the cross 'but *he bounced back*'; and patients do not *suffer* from an illness, they are *fighting* it. The problem with this last expression, for example, is that when the illness is not curable, and the patient dies despite all efforts, or gives up because carrying on is unbearable and pointless, such patient is said to have '*lost* the battle' with the illness, which suggests being a *loser*, a word used in American English as an all-purpose insult – or being a *quitter*, another American term interestingly used as a put-down, with no translation in most languages. From that cultural mould come also, conversely, the metaphorical use of the term *fighter*, very common in American English, with strong approbative meaning, and the frequent description of anything excellent as a *winner* ('this sauce is a winner'), as if every alternative was part of a competition. Words like *winner* and *loser* do have a literal translation into many languages, but they would not be used in this way. The laudatory use of terms like *battle*, *fighter*, or *winner* is, moreover, in line with an insistent use of military metaphors that is widespread in American English: mundane actions and plans are conceptualized and described in terms like *strategy*, *target*, *campaign*, *attack*, *frontline*, *invasion*, *bombard*, *firing line*, *weapon*, *battleground*, *crossfire*, *recruit, ammunition, make a killing,* and of course with the term *war* applied to any effort to handle or contain a problem (we heard of the 'war on' drugs, on cancer, on poverty, on inflation, on plastic). This military lens has now been adopted also in Britain. For example, the British response to the coronavirus outbreak – which was tardy, weak, chaotic, and with disastrous results – was described, in a briefing by the UK Secretary of State for Health, in terms of 'this war', 'national effort', 'strategy', 'frontline', 'target', 'challenge', 'fightback', and 'victory'.[10]

Linguistic notions of (im)politeness

Different cultures differ in the way they report events, articulate requests, make suggestions, express dissent, phrase refusals, issue orders, give rebukes, or ask questions. It is true that a role is played in this also by the personality and mood of the individual speaker, which make someone more forthright or more indirect, more yielding or more confrontational, and so forth. Listeners too are guided (or mislead) not only by the conventions of their own background but also by their own psychological position: they are prone to interpret your behaviour in the light of their fears, hopes, habits, and complexes. Some may therefore think that you are supercilious if you are quiet, others flirtatious if you are chatty; some may feel that you are being invasive or accusatory if you ask questions, others that you are uncaring and self-centred if you do not. Context is also key: depending on that, the same culture may view a formal style as courteous or as pompous, and an informal style as friendly or as rude. And what particular tone or style is regarded as appropriate or acceptable in a given context depends also, in culture-specific fashions, on other status determinants such as the speaker's and the listener's age, sex, class, title, role, and position in a hierarchy.

Nonetheless, there are usually shared conventions in the way a community of speakers talks and converses. This is why verbal responses to other people may sound either normal and innocent or curt and aggressive depending on the language. So, if what you said has not been heard in full, in a context where 'I beg your pardon?' would be the routine neutral response in English, a Greek could say 'what are you saying?' (τι λες;) and an Israeli simply 'what?!' (?מָה) – which in English may sound rather cold, rude, or confrontational. In Greece, the shop assistant meeting the customers may say just 'say!' (λέγετε!) in situations where English would say 'how can I help?'. In Serbia, they may just say 'what do you want?' (шта желиш?). In response, in Modern Greek, it is fine to address the shop assistant or a waiter using informally the second person singular, and saying simply 'right, you shall bring us … ' (λοιπόν, θα μας φέρεις …). In Serbia too, you can simply say 'you will give me … ' (даћете ми). Russian, in like manner, uses constructions that, if translated literally, would sound terse and bossy to English ears (cf. Gladkova 2015: 45) but they are not so to Russians. In Russian, as in Greek, or Turkish, bare imperatives, like 'go now' or 'sit', for example, are not considered rude. Turkish friends have advised me to stop saying 'please' (*lütfen*) in

---

[10] Matt Hancock, 3 April 2020, briefing on BBC News.

Turkish, describing it as linguistically correct but un-Turkish; in Greek too, 'please' (παρακαλώ) and 'thanks' (ευχαριστώ) are words used far less often than in English. Russians, similarly, recognize that they thank and apologize less than the French, the Germans, or the English (Zemskaja 1997: 298). It is also normal, in Modern Greek and Serbian, as in Turkish and Hebrew, to ask for items in a shop saying simply 'I want' (θέλω, желим, *istiyorum*, אֲנִי רוֹצֶה) whereas in English we feel the need to say at least 'I would like' or 'could I have'. Wierzbicka (2006: 51–3) suggests, quite plausibly, that the indirect formulas used in English to express requests are part and parcel of the 'Anglo' emphasis on respecting individual autonomy, personal space, and open choice. Because of that emphasis, we can add, English uses also formulas like 'for your comfort and safety' to announce a legal obligation (like wearing seatbelts), or says 'helping police with their inquiry' when meaning 'under arrest and interrogation and thought to be the culprit'. All this is culture-specific. In terms of politeness theory (Brown and Levinson 1987: 61), we can say that, while in some cultures politeness is primarily focused on not imposing or intruding on someone ('negative face') in others it is focused on inclusion and therefore informality ('positive face'). English requests introduced by 'could I ask you to', 'would you (terribly) mind to', or 'could you be so kind as to' would sound funny if translated *verbatim* in many other languages. Utterances like 'can you be quiet for a minute?', which in English usually constitute indirect orders, would be interpreted literally, as genuine enquiries (or as sarcasm). And common English litotes, like 'I am not really sure I like it very much', in many languages may even provoke laughter.

Of course, English phrases like 'can you be quiet?' can be said with a particular intonation that gives away the disapproval and irritation of the speaker; yet, the wording remains polite, and may even express pride in one's own observance of good manners. If a person suddenly enters someone else's room or a private area in a way that is perceived as unexpected and unwarranted, the response in English can be a stern 'may I help you?' which, contrary to what the words may suggest, is a dismayed rebuke, as perhaps a cold tone of voice makes clear. Such polite wording might also be used in order to stress the contrast between one's respect for manners and the unlicensed intrusion of the interlocutor – as we noted before, people use language divergence to affirm their superiority. Uttering a solicitous-sounding phrase like 'may I help you' in those circumstances, however, would sound utterly out of place in many other cultures, in which a more curt response would be standard. I remember, when I was a child, my uncle in Switzerland said to me that the English 'may I help you', translated into Italian terms, means 'what the f*** do you want?'; at the time I thought of this as a joke, but I subsequently realized that, at times, it is not entirely inaccurate – especially if we accept that translation, as was already argued in antiquity by the likes of Cicero and Horace, ought to be a close rendering of the overall intent and meaning of the original phrase, rather than a literal reproduction of its wording – as Saint Jerome said, 'not word-by-word but sense-by-sense'.[11] Besides, swearwords sound less aggressive in many European languages than they do in English.

---

[11] Ep. LVII, 5: 'ego enim non solum fateor, sed libera uoce profiteor me in interpretatione Graecorum … non uerbum e uerbo sed sensum exprimere de sensu'.

Swearwords, precisely because they are a lexical category subject to strong social norms, are used in a way that reveals culture-specific pragmatics. Terms that have the same literal meaning in different languages can differ in their degree of perceived vulgarity and taboo status. In Modern Greek, among young men, it is very common to call affectionately any of your mates *maláka* (μαλάκα, lit. 'wanker'), but in English that noun is only hostile and offensive. It is impossible to demonstrate, and yet it is hard not to surmise, that the Greek usage is connected to certain aspects of Modern Greek culture, such as a jokey machismo in male interactions, a prevalence of the male viewpoint in public discourse, and – in comparison with Britain – a longer-standing (relative) openness about the body and about canonical sexual interests, and therefore a more established explicitness in sexual references. This may also explain a greater admissibility of swearwords in Greek, which gives them a wider use and more neutral register – though Greek has also extraordinarily lofty, elegant, and courteous styles. For the same reasons, the Modern Greek exclamation *ghamó to* (γαμώ το), which means literally 'f*** it!', sounds much milder and is more acceptable than its English literal translation; it is more similar to its literal equivalent in other Balkan languages, such as the Serbian/Croatian *jebi ga*. After all, if one does want to sound offensive and aggressive, it is always possible to up the ante: Balkan languages such as Modern Greek, Serbian/Croatian, or Albanian, have common obscene exclamations and imprecation that simply have no equivalent or match in English. In these languages, some speakers may, for example, voice their annoyance at someone with phrases like 'I (will) f*** your mother' or 'your family', 'your god'. However, such expressions (rare or absent in English) should not be interpreted as reflecting an unbridled and unconservative outlook: they presuppose, ultimately, a far more family-oriented and religious culture than modern Britain. Besides, they can be just a form of venting, and express an anger milder than it may sound. The fact that swearwords in several languages sound less forceful than in English raises therefore also problems of translation and of international communication. Foreigners who swear in English, or who are heard swearing liberally in their own languages by English learners of that language, are likely to be perceived as needlessly rude because of that difference: two words that have, in two languages, basically the same meaning, are not equivalent, because cultural norms differ.

Language-based collective images

Such dissimilarities in the use of language also colour the impressions that different nationalities form of each other. I often noticed this, for instance, in comments made to me by some Greeks about the Brits and by Brits about some Greeks (Greeks speak freely to me about the Brits because, although I have lived in England most of my life, I am not British in origin; and Brits openly comment to me on the Greeks because, although I speak Greek with total fluency, I have no Greek background). The Greeks who have not adapted at all to English ways are sometimes described to me by monocultural Brits as rather invasive, bossy, impetuous, and melodramatic – although such perceived traits are often considered by the British forgiveable in the light of Greek warmth and generosity. The British are likely to feel that Greeks who, for example, give you a third helping of food despite your protestations may be warm and generous but insufficiently polite; but, to Greeks, that behaviour *is* politeness. Conversely, the British who are unable to interact with the same directness and extroversion of the Greeks are sometimes described to me by Greeks as unfriendly, aloof, wooden, and unfeeling (κρυόκωλοι, lit. 'cold-arsed'), even though the same Greeks may also extol many aspects of the British way of life. Greeks are likely to feel, for example, that a host who simply gives you a set of keys and does not spend much time with you is accommodating but unwelcoming and uninterested. But, from a British perspective, keeping out of someone else's way can also mean being respectful of their private space and privacy, not being frosty and uncaring; to most British, this *is* how you care about a guest. As Stoic philosophers thought, what upsets people is not reality but their own judgements of it, and life is all an impression.[12]

The perception Greeks and Brits have of each other's use of language, if they are not very familiar with it, is somewhat in line with the image they often have of each other as people. Those watching Greek conversational style from a British perspective are bewildered by Greeks who say to their misbehaving small children 'I am going to eat you alive' (θα σε φάω ζωντανό) or say to a friend who hesitates to say something 'tell me, lest I smash your head' (λέγε, μη σου σπάσω το κεφάλι). But, in a sense, these are mistranslations because, although literally correct, they are not socioculturally equivalent to the original. English speakers who learn Greek may take such phrases at face value and regard them as hostile and as alarming. There are, however, key cultural differences at play: Greeks tend to use playful aggressiveness as form of bonding, regard it as evidently tongue-in-cheek, and expect hyperbole to be a shared code. As a broad rule, Greeks – like Arabs, and many others – accept exaggeration as a way to express the correct extent of something while adding emphasis in a culturally approved (and easy to decode) way. Monocultural Brits are more likely to process what is being said literally, and therefore may misjudge that talking style as bullying and bullshitting. In turn, Greeks are liable to perceive Brits as stand-offish, inhibited, and, above all, as hypocrites who do not spell out what they think. Either side, therefore, may see the way the other uses language as dysfunctional and untruthful, and as confirming a general stereotype: the histrionics of the wild south-eastern European, or the narrow-mindedness of the emotionally stunted northern European. The implicit adherence to a different behavioural script on the part of one is perceived as a violation of norms of sensible conduct by the other. Even when some shared norms are broadly recognized across cultures, the very role of norms may be seen very differently: a flexible attitude to rules is regarded as reasonable and normal in one culture and as dishonest and disturbing in another. In Germany or Switzerland, rules are often considered the supreme and indisputable arbiters of communal life; in the Balkans or the Middle East, the understanding is often that, as I was once told by an Israeli, 'rules are the starting point for a negotiation' (הַכְּלָלִים הֵם נְקוּדַת הַמּוֹצָא לְמַשָּׂא וּמַתָּן).

---

[12] Cf. e.g. Epict. Ench. 5.1: 'ταράσσει τοὺς ἀνθρώπους οὐ τὰ πράγματα, ἀλλὰ τὰ περὶ τῶν πραγμάτων δόγματα'; M. Aur. Med. 4.3: 'ὁ βίος, ὑπόληψις', etc.

In everyday life, the semantics of an utterance can rarely be understood without pragmatics: meaning is shaped by verbal context, cultural conventions, social dynamics, background history, the relationship between speakers, the occasion, the location, and more besides. Full linguistic competence – contrary to what some linguistic theories seem to assume – is communicative competence, a larger package than grammar and lexicon, and includes a host of tacit rules of a social kind. These need to be adhered to for the exchange to be effective, and should therefore be considered a fundamental part of learning a foreign language. After all, learning to speak in the terms, tones, places, and moments deemed suitable by the community that speaks that language is a key part of language acquisition in children (Hymes 1972: 277–8). The fact that such information is not regularly included in second-language teaching results in serious *gaffes* made by even highly fluent visitors, who often never understand why others appeared to be offended or to be behaving in seemingly offensive ways.

We should mention, at least incidentally, that differences among cultures in the correlations between signs and meanings are not limited to language. Many tourists and travellers appear to assume that, if they do not know the language of the countries they visit, they can rely on the universality of gestures to communicate successfully. However, while a few gestures may be universal, many others have markedly different meanings in different cultures: a thumb up is a signal of friendly endorsement in Britain but of hostile (and vulgar) dismissal in Iran; all fingers up, tip touching, forming an inverted cone, can mean 'excellent' in Turkey, 'what's this?' in Italy, and 'wait' in Egypt.

How to not say things

Another simple consideration will make it even clearer that communication is subject to cultural conventions. There are ways to say something *without saying it at all*, and such implicit transmission of meaning obviously can only occur thanks to culturally agreed strategies. Muriel Spark (1961: 37), in her most famous novel – with a partial nineteenth-century antecedent in Artemus Ward – has her central character, Miss Brodie, respond to an idea she disliked by saying: 'For those who like that sort of thing, that is the sort of thing they like'. Taken literally, this is an entirely uninformative tautology. And yet, in English, it is an unequivocal put-down. In British English, unlike in many other languages, it is also not usual to phrase one's own wishes as enquiries about someone else's. A co-worker asking you 'would you like to have a tea break in a short while?' is probably not posing a genuine question, but signalling that he would like a break soon. While I was a graduate student, one year I rented a room in a Yiddish-speaking, ultra-orthodox Jewish (Hasidic) household in north London; I was the only non-Jew there, and therefore could be the *shabbos goy* (שַׁבָּת גוֹי), the 'Gentile for the Sabbath' able to do for religious Jews things forbidden to them, such as switching on a light on Friday nights. Many observant Jews hold that saying explicitly to a non-Jew 'put that light on for us' during Sabbath is a rule violation, though by proxy; however, to say hintingly 'it is very dark in here' is a recognized, accepted, and not uncommon way to achieve the same result – provided that the resident outsider has learnt that this is how the request is conveyed. That is the difference that semanticists make between meaning and implicature.

Smooth communication through a language presupposes not only some shared implicit understanding of what the half-said or unsaid means, but also of the extent to which things are to be left unsaid. Those who, owing to their linguistic background, are accustomed to full and explicit interchanges, when meeting those who communicate extensively in indirect ways, not only cannot guess the subtext, but might even not suspect that there is one. Societies in which the use of language is explicit usually also teach that being forthright is praiseworthy; societies in which conversations leave much unsaid highly prize the skill of guessing what a speaker silently means. In such cultures, the ability to sympathize and act in a considerate and appropriate manner, and thereby to please one's interlocutors, is linked to tacit empathetic perceptiveness. Japanese culture, which relies extensively on implicit communication (腹芸), expects and appreciates the ability to assess well the subtext of interpersonal situations and, crucially, to infer what your interlocutor thinks or feels but does not say; and Japanese even has a verb for this (察する).

At the same time, to a culturally variable extent, conversations can, conversely, include statements that are made explicitly but are to be understood to mean very little – and this is another source of international misunderstandings. Compare the meaning, say, of a social phrases like 'we should have lunch (together)' or 'come over at any time' among Germans and among Americans: in German culture, it is an earnest and concrete suggestion; in the United States, it is often merely a social pleasantry not to be taken literally.

Indeed, one of the clearest indications that meanings are located in the culture and not only in the words uttered is provided by statements that say the very opposite of what they actually mean. Two sources close to Buckingham Palace told me, independently, that when a person who was meeting the Queen did not, against royal etiquette, remember to switch his mobile phone off beforehand, and the phone suddenly rang during the meeting, the Queen said to him: 'perhaps you should answer it; it could be someone important'. Someone unfamiliar with English ways might take this utterance literally, as a friendly and reassuring permission to take the phone call; that would be under-interpreting, as semioticians say. Someone with a better understanding of the culture around the English language would realize at once that, *au contraire*, that statement was a gently sarcastic reproach, which communicated, through conversational implicature, the opposite of what it literally stated. This can be true even of single words. The English term *clever* is positive, but is also laced with disapproval: the writer George Mikes reported ([1946] 1952: 32) that, shortly after he emigrated from Hungary to England in the late 1930s, he was once told by an English lady: 'you foreigners are so clever'. Since he only knew the pocket dictionary meaning of the word (*clever = intelligent*), he took the phrase to be an emphatic compliment. He learnt only much later what insult had been delivered to him. A radical ambiguity exists even in parts of speech other than nouns and verbs: contrary to what language learners may expect, in English, an adverb like *surely* often means not surely at all: 'surely they will not do such a terrible thing' means that they indeed may, and that the speaker fears that they will. Again, visitors from a different culture who have only a literal understanding of English may not be attuned to such implicatures.

As we discussed in the last chapter, we tend to judge other people's speaking style (and assume that they will judge ours) by our own standards, which we automatically treat as universally applicable. As a result, many Westerners report finding the Japanese disconcertingly, at times maddeningly, inscrutable, and many Japanese admit finding Westerners embarrassingly talkative and explicit. The deviations from our customs which we see in others may occasionally strike us as good ideas but, most often, strike us as wrong. And since such deviations (i.e. different conventions) are likely to be shared by a whole group, they become part of the stereotype that we develop of that group. The impression one forms depends on one's background. Individuals who talk fast, talk loudly, talk a lot, and interrupt a lot might think that we see them as articulate, confident, enthusiastic, interesting, engaged in the conversation, and with an eventful life; but we might see them as manic, rude, deafening, uninterested in what others have to say, overbearing, and pushy. When, on the contrary, we meet people who speak slowly, are taciturn, and let us talk at length before saying anything, we may judge them to be inobtrusive, reflective, good listeners, even profound; but if we came from a different culture, we would think that they are dull, slurred, without much to say, or haughty. When I went to Greece as a teenager, and stayed with a lovely Greek family, I was baffled because my hosts, always very jovial and loving with one another, seemed to have also intense and loud quarrels among themselves for trivial matters. On one such heated occasion, I quietly headed back to my room to leave them to it; but this did not go unnoticed, and they all came to ask me why I had left; when I explained that I just did not want to be in the way of their row, they all looked at me mystified: 'what row?' they asked. One easily fails to realize or bear in mind that speakers of other languages – and sometimes even speakers of the same language, perhaps if from a different region, ethnic background, gender, or class – may use language with different conventions concerning what and how much to say or to ask; when to do so, to whom, and how; when to interrupt or take the floor; what volume, speech rate, frequency and length of pauses, and tone of voice is normal; what accompanying body movements and amount of eye contact are proper. The way in which something is said, therefore, also has a variable meaning: to Greeks, particularly among men, explicit dissent and aggressive tones can be a signal of intimacy, engagement, and liking.

Such differences in conversation style are not just accidental variations: they reflect different schoolings, traditions, conventions, concerns, and values. For instance, the speech style used among Israelis tends to be assertive, blunt, forceful, and argumentative (Ellis and Maoz 2002: 182). Others may experience it as disrespect and bullying, but Israelis see it as plain speaking (לְדַבֵּר דּוּגְרִי 'to talk straight'). Among Israelis, such style is automatically accepted and actively fostered. After all, traditional Jewish education is based on fierce debating: the teaching in *yeshivot* (religious schools) and *batei midrash* ('houses of study') entails a lot of animated discussion, which is considered integral to learning: the root of the very term *midrash* (Aramaic דְּרַשׁ) means 'study' but also 'discuss, argue'. Studying was done traditionally in a pair (חַבְרוּתָא), with a co-discussant; and the Rabbinic texts that were studied contain commentary and responses by multiple authors and reports of dissenting views. The Arab communication style, on the other hand, though often hyperbolic, formulaic, and prolix, avoids interrupting, and tends to be unconfrontational, indirect, vague, ceremonious, deferential, and warm. This (Mizel 2016: 274–5) correspond to the Arabic concept of *musāyara* (مُسَايَرَة 'going along with, keeping the pace of, adapting oneself to, being willing to please'). The cultural roots of that style too can be identified, at least tentatively, in a number of rather culture-specific notions that are hard to translate. The Arabic way of talking is meant to be cautious, conciliatory, and is based on the understanding that one shows 'courtesy' (مُجَامَلَة) by being complaisant, ceremonious, and verbally effusive. It is, ultimately, part of a culture that is careful to save both the speaker's and the interlocutor's face, and that is intensely concerned about reputation and 'honour' (شَرَف). Arab societies, furthermore, have a traditional appreciation for persuasive rhetorical eloquence (فَصَاحَة), a religion that preceptually accepts 'defensive dissimulation' (تَقِيَّة), and a collectivist ethos of sociability and interdependence that dislikes clashes and famously prizes an extreme idea of hospitableness (ضِيَافة). In that outlook, phrasing statements – and, above all, any requests – in a very indirect way is considered tactful and polite, not crafty and underhand. Westerners, and the British in particular, often misperceive such speech style as over-the-top, rambling, insincere, unctuous, and even devious, because the conversation style that they would use, or anyway deem appropriate, is more understated, organized, informative, succinct, restrained, and focused on the facts to be communicated; the belief that this latter (English) style is normal, generally shared, clearly reasonable, and to be prescriptively recommended is even found in British philosophers of language such as Grice (1975: 48).

All this also shows that, although – as we saw earlier – many people, notably in Britain, are put off by a blunt and curt tone, they are also repulsed by a tone that is excessively reverential and complimentary. And when the use of such tone is clearly insincere, they will not accept it as being mandatory politeness – since, in their culture, it is not – but will see it as manipulative and therefore as creepy. The corporate representatives who use unrealistically pally, obsequious, and flattering words will be seen as shamelessly fawning, false, and self-interested. For example, a 'Corporate Customer Care' agent of an American airline which had cancelled my flight causing me to reach my destination a day late wrote to me trying to induce me to accept credit vouchers redeemable towards future tickets with the same airline – instead of the cash compensation that I was owed under European law and that I had requested. Her email concluded:

> We consider it a privilege to serve as your preferred travel partner and look forward to the opportunity to see you aboard the friendly skies of [Airline name] soon. I truly hope your next travel plans with us delivers [*sic*] the seamless customer experience you deserve. Thank you again for your business

Many Brits are, as yet, less used to language such as this, and find it toe-curling. And this highlights also something else that, though seemingly obvious and even banal, we should reflect on: different linguistic perceptions exist even among populations who speak, at least in terms of grammar and lexicon, essentially the same language. The signs – the words of their language – may be the same, but the interpretations can differ significantly. I shall return to this when we analyse the role and importance attributed to languages in nationalities. This chapter has emphasized how different communities use language in dissimilar ways, and how their languages can differ in their social use and, in some small respects, even in the worldview that they appear to presuppose; however, several of the examples I cited, including this last one, also suggests that, as we shall discuss more extensively later in the book, a common language is no guarantee of a common mentality. That is why, in the next chapter, before we move onto the subject of nationality, we shall appraise a popular old theory: that the particular language that we acquire as mother tongue constrains our cognition, and prevents us from thinking in alternative ways.

6

The effects of languages on cognition

We noted in Chapter 3 that, in bilingual individuals, changing language in conversation sometimes appears to switch on a different cultural frame, and to activate a different set of manners, habits, social norms, and judgements. Several studies report that the description and the affective content of events narrated by bilinguals vary significantly according to which of their languages they are using (Burck 2005: 17). Certain behavioural conventions, emotional responses, and culture-specific judgements seem associated in their minds with a particular language. Presumably, this is, at least in part, because that language reconnects them to a particular social circle of present or remembered interlocutors with whom they spoke it, or to the time in their life when they learnt it or used it more. But is the association between language and outlook merely one of personal social history, or is there something *within the structure of language itself* that forces a person's thinking into a certain mould? For example, when, in Chapter 4, we looked at colour terms and at evidentiality markers, we saw that languages can partition a descriptive continuum differently and either spotlight or gloss over certain aspects of an event. And as we saw in Chapter 5, some of the differences between languages reflect, and arguably promote, a given cultural outlook. This raises the question of whether our language shapes only the verbal expression of our thoughts, or whether it constrains the very way we think.

The 'Sapir-Whorf' hypothesis

Does our language (whichever that happens to be) impose on us a cognitive grid that limits how we understand reality? For a long time, the answer to this question was assumed to be yes – so much so that the question was barely asked. The certainty that languages affect thought was voiced incidentally, as an established fact. In the writings of philosophers, cultural critics, and philologists of the past, there are frequent, if casual, assertions that each language makes the speakers think in a particular way. To quote one philosopher, almost at random: Schopenhauer (1851: 463) stated that 'one thinks differently in each language' and that 'with each language that we learn, our thinking is therefore modified, and takes on a new colouring'.[1] Indeed, it was assumed

---

[1] 'Hieraus nun folgt, daß man in jeder Sprache anders denkt, mithin unser Denken durch die Erlernung einer jeden eine neue Modifikation und Färbung erhält'.

that we cannot think outside what Nietzsche ([1886] 1988: 193) described as the 'constraints of language'.[2] A number of linguists too, at that time, espoused the theory that the structure of a language fetters thought, and that since we all look at the world through our language, speakers of a different language experience reality differently. Von Humboldt ([1820] 1843: 262), pointing out differences between the languages of different nations, proclaimed that 'their diversity is not one of sounds and signs, but of world-views themselves'.[3] In the early twentieth century, reflections on this topic were fuelled by the discovery of how different the native American languages were from European ones. Though scholars accepted that all languages share certain features owing to universal traits of the human brain, they became ever more convinced that linguistic dissimilarities can lead to diverging conceptualizations and interpretations of reality, with ensuing differences also in non-linguistic behaviour. The hypothesis that different languages may induce different thinking styles was, in particular, voiced by a student of Franz Boas, Edward Sapir, and, above all, by Sapir's own student, Benjamin L. Whorf. For this reason, the hypothesis has come to be referred to as the 'Sapir-Whorf hypothesis', although it is not a co-authored theory and not even a clearly defined position, but a hazy idea that has been reformulated in many guises, each entailing a variety of claims. The hypothesis, as usually understood by academics, is the suggestion that the structure of a language makes it arduous or impossible for speakers to conceive of something not marked by their language. The fact that an idea of this kind was expressed before Sapir and Whorf means that even objections to the 'Sapir-Whorf hypothesis' are older than Sapir and Whorf; more importantly, to what extent Sapir and Whorf actually believed the idea now named after them is a hotly contested issue. This needn't be explored in detail here, but it should be mentioned that the textual evidence justifies the conclusion that 'Sapir-Whorf hypothesis' is rather a misnomer. There are statements in Whorf that appear to refute the very theory attributed to him (Alford 1978: 489–90), and the same applies to Sapir. However, Sapir did write, among other things (1929: 209–10):

> It is an illusion to think that we can understand the significant outlines of a culture ... without the help of the language of its society ... Language ... powerfully conditions all our thinking about social problems and processes. Human beings do not live in the objective world alone ... but are very much at the mercy of the particular language which has become the medium of expression for their society ... the "real world" is to a large extent unconsciously built up on the language habits of the group. No two languages are ever sufficiently similar to be considered as representing the same social reality. The worlds in which different societies live are distinct worlds, not merely the same world with different labels attached.

Whorf ([1940] 1956: 212–3) followed:

---

[2] 'Wir hören auf zu denken, wenn wir es nicht in dem sprachlichen Zwange thun wollen'. The key term *Zwange* is best rendered as 'constraints', and not as 'prisonhouse', as it is usually translated.
[3] 'Ihre Verschiedenheit ist nicht eine von Schällen und Zeichen, sondern eine Verschiedenheit der Weltansichten selbst'.

[T]he grammar ... of each language is not merely a reproducing instrument for voicing ideas but rather is itself the shaper of ideas, the program and guide for the individual's mental activity, for his analysis of impressions ... Formulation of ideas ... is part of a particular grammar, and differs, from slightly to greatly, between different grammars.

Most claims of this kind, especially those made in the past, were vague and untestable. Given that evidence provided for the 'Sapir-Whorf hypothesis' was unreliable and occasionally even spurious, in the latter part of the twentieth century the conjecture that individual languages affect a person's (non-linguistic) thinking style came to be seen as entirely fanciful and unscholarly. Besides, with the advent of the Chomskyan paradigm, much of linguistic research turned its attention to universals, and postulated a neurologically distinct 'language faculty' shared by everybody regardless of language and culture. Meanwhile, various cognitive sciences, such as psychology, neuroscience, and artificial intelligence, made strides in the investigation of cognition as a system genetically inherited by all humans. The 'Sapir-Whorf hypothesis' appeared misguided at its core. It was gingerly taken up again by a few researchers only in the 1980s, helped by the rise of Cognitive Linguistics, and by new intriguing – though never dramatic – data that had started to emerge. Many high-profile linguists, however, have continued to lambast the hypothesis in both its radical and milder versions (e.g. Pinker 1994: 57). Those completely opposed to the 'Sapir-Whorf hypothesis' contend, in essence, that languages, in principle, are independent of cultures, and do not invite, let alone dictate, different thinking styles and sociocultural practices, although they may perhaps reflect them (cf. Björk 2008: 100–28), and that any thought can be expressed equally well in any language.

Popular perceptions and Sapir-Whorf

There are a few factors that may explain the common-sense feel of the idea that the language you know determines how you think. We shall now consider three such factors. The first is the apparent link between articulacy and mental brilliance. In Chapter 4, we talked about the disputable tenet that the complexity of different languages is equal; but there is also another linguistic complexity that, partly for ideological reasons, is commonly asserted to be equal: the complexity of the language spoken by different speakers of (what we think of as) the same language. The English of all native English speakers, like the French of all native French speakers, or the Arabic of all native Arabic speakers, is often postulated to be complex to the same degree. However, there are strong indications that it is not (Sampson 2009: 12–14). Even different (native) varieties of the same language – English – have also been reported to vary in complexity across the world (Kortmann and Szmrecsanyi 2009: 281). Besides, where a *written* form of the language has been extensively developed and most speakers can write it fluently, this may have an impact also on oral usage, and therefore on the language as a whole; if so, since written languages tend to be more carefully constructed, honed, and embellished, this may result in the spoken form of those languages becoming more elaborate and rich (Kalmár 1985: 153). This is not news to the non-specialist: lay people, in the main, consider it obvious that individuals differ in their command of their native language. Some speakers can verbalize and elaborate their thoughts (opinions, recollections, instructions, etc.) more fluently and effectively; others speak with more false starts, anacolutha, grammatical inconsistencies, hesitations, and with less precise vocabulary. This is a fair observation, but what people may infer from this may not be. In the perception of many, that difference betokens also different degrees of intelligence, and therefore establishes a link between language and cognition. There is both something obviously true and something profoundly mistaken in this perception. On the one hand, a person's higher brainpower is indeed likely to come through more clearly if such person is more articulate. Although intelligence is a fuzzy concept, and there is no agreement among clinicians on its definition, the key signs of intelligence most frequently cited include not only the ability to learn, understand issues, extract meaning, reason with abstract concepts, draw analogies, and apply knowledge, but also verbal comprehension and fluency. Using a grammar that marks more nuances, and a lexicon that is larger and more specific, allows people to express their thoughts in a way that is more precise and richly textured, and therefore more satisfying for the speaker/writer, and usually more informative and aesthetically enjoyable for the listener/reader. A richer grammar and vocabulary may also seem to provide additional thinking tools and to enable finer and more accurate reflection. But is it so? Assuming that you are monolingual, does enlarging or enhancing your knowledge of your native language also sharpen your cognitive abilities? It is easy to see why one may imagine this to be the case. In our evolution as a species, it is likely that language and intelligence fuelled each other's development, and we know that babies' cognitive development goes hand-in-hand with their linguistic development. In adolescents and adults, the effort and the training to be linguistically exact is usually interlinked with learning to be conceptually and descriptively precise. For example, through the extensive reading of dictionary entries, one not only acquires a larger vocabulary but also discovers novel concepts, learns how to articulate more pithily, clearly, and comprehensively a particular meaning, and becomes aware of the different nuances of alternative ways to summarize and convey a thought. And yet, this is not quite the same as being more intelligent in a comprehensive sense. To make a facile but painfully true point, there is no shortage of people with the gift of the gab but with limited discernment or wisdom: *satis eloquentiae, sapientiae parum*, to use Sallust's (Cat. 5.4) phrase.

The second factor that fuels the belief that each language steers cognition in a particular way is the fact that the choice of words employed to say something can indeed affect someone's perception of reality, although the effect is not inescapable. An experiment showed footage of a car accident to a number of people; they were then asked to estimate the speed of the two cars involved when they *hit* each other or *smashed into* each other; people gave different estimates depending on the verb used, even though they all had seen the same footage (Loftus and Palmer 1974: 586). In another experiment (Carmichael, Hogan, and Walter 1932: 79–81), the same drawing was presented to two groups of subjects, but verbally characterized to them in different terms: the same incomplete circle was described to the first group as resembling a 'letter C', and to the second group as resembling a 'moon crescent'. Subjects were later asked to redraw from memory the object they had seen; those in the first group tended to reproduce a very round thin circle with a small opening (in line with the prototype of a letter C), while those in the second group often drew a wide open and thicker concave figure tapered at its ends, like a moon crescent. In another case, a picture of two circles connected by a line was presented to two groups but was described to one group as resembling 'eyeglasses' and to the other group as resembling 'dumb-bells'; those in the first group later tended to produce a picture more resembling a pair of spectacles (e.g. the two circles now had a shorter, curved line between them), while the second group tended to draw something more resembling a gym dumb-bell. What the experiment's subjects remembered, therefore, was shaped not only by what they saw (presumably they all saw the drawings in the same way), but also by how the picture had been described to them linguistically. Other experiments have produced the same result: using language to describe something seen previously – from a colour to a face – has been shown to interfere with later recognition (Schooler and Engstler-Schooler 1990: 56, 42): verbalizing our memories impairs subsequent recollection. We suppose that reality guides our choice of befitting words, but our choice of words can shape our perception of reality. This has long been clear to literature writers: Nobel laureate writer Herta Müller (2003: 86) wrote that 'what has truly happened never lets itself be caught in words that match it; in order to be described, it must be tailored for words and be re-invented entirely'.[4] There is no doubt that the manifold ways in which we can all use language – for instance, the different formulations that we can give to a statement – lead the listeners, and perhaps the speakers as well, to see what is being discussed in a different light. The terms that are used can frame the thinking, or at least the discussion, as rhetoricians have always known. In any politically relevant dispute, in particular, language can slightly hamper the forming of views and responses not in keeping with a given belief or culture. And a certain outlook is embedded not just in the answers but already in the questions. This is observable in many of the fiercest political debates of the present. Compare these two versions of what is, ostensibly, the same query about the same person:

> Do you think that *this man, who calls himself Joanna and, though born male, identifies as a woman, or any man like him,* should be considered a woman?
> Do you think that *Joanna, the woman over here, who was assigned male gender at birth, or any trans woman like her,* should be considered a woman?

Stark evidence that the general public is aware that the use of particular words can guide our thinking and influence our outlook is provided by the current campaigns for the replacement of part of our social vocabulary. Despite a few laughable excesses in politically correct word-coining, it should be obvious to anyone that the different terms that people use to describe the same referent do express different understandings: the term 'wheelchair-bound' implicitly suggests helplessness, 'wheelchair user' suggests

---

4   'Wirklich Geschehenes läßt sich niemals eins zu eins mit Worten fangen. Um es zu beschreiben, muß es auf Worte zugeschnitten und gänzlich neu erfunden werden'.

agency; 'free speech' suggests liberty, 'hate speech' suggests a crime. And different terms also prompt different responses: it is arguable that 'refugees' implicitly urges sheltering, 'illegals' urges repatriation; 'freedom fighters' urges support, 'terrorists' urges suppression, and so forth. Words can have implicit postulates and invite us to accept a certain view. And this is true also of verb phrases: compare 'he was murdered' with 'he was executed', or just 'she fell' with 'she had a fall'.

To take another sociopolitically significant example, consider the existence, in the grammar of very many languages, of multiple forms of address that differ in degree of formality, from pally to deferential. It is fair to surmise that these forms indicate that the population speaking that language is (or, at the very least, was) socially stratified. It is also reasonable to posit, conversely, that the continued use of those different forms of address reinforces, or at least naturalizes, such social compartmentalization. What is noteworthy is that, right or wrong, this has clearly been the understanding of the speaker themselves. When the wish to abolish or to soften those social divisions has prevailed, time and again there has been an effort to abolish, as a means to that end, the different forms of address. In France, after the revolution, there was a promotion of a generalized use of *tu* (the second person singular form of address, more direct and informal, as opposed to *vous*, the second person plural form, which is deferential and formal when used to address a single person). In Sweden too, at the end of the 1960s, a generalized use of the informal *du* was successfully encouraged in replacement of a multilayered system of address forms; the express goal was, one again, to make society more egalitarian. The same, in essence, was thought in Russia, after the revolution: the distinction between ты and вы as forms of address was officially disfavoured in the belief that it reinforced class distinctions. And after the dissolution of the Soviet Union, in the countries of Eastern Europe, there has been a sharp decline in the custom of addressing others with the term usually translated into English as 'comrade' (Russian товарищ, German *Genosse*, Hungarian *elvtárs*, Estonian *seltsimees*, Latvian *biedrs*, Romanian *tovarăș*, Georgian ამხანაგო, etc.). This is not only because the term is less plausible in a market economy, but also because it is felt to affirm the social outlook of the disbanded communist system. In general, the changes of terminology that are sometimes recommended – especially of terms used to refer to people – aim explicitly at changing not only a language's vocabulary and its application, but public perceptions and style of interaction.

The third factor that may seem to lend credence to the hypothesis that our language imposes limits on our perception and understanding is the fact that this appears to be true in the domain of phonetics. One can see how the argument can run – although, even if the hypothesis that a person's native language is a mental constraint proved to be correct in one linguistic domain, to assume that it must therefore be correct also in others is a bit of a *non sequitur*. Infants (in the Latin literal sense of *in-fantes*, i.e. those who do not yet speak a language) are able to notice and, potentially, to learn to reproduce the phonetic distinctions of any language; however, adults fluent in their mother tongue seem to have become unable to pronounce or even distinguish the linguistic sounds that are absent in their particular language(s). Phonetic distinctions regarded as clear by speakers of one language can seem simply non-existent to speakers of another. For instance, most western Europeans cannot hear the difference between

Serbo-Croatian č and ć (in Cyrillic, ħ and ч), or between Polish *cz* and *ci*, because it does not exist in their languages: they just hear a sound like English *ch* in both cases. When faced with a language like Arabic, they struggle to distinguish a whole triad of sounds, like خ /x/ and ه /h/ and ح /ħ/. Conversely, many monolingual speakers of Serbo-Croatian, Spanish, or Japanese hear little difference among English words like *hat, hut, heart, hurt* (pronounced as in Standard English, without r) and *hot* (if pronounced the American way). Even if they do hear a difference, they cannot easily reproduce it: people who are able to identify a particular foreign sound are often still unable to pronounce it. Quite a few English monolinguals, for example, hear distinctly the tapped /r/ of Spanish (and of Polish, Finnish, Arabic, Latvian, or Malay) but say they could not possibly articulate it.[5] The result, as we all know, is a foreign accent, because pronouncing those languages with a typical English R (phonetically /ɹ/, a postalveolar approximant), sounds markedly foreign and distinctly English to native speakers of those languages – whose own foreign accent in English usually includes, at least initially, the pronunciation of English Rs as a tapped /r/. Similarly, English /t/ and /d/ are *alveolar* plosives; in many languages, such as French, Swedish, Finnish, Slovenian, Latvian, Turkish, Armenian, or Indonesian, /t/ and /d/ are audibly closer to dental. One of the traits of the accent that speakers of these languages may have in English is their dental or nearly dental articulation of Ts and Ds. Conversely, one of the hallmarks of an English accent in all those languages is the alveolar Ts and Ds. To a large extent, a foreign accent consists in this: people process the sounds of other languages through the grid provided by their own language; they reproduce foreign sounds as sounds of their native language. They also import phonological and phonotactic rules from their native languages into the language they are learning: some Spaniards may add a prosthetic /e/ vowel in front of the cluster /sp/, as done in Spanish; some Greeks may pronounce /p/ as /b/ if preceded by /m/, as in Modern Greek. In some cases, a particular sound of the language being learnt may well exist in the learner's mother tongue, but only as a contextual variant (an allophone), not as a distinctive sound (a phoneme). This can be enough to create problems for the learner. Take the velar nasal consonant [ŋ] that English writes as <ng> in words like *singer* (unlike in words like *finger*, in which the <g> is pronounced): in English, this sound has phonemic status, as it distinguishes the members of pairs like *sin/sing, thin/thing, banned/banged*. Hungarian, Portuguese, Serbo-Croatian, Turkish, and many other languages do have the sound [ŋ], but only as an allophone of /n/, before velar stops (/k/, /g/) which are pronounced in full. So, for example, the Hungarian word *hang* 'voice' is pronounced [hɒŋg], unlike the unrelated English word *hang* /hæŋ/. The result is that many speakers of those languages, guided also by spelling, tend to pronounce any English *ng* as [ŋg]. All this suggests that the language that people learn natively affects their ability to make the distinctions that speakers of other languages take for granted, which may seem to corroborate the 'Sapir-Whorf' hypothesis. However, two points must be borne in mind. One is that our ability to learn languages to a native

---

[5] Some can, of course, and some Scousers, Scots, Welsh, South Africans, and even old speakers of advanced RP use that sound natively for English r.

level diminishes dramatically as we grow up: small children, though already fluent in a language, can easily learn another with no accent, no matter how different its phonemic inventory; whereas adults brought up with no language at all (there have been a few such cases), when they learn a first language, at a mature age, struggle and usually never learn it very well. The second is that, as we said earlier, the decline in our learning abilities varies according to domain: it is dramatic in phonetics but less in syntax or morphology and almost untrue for the lexicon. If our particular language seems to make us unable to produce and even to hear the phonetic distinctions it lacks, it does not make it impossible for us to understand or express the semantic and conceptual distinctions that it lacks and that we may discover in another language.

Concrete evidence for linguistic relativity

Is there, then, any evidence that being speakers of a particular language rather than of another, owing to the structure of that language, affects our thinking in general? Consider the following. Languages like English or Spanish grammatically distinguish count nouns (i.e. items that can be pinpointed individually, e.g. a book) from mass nouns (e.g. sand), but languages like Japanese or Chinese do not. Various tests have suggested that speakers of the latter type of languages pay less attention to the discreteness of entities, and are more likely to classify objects by material than by shape (Pavlenko 2014: 69). There are also indications that, if your language marks certain distinctions (lexically or morphologically), this makes those distinctions more accessible in your thoughts. Speakers of languages that use only cardinal (i.e. compass) points to communicate spatial location, rather than relative terms like left and right, are reported to have a better sense of orientation than the average westerner (Levinson 2003: 33, 39) and to make geographically accurate unreflective gestures; if so, they are subconsciously guided and helped by the structure of their language even in non-linguistic domains. Conversely, speakers of Pirahã, an Amazonian language with no exact numbers, in certain tasks are disadvantaged by this lack: they do not do well when asked to perform tasks like copying a set of lines if the lines are more than two or three (Gordon 2004: 498). Furthermore, the individual words of a person's language, *even when not mentioned*, apparently can influence perception: in an experiment by Hoffman, Lau, and Johnson (1986: 1104), bilinguals were given the description of a person which fitted a term that exists in only one of their two languages – but the term was not explicitly used; it was noted that, if the description was processed in the language in which the term existed, a whole set of characteristics evoked by the term (characteristics not indicated in the description provided in the experiment) was attibuted to the person being described. This suggests that language-specific words, just by existing and being known to a speaker, can create lasting mental pictures and associations that affect our understanding of things – and of people.

We previously touched upon the intricate and elusive problem of colours, noting the different ways in which languages apportion the colour spectrum to lexical labels. Such variable segmentation of the colour spectrum does not corroborate the 'Sapir-Whorf hypothesis': speakers of different languages may still have the same visual perception of a colour, regardless of the colour categories of their particular language (assuming that they are either monolingual or speak two languages with overlapping colour categories). But do they think of that colour in the same way? Let us take English as an example. When English speakers look at an object, do they spot that it is not quite, or not simply, *blue*, but *azure*, or *celeste*, or *cyan*, or *ultramarine* only if such uncommon terms are part of their active vocabulary? Does lacking such terms and such concepts affect their ability to distinguish, or recognize, or remember that particular (variant of) colour? We saw earlier that languages such as Russian and Modern Greek have two colour categories corresponding to the English single category *blue*. Russian speakers, in comparison with English speakers, have been proven to be faster at matching two blue colours out of three when the third, to them, belonged to a different linguistic category, i.e. when, in their language, it was a differently *named* colour (Winawer et al. 2007: 7781–2). Moreover, tests on perceptual deviancy detection have found that Greek-speaking subjects spotted distinctions across shades of blue (as compared to shades of green, for which they have only one word) as early as 100 milliseconds after the stimulus, while English-speaking subjects did not (Thierry et al. 2009: 4568–9). This demonstrated a link between native language and unconscious, preattentive colour discrimination, even in situations where colour distinctions are ostensively immaterial to the task. Colour terms, it would therefore seem, draw our attention, even subconsciously, to the lexically distinguished differences in colour, facilitating memorization and retrieval. Having a word that encapsulates a given concept makes it, arguably, more salient, common, and readily accessible: comparisons between children whose native language was English or the Himba language of southwest Africa (Roberson et al. 2006: 165) has shown that, across time, they tended to re-identify colour samples correctly when these corresponded to a recognized focal colour term in their own language. In other experiments (Kay and Kempton 1984: 70; Roberson 2005: 63), participants were shown sets of three different colour chips and were asked which two were most alike. Two chips were very similar but, for that particular language, they were on different sides of a category border – they were such that they would be *called* different colours; the third chip was chromatically more different, but was within the same category as one of the others. The *linguistic label appeared to override vision*: the colour chip declared to be the more similar was often the one of the same lexical category – not the one that was physically more alike in colour but was, in the language of the person tested, labelled as a different colour.

In Chapter 4, we also saw how languages like Turkish distinguish, in their verbal conjugations, first-hand and reported or inferred knowledge. It could be objected that in English one can express roughly the same evidential distinction, using lexical rather than grammatical means, i.e. introducing a sentence with formulas like 'I hear that', or 'I am told that', or 'I found out that', or just 'apparently'. This is correct, but is not the whole story. It is, of course, true that the conceptual distinction between first-hand and reported or inferred knowledge is not unknown or obscure to English (monolingual) speakers, even though English cannot express it through verbal inflections. It is worth emphasizing that the structure of a language – whichever language that be – does not make it forever impossible for its speakers to understand what it does not articulate explicitly. And in this fundamental sense, the 'Sapir-Whorf hypothesis' is wrong. Nonetheless, as we noted for other domains, having a particular verbal form or noun for something, which another language may lack, focuses the speakers' attention on a certain aspect of reality. Studies on Turkish have found that the fact that Turkish verbal morphology distinguishes reported events from witnessed ones causes speakers to remember less well their sources of information about non-witnessed events – which was not found to be the case for English (Tosun, Vaid, and Geraci 2013: 131–2).

And then there is grammatical gender. Many English-speaking students of foreign languages think that the assignment of all nouns into gender classes in French, German, Spanish, or Gaelic entails only the obligatory use of certain endings and articles, but that the classification into gender classes is otherwise semantically empty. One can see why they would think so: although these classes are given names such as 'masculine' and 'feminine' because terms like *man, father, brother,* and *male* belong to one class, while words such as *woman, mother, sister,* and *female* belong to another, not only are there exceptions (in Scots Gaelic, the word for 'woman', *boireannach*, is masculine) but, above all, the vast majority of nouns with a gender have no biological sex. There is no biological reason why, in French, a fork is 'feminine' (*la fourchette*) and a knife is 'masculine' (*le couteau*). Indeed, grammatical gender ignores and overrides sex: in French, the equivalent of the word 'trout' is always feminine independently of the animal's sex, and the equivalent to the word 'salmon' is masculine independently of the animal's sex, and any word that refers to these nouns also bears their grammatical gender regardless of the animal's sex:

- the salmon is good, big, and shiny > *le* saumon est *bon, gros, et brillant*
- the trout is good, big, and shiny > *la* truite est *bonne, grosse, et brillante*

Despite all this, if you think that grammatical gender is just a misnomer for noun classes that have no connection to biological sex *in our heads*, think again. There is some evidence that grammatical gender can affect our conceptualization of objects in ways that are irrationally linked with biological sex. This can be seen, for example, in personifications of genderless concepts. Ancient Greeks deities and other personifications of abstract concepts were portrayed as female or male largely for grammatical reasons. *Bía* 'Violence' and *Níkē* 'Victory' were nouns of feminine grammatical gender and were conceptualized as females; *Éleos* 'Compassion' and *Hýpnos* 'Sleep' were nouns of masculine grammatical gender and were conceptualized as males. If you ask children who speak a language with genders to give an anthropomorphic representation of abstract concepts (e.g. write a story in which the characters are, for example, motor vehicles) they will tend to match grammatical gender with sex stereotypes: if, in their language, *car* is a feminine noun and *van* is masculine, children will tend to portray cars with conventional feminine traits and vans with male ones. In an experiment conducted in English (Boroditsky, Schmidt, and Phillips 2003: 70), Spanish and German speakers were asked to provide adjectives appropriate to a *bridge* and a *key* – the choice of objects, unbeknownst to the interviewees, was due to the fact that in Spanish *bridge* is a masculine noun (*el puente*) and *key* is feminine (*la llave*), while in German *bridge* is feminine (*die Brücke*) and *key* is masculine (*der Schlüssel*). Speakers of Spanish reportedly described bridges as *big, strong, sturdy, dangerous,* and *towering*, while speakers of German described them as *elegant, slender, fragile*, and *pretty*. Keys, on the other hand, were deemed to be *little, shiny*, and *lovely* by Spanish speakers, but *heavy, hard*, and *jugged* by German speakers. There is also a carry-over between languages: native speakers of a language with gender, when they learn English, quickly learn to refer to all inanimate objects as 'it', but often still use gender when talking of animals. For example, in Spanish and in Italian the word for 'spider' is almost the same, but it is feminine in Spanish (*araña*) and masculine in Italian (*ragno*); speakers of such languages may, accordingly, refer to any spider automatically as *she* ('don't kill *her*') or as *he* ('don't kill *him*'), without knowing whether the spider is male or female. This does not mean that the language deterministically prevents such speakers from comprehending that the spider could be of a different sex; but nonetheless shows that grammatical gender leads to a default conceptualization of the referent in gendered terms. For very moderate formulations of the 'Sapir-Whorf hypothesis', therefore, there is now some evidential corroboration; each particular language may slightly affect the speaker's conception of the world in certain domains (cf. Xu 2002: 225).

Imposing an outlook together with a language?

If each language, in some very small respects, predisposes speakers to think of certain things in a particular manner, it is not surprising that a question that elicits great interest, and indeed political passion, well beyond academia, is that of whether the adoption, or the imposition, of a given language alters the mindset of the speakers in politically significant ways. A concern raised often is that when the political and economic clout of a country leads other populations to assume its language, partly or entirely, this will also implant in these populations a particular outlook, a perspective with implicit metaphysical postulates, moral values, social biases, existential goals, consumption patterns, and so forth. After all, western countries that spread their language among conquered populations often thought of it, presumptiously, as a *langue de civilisation*. A number of intellectuals born and raised in European colonies have not failed to notice the issue. Derrida, who had grown up in French-ruled Algeria, and whose main language was French, said insistently and plaintively, in a book significantly titled *The monolingualism of the Other* (1996: 13–15): 'I have but one language, and it is not mine.'[6] Fanon ([1952] 1971: 14–16, 30), discussing the use of French by colonized populations, believed that 'a man who has a language has, as a result, the world expressed and implied by that language'; he argued that although, for West Indians, learning to speak French well was a necessity,

> In a group of young West Indians, the one who expresss himself well, who has mastery of the language ... is a semi-White. In France one says 'to speak like a book'; in Martinique, 'to speak like a White'.[7]

---

6   'Je n'ai qu'une langue, ce n'est pas la mienne'.
7   'Un homme qui possède le langage possède par contrecoup le monde exprimé et impliqué par ce langage... Dans un groupe de jeunes Antillais, celui qui s'exprime bien, qui possède la maîtrise de la langue... c'est un quasi-Blanc. En France, on dit parler comme un livre. En Martinique: parler comme un Blanc'.

This is also why many people who otherwise care little about linguistics oppose the demise of many 'small' languages: usually, the possibly different constructions of reality that are assumed to inhere in those languages are what those who mourn the extinction of languages really lament: they decry the loss of linguistic diversity as a loss of cultural diversity, a loss of alternative world views. They deplore the spread and clout of colonial languages like English or French because they fear that these come with various forms of cultural (and therefore also political and economic) domination. Their fear, as we saw also in Chapter 5, is not altogether groundless.

One should, nonetheless, also note that local pre-colonial languages have sometimes constituted an imposition too: in India, pacifists such as Gandhi promoted Hindustani as a composite, native, and inclusive alternative to English – but a hundred million people in India spoke languages of other families, and experienced the top-down promotion of Hindi as oppressive and alien. In the United States, Hispanic intellectuals understandably inveigh against the pressure to abandon Spanish and to switch to English; the irony, however, is that, in America, Spanish too is a language of colonization, and therefore was originally an obtrusion. Furthermore, while linguistic colonialism is clearly objectionable, to conceive of some (other) language as a freely chosen medium that enables authentic self-expression is somewhat misleading. What gradually becomes 'our' language as we grow up is a code that we all find ready-made. A few of us succeed in introducing into it, at most, tiny innovations; but, otherwise, we learn to accept it as it is. Most people do not wonder whether their mother tongue can constrain or bias their thoughts, and treat it as having a direct and objective correspondence to reality. But that correspondence has long been doubted. In Plato, the question of whether language is a valid epistemological tool is famously raised, though with a rather inconclusive debate as to whether there is an intrinsic correctness in the names of things, or such correctness exists only in reference to a conventionally agreed standard.[8] Later, Aristotle stated less equivocally that the words that different peoples use to refer to things are utterances that have meaning by virtue of convention.[9] A few other traditions took a critical stance earlier: Taoism proclaims that language limits self-expression and even hampers and misleads thought. The *Tao Te Ching* begins with the assertion that 'the Way that is verbalized is not the eternal Way; designations that can be named are not the timeless designations'.[10] Other traditions inclined to a different view. In Classical Indian philosophy, there was much discussion of the role of words as means of knowledge (प्रमाण); the Mīmāṃsā school of classical Hindu philosophy argued that the Veda, the ancient scripture of Hinduism, being supposedly authorless and the eternal truth, was written in words that were perennial and accurate, and whose meaning was consequently timeless, factual, and universal; so was, therefore, the relation between words and their referents. Meaning was thus posited to be inherent

[8] Plat. Crat. 383a–d: ὀρθότητά τινα τῶν ὀνομάτων πεφυκέναι καὶ Ἕλλησι καὶ βαρβάροις... - οὐ δύναμαι πεισθῆναι ὡς ἄλλη τις ὀρθότης ὀνόματος ἢ συνθήκη καὶ ὁμολογία.
[9] Aristot. De Int. 2.1: Ὄνομα μὲν οὖν ἐστὶ φωνὴ σημαντικὴ κατὰ συνθήκην.
[10] 道可道 非常道. 名可名 非常名.

and stable in the words, not arbitrary or conventional, and the reality of being (सत्) to be directly connected to utterance (शब्द). Although there were alternative opinions on this, even some Indian grammarians took that position. For example, Kātyāyana (c. 300 BC), thought that the link between word and meaning was not a contingent accident but a fact proven and invariable (सिद्ध).

Modern linguistics, especially since the shake-up brought in by Saussure, stresses that each language is an arbitrary convention. Some western modern theorists incline to the view that language is arbitrary and distorts reality, or restricts access to it. Their concern is not only epistemological but also social and political, since language is the main social structure through which our inter-subjective relations are negotiated and managed, and is the main medium through which we develop and articulate a sense of who we are. As we mentioned in Chapter 1, there is an argument that all languages are forced on their speakers. Babies realize, if subconsciously, that, in order to survive, they need to learn to communicate, linguistically and otherwise, by following codes and norms that others have already set – what Lacan called the signifiers of the Symbolic Order. In a Lacanian interpretation, to grow up in a culture and to acquire language, as we all do, entails entering an external, alienating, regulatory structure. In that line of thought, any culture, including the one that we consider our own, and any language, including our mother tongue, whichever that be, is to us 'Other', and in a sense colonial, because originally not our own but foreign, imposed, and limiting – although most of us do not realize this fact, and do not reflect on its consequences. One of those consequences is that we learn to understand and describe ourselves in terms not created by us. If that is correct, people cannot be the fully self-aware, self-determined, free agents that most of the western tradition, from the Greeks to the Enlightenment, had envisaged. If we are all forced to adopt someone else's words and meanings – the argument goes – we thereby also adopt the point of view that these may imply. Several thinkers have expressed such perception. Bakhtin is a ready example: according to him, language is a mix of the voices of others (разноречие), because it is learnt from the usage of others and is imbued with their vision of things.

There is something obviously true, though hugely overstated, in this idea. Feminist thinkers of the twentieth century (e.g. Rich 1977: 53–4) have described in similar terms the linguistic experience of women: they wanted to speak or write as women and about women's lives, but 'they have only male language with which to do it' (Heilbrun 1988: 40). Phrased in this way, the claim is hyperbolic, but women did have to use a language peppered with elements that universalize the viewpoint of men, and in which many words and their definitions and connotations were not developed by women. Evidence of this is not difficult to spot: the overwhelming majority of books, films, articles, and public speeches were made by men; many traditional grammatical constructions, like the generalized use of masculine pronouns (e.g. 'every person should have his rights respected'), reveal an assumption that speakers and listeners are male; negative terms for women like *slut* have no male equivalent; others terms have both a female and male form but with a value-laden difference, as in *mister* vs *mistress*;

words like *policeman, fireman, postman, barman,* or *chairman* did not even have a form for women – and this not only reflected descriptively the paucity of women in those roles, but also perpetuated that absence by describing those roles as inherently male.

Considerations against the 'Sapir-Whorf hypothesis'

Whether the 'Sapir-Whorf' hypothesis and various claims of 'linguistic relativity' can be said to have any truth to them depends on which features of a language are being claimed to affect our thoughts, which aspects of our thinking are said to be influenced, whether inevitably or not, and with what results. There is clearly mileage to the notion that language, by framing reality in a given way (which is done not only by terms like *slut* or *insane*, but ultimately also by terms like *French* or *patriot*), can nudge our thinking in particular directions – the whole art of rhetoric is born of that realization. There is therefore *some* truth to the postmodern idea that many perceptions and social realities are constructed and reinforced by a discourse that we take for granted. In certain circumstances, the invention of words has considerable sociopolitical power; as Austin noted, words can, in the right context, even make true or bring about what they say. The presence of certain words, as we saw, suggests that a culture is aware or attuned to certain facts, that it believes certain categories to be ontologically real; if the word, besides its denotation (the reference to something) has also a connotation (an implicit judgement), this may well indicate a common attitude within a culture, which the word teaches to those growing up in that linguistic community.

There are, nonetheless reasons to be very skeptical about the 'Sapir-Whorf hypothesis' as it is usually understood. The deterministic idea that our native language(s) forcibly limits what we can grasp with our minds is not well supported by the data. Nor is there valid reason to accept the presupposition that we cannot think outside of language, or the conjecture that having a language is a precondition for having concepts – let alone the sweeping claim that all reality is just a construction of language.

While it is true that words can reify and confer apparent legitimacy to ideas and to attitudes associated with them, the lack of words does not impede alternative thinking. Giving a lexical label to a category does make it easier for us to learn that category and solidifies it in our mind (cf. Lupyan 2006: 196), and *habitually* we categorize things in line with our language (cf. Majid 2002: 504); but if a certain concept has not been lexicalized or grammaticalized in our language, that does not necessarily mean that we cannot conceive of such concept (cf. Slobin 1996: 81–2, 86). Indeed, we may even have that concept already, without having a term for it. One must distinguish words from concepts. What is within everybody's experience may be understood even without a word for it: the same meaning may also be roughly conveyed through a paraphrase or a lengthier explanation. Even Whorf, who so stressed the uniqueness of individual languages, provided translations when reporting on little-known languages like Hopi (an Uto-Aztecan language of north America). There can be what Grace (1987: 63) called perlocutionary intertranslatability. For instance, in most European languages there is one-word term for 'the day after tomorrow':

Table 6.1 Example of a common concept expressed monolectically by many languages but not by English

English	Dutch	Lithuanian	Albanian	Estonian	Serb/Croat
the day after tomorrow	*overmorgen*	*poryt*	*pasnesër*	*ülehomme*	*prekosutra*
Hungarian	**Italian**	**Czech**	**Romanian**	**Mod.Greek**	**Georgian**
holnaputàn	*dopodomani*	*pozítří*	*poimâine*	μεθαύριο	ზეგ

Modern English does not have a single word for this, though it would have been easy to create one (most of the languages above have combined 'over/after' with '(to) morrow'); nevertheless, despite such lack, the concept is not only easy to grasp for English speakers, but thoroughly familiar to them. More radical examples can be cited. The majority of languages in the world do not have the verb 'to have'; but we should not rush into claiming that their speakers do not have or struggle to understand the concept of possession or ownership. The languages that lack the verb 'have' use other ways of conveying the idea of possession and ownership (cf. e.g. Bortone 2010: 67–8). Many, for example, use locative constructions; thus they phrase a sentence such as 'I have a house' like this:

Table 6.2 Examples of alternative constructions for expressing possession

Language	phrase	literal English translation
Irish	*tá teach agam*	'is house at-me'
Finnish	*minulla on talo*	'on/at me is house'
Swahili	*nina nyumba*	'with-me-is house'
Mongolian	надад байшин байна	'to-me house exists'
Hebrew	יֵשׁ לִי בַּיִת	'there-is to/for-me house'

Similar considerations can be made about grammatical structure. There are many languages that are tenseless altogether, including Mandarin, Thai, Burmese, Vietnamese, and Dyirbal; this does not mean that they have no way at all to convey the location in time of an event, let alone that the speakers have no notion of the passing of time. It is that they have not *grammaticalized* the marking of the time-location of events.

It is also common for a language to lose grammatical (morphological) distinctions or words without losing concepts. Standard English has lost, for example, the distinction between the second person singular and second person plural. So we now say, for example, *you sing* in both cases, whereas in Middle English one said *thou singest* when addressing one person and *ye singen* when adressing more than one (to this day, German separates *du singst* and *sie singen*, and that contrast is usefully marked also by countless other languages, from Arabic to Zulu). This perhaps shows a sociocultural shift among English speakers at the time when *thou* was lost, but does not mean that contemporary English speakers cannot mentally grasp the difference between having one interlocutor or many. Similarly, the modern English third-person possessive adjectives (*his, her, their*, etc.) are ambiguous, as they do not make clear whether the referent is the subject of the sentence or someone else. So, in an utterance like *Jack spoke to David about his book*, the word *his* does not clarify whether the book is Jack's or David's. Old English did have an alternative term that could mark that distinction (*sīn* vs *his*), but the distinction was not strictly observed and was eventually abandoned. Other ancient European languages also had separate words that made that distinction, and many modern languages still do, notably Scandinavian and Slavic ones. In English, the ambiguity of *his book* may create semantic confusion, but does not create a cognitive incapacity or difficulty to understand the distinction that is no longer marked linguistically.

The same can apply to vocabulary. Those who study ancient texts often discover that their own language used to have words for certain objects, actions, qualities, or feelings but later lost them, although those words refer to something that is still part of the speakers' experience. Latin distinguished *patruus* 'uncle on one's father's side' and *avunculus* 'uncle on one's mother's side', a distinction for which the languages that continue Latin, like Italian, French, and Spanish, do not have a word (unlike Arabic, Hindi, Chinese, and a few Slavic languages). One may reasonably argue, as we mentioned before, that such loss in Romance languages reflects a decline in the specificity of roles or of hierarchical differences in the kin positions within an extended family; but one cannot argue that the lexical loss leaves one unable to think of the relevant concept: Italians, Spaniards, and the French do have, and are well aware that one can have, uncles on both parents' side, just as the ancient Romans did. Many other lost words could be cited to corroborate this point. Latin also had, for instance, the word *contĭcĭnĭum*, which indicated the time when everyone and everything falls eerily silent, i.e. the first hours of the night. This is a concept readily graspable by virtually anybody, but has no corresponding word in French and Italian. On a similar note, Old English had the word *ūhtcearu* 'pre-dawn dread/sorrow', i.e. despondency and fear engulfing someone alone in the dark early hours of the morning. The phaenomenon of people being seized by a nameless dread and hopelessness when alone at that time of the night has apparently not disappeared: it is considered widespread by psychologists (cf. Rowe 1991: 190), it is known as 'the hour of the wolf' in several languages (Swedish *vargtimme*, Finnish *suden hetki*, Polish *godzina wilka*, etc.), and is also often alluded to in popular culture (Troye Sivan sings: 'I can't trust myself with my 3am shadow'[11]). And yet, English no longer has a word for that concept.[12]

---

[11] Troye Sivan, *Talk me down*.

[12] The word *ūht-cearu* (for *ūht-* cf. modern Dutch *ochtend* 'early morning'; and for *-cearu* cf. modern English *cares*) is, for us, a *hapax legomenon* even in Old English; but in Old English poetry the concept of an anxiety and despondency gripping one towards morning is recurrent.

We noted before that language may have, or lack, or lose words for something cross-culturally common, and that we may attribute this to a peculiarity or a shift in the culture and lifestyle of the speakers; but we should tread carefully. A word may not be enough for us to draw vast inferences about the social structure, or moral values, or gender politics of a culture. For example, in order to describe sexual activities, Classical Latin has the nifty term *crīsō*, a verb that indicates the willful movement of the haunches made by a woman during vaginal intercourse so as to control and manage penetration as she pleases. In the absence of more information about the culture of ancient Rome, one could be tempted to read the existence of the verb *crīsō* in Latin as a sign that, in Roman culture (as compared with, say, French culture – given that the verb *crīsō* has not survived into French), there was a clearer recognition and validation of women's viewpoint and will, a greater acknowledgement and acceptance of women's sexual desire and sexual agency, or a custom that women would take charge in their sexual activity with men. But that would be decidedly mistaken. In the same way, inferring a cultural outlook from the presence or lack of a grammatical distinction in a language must be done with extreme caution. Consider the presence of a gender-specific lexicon in many languages. The concern that it can foster sexism is understandable. However, languages like English, Dutch, or Swedish have distinct words for 'he' and 'she'; and that distinction is lacking altogether, and only one word is available, in Persian (او /u/) and in Turkish (*o*), as also in Georgian (ის /is/) and Malay (*dia*); in Bengali, third-person singular pronouns distinguish two degrees of formality and three of proximity (এ /e/, ইনি /ini/, ও /o/, উনি /uni/, সে / ʃe/, তিনি /tini/) – but with no gender distinctions. This does not reflect nor cause a less strict distinction between men and women in Iranian, Turkish, Georgian, Malay, or Bengali culture, and does not demonstrate nor promote more gender equality in the countries where those languages are spoken. Turkish has, furthermore, several gender-neutral forenames (*Burçak, Deniz, Tümay*), while in Finland giving to babies any names used for the other sex is prohibited by law.[13] This is no ground for claiming that Finland has a more sexist culture than Turkey. In the same way, we cannot argue that nineteenth-century England was egalitarian because it had, in essence, one pronoun (*you*) and one verbal form to refer to a singular addressee, instead of two as we find in French or German.

Some experiments have confirmed that our mental categorization of what surrounds us in everyday life is not guided only by language. Studies have found that monolingual speakers of different languages, although showing substantially different patterns in the way they name objects, can recognize the material properties shared by those objects in the same way as speakers of other languages. In American English, various small containers are classified into categories such as *box*, *jar*, *can*, *tube*, *jug*, or *bottle*, while in Spanish and in Chinese the same objects are grouped differently into named categories; and yet, when asked to sort the objects according

---

[13] Nimilaki/Namnlag (1991 §32b): 'Etunimeksi ei voida hyväksyä nimeä, joka on sopimaton tai jonka käyttö muutoin voi aiheuttaa ilmeistä haittaa... pojalle naisennimeä eikä tytölle miehennimeä' / 'Såsom förnamn kan inte godkännas namn som är olämpliga eller vilkas användning annars kan medföra uppenbar olägenhet... kvinnonamn för pojkar eller mansnamn för flickor'.

to physical or functional similarity, speakers of different languages group the object in very comparable ways (Malt et al. 1999: 242, 244). Similarly, French- and Dutch-speaking monolinguals (Ameel et al. 2005: 69–70) seem to agree, to a considerable extent, on the similarities among items such as bottles and dishes. Although the boundaries of linguistically named categories (i.e. the set of all objects called by the same word) vary cross-linguistically, this is no guarantee of a radically different perception of the objects.

Thinking beyond language

To claim that we can experience and conceive only what our language allows is a very intellectual idea. And a rather myopic one too. For a start, it is clear that human beings have pre-linguistic and extra-linguistic thinking. In evolutionary terms, the structures of human thought and symbolic cognition long predate the development of language. Although much of late-twentieth-century linguistics has treated language as being primarily for thinking rather than for interpersonal communication, there are good indications that thought is, at least largely, not linguistic to begin with, not only phylogenetically but also ontogenetically. Babies do have thoughts – though, of course, far less complex than those of adults. A large body of research with infants indicates that humans think also outside of language, and the same is clear about other species. Just by observing pets or wild animals in your garden you can see that they too, at some level, think: they recall places and people, dream when asleep, navigate directions, understand causality, gauge the feasibility of actions, plan (e.g. hiding nuts for later retrieval), engage in problem-solving, employ tools, learn tasks, choose to cooperate, guess goals, and even deliberately deceive. Lack of language does not prevent thinking. In human adults too, even in the most articulate ones, a great deal of thinking is carried out non-linguistically. As we noted before, we have all, on some occasion, struggled to put some thought into words, i.e. entertained concepts for which our language has no word. If language and thought did coincide entirely, we would probably never notice the limits and limitations of our language. This, of course, does not mean that, in the average person, all thoughts are independent of language. Certain parts or types of thinking do seem to contain language, particularly when the activity of thinking is employed in the activity of speaking (Slobin 1996: 76); but that is just one kind of thinking, and there are many others. We may find this counter-intuitive because, phenomenologically, most of us think in ways that, at least partly, feel like silent inner speech; some people even verbalize their thoughts out loud when alone. The act of thinking was therefore long believed, wrongly, to be a silent use of one's language. But the language we hear in our heads when thinking is not the thought itself: it is the conscious formulation of it (cf. Jackendoff 1994: 187). The conceptual structure of our thoughts receives only subsequently and partly a phonological garb which we experience as our conscious inner monologue (Jackendoff 2011: 613).

Languages are not inescapable grids that set the confines and terms of all our cognition. Such an extreme view is implausible – and, as we mentioned, is often a strawman version of what Sapir and Whorf themselves believed: Sapir himself (as we saw above) spoke of language habits, not mind prisons. Besides, although language is a convention, it does not lack room for creativity, transgression, individuality, and adaptability to new ideas, new objects, and new needs. And this clearly happens – otherwise, languages would never change; but they do, ceaselessly. Languages constantly cross their own confines: they can expand their vocabulary, phraseology, semantics, and range of syntactic options, and thereby, arguably, their conceptual and expressive powers – we noted this process in Chapter 4. And it is not only the conscious word-smithing of academics and poets that stretches languages in novel ways, but also the spontaneous usage of each new generation. If languages really hamper our access to reality (assuming there is an objective reality), they do so only to a small degree while, to a larger degree, they enable us to grapple with it. And anyway, we express ourselves (and others express themselves with us) in many ways other than linguistically, from body language to art. In any society, language is neither the foundation of all communication, nor of all culture.

The observations made so far in this book ought to provide a helpful background for the reflections, which we shall make in the coming chapters, on language's contribution in the forging of a national culture and identity, on the idea that language indicates and designates a nationality, and on the equation therefore often postulated between languages and nationalities. First, in the next chapter, we will look at what else forges nationalities – and at how the existence of nationalities forges our outlook.

7

Let there be a nation

In this and the following chapters, we will spotlight, alongside language, the second subject of the book: nationality. First, in this chapter, we shall need to look, albeit briefly, at what factors are usually deemed necessary for a community to amount to a nation; and thence at what the definition of *nation*, in broad terms, is assumed to be. In this connection, we will ask also when various populations first came to constitute, or anyway to be considered, nations; and we will make a few remarks on the consequences that the establishment of nations has had both in practice and, crucially, in our perception of other people. In later chapters, we shall discuss how a national identity is promoted, and look at the role that, in the making of nations and in the construction of national identities, has been played by language – especially by the development of a standardized language designated as national. We shall then consider the consequences that such languages have had on our understanding of the nature of both nations and languages themselves. Finally, we will assess merits and faults of the equation, commonly postulated, between nations and languages.

Nations and ethnicities[1]

The question of when nations first formed has exercised scholars intensely, and received a variety of responses. At one end of the spectrum, we find scholars, in academic literature often termed primordialists or perennialists, who assert that nations are a timeless feature of humanity, and that they developed naturally from long-standing ethnic communities (we shall return to the concept of *ethnicity* and its definition shortly). This view is usually also part of the ideology of nationalists – though it should not be simply equated with it – who see their nations as eternal, and believe that it should be composed of people with the same ancestry, and generally homogenous. Many of them are keen to trace their nation as far back in time as possible, and treat an early date of first attestation as a status-enhancing pedigree (as well as a legitimization of territorial possessions or claims). At the other end of the spectrum, we find scholars, often labelled modernists or constructionists, who see nations as historically recent and often artificial entities, which have grown, both physically and culturally, from

[1] I thank Dr Mark Pottle for a helpful exchange on some of the points I made in the first part of this chapter.

mixed origins, and which date mostly no further back than the eighteenth century. A corollary within this second view is that all writings that deny the contingent and largely made-up nature of nations is to be dismissed as unscholarly (cf. Hobsbawm 1992: 12; Gellner 1997: 5). The majority of contemporary academics, unlike the broader public, take positions relatively close to this end of the spectrum. Some academics, however, though leaning towards a modernist view, have argued that there have been a few peoples, long before the modern age, that fitted rather closely to our concept of nation (Smith 1998: 190). England is thus said to have been a nation already in the sixteenth century, the first nation in the world and the model after which other nations were fashioned in Europe and America in the eighteenth century (Greenfeld 1992: 14, 23). More conservative authors claim that the English nation started in 1066, albeit it absorbed later waves of invaders; and that the English, the Germans, the French, the Italians, the Danes, the Spaniards, the Dutch, and the Scots were 'all firmly in place' by the end of the fifteenth century (Hastings 1997: 43, 114). Others trace the existence of nations, as a typology, back to the dawn of history (Gat 2013: 23), though recognizing that some nations are recent and some have vanished.

Which of these views is correct depends largely on the definition of *nation* that one adopts. What makes a particular collection of individuals a nation? Most scholarly sources now tend to define a nation as a community whose members share a culture, a name, a belief in a common origin, a collective historical narrative, and a sense of belonging together (which presupposes the exclusion of some others).[2] There are two main things that are noteworthy about a definition of this kind. One is that, if such communities are what nations are, then some nations have indeed existed well before the development of countless modern nation states from the eighteenth century on. The second is that, by this definition, the existence of a nation, unlike the existence of the people that compose it, requires that its members *identify* as a nation. The Latin term *natio*, from which the English word *nation* derives, originally indicated any set or stock of humans (or even of animals) who may have not concurred or been aware that they constituted a particular group; the English term *nation* had the same broad meaning until the seventeenth century. Now it typically denotes a kind of social unit that, among other things, perceives itself as one, and professes to be one. It must be stressed that, since a nation is a concept, a cultural idea, here we are not stating that this is, prescriptively or objectively, what a nation is; we are observing, descriptively, that this appears to be the conception of *nation* most widely held.

Furthermore, many sources add other features to the definition of a *nation*. They often include location in a specific territory, in a land where the nation either currently resides, or did so in the past, or which it aims to inhabit in the near future. Very many scholars have described the *nation* as differing from other clusters of people precisely because of its 'desire to control a territory that is thought of as the group's national homeland' (Barrington 1997: 712–3, and others there cited). The conceptual

---

[2]   Note also the distinction implicitly made between a *people* and the related term *population* (as also in German between *Volk* and *Bevölkerunk*): the latter lacks connotations of unity, shared descent, or common spirit (Blommaert and Verschueren 1992: 196).

association between land and people is clear also in the vocabulary that we employ informally: the term *country* is often used as a synonym for *nation*.

More importantly, the term *nation* usually has an additional crucial entailment: it denotes a population that constitutes also a political entity, with its own common organization of the economy, of labour, and a set of equal obligations and rights for its members. And again, everyday usage confirms this: the word *nation* is frequently used as a synonym for *state* (although a *state*, strictly speaking, is a centralized political, administrative, legal, and military entity, rather than the people that such apparatus governs). There are even official names such as *The United Nations*, which in truth indicates a union of states.

Since *nation*, as we said, is often treated as a synonym for both *country* and *state*, by what mathematicians call the transitive property of equivalence relations (i.e. the observation that, if $a = b$ and $a = c$, then it is also the case that $b = c$) one can expect that *country* and *state* also be sometimes used as equivalent terms. And so they are: in English we talk about the 'president of a country' when referring to the president of a state, and conversely, about 'entering a state' when entering a country. In other western languages too, even though there is a separate word for *state*, the term for *country* can informally mean *state*: this is true of the German word *Land*, the Hungarian *ország*, the Italian *paese*, the Modern Greek χώρα, the Romanian *țară*, and several others. None of this is accidental: it betrays the assumption that states are territorially defined.

We can now come to the question of ethnicity. Does the *nation* have an *ethnic* basis? If we take the concept of *nation* as just described, and we leave out of such a concept the semantic feature of having (or aspiring to have) self-government, and perhaps that of professing publicly a collective identification, we do get close to what many would call an *ethnicity*. This is another term whose definition we must briefly discuss. Spotlighting *ethnicity* for a moment here, in a discussion of the idea of *nation*, is important because many people define, and want others to define, the nation in ethnic terms, and their choice to do so has profound, sometimes explosive sociopolitical consequences. The term *ethnicity* usually denotes a population that is said to have a distinct outlook and communal practices, a (presumed) common descent which gives to its prototypical members some phenotypical similarity, and a (truthful or fanciful) collective history – even when the members of that ethnicity do not themselves articulate any of this, and perhaps not even have a collective emic name for themselves. To some, the meaning of *nation* is not merely a body of citizens, but something close to *ethnicity* or even *race*. The latter term conceptualizes a human group thought to be biologically distinct in marked and visible ways – though the racial categories we commonly recognize do not correspond to a significant biological distinction (cf. Templeton 2001: 51); however, *race* has occasionally been used merely as a loose term for a people, or a line of descent, without implying phenotypical distinctiveness.

Here too, there are the two opposite, politically charged views. Some claim that ethnic groups, like nations, are a reality neatly defined by biology and in vain denied by political correctness, and that their cultures are a carefully preserved heritage specific to them. Others contend that ethnicities are just a socially constructed fiction, a fantasy that reinforces distasteful notions of racial distinctiveness, and that their culture is an ever-changing farrago replete with borrowings from other peoples. Both views, again, are partly correct and partly false. On the one hand, as the former view implies, the fusion of some large family units did create the original core of many populations that many would now call *ethnicities* or ethnic groups; in pre-modern times, moreover, people married and reproduced mostly locally; this may contribute to explaining why 'ethnic' backgrounds can usually be roughly established by DNA analysis. In that light, ethnicities have some concrete reality to them, and are, to a limited degree, often biologically identifiable. It is also correct that human collectivities roughly equivalent to the modern idea of an ethnic group have existed through most of human recorded history, and it might conceivably even be the case that 'ethnic collectivities will exist as long as human societies exist' (Fishman [1977] 1989: 48). It is likely true, moreover, that a number of nations developed from such ethnic groups, though only partly so, and anyway from a combination of such groups. And we can also say that such development can be seen already in some ancient populations. Those of us who have studied cultures of the past know that ethnicity-based collectivities resembling nations existed before modernity. Already in antiquity – notably, in Ancient Greece – there were politically autonomous communities that claimed a common descent and saw others as foreigners, though often by degrees, and that usually discriminated against them, though they sometimes incorporated them by assimilation. However, it is possible to object that applying the term *nation* to these populations may be inapposite because only some members of such communities had citizenship and equal rights in law such as the ability to vote, own property, or hold public offices; for that reason, those communities perhaps did not constitute a *nation* as most now understand the term. If so, we are back to the problem of definitions.

Above all, it would be specious to conclude that a whole ethnic group has an ancestry common to all its members (the 'blood' invoked by nationalists), and that nations, with the exception of modern multi-ethnic ones whose membership is supposed to be based purely on civic principles, such as the United States or Australia, are purely ethnic groups with added political autonomy. Ethnic groups and nations (whether past or contemporary) have often claimed a long and distinguished lineage preserved by a history of exclusive endogamy (and therefore racial distinctiveness or even purity), and a time-hallowed identity preserved unchanged over time. But all of this, in most cases, is to be taken with a large pinch of salt. Communities of the past were far less stable and watertight than is usually acknowledged by those who assert to be their descendants; outsiders could be accepted as new members through marriage and acculturation, like in-laws in a family, or got blended in quietly. Various groups can gradually coalesce and come to be regarded as an ethnicity – even whole multi-ethnic civically defined nations such as Australia or the United States are now sometimes referred to as ethnicities; and in the past too, among many populations, the cultural similarity of another group has often been treated not only as a sign of compatibility but of kinship, without other evidence. A unique and unalloyed bloodline is normally a myth, and so are the concomitant claims that the group's culture is purely an internal creation, or that its professed national identity has existed, uninterruptedly and unaltered, since time immemorial. In truth, the descent or ancestry that is claimed may be historically incorrect, not only in the case of particular individuals but also in the case of entire communities.

The census that many states conduct, asking the population to declare their ethnicity, has sometimes found that siblings earnestly declare different ethnicities (Romaine 2000: 40), and that individuals sincerely profess a different ethnic background from survey to survey (Waters 1990: 16, 36). Above all, most civilizations have received, both biologically and culturally, vast inputs from elsewhere, and whatever is thought to be a unique and age-old national identity is likely to have undergone profound transformations over time. Nevertheless, while unhistorical claims sometimes are part of a conscious political ploy, often they are made in good faith. The resulting notions of national lineage, national character, and national unity, even if based on fictions or on heavily edited history, are therefore not necessarily insincere nor flimsy. The fact that national identity is, to a considerable degree, a construction, should not lead us to assume that it is fake; for countless people, it is very real and very meaningful.

The emergence of nations

We can circle back to the question of when the nations that are now with us were formed. One may be tempted to rely on medieval texts, written by local men of letters, which name some such nations in their writings. Many present-day nationalists cite these as proof of the antiquity and solidity of their nations. For example, long before the unification of regions of southern Europe into Italy in the nineteenth century, Dante (thirteenth—fourteenth centuries) spoke of Italy as a country, and Machiavelli (fifteenth–sixteenth centuries) not only spoke of 'Italians' and of an 'Italian spirit', but ended his work ([1513] 1550: 79) with an exhortation to liberate Italy from foreign rulers, whom he described as Barbarians.[3] Similar references to the English, the Germans, the French, or the Spaniards can also be found in the literature of the pertinent regions, as can derogatory remarks by one group against the other; histories of this or that particular people ('nation') also predate the 'Age of Nationalism', as do mentions of 'national character' (Burke 2013: 24, 31–2). But in such cases too, prudence is called for. In several countries, the national identity now taken for granted was developed and promoted by a restricted circle of intellectuals (cf. Hann 1995: 106). This was the case in England, in France, in Italy, and in Sweden, as it was in Greece, in Bulgaria, in Russia, in Bohemia, and in Bengal. National consciousness long remained patchy by class and area (Hobsbawm 1992: 12). To call 'national identity' or 'national consciousness' the sentiment that some authors expressed in the Middle Ages can be misleading, and not just because those terms now have political and cultural connotations that they could not have had then. The main issue is another: those terms suggest a mass phenomenon, rather than an élite one, and consequently somewhat distort the picture, as Connor (1990: 97–100) argued: academics reconstructing the history of national sentiments have taken the written comments left by the intellectual class as representative of the whole population, but the opinion of the masses is mostly lost to us. It is hard to tell

---

[3] 'Esortatione à liberare la Italia da i Barbari'.

when enough people adopted the same view, and when an entire population should, therefore, be considered a nation – particularly if one wishes to abide by the modern tenet that the only correct 'identity' labels are those self-declared by each individual. Our tangible evidence for some kind of national consciousness in the distant past often covers only a tiny stratum in the population. For instance, there is no proof of a large-scale 'national consciousness' among Baltic, Germanic, and Slavic peoples before the nineteenth century (Connor 2004: 40). We should also bear in mind that nationalities are fundamentally contrastive; a community is unlikely to have a very marked national identity as such if the other communities with which it comes into contact do not manifest one either. The *intelligentsia* of Medieval Europe did often have a rudimentary sense of national identity, either acquired through historical awareness, or elaborated for political aims; but if we look for the earliest time when a whole people embraced a national identity, we cannot confidently assume that the thoughts occasionally voiced by a handful of intellectuals had immediately mass currency – let alone mass concurrence – in the wider population. Most people were barely literate; they lived separate lives from the intellectual élite, and did not count much in its eyes. Besides, not only the ideology of nationhood, but also the right of membership of the nation often extended primarily to the higher classes. In France, for example, the 'nation' was usually assumed to be the circles with cultural and political clout, and the concept was only much later fully extended to 'the people' (Greenfeld 1996: 11–2). A problem with attributing, already in the Middle Ages, a nation state and a modern national consciousness to the French, the Italians, the Danes, or the Greeks, is therefore, a problem of definition also in that sense: who and how many people do we count as French, Greek, Italian, or Danish? These national epithets covered a different area than they do today.

In pre-modern societies, before urbanization, industrialization, mass transport, mass communication, and literacy, the majority of people were, physically and culturally, locally grounded, and so were their main loyalties and solidarities. They were socially quite detached from the educated, wealthier, and politically influential classes – in feudal societies, social positions were neatly separate and rarely changeable, and people were rather isolated vertically as well as horizontally. Establishing a homogenized collective culture on a large scale became easier only once means for mass education were available, namely in the nineteenth and, in many lands, the twentieth century. While people probably felt attached to their locality and their immediate community, we should not presume that they cared for the rather abstract concept of a 'country' – at least, not before being taught to do so. The aim of these observations is not to suggest that *any* national identity is entirely a recent development; it is to underscore, for those not aware of this, that the national labels that are banded around (and placed on everyone) today can be more superficial, precarious, recent, and artificial than they may seem. A couple of examples of this will be instructive – even if what is true of a few is not necessarily true of all. Although we should beware of the danger of making overbroad generalization from a few particular cases, the fragmentation that there was (and, to a small extent, there is) in large parts of Europe is undeniable and, while not a universal norm, it is a salutary reminder that collective 'identities' and the discourse that asserts them cannot be just taken at face value.

As late as the 1870s, the majority of the population of France, for instance, lived in poorly interconnected villages and had no French identity, although a widespread national French identity was later postulated to have existed since the Middle Ages by many scholars. As detailed in Weber's now classic study (1976: 4–7, 67–70), life conditions, outlooks, communication, and social identities in France had remained relatively constant for centuries, until the Revolution and its aftermath at the end of the nineteenth century. Then a sea change swept through the country, slowly integrating it with the worldview of Paris. A French identity took root especially in the early twentieth century with the growth of centralized systems of administration, communication, transportation, and education. Before, the peasants of France were described by the French educated élite as an unrelated race or as wild animals with no mental life – and with no knowledge of French: at the advent of the Third Republic (1870), French was a foreign language to half of the French citizens, and the upper class who spoke French did not see linguistic unity as necessary.

The situation in Italy was analogous, and this was recognized even by those ardently advocating the creation of a single Italian state. As we noted, a number of writers across the centuries had made references to an Italian nation, and those references were later cited to buttress the demand for a self-ruling state. Supporters of the idea of a unified Italian state had also the advantage that they could point to a literary tradition written in Italian going back to the fourteenth century. But that literary tradition was accessed by – and accessible to – very few. An intellectual who played an influential role in the unification of Italy in the nineteenth century, Gioberti (1843: 80–1), while arguing that it was attainable and advisable, and that around Italy there was already an 'illustrious' common written language, nonetheless acknowledged that any notion that there was already also an Italian *people* was misguided:

> The Italian people ... is a wish and not a fact, a presupposition and not a reality, a name and not a thing ... the Italian nation ... is a mere abstraction ... the Italian people ... does not exist.[4]

Although Italy was the earliest area of Europe to develop a written language that aimed to be shared across regions and therefore be national, the regions that now make up Italy were among the last to unite into a western European state and to forge a self-identified nation. Activities leading to unification gathered momentum at the end of the eighteenth century, under French influence; most of Italy was unified only in 1861, and the rest (including Rome) even later – some parts only after the First World War.

Surveys on group identities of European migrants to the United States in the nineteenth and early twentieth centuries show that national labels such as 'Italian', 'Croatian', 'Norwegian', 'Polish', 'Ukrainian', or 'Lithuanian' were mostly unknown to the people we now designate as such (Connor 2004: 40). Before the Second World War, in multi-ethnic Poland, when people were asked to state their national identity

---

[4] '[Il] popolo italiano ... è un desiderio e non un fatto, un presupposto e non una realtà, un nome e non una cosa ... [la] nazione Italiana ... è una mera astrattezza ... [il] popolo italiano ... non sussiste'.

for a census, many could not understand the question because they apparently had no such notion (Bauman 2004: 17). At the 1848 Pan-Slavic Congress in Vienna, it was reported that peasants in the district of Sącz in West Galicia, being questioned as to what people they were, were puzzled; asked whether they were Poles, they had answered, bemused, 'we are quiet folk'; when asked whether, if not Poles, they were Germans, they simply replied: 'we are decent folk' (Namier 1944: 107). Considering the now common perception that national identities stem from time immemorial and that belonging to a nationality is only natural and inevitable, it is sobering to realize that in nineteenth-century Europe there were people with reputedly no concept of nationality, no clear national identity beyond, presumably, a generic sense of *Landesgemeinschaft*, and who did not miss or seek one. But all this was lost to those asking the question for the census: they insisted that such a population was of a given ethnicity or nationality even without knowing it.

While it is definitely true that, in some cases, the untutored populace partook fervently in fights for national independence, it is also true that, in several countries, local communities experienced the arrival and the demands of the state as an alien, self-interested enterprise, often comparable to the explicitly foreign domination that they had endured in previous years. The new state imposed a political structure and an identity, inclusive of a language or a variety of the language, often unwanted by the people. In what now are regions of some European states, the rejection of the state is still palpable.

Maps and borders

Passports, visas for limited stay, nationality-dependent differences in the right to enter or reside in another country, immigration quotas, and border checks are primarily a feature of modern life. In the last century, borders proliferated like never before. The borders of lands used to be, overall, less marked and less policed. This, in many regions, probably fostered and reflected a fuzzy feeling of belonging locally, instead of a strong sense of national divisions. In many instances, residents of border zones think of the whole local area on either side of the border as part of their social space, and at times also regard the people immediately across the border as part of their community. Even the local authorities sometimes take that view, and allow foreigners who live just past the border to cross it more freely than travellers from deeper inside the other country. The classic case was that of West and East Berlin: documented West Berliners could cross into the East with relative ease, unlike all other Germans. Somewhat analogous was my childhood experience when I lived some thirty miles from the Swiss/Italian border: many local people crossed it daily to commute to work or go to school or visit family, and local guards were much more likely to let them come and go with little inspection.

If we compare original old maps of the pre-national era, down to the Renaissance period, with modern maps – even with some of the modern maps depicting the world of the past – one difference should immediately strike us. Old maps very often indicate no borders, whereas modern maps invariably do. Admittedly, in cartography, the data included is by necessity simplified and limited to a selection; but it is also true that such simplification is not without ideological underpinning or conceptual consequences: 'maps are the products of power and they produce power' (Kitchin, Perkins, and Dodge 2009: 9). As Barth (1969: 13) argued, ethnic identity is more determined by its boundaries than by its specific content; setting up and maintaining the boundaries of a social category like nationality are, in a sense, what establishes and preserves the category itself. Upon reflection, there is much that is remarkable about many modern political maps. They draw unrealistically thick borders around countries, as if there were a neat and vast separation between them; they usually mark every country with a dramatically different colour from the next, as if, the moment you cross the border, you enter a totally different world; and they fill each country with unvarying inner colouring, as if each country was internally uniform. They thereby suggest both clear-cut distinctions between countries and homogeneity within each of them. The importance of this will be clear if we think back to the unrelated experiments concerning colour perception that we mentioned in Chapter 6: people wrongly saw a greater difference between two colour chips if their hues fell at opposite sides of the border between two colour categories in their language. The linguistic distinction, and therefore the conceptual border, apparently, made them see a much bigger difference in reality. Psychological tests have demonstrated that the very act of imposing categories on reality, of giving to separating labels to groups, tricks both insiders and outsiders into seeing greater similarities within groups, and greater differences between groups (Hogg 2001: 60; Yzerbyt and Rocher 2002: 46–50). This must be why we talk of 'white' grapes or 'white' potatoes – not, more accurately, of 'green grapes' or 'yellow potatoes': it is because we identify the two varieties by overstating their contrast. In a comparable way, most English speakers describe people of brown, even very light brown, skin as 'black', and those of pinkish skin as 'white'.

From our school days up, national borders are presented to us as solid and lasting, and they are a defining element of the picture that we form of the world. We tend to perceive the militant secessionist movements reported in the media as unreasonable also because they strive to alter familiar geopolitical maps, and contest divisions that we have come to see as natural, objective, logical, and inherent. But many borders have unceasingly, if quietly, been contested to this day. In many areas, borders have been redrawn in relatively recent times, and local identities straddle them. We should not forget that, in the twentieth century alone, countless significant border changes have occurred on all continents and especially in Europe, and this entailed a change of nationality – though not necessarily of national identification – for the local population. Many times, imposed borders create minorities that are perceived as extraneous by the national majority, but also by their own co-ethnics across the border. In America, the original native Mexicans of Texas, for example, once Texas was captured by the Americans in 1836, 'overnight, became the foreigners' (Anzaldúa 1987: 6). European states colonizing Africa decreed national categories regardless of local sentiments: many 'nations' of Africa – i.e. the names that postulate the existence of such national groups – were a colonial invention imposed across linguistically and culturally diverse groups. And yet this act had some performative power: the nationalities were, in several cases, gradually internalized by the populations so autocratically named (Hylland Eriksen 2004: 51), another instance of ideology creating nations rather than vice versa (Gellner 1983, 1997: 5: 55; cf. also Hobsbawm 1992: 10; Kedourie 1993: 141).

The rise of nations

The rise of the nation state as we know it – the genesis of the idea of it and, above all, the emergence of its concrete instantiations – has had a traceable intellectual and political history, of which we should be aware, at least in a very simplified outline. Many scholars posit an 'Age of Nationalism' (Francis 1976: 68; Kedourie 1993: 1; Gellner 1997: 51) from the mid-eighteenth century until at least the twentieth, though some important premises took shape earlier. From the fourteenth century, with the Renaissance, educated discourse on human social organization, until then conceived more in religious terms, returned to a more classically inspired ideal of democracy and republicanism.[5] In the fifteenth century, the advent of the printing press in Europe greatly facilitated the diffusion of information and new ideas (and was crucial also in the establishment of local vernaculars and, later, of standardized national languages). In the early sixteenth century, with the Reformation, disaffected Catholics strove to reform the Catholic Church and ended up with a schism, thereby giving rise to new, independent, Protestant churches, of a more localized, near-national kind – and generating an unprecedented attention to local languages. The Catholic response, the Counter-Reformation, also contributed to that trend. The ensuing Thirty Years War between Protestants and Catholics ended with the consolidation of several European states. The Enlightenment movement of the eighteenth-century revolutionized intellectual discourse in Europe, rejecting tradition and championing the ideals of science and reason against those of religion; the latter had constituted, for very many, a stronger fulcrum than nationality for what we would now call 'identity'. A modest secularization then curbed the political power of the Church and of religious institution, and attenuated transnational religious allegiances. The advent, by the end of that century, of Romanticism, although it was essentially a reaction against the Enlightenment, in some ways helped to prepare the ground for the rise of modern nations, as it brought a new appreciation of local cultures and of folk artistic expressions. A key turning point is usually identified in the French Revolution, at the end of the eighteenth century, a period of widespread revolt promoting, across Europe, the principle of the sovereignty of the people. After the Revolution, Napoleon the 1st (Napoléon Bonaparte) enshrined such principle in a civil code that was applied also in many other countries, and which aided the development of states as normally envisaged in modern times: with a pervasive legal, bureaucratic, and school apparatus that instils in all citizens civic values and a national identity, and that does so through a unified and standardized language. This was also

---

[5] Though it should be noted that terms such as *republic* and *democracy* had different meanings originally (cf. Latin *res publica* and Greek δημοκρατία), and that the unqualified use that is often made of them, drawing analogies between modern times and antiquity, can be misleading.

the time of the Industrial Revolution, notably in north America and northern Europe (including Britain), which caused mass migrations from rural localities to factories, with inter-regional mixing of the people and the development of cities. In 1776, the United States declared independence from Britain, followed by American colonies previously held by France, Portugal, and Spain. By the nineteenth century, the Russian Empire, the Austro-Hungarian Empire, and the Ottoman Empire were ruling over a vast assortment of increasingly restless populations. Many nations, from Bulgaria to Finland, date their 'national awakening' to this period. The First World War, which started with the assassination of the heir-presumptive to the Austro-Hungarian throne by a Bosnian Serb nationalist, was followed by the disintegration of the German Empire and of the Austro-Hungarian Empire, soon followed by the Ottoman Empire. Already during the war, the Russian Empire had crumbled. By 1922, British rule over most of Ireland ended and, in 1932, Canada and New Zealand achieved *de facto* independence from Britain. The first half of the twentieth century saw also Australia's slow journey to independence. The period after the Second World War saw also vast campaigns for national independence in a process of partial de-colonization of the Middle East, Africa, and the Asian subcontinent. Nationalist principles, however, had started to undercut the imperial vision much earlier. In the following decades, this trend continued across large parts of the world. Starting in 1989, the Soviet Union shattered into over a dozen states besides Russia, a process that continued into this century. In western Europe, despite supranational political memberships and de-territorialized alliances enabled by global connections, many more populations continue to affirm distinct nationhood and advocate separate statehood, as in Scotland, Wales, Alsace, Basque Country, Corsica, Flanders, Catalonia, northern Italy, Transnistria, and Friesland.

We noted earlier that the nation state is so deeply embedded in modern perceptions that the concepts of *state* and *nation* are often used interchangeably. The theoretical postulation that state and nation should tally with each other is, technically, the very definition of the term *nationalism* (Hobsbawm 1992: 9; Billig 1995: 77; Kupchan 1995: 2; Gellner 1997: 45; Kedourie 1993: 9; Edwards 2009: 163). Academics who defend the ideal of the nation, like Miller (1995: 90) have argued that 'the thesis that a nation should want its own state is at one level tautological, since the ambition to be politically self-determining is built in to the very idea of nationhood'. However, the principle that states and nations should be in a one-to-one relation is a belief developed primarily in late-eighteenth-century Europe, and uncommon before the nineteenth century (Haas 1986: 727). In the affirmation of one's collective identity as a distinct nation state there is, therefore, a paradox worth underscoring. For all their assertion of autonomy, their rhetoric of cultural uniqueness, and even expressions of xenophobia, in most communities, the modern nation state is a political ideal largely derived from foreign cultures and modelled on other countries. In many nation states now long-established, the campaign for a nation state was introduced primarily by those whose education, social contacts, and life experience was decidedly non-domestic. In the most recently recognized nations too, and in populations currently striving to achieve national status, we can see the imitation of other states: the concepts, formats, and strategies used are not native. During the nineteenth century, in several instances, the educated élites who launched and sustained nationalist movements were living abroad, were educated abroad, and their vision was shaped by political models developed abroad. Many key figures of such élites would have been considered culturally, or even ethnically, alien by the peoples they wanted to convert to their nationalist cause. The leaders of many modern independence movements of the twentieth century were educated in the West: this is true of southeast Asia (Indochina's Ho Chí Minh studied in France and lived in England and the United States), of India and Pakistan (Gandhi studied in the UK, as did Mohammad Ali Jinnah), and of Africa (Kenya's Kenyatta studied in England, Senegal's Senghor studied in France, Ghana's Nkrumah studied in the United States). And, in a somewhat similar way, the Jewish, the Armenian, and the Irish diaspora have fuelled – intellectually and materially – nationalist movements in what was or was to become the independent country of their co-ethnics. In recent years too, in Africa, Asia, and Europe, it has often been university students, educated in the ways of other countries, who have spearheaded nationalist revolts. In some cases, such as that of Finland, those who were spearheading the national 'awakening' were of foreign extraction.

Consequences of the ideal of the nation state

A few more basic remarks about the nation state are in order, though they will have to be limited to observations useful for later discussions about language. There have been, in principle, positive and democratic sides to the nation state. Nationalism in the eighteenth century postulated popular sovereignty, which at the time was not a commonly held view. With the establishment of the nation state, a larger part of the citizenry usually was given some rights and a symbolic voice, and there was often some redistribution of wealth. And in this light, it is perhaps more understandable that many people who feel impoverished and disempowered by the effects of 'globalization' reaffirm the nation state. However, since a nation is traditionally conceived in ethnic or ethnic-like terms, the ideal of a nation state typically suggests, implicitly or explicitly, that ethnic uniformity within a country is desirable. Those who are markedly different, especially if similar to the prototype of another nationality, are likely to be considered out of place. Given that it is extremely rare for a sizable state to be naturally monoethnic from the start, the danger that native ethnic minorities become the target of mistreatment is, as history well substantiates, very real. Those minorities too, on the other hand, may adopt a nationalist view, and embrace the belief that, since they constitute a distinct ethnicity, they ought to have their own state. While we may be inclined to perceive this in a romantic light, as a journey of self-realization and liberation, we should also be mindful that, if all ethnic groups were granted the right to secede and set up their own states, global chaos and bloodshed would ensue (Vincent 1997: 287). We should also be aware that many ethnic minorities have no secessionist aspirations whatsoever; not every ethnic group that does not have a state of its own finds this distressing, humiliating, and abnormal. The wish for political and ethnic units to coincide is not quite universal and timeless. In pre-national times, ethnic communities were often subsumed by large states or empires, and many indicated little or no desire to be independent. Many did well without a separate homeland or political independence. But the doctrine that states should coincide with nations, being treated as a natural one, is attributively projected also onto those who do not share it. There is a widespread assumption that any native minority with a different ethnic identity is, *ipso facto*, an embryonic secessionist movement, inactive only because lacking in self-awareness. Some governments, therefore, assume that indigenous ethnic minorities want political independence and represent a potential hazard for the larger state they live in. This engenders not only public suspiciousness towards them, but oppressive legislation – including against their languages.

Xenophobia nowadays is habitually blamed on far-right subcultures, or on individual psychology, or on contingent crises; but we should not overlook the larger political structure that contributes to it. The very idea of the nation state presupposes that some people do not belong in it. Ethnic, national, and racial discrimination and exclusion have been, in a sense, constitutive of the nation state. It may be counterargued – not without foundation – that for a nation to be united, to make common cause, and to last through time, some visceral binding factor is needed; and that a perceived common ethnicity may provide this, as it can foster solidarity and cooperation. For native minorities who found themselves within the borders of a newly founded state, though, the new emphasis on invariance and uniformity has usually been a baleful development, as it became a rationale for marginalization, suppression, or expulsion. We must and can say that this is abhorrent without maintaining, disingenuously, that the alternative approaches are entirely unproblematic. One alternative recurrently put forth is that minorities ought to be accepted and absorbed into the mainstream; but this has been opposed not only by xenophobes and racists, but also by many members of those communities and their advocates, who contend that different communities should be allowed to maintain their distinct practices and beliefs without challenge. The paradox, important also for the language issues that we shall discuss in later chapters, is that in a society that embraces minorities, these will succeed in preserving their cultural (including linguistic) differences only if they make vigorous and sustained efforts to do so. Where there is ample social mobility and much interpenetration between communities, individuals increasingly change their customs, their views, and their 'identity' labels – their ethnic, cultural, religious, linguistic, or class affiliations. As Lévi-Strauss (1971: 665) noted, not without being contested, 'one cannot, at the same time, melt oneself into the enjoyment of the Other, identify oneself with him, and keep oneself different'.[6] Another alternative, advocated by many liberal thinkers and – notably – by religious leaders, is that a different community should be welcomed without being asked to alter or question its way of life, social attitudes, and traditional world view, and that two cultures can peacefully thrive alongside each other. Those disagreeing, perhaps in an attempt to beat their opponents at their own game, object that this presupposes an essentialist and exclusionary outlook, and grants unequal privileges. More conservatively

---

[6] 'on ne peut, à la fois, se fondre dans la jouissance de l'autre, s'identifier à lui, et se maintenir différent'.

minded commentators, in several European countries, contend also that a multi-cultural society is a contradiction in terms; they point out that multiculturalism expects us to be ethically blind, and that it creates mutually averse social bubbles that coexist without communicating. In Germany, there has been much talk of *Parallelgesellschaften*; in the Netherlands, a bill presented to the senate by the Minister for Domestic Affairs and Kingdom's Relations, J.P.H. Donner (2011: 7), affirmed:

> The government distances itself emphatically from the relativism implied in the concept of a multicultural society ... An integration policy entailing more obligations is necessary and justified, because otherwise society gradually grows apart, people will live alongside each other, and in the end no one feels at home in the Netherlands anymore.[7]

Although these observations can at times mask antipathies due to prejudice, it would be naïve to deny that different cultures can, in some respects, be irreconcilable, and that some communities, in several Western countries, rather avoid each other.

Such concerns and debates about social unity and shared norms have also linguistic reflexes. In later chapters, we will see that states that have developed a standardized and distinctive national language as a unifying medium, have often also shown antagonism to minority languages, and treated even bilingualism as a sign of disloyalty. Moreover, not only political figures but also scholars, including linguists, have thought that languages can be equated with nationalities. Before we discuss all that, however, we need to become fully aware of the effects of seeing reality in terms of national categories.

The nation-based outlook

A view of the world as naturally and exhaustively divided into nations is a central feature of the historical period that many historians and social theorists call modern. Greenfeld (2005: 326–7) remarked:

> Modern consciousness ... has at its core the nationalist world-view and ... projects this world-view on every sphere of cultural/social activity ... [such world-view] represents the cultural foundation of modern social structure, economics, politics, international relations, education, art, science, family relations, and so on.

That world view, and the assumption that it is objective and unavoidable, has far-reaching repercussions. Nowadays, lack of citizenship, as the *sans papiers* immigrants

[7] 'Het kabinet neemt nadrukkelijk afstand van het relativisme dat besloten ligt in het concept van de multiculturele samenleving ... Een meer verplichtend integratiebeleid is nodig en gerechtvaardigd omdat anders de samenleving geleidelijk uit elkaar groeit, burgers langs elkaar heen gaan leven en uiteindelijk niemand zich meer thuis voelt in Nederland'.

know well, is an unsustainable lifestyle – and most people treat this as logical and natural. Moreover, those who would prefer not to have, not to be defined by, not to be bound to one particular nationality are frequently treated as morally dubious, like someone opting for sexual promiscuity instead of an officially sanctioned and monogamous marriage. At best, they are given short shrift as delusional. In a speech at the Conservative Party Conference in 2016, British Prime Minister Theresa May stated disapprovingly: 'If you believe you are a citizen of the world, you're a citizen of nowhere'. In the eyes of many, foreigners who are blindly patriotic towards their own country are more acceptable than someone who rejects the concept of nationality altogether. As pointed out by Bertrand Russell ([1928] 2004: 3), 'people hate sceptics far more than they hate the passionate advocates of opinions hostile to their own'; individuals with strict religious views are usually more sympathetic to other religions than to atheism.

A dislike for those with loose or multiple national attachments has been quite prominent also in anti-Semitic discourse. One of the claims traditionally advanced by anti-Semites was that Jews were 'wanderers' not fully devoted to one country, that they had primarily links with other Jews of other nations, and were therefore of questionable loyalty, uncontrollable, selfish, and untrustworthy. No matter how well-integrated, they were seen as potential dissenters, also because of their international, universalist *Bildung* (cf. Mosse 1985: 3). The classic accusations levelled at Jews were that they were 'rootless … dishonest, unassimilable … sneaky … opportunistic … alien' (Gordon 1984: 25). Being perceived as having no single collective national attachment, Jews have also been cited as a by-name for everybody despised for lacking a national allegiance; Mazzini (1860: 57), a key figure in nineteenth-century nationalism and one of the masterminds of the Italian state, addressed those who did not claim affiliation to one country as 'the bastards of humanity, soldiers with no flag, Israelites of the nations'.[8]

The nation-based outlook means that when people meet someone from abroad, they regard nationality as crucial information, and as a key to guessing countless other characteristics of that person. This is a tendency towards generalization and essentialism that comes with thinking in broad categorial terms; it produces a homogenized image of each nation, and tends to trigger a uniform approach to all its members. Besides, whenever someone is described in general abstract terms of any kind, the descriptors used seem more context-independent, and therefore more informative (Walton and Banaji 2004: 194). Only members of one's own nationality are usually perceived in more varied, individualized terms, as if regardless of nationality; foreigners are more likely to be liked or disliked depending on their category label. And they are usually quite aware of this. Some foreigners, as a consequence, endeavour to pass as native locals; if their appearance or language skills rule that out, they admit to being foreigners but sometimes claim to be of a nationality that they feel will get a better reception than their own. I have often met people who asserted to me that they were from one country but, when I switched to the relevant language, they could not speak it natively and confessed to being from somewhere else: 'Greeks' who turned out to be Albanians, 'Italians' who turned out to be Romanians, 'French' who

---

8 'Senza Patria, voi … Siete i bastardi dell' Umanità. Soldati senza bandiera, israeliti delle Nazioni'.

were Arabs, 'Turks' who were Iranians, and so on. A nation-based outlook, after all, attributes to people the merits, misdeeds, and social status of their nation, regardless of their individual conduct, personal history, particular social position, and possibly dissenting views. So when you travel abroad, someone who does not know you, your personality, your biography, or your opinions may give you a friendly, or indifferent, or cold reception depending on how people unknown to you but bearing the same type of passport have behaved on a different occasion. By projection, the nation-based outlook also expects that foreigners will tend to support and agree with any unknown person classified as the same nationality as themselves, while not feeling that same way towards other strangers. This is also a political issue. Kidnapping or assaulting people, including civilians, or just passing tourists, because they are from a particular country stems from the same logic. Even within one's own country, one may be considered by some to be a legitimate target of terrorism for being part of that nation. Such attacks are widely recognized as savage, but – interestingly – not readily recognized as absurd. One is considered co-responsible for the actions of a government that one does not control and perhaps has not voted for. And again, as a result, some people hide their nationality if their government has engaged in disreputable international or interethnic behaviour: some Germans, although born well after Nazism, confess that, on foreign trips, they let others think of them as Dutch or Scandinavian; in the early 2000s, at the time of the contested and pretextuous invasions of Afghanistan and Iraq, some Americans travelled around Europe with Canadian flags sown on their backpacks; Israeli tourists often allege some other nationality to deflect possible hostility.

In the same vein, a nation-based outlook presumes – and teaches – that people should be ready to defend the track record and reputation of 'their' country regardless of the facts, to take offence at criticism of it, and be unwilling to concede faults and misdeeds. And many indeed do mount knee-jerk defences when something about their nation, state, or country is criticized. If an individual's sense of pride and loyalty is blindly bound up with nationality, this will regularly override rational thinking: in the United States, many declared that George W. Bush needed to be supported in his Iraq policies, even if dangerous and based on lies, for the sole reason that he was the President, and that patriotism is part of being American. In national(ist) ideology, not only does the nation become undistinguishable from the state, as we saw, but allegiance to one becomes indivisible from allegiance to the other. Historically too, a key function of the campaigns to promote the ideal of a nation state has been to make people identify with – and therefore recognize as legitimate, and delegate power to – a particular state power (Addi 1997: 111–2; A. W. Marx 2003: 5–6). This may leave in a friendless limbo those who disagree with the policies of their own state. Etgar Keret, liberal left-wing Israeli writer and commentator, openly condemnatory of Israel's treatment of Palestinians, lamented: 'in Israel people would boycott me saying I'm a traitor, and overseas people would boycott me because I'm Israeli'. He reported that he received death threats for writing excoriatingly about Israel's Gaza war, but also that, when travelling outside Israel, he has been shunned by people who asserted that he is guilty because of his nationality.[9]

---

[9]   *The Guardian*, 1 August 2015.

It is not difficult to see, on the other hand, that such assumptions of collective responsibility and moral ownership have also their rewards. And the way we *talk* with a nation-based outlook is, again, revealing. We can start by considering how people – very commonly but, upon reflection, very bizarrely – refer to famous individuals (such as writers, actors, or athletes) born roughly in the same land, to whom they are not related, and do not personally know, as 'our'. It must be stressed that, contrary to common academic assumptions, this conceptualization is not purely a product of the modern nation state, but of any conceptualization of a large polity as 'we'. Comparable behaviour could be found among the Ancient Greeks with reference to their particular city state, as Plato (Resp. 463e) attests:

– Then, of all cities, in this one in particular, when somebody does well or badly, they will all use the expression we were now discussing: *mine* is doing well, or *mine* [is doing] badly.
– Very true, he said.
– And together with this outlook and terminology, we said that collective pleasures and sorrows also ensue.
– And we said correctly.
– So, will the citizens have in common the same thing in particular, and call it *my*? And, having that in common in this way, they will especially share displeasures and pleasures?
– Very much so.[10]

In an analogous way, countless people talk with a tone of familiarity and personal possession about their country's dominions, such as lands, rivers, animals, cities, or antiquities – even if they are unlikely to ever see most of them. And, above all, although they realize that their own nation is made of millions of people about whom they know nothing other than their nationality (cf. Anderson 1991: 6), they refer to the whole nation collectively as 'us'. They conceptualize (cf. Gellner 1983: 74) a modern abstract society as a pre-modern, personally known community; to apply Tönnies' terms, they envisage a *Gesellschaft* as a *Gemeinschaft*. Such fantasy has long been noticed (cf. Allport 1954: 30) and was well-captured by Anderson's (1991) ubiquitously quoted phrase 'imagined community'. A personal self-identification with the nation is made also on a diachronic scale, which is all the more absurd, but no less common. I recently went to see the relic of the *Mary Rose*, Henry VIII's flagship, which sank with hundreds of men aboard in a naval battle between English and French forces in 1545; the museum guide referred to the men who were on the ship as 'our boys'; the conflicts between Ancient Greeks and Persians in the fifth century BC are now

---

10 '- [463e] πασῶν ἄρα πόλεων μάλιστα ἐν αὐτῇ συμφωνήσουσιν ἑνός τινος ἢ εὖ ἢ κακῶς πράττοντος ὃ νυνδὴ ἐλέγομεν τὸ ῥῆμα, τὸ ὅτι τὸ ἐμὸν εὖ πράττει ἢ ὅτι τὸ ἐμὸν κακῶς. - ἀληθέστατα αὖ, ἦ δ' ὅς. - [464a] οὐκοῦν μετὰ τούτου τοῦ δόγματός τε καὶ ῥήματος ἔφαμεν συνακολουθεῖν τάς τε ἡδονὰς καὶ τὰς λύπας κοινῇ; - καὶ ὀρθῶς γε ἔφαμεν. - οὐκοῦν μάλιστα τοῦ αὐτοῦ κοινωνήσουσιν ἡμῖν οἱ πολῖται, ὃ δὴ ἐμὸν ὀνομάσουσιν; τούτου δὲ κοινωνοῦντες οὕτω δὴ λύπης τε καὶ ἡδονῆς μάλιστα κοινωνίαν ἕξουσιν; - πολύ γε'.

discussed online between Iranian and Greek teenagers in terms of 'we did' and 'you did'; quite regularly, one can also hear the offspring of recent immigrants to the UK or the United States (whose ancestors were, therefore, not British or American) refer to achievements by American or Brits of previous centuries as things 'we' have done.

The culture of many nations encourages you to portray your positive performances (a scientific discovery, a sport record, or an international award) as somehow reflecting on the whole nation, and to present the negative ones (your involvement in a crime, other acts drawing condemnation, or any fiasco in an international setting) as personal matters that only say something about you. And this too is not new. The ancient orator Polycratidas, who was sent, with others, as an envoy to the generals of the Persian King, when asked whether they were there in a private role or had been sent in a public capacity, answered: 'if we succeed, public; if we fail, private'.[11] There is a well-known tendency to publicize one's association with people who have positively distinguished themselves in some respect or other, as if their personal merits rubbed off on everyone who happens to share their nationality, ethnicity, or profession, or place of residence, or another extrinsic factor. Spotlighting and glorifying those people can be an indirect way to spotlight and glorify oneself. The readiness to bask in reflected light, *luce lucere aliena*, as Cicero (Somn.Sc. 6.16) says of the moon, is particularly conspicuous in sports. Unsurprisingly, research has found that team supporters are more likely to wear apparel of the team they support, or to refer to that team as 'we', after the team chalks up a victory than after it suffers a defeat. Even more tellingly, fans are more likely to stress their affiliation to a winning team after a personal failure (Cialdini et al. 1976: 369, 372, 374).

Thus, nationality is comforting to many because it gives them imaginary possessions, imaginary abilities, and imaginary successes. The Hungarian constitution, the Fundamental Law of Hungary, produced under the right-wing *Fidesz* party in 2011, begins with a 'national profession of faith' (*Nemzeti Hitvallás*) that lists things Hungarian nationals take pride in, and proclaims 'we are proud of the Hungarian people's magnificent intellectual creations'.[12] Hungary's culture indeed includes admirable creations, which the international public should appreciate more, such as an insightful literature, a rich musical tradition, and ingenious inventions; but being Hungarian – or British, Italian, Japanese, etc. – does not automatically mean that one has exactly the same talents as, or even an in-depth knowledge of, that country's writers, composers, or inventors, let alone that one should be personally admired for their accomplishments. And yet, it is an internationally common practice for individuals to boast about some thinker, scientist, artist, actor, sport champion, model, or other grandee of the same nationality, as if they automatically shared the qualities and merits involved. The converse is also true: those hostile to a particular (perhaps rival) nationality may belittle the qualities and achievements of someone who happens to be of such nationality. If people outgrew such mindset, they would

---

[11] Plut. Lyc. 25.4: 'Πολυκρατίδας δὲ ὁ πρεσβεύων πρὸς τοὺς βασιλέως στρατηγοὺς μεθ᾽ ἑτέρων, ἐρομένων αὐτῶν πότερον ἰδίᾳ πάρεισιν ἢ δημοσίᾳ πεμφθέντες, εἶπεν 'αἴκα τύχωμεν, δημοσίᾳ, αἴκα ἀποτύχωμεν, ἰδίᾳ'.

[12] 'Büszkék vagyunk … Büszkék vagyunk a magyar emberek nagyszerű szellemi alkotásaira'.

see that the only honest position one can take, as Arthur Schnitzler elegantly noted in 1914 (Bergel 1956: 207), is to 'affirm explicitly that to him the beautiful will always remain beautiful, the great always great, even if it belongs to nations, or was developed or grew inside nations, with which his country is even embroiled in a war'.[13] Unfortunately, those who look at people, including themselves, in categorial (and therefore comparative and competitive) terms become invested in the relative prestige of their own category as a key indicator of their self-worth; and once that category acquires for them such existential significance and emotional charge, a realistic assessment of its merits becomes unlikely.

What needs to be highlighted is that nationality determines a person's principles, aspirations, and mentality less than it is thought. Research into people's values, goals, or outlooks has found that these *vary less between countries than between individuals*: nationality accounts for less than 12 per cent of the variance, a fact which is deeply 'problematic for claims that national cultures are the primary determinant of individuals' value priorities' (Fischer and Schwartz 2011: 1133–4). Research on European countries, for example, has confirmed that within each of twenty-nine countries examined, citizens vary substantially in their outlook and values from their compatriots (Magun, Rudnev, and Schmidt 2016: 196). Therefore, when we try to guess what a person's opinion and behaviour will be, we ought to bear in mind that the epistemic value of a category like nationality is limited. Nevertheless, studies of cross-cultural psychology have traditionally relied on countries as cultural units of analysis.

Having briefly looked at when and how nations arose, at some repercussions of their establishment, and at the consequences of thinking of humankind as being naturally divided into nationalities, we need to consider how a nation-based outlook is promoted and learnt. We will see that language, both in obvious and in covert ways, has a special role in bringing a nation into existence and securing its continuance.

---

[13] 'ausdrücklich versichern zu müssen, daß ihm das Schöne jederzeit schön, das Gröse jederzeit groß bleiben wird, – auch wenn es Nationen angehört, oder innerhalb von Nationen geworden und gewachsen ist, mit denen sein Vaterland eben in einen Krieg verwickelt ist'.

8

Creating nations and languages

Teaching a national identity

Having reviewed, in the last chapter, a few effects of the development of nation states and of the widespread perception that nationalities are objective and highly informative divisions, it behoves us to observe how fashioning and preserving a national identity is, to a significant extent, an active endeavour, and how several semiotic elements – language prominently among them – are utilized for fostering and teaching a sense of nationality.

The citizens of a country rarely notice the national framework in which their lives have to be conducted. They usually do not consider that such framework is not naturally given, and so do not reflect on how influential it is. While nationality can bestow on them rights and clear benefits, it has also very personal implications beyond their control – after all, they may, for example, be forcibly drafted into an army and required to kill and risk being killed.

Concerted efforts are made to teach us, and periodically to boost in us, a national identification. Schools have been most commonly at the frontline in the efforts. The argument that education should be used for instilling in people a strictly national view has not been put forth only during the 'Age of Nationalism', nor only by right wingers, nor only by those who wanted it to benefit their own country. This is what Rousseau ([1772] 1782: 435–6) said with reference to Poland:

> Here is the crux: it is education that gives to souls a national form ... An infant, the moment he opens his eyes, must see the fatherland, and until his dying day he must not see anything else ... the love of his fatherland ... is his whole existence; he does not see anything but the fatherland, he lives for nothing else ... if he no longer has a fatherland, he no longer exists ... At the age of twenty, a Pole must not be otherwise: he must be a Pole. When he learns to read, I want him to read about things of his own country; at ten, to be familiar with all its products; at twelve, with all its provinces, roads, and cities; at fifteen, [I want] him to know its whole history; at sixteen, all its laws; there should not be any beautiful action or illustrious man in the whole of Poland of which his memory and heart are not full, and on which he cannot expound at the drop of a hat ... The law must regulate the subject, the

order, and the form of [children's] studies. They must have only Poles for teachers, all married.[1]

A nation-based view has become the norm. And maps, again, reflect this. In many countries, the maps displayed when addressing the public – from those used in the weather forecast to those pinned to school walls – have traditionally shown only one country. This choice is not innocent, as one can see in lands that are in conflict. In both Palestinian and Israeli school textbooks on any subject, the vast majority of maps omit the existence of the other entity. In Israeli textbooks, 76 per cent of maps show no boundaries between Palestinian territories and Israel, although borders between Israel and other countries are indicated; Palestinian areas are not labelled as such, as if they were all simply part of Israel. In Palestinian textbooks, 58 per cent of the maps indicate no border, and label the whole area as Palestine; 33 per cent mark the Green Line (the borders set in 1949) but make no reference to Israel, and refer to the entire area as Palestine; another 9 per cent mark the Green Line, and separate Israeli and Palestinian areas by colour – but still do not use the label 'Israel' anywhere: Israel is so identified in only 4 per cent of Palestinian maps (CRIHL 2013: 42–3).

Promotion of a national outlook is not limited to schools or to the nation's school years. Teaching a national identity is a pervasive and open-ended process. As Billig stressed (1995: 43), nationalism is not only the struggle to establish a state once for all, and to obtain a people's identification with it; it is also the ongoing endeavour to conserve that state and to maintain the people's identification with it. Insofar as nationalities are – at least to a good extent – artificially created, they need also to be actively regenerated through discourse and praxis. States therefore take continual measures to determine, shape, and control the national identity of their citizens, and to teach them a particular interpretation of history and politics that legitimizes, and often glamourizes, the nation and its institutions. States also need to present these measures as being the result, rather than the cause, of national identification. And they are mostly successful in this. The national hallmarks in people's lives, the daily objects and routines that tag everything and everyone as being of a given nationality, that affirm and reaffirm nationality, the seemingly unobtrusive symbols of what Billig termed 'banal nationalism', are typically treated as normal and inevitable, and are taken for granted because they are very familiar. They are effective precisely because they appear inert. Symbols are central in a culture

---

[1] 'C'est ici l'article important. C'est l'éducation qui doit donner aux âmes la forme nationale ... Un enfant en ouvrant les yeux doit voir la patrie & jusqu'à la mort ne doit plus voir qu'elle ... l'amour de sa patrie ... fait toute son existence; il ne voit que la patrie il ne vit que pour elle ... si-tôt qu'il n'a plus de patrie, il n'est plus ... À vingt ans un Polonois ne doit pas être un autre homme; il doit être un Polonois. Je veux qu'en apprenant à lire il lise des choses de son pays, qu'à dix ans il en connoisse toutes les productions, à douze toutes les provinces, tous les villes ... qu'à quinze il en sache toute l'histoire, à seize toutes les loix, qu'il n'y ait pas eu dans toute la Pologne une belle action ni un homme illustre dont il n'ait la mémoire & le cœur pleins, & dont il ne puisse rendre compte à l'instant ... La loi doit régler la matière, l'ordre & la forme de leurs études. Ils ne doivent avoir pour instituteurs que des Polonois, tous mariés'.

because, as Geertz (1973: 89) pointed out, they are used to structure daily life, to frame thoughts, to trigger emotions, and to direct behaviour, but their influence goes undetected. People thus consider it natural that a government issues everyone with *identity* cards or passports proclaiming a nationality, which in many countries must be carried at all times. They do not spend time pondering the fact that 'their' state has not only national borders (or even walls) and often a national currency, but also a national anthem, a national flag, national heroes (streets, schools, and airports are named after them), national memorial monuments, national stamps, national car number plates, national airlines. In many countries there is also a national dish, a national drink, a national animal or flower, sometimes a national church or religion. There are also national teams for several sports; those teams, with an unquestioned synecdoche, are referred to as whole countries: 'France won the cup'. And sport is practised competitively against another country, although it may have been adopted from there; international oppositions are emphasized, while cultural connections are not. And there are also national holidays, including for celebrating the established state, which are presented as expressing a pre-existing popular joy at existence of it, but which also help to establish it, reaffirm it, and legitimize it. Chile's dictator General Pinochet made the day of his 1973 coup d'état into a holiday (it was scrapped when a democratically elected president replaced him in 1990); when United States troops arrived in Baghdad in 2003, and Saddam Hussein was toppled, the Iraqi Governing Council opened its first meeting by announcing a new national holiday: 9 April, 'Baghdad Liberation Day', another example of how language is used to put events in a particular light. A general national day is on the calendar in Sweden, Hungary, Switzerland, Austria, Norway, Portugal, Luxembourg, Spain (and, separately, in Catalonia and in the Basque countries). Many states have a day that commemorates the country's attainment of independence, for example Poland, Finland, Croatia, Greece, Lithuania, Estonia, and the Czech Republic. Several have a day marking their rebellion against, or liberation from, foreign occupation, for instance the Netherlands, the Czech Republic, Italy, Greece, and Croatia. Quite a few have a day celebrating their attainment of statehood or of status as republics, including Hungary, the Czech Republic, Lithuania, Croatia, Italy, and Portugal. Of course, dissenting views of those events also exist: Israel's 'Day of Independence' (יום העצמאות) is marked also by the Palestinians as the 'Day of the Catastrophe' (يوم النكبة). One type of national symbol is also invoked to reinforce another: quite commonly, states have a day dedicated to the national flag: examples include Ukraine, Sweden, Philippines, the United Arab Emirate, Estonia, Argentina, the United States, Thailand, Lithuania, Ecuador, and Australia. Many countries have also a day celebrating the national language; this is the case of Hungary, Greece, Moldova, Germany, Brazil, Thailand, and Estonia (in Estonia, the country has the same name as the language, *Eesti*). New or aspiring nations realize that there is a set of symbols that they need to have in order to be recognized as nations – and they usually come up with them.

Besides, in order to engender a shared sense of nationality, it is important to create a nationally shared set of cultural references with strong affective content: you are likely to feel a sense of empathy and affinity when you meet someone who knows and loves the old songs that still move you, the national dishes that your mother prepared, and the local TV programmes that you watched in your childhood.

The creation of a body of common objects and routines that symbolize a national culture has greatly contributed to the reification of such culture into something seemingly external to human agency, and seemingly fixed. It has partly counteracted and partly masked the fact that all cultures are syncretic, protean, and actively re-negotiated. Many people find those symbols gratifying, inspiring, reassuring. Such symbols have a function, we could say, opposite of the *vanitas* motifs (such as hourglasses, rotting fruit, or skulls) that were often included in late medieval paintings to remind the public of the transience and decay of everything. National symbols implicitly convey a sense of spatial and temporal continuity, of solidity, significance, permanence; they provide, in essence, transcendence, the feeling of being connected to something wider, older, more important and more lasting than the individual.

The importance of writing

When it comes to language, what turns language into a visible, tangible symbol and gives it an air of solidity and permanence, is *writing*. And among the cultural items that are believed to make up, and also to impart, a national heritage, a special place is occupied by texts. The importance of the written word, in this, cannot be overstated. This is because, apart from being potentially the medium of illustrious literature, it formulates and passes on collective memories, it records and promotes traditional customs, it devises and champions behavioural models, and it gives a canonical form to the language itself, making that form more homogeneous across time and space. More specifically, the development of written languages has been instrumental in spreading a national outlook and fostering a national identification. And, as we will see, the power of language in that domain goes beyond the obvious: language has ways of talking about the nation as a solid and lasting reality, which contributes decisively to its birth and perdurance.

The invention of writing (long before modern nationalism) allowed humans to preserve and spread ideas, instructions, and information like little else before. Combining the letters of the alphabet enabled 'the memory of everything', as already Aeschylus had intimated.[2] As Galileo, among scientists, concluded (1632: 98):

> Yet, surpassing all the splendid inventions: what stroke of genius had the man who dreamt up of finding a way to convey his innermost thoughts to any person whomever, though distant by a most extensive gap in space or time? To talk with those who are in India, to talk to those who have not yet been born, nor will be except in a thousand or ten thousand years? And with what ease? By cobbling

---

[2] Aesch. Prom. B. 460 -1: ʻγραμμάτων τε συνθέσεις, / μνήμην ἁπάντωνʼ.

together in various ways twenty little signs upon a piece of paper. Let this be the seal of all marvellous human inventions.[3]

In their efforts to preserve an ethnic identification and the culture associated with it, some human groups have had the decisive help of a tradition of written texts. To a large extent, it was for the very purpose of preserving a way of thinking and living that such texts were written: *scripta manent*. Some populations, in their search for a sense of who they are, have been able to turn to a vast body of (often self-referential) literature in their language. Some also had the foundational text of their religion written in their language; if one's cultural code and collective identity is traced back to divine command, this will greatly help to preserve it, at least nominally.

Religious texts

Christianity, for example, relies on its holy scriptures and on an extensive textual (and intertextual) tradition regarded as an unbroken chain that preserves the essence and the authority of the source. This has constituted an ideological, behavioural, and literary blueprint. Greek Christian Orthodoxy, for instance, in this respect (as in many others) bears affinity with Judaism and differs considerably from Ancient Greek religion. The latter had no canonized holy books: the ancient texts detailing what we call Greek 'mythology' are our main source of information on Ancient Greek religion, but they did not provide an official creed or formal precepts to readers in antiquity. Ancient Greek religion, also owing to its polytheistic nature, had anyway an elasticity that allowed adjustments, additions, reinterpretations, variations, without scandal or crisis. After all, 'Paganism' is not a self-defined doctrine to which one could convert: it is a Christian label which would have made little sense (even when stripped of its frequent belittling connotations) to the Ancient Greeks. The ancient religions of southern Europe were porose and changing, and so were those of northern Europe: divinities were added and dropped over time. A body of texts regarded as holy and authoritative, on the other hand, can make a difference.

In the case of the Jews, aptly named 'people of the book' (עַם הַסֵּפֶר), a strong focus on studying a textual tradition of thought, and on remembering one's group history and customs, has been a cardinal factor in identity retention. In a traditional Jewish setting, attendance of Hebrew school was a requirement, although limited to males. The immense perceived authority of the scriptures resulted in a close relationship between practical life and book, in an emphasis on learning common to all social classes, and in

---

[3] 'Ma sopra tutte le inuenzioni stupende, qual' eminenza di mente fu quella di colui, che s'immaginò di trouar modo di comunicare i suoi più reconditi pēsieri a qualsiuoglia altra persona, benché distante per lunghissimo interuallo di luogo e di tempo? parlare con quelli che son nell'Indie, parlare a quelli che non sono ancora nati, nè saranno, se non di quà a mille, e dieci mila anni? e con qual facilità? con i varj accozzamenti di venti caratteruzzi sopra una carta. Sia questo il sigillo di tutte le ammirande inuenzioni umane'.

an antipathy to change. The Massoretes, the Jewish grammarians who worked on the Hebrew scriptures, reproduced the received text unchanged even when they thought it clearly wrong; such was the reverence for the written word. They left scrupulously untouched the version they found written, called the Kᵉthîv (Aramaic כְּתִיב *scriptum*) and indicated in the margins of the text the form to be read in its stead, called the Qᵉrê (Aramaic קְרִי *legendum*). Many modern Biblical translations take a different approach and often simply incorporate the Qᵉrê form within the text, in replacement of the Kᵉthîv altogether; but in the Torah scrolls read in synagogues, not only is the Kᵉthîv form left in the text, but no Qᵉrê form is written at the margins – although it is, nonetheless, the form read out: the reader is expected to know it. In Massoretic scholarship, the Qᵉrê annotations themselves played also a conservative role: while sometimes they provided alternative vowels for the consonantal text handed down through the centuries, or a different spelling of it, or an oral replacements altogether for taboo words (e.g. the name of God, or terms deemed crude), they sometimes collated, and therefore preserved, variant versions of the main text found in other manuscripts. Religion, text, and language intertwined also in another way. Among Jews, retaining the community's language was declared to be in itself a commandment and pious deed, a *miṣwah*. According to a halakhic midrash to the book of Exodus (the *Mekhilta* attributed to Rabbi Ishmael ben Elisha, tractate Pisḥa 5:14), in the late second century CE, Rabbi Eliezer ha-Qappar had explained that one *miṣwah* among Israel's most worthwhile was that Jews 'did not alter their name and did not alter their language'.[4]

Indeed, the Jews' emphasis on a holy scripture, and on a body of sacred literature to be studied continuously and from which to glean guidance for all aspects of ordinary life, was a model for Christianity (Ling 1968: 167). In the case of the Jews, there were, of course, also other determinants preserving their separate identity, including a more exclusivist religion, which once even forbade them to teach Talmud and Hebrew to non-Jews – just as in the Middle Ages, Jews were at times not allowed to learn the local language by the Gentiles (cf. Spolsky 1996: 182). And another factor has been a history of forced confinement and of extreme persecution, which has strengthened the oft-affirmed imperative to preserve memory of the past. Even in secular Jewish culture, the decisive experience of the Holocaust triggers frequent references to the injunction in Deuteronomy: 'remember ... don't forget'.[5]

In the Muslim tradition, the Qur'ān has, in a sense, an even more sacred status than the Bible in Christianity, as it is believed to be the unmediated word of God and to contain and provide complete knowledge and guidance on everything. Reading it is considered, in itself, a form of devotion. The Qur'ān relies strongly on a textual tradition: it is supplemented and elucidated by a crucial body of many a *ḥadīth* (حَدِيث): reports of statements or acts, and therefore of opinions and endorsements, by the prophet Muhammad. A *ḥadīth* typically consists of its *matn* (مَتْن), which is the narrative, and its *isnād* (إِسْنَاد), namely its sources going back to the Prophet in a chain: the sequence of authoritative people reporting the narrative and, therefore,

---

[4]   In Lauterbach's edition (1949: 34): 'לֹא שִׁינּוּ אֶת שְׁמָם וְלֹא שִׁינּוּ אֶת לְשׁוֹנָם'

[5]   Deut. (25:17–19): 'זָכוֹר...לֹא תִּשְׁכָּח'

to a variable degree, validating the story. The reliability is variable because reports about the life of the Prophet Muhammad and about the early history of Islam were passed down only orally for over a century after his death (632 AD); great value is therefore attached to the continuity and authenticity of the tradition. Consequently, in Islam, as in Judaism and in Christianity, a vast field of self-referential scholarship grew, with a class of experts (Muslim ulema, Jewish rabbis, Christian clergy) whose focus was the exegesis and the safeguarding of the tradition. And the duty to preserve memory is central in Islam too: the Qur'ān is referred to, including in the book itself, as *dhikra* (ذِكْرَى), 'reminder' or 'remembrance'. Muhammad did not think he was launching a new religion but only restoring and bringing to completion a pre-existing, indeed eternal religion (cf. Hourani 1980: 5). Learning Islam was understood as recalling that religion. In Plato too, there is the idea that philosophical knowledge is a rediscovery, that 'what we call learning is recollection', that what we do not know is simply what we do not remember, and that our efforts to find it out are efforts to recall it.[6] One of the key subtleties of human language – as opposed to most animal communication – is its ability to refer in detail to events set in another time and place. Because of language, the act of remembering, rather than merely a private and silent reflection, can entail the retelling of an event to others; memory is thus reconstructed through conversation and interactive negotiation; this is what is habitually done by parents with their children, and perhaps by teachers with their pupils, who thus *teach* remembering (Edwards and Middleton 1988: 21). Older family members, and anyone in a didactic role, teach children how, why, what, and which aspects to remember, what moral lesson to draw from the memories presented, and what image of oneself and of others to glean from them, and how to classify oneself according to certain categories, including nationality.

The role of religion in nationalism can, nonetheless, also be overstated. Hastings (1997: 151), who was a priest, went as far as to argue that nations and nationalism were, in themselves, due to Christianity, and specifically to the Bible, for two reasons. One is that the Old Testament provided and promoted a model of polity based on ancient Israel, with its emphasis on a special land and on an elected people with a mission; the second is that it required translations in different languages, and these established distinct (later national) written languages. The Bible was once not only the most read book in the West, but one whose word bespoke authority, also linguistically: to this day, not all Christians realize that the Bible that they read in their own language is a fallible translation, and often a translation of a translation. The Protestant campaign to provide *the* Book, and thence books in general, in the vernacular language, started a tradition of writing, which largely overlapped with the invention of printing around 1450. Hastings considered this the foundation of nationhood. His theory makes good points but is not watertight: although it is true that, in the history of many languages, Bibles were either the first book or among the first books to be printed, the idea that the Old Testament, owing to the vernacular traditions that it started, created the modern nation appears bizarre if one – instead of focusing on the history of Modern

---

6 Pl. Meno (81e, 86b): 'ἣν καλοῦμεν μάθησιν ἀνάμνησίς ἐστιν … χρὴ ὃ μὴ τυγχάνεις ἐπιστάμενος νῦν – τοῦτο δ᾽ ἐστὶν ὃ μὴ μεμνημένος – ἐπιχειρεῖν ζητεῖν καὶ ἀναμιμνῄσκεσθαι;'.

English – looks at ancient languages. A Greek translation of the Old Testament, the Septuagint, was available since the second century BC but did not generate anything like a nation state: the Byzantine Empire was conceived of as a Christian state, but was hardly a nation in the modern sense. Moreover, although translated Bibles (and, more generally, the Reformation and the Counter-Reformation) may have underscored linguistic differences, they also reaffirmed religious differences as the most important distinctions. Besides, if possessing a written language with a literary tradition makes a population a 'nation', then the Egyptians, the Assyrians, the Ancient Greeks, the Persians, and many others would have to be claimed to have been a single unified nation. This would not only date the birth of nations much earlier than Hastings himself wanted it, but would also undermine his central claim that modern nation states and nationalism as we know them are a Christian product, and a European invention – a claim that is, to a degree, correct. Claiming that printing and the spread of literacy aided an unprecedented diffusion of a common culture is also basically correct – in early Egypt or early Mesopotamia, only a restricted élite could read and write – but the promulgation of literacy, printing, and communication channels, useful as it was to the spread of a state-sponsored world view, could also have been a potential threat to that, because it could have been also the conduit for alternative ideologies and counter-information. The suggestion that nations are essentially *due* to Christianity clashes also somewhat with the fact that the consolidation of European nations was aided by the disintegration of Catholic central rule and by the Reformation; above all, the Church often opposed (and was opposed by) those who fought to establish a national state.

Very many religious traditions, being based on texts, have led people to study, reproduce, revere, and endeavour to keep alive and relatively unchanged also the language itself of their holy writs. Among Jews, Hebrew (and Talmudic Aramaic) has been termed 'the holy language' (לשון הקדש) since antiquity, and that remained its name in Yiddish. The Qur'ān, although it was spoken word for a considerable time before becoming written text, has become, for Arab speakers, the book *par excellence* and a linguistic point of reference. In the Arab world, even today, the language used as written language and as formal spoken medium is not the local vernacular, but a variety of Arabic relatively closer to the classical idiom of the Qur'ān (7th century); and this fact has buttressed the link with Islam (Holt 1996: 20). Among Hindus, Sanskrit, the language of the Vedas, is the main language of liturgy, and is also an important language in the Buddhist and in the Jainist traditions, although it is also the medium of non-religious literature; as a result, Sanskrit is described as *devabhāṣā* (देवभाषा) 'divine language', and is cultivated to this day. In Europe, after the demise of the Roman Empire, Latin, which was the language of authoritative versions of the Scriptures and of the writings of foundational figures in Western Christianity, continued to be used by the Church for centuries. The belief that Latin promoted an eternal and unchanging religion fuelled the persuasion that Latin had to remain in use and unchanged (cf. Clackson and Horrocks 2007: 295). Thus, in many traditions, concerns about 'correct' exegesis of religious texts fostered also attachment to an obsolescent or obsolete language. Several languages that had ceased to be spoken in the form in which they were employed in religious texts continued to be studied and used in religious contexts. These include (Biblical) Hebrew, (Koiné) Greek, (Qur'ānic) Arabic,

Old (Church) Slavonic, (Church) Latin, Syriac, Ge'ez, Pāli, Sanskrit, and Avestan. Even where the believers speak only a totally different language, they may learn a smattering of the language of their scriptures: non-Israeli Jews and non-Arab Muslims learn at least basic blessings and prayers in Hebrew and Arabic, respectively; Protestants and Catholics used to learn prayers and religious phrases in Latin, as Greeks learn them in Koiné Greek, the Hindus in Sanskrit, and Zoroastrians in Avestan. When someone converts, if a new name is given, it is usually in the language associated with the religion adopted: Sanskrit if Hinduism, Arabic if Islam, Hebrew if Judaism, even if the language is not known to the person. It has proved possible to resuscitate (to re-vernacularize) Hebrew into a living modern language because religion had kept it alive, though *in vitro*, as a language of prayer and learning (Spolsky 2009: 31).

The supposed holiness of the texts was transferred to the language – and even to the script: the *nāgarī* script used to publish Sanskrit texts thus came to be thought as divine and to be termed *devanāgarī* (देवनागरी). The alphabet adopted by a people (e.g. Latin, Cyrillic, Arabic) has often matched a community's religion regardless of the language, as can be seen in the case of language varieties that were barely distinguishable. While Croatian is only written in the Latin alphabet (reflecting the Catholic faith), Serbian is written also in the Cyrillic alphabet (Orthodox faith). Similarly, while Hindi is in the Devanāgarī script (Hindu faith), Punjabi is in the Gurmukhī script (Sikh faith), and Urdu in the Perso-Arabic script (Muslim faith). In all these cases, although minor differences in the use of the language also exist, it is mainly the alphabet that immediately identifies the written language. Somewhat comparable is the case of Yiddish: Jews used the Hebrew (Aramaic) alphabet when writing their own distinct variety of Germanic, and this inevitably marked it, at a glance, as Jewish. In the Middle Ages, many Jews who wrote in Arabic used, likewise, the Hebrew script. Another parallel, to a degree, is Garshuni, the Christian literature in Arabic written with the Syriac alphabet – often by authors who were highly literate in Arabic but who chose to use the Syriac script (with Arabic elements). And many languages unrelated to Arabic but spoken by Muslim populations have been written by them in the Arabic script: Urdu, Persian, Ottoman Turkish, Kurdish, Pashto, Swahili, Hausa, Malay, and even Spanish (and all these languages are now marked by Arabic loanwords).

In the history of the Western world, religion has also constituted one of the most powerful and earliest impetus to make *translations*, and to reflect on the practice of translating. Sometimes the awe felt for the original text was transferred to the translation, which came to be attributed immense religious and linguistic authority. This happened with the Peshitta translation of the Bible (second century) for Syriac; with Cyril and Methodius' Old Church Slavonic Bible (ninth century) for Slavic; with Luther's Bible (sixteenth century) for German; and with King James' Bible (seventeenth century) for English. Some languages that had already been in written use for a long time, but were later employed either in the composition or the official translation of scriptural works, became associated with a particular religion and religious community. Thus Greek and Latin, despite their vast, magnificent, influential, and much-admired pagan literature, came to be seen by many as a symbol of Christian Orthodoxy and of Catholicism, respectively. And since a language can have very strong associations with a particular faith, believers may also, for religious reasons, claim that language as their own language: the Muslims of Mauritius (Eriksen 2004: 53), who centre their identity on their religion, in the 1983 Census, though of north Indian descent, mostly declared Arabic as their 'ancestral language', which is historically false. And because each religion presents itself as *the* way to live and think that makes sense and is proper, speaking in a way deemed clear and sensible is sometimes described in religious terms: a traditional way to say 'to speak plainly' in Spanish is *hablar en cristiano*.

The cachet and authority of the written language, as well as its tangibility and stability, also meant that it was often treated as the 'real' form of the language, while speech was perceived as a pale and unreliable shadow of it – rather than the reverse, which is how modern linguistics would see it. Until relatively recently, learning a foreign language was understood as entailing the study of the literary tradition of a country. There was an implicit understanding that the correct language and *le bon usage* was the one found in the good literature of different historical periods, and that the true form of words was the old one. This is the meaning of the word *etymology*, after all: in Greek, *etymos* meant 'true'. In order to write and speak 'better', people were encouraged to imitate older usage. Such instruction has, in itself, a long history. Just like Late Greek grammarians, late Latin grammarians enjoined their readers to use the older, 'classical' form of words, and to shun contemporary forms in which the pronunciation had evolved (and had become rather like what we see in Romance languages): they urged readers to say *mensa* and not *mesa* for 'table, meal' (cf. Portuguese *mesa*), *calida* and not *calda* for 'hot' (cf. Italian *calda*), *oculus* and not *oclus* for 'eye' (cf. Aromanian *ocljiu*), and so forth. Contemporary languages were thus seen in an inescapably historical perspective. Saussure, widely regarded as the founder of modern linguistics, separated conceptually how languages are at a given point in time, like the present, from their historical development (as recorded in texts or reconstructed), but such categorical sundering of synchronic and diachronic happened no earlier than the start of the twentieth century.

In regions of the world whose past civilization is extensively recorded and is internationally well-known and much acclaimed, the stance of the local population towards it sometimes is a rather fetishistic preoccupation, permeated by a sense of inferiority, with the preservation of the cultural and linguistic features of their presumed ancestors. In Modern Greek there are even words for this attitude.[7] Like, and sometimes alongside, the spread of nationalist ideals, the spread of such attitude, it should be noted, has often been partly or largely due to *foreign* intellectuals, who were educated in ancient languages. For example, in Iceland, the movement calling for national independence from Danish rule was inspired by the nationalist ideas and campaigns of continental Europe, and was introduced into Iceland, paradoxically, by Danish-educated men of letters. For the language too, the author of the first Icelandic grammar, who also convinced Icelanders that stressing and increasing the similarities between Old and Modern Icelandic would win them international regard, was the eminent Danish philologist Rasmus Rask (1787–1832). In a comparable fashion,

---

[7]   E.g. αρχαιοπληξία, προγονοπληξία, αρχαιολατρεία, αρχαιομανία, etc.

the population of modern Greece, at the turn of the nineteenth century, realized – from the condescending attitude of educated foreigners (German, British, American, French, and Italian intellectuals), who were in total awe of Ancient Greece – that western respect and support for the nascent modern Greek state was only possible if those who now lived in Greece and their language were internationally perceived to be the same people and language as those of Ancient Greece.

We might incidentally also note that our very construal of languages as distinct entities is something that has a lot to do with the existence of writing and with its spread. Writing defines and reifies languages, makes them distinct and palpable and presents their individual features as invariable across time and space. In societies with lower levels of literacy, where different languages and dialects are used and mixed, speakers may not exactly distinguish – neither in practice nor in concept – what outsiders categorize as two distinct languages.

National literature, arts, and history

Of course, language is important in the creation of a national identity also because, among the many official national symbols, there is usually a national literature, and often even an individual national writer or poet. Sometimes there is a specific text that is touted as the national poem. Not infrequently, such text has the explicitly stated aim to intone (and record in writing) a narrative about and for the national group, presenting it as naturally defined by a shared kinship, and therefore as objectively existing and legitimate. Thus it seeks

'to set out to sing,
to dictate my words,
to produce a poem of the nation,
to sing a poem of the kin'[8]

as proclaimed at the outset by the *Kalevala* (1: 3–6), the Finnish national epic – which was compiled in the nineteenth century, the time when Finland's *intelligentsia* was striving to limit Russian and Swedish influence, and Finns came to see themselves as a nation.

Literature is also connected with other forms of artistic expression that can be used to advance the same message. Music has often been deliberately constructed as national, and has been made part of nation-building projects, either by the composers themselves, or by others who later promoted it as such. To stay with the same example, Finland also had a national composer, Jean Sibelius (1865–1957), and some of his patriotic compositions (as also those of later Finnish composers, like Uuno Klami) were explicitly inspired by the *Kalevala* – again, one type of national symbol is often invoked to reinforce another.

[8] 'Lähteäni laulamahan / saa'ani sanelemahan / sukuvirttä suoltamahan / lajivirttä laulamahan.'

Sibelius's work was performed abroad with a view to win international sympathy for Finland's pursuit of independence. Right or wrong, not only the Finn Sibelius, but the Norwegian Grieg, the Hungarian Bartók, the Czech Smetana, the Romanian Enescu, and many others have either seen themselves or have been portrayed as national composers. In pre-unification Italy, Verdi's compositions were used by some Italians as allegories to express their wish to shake off Austrian rule and to have an Italian king, and crowds used to chant Verdi's name as a coded acronym for 'Vittorio Emanuele, Re D'Italia' (Victor Emmanuel, King of Italy). National music has also often drawn on traditions of folk music or has been inspired, allegedly, by the national landscape. In England, an example of this is Vaughan Williams. He considered music `the expression of the soul a nation', and his most popular pieces are meant to evoke images of the English countryside. Those are also the representations of 'characteristic national landscapes' found in visual art – and later in touristic brochures, websites, posters, and so forth.

The other main form of writing that has been pivotal in the construction of nations – to state concisely the obvious – has been history. In many nations, a key role in nation-building was played by historians: suffice it to think of the importance, in this respect, of František Palacký for the Czechs, of Constandinos Paparrigopoulos for the Modern Greeks, or of Nicolae Iorga for the Romanians. Much national history writing, besides being necessarily a selection and a simplification of the available information, has an aetiological and explicative structure, if not a justificatory and exonerative aim, and a celebratory and moralizing tone. A well-crafted account of the past can be made to corroborate the political legitimacy of the nation state, to vouch for the nation's ancient, illustrious, and 'pure' lineage, to put its undertakings in a glorious (or at least forgivable) light, to sanction the *status quo*, and to portray the nation's identity as diachronically ever-present and consistent. Furthermore, historical accounts, consisting primarily in texts as they do, are also affected by language usage and by literary forms. They are thus likely to contain rhetorical devices, a structure like a plot, genre-typical conventions, inter-textual borrowings – and, crucially, an implicit lesson to be drawn: a historical account is usually written for a reason, and aims to be convincing in its message. For any political effort, public agreement that things are or should be in a certain way is needed, and is obtained through campaigns of persuasion, i.e. through language. Persuasion is far more effective than coercion, and this is why rhetoric is closely associated with politics, as already Aristotle (Rh. 1356a) had noted.[9] Of course, this also means, as the Ancient Greeks knew, that what gets accepted as knowledge (*sophía*) can also be just casuistry (*sóphisma*). There is a debate as to whether 'history' as such exists: whether sequences of historical events form a coherent story, and follow diachronic patterns and laws; and whether, therefore, a single account can be an adequate 'history' and allows us to extract a lesson, as we may do from a tale. Some theorists, especially those in a post-structuralist vein, dismiss history as mere language. This may be academic posturing, or anyway a case of the proverbial throwing the baby out with the bathwater. We cannot discuss this question extensively here, but we must stress that historical

---

[9] 'συμβαίνει τὴν ῥητορικὴν οἷον παραφυές τι τῆς διαλεκτικῆς εἶναι καὶ τῆς περὶ τὰ ἤθη πραγματείας, ἣν δίκαιόν ἐστι προσαγορεύειν πολιτικήν· διὸ καὶ ὑποδύεται ὑπὸ τὸ σχῆμα τὸ τῆς πολιτικῆς ἡ ῥητορική'.

proclamations about a nation can be connected to the truth also in a different way, which is worth discussing at some length – as we shall now do.

Language creating nationality

We have mentioned, and will review in later chapters, instances of language being openly used to establish a nation; but there are also covert ways in which language can almost spirit a nation into existence. We emphasized from the start of the book that any statement that one makes does not simply report information: it also shows that the speaker chooses to make that statement, chooses to make it in a certain way, chooses to make it at a certain time and place, and so on. We also noted that what a statement says literally and what the speaker means by saying it are often not the same thing. And there is more to this. Ordinary utterances do not simply imply a commitment to their content but, usually, intend to have some effect in the mind and perhaps the behaviour of the hearer. Rather than contrasting words with actions, we can regard words as concrete actions: for example, insults do not just express hostility, they are acts of hostility; when pupils say to each other 'the teacher is coming', they are not simply making a factual announcement, but probably also urging a change of conduct in their friends. We tend to think of utterances as being inert accounts (true or false as they may be) of an independently existing state of affairs; but this overlooks their power to *change* reality. Public commentators (as it has often happened in politics or economics) can initiate new events by ostensibly describing them as already happening. Language can start as a mere *flatus vocis* not corresponding to a reality but can make that true by affirming it. Linguists have long been pointing out that the way in which languages such as English are used, besides being constative and perlocutionary (i.e. a mere statement of fact), can have performative power: it may lead to the production (and thereafter to the maintenance) of the reality that it appears to be simply reporting. The very act of saying something (what John Austin termed 'speech-act'), if someone says it in the appropriate circumstances and has or achieves the necessary authority, can sometimes *make* that thing real. Conspicuous daily examples are phrases such as 'I apologize', 'I promise', 'I bet you a fiver', 'I wish you goodnight', 'I declare the meeting adjourned', 'I pronounce you man and wife', 'I baptize you in the name of the Father', 'I sentence you to two years in prison' (cf. Austin 1975: 5–6); each of these state something that is true purely because they state it. And that is usually the intention in making the statement: we use language to alter or manipulate our environment. George Steiner had a point when he asserted (1975: 217) that 'Language is the main instrument of man's refusal to accept the world as it is'.

The performative power of words is not a modern insight. Indeed, one reason why the performative use of words is common is that it is well recognized in many cultures. In the Christian tradition, the *Word* is at the origin of all, and speaks all into existence.[10] Buddhism suggests that objects exist thanks to the words that designate them (Bronkhorst 2011: 37). The Jewish God brings everything into being by utterance: 'for

[10] John 1:1, 1:14: 'ἐν ἀρχῇ ἦν ὁ λόγος … ὁ λόγος σάρξ ἐγένετο'.

He spoke and it was; He commanded, and it stood'.[11] This is said also of the divinities of many other religions, from the god Ptaḥ of the Egyptian to the god Prajāpati of the Hindus. In the Babylonian *Enûma Eliš* too, things are created by speaking their names: the utterance makes the thing real. Similarly, if something is no more, speech is believed to be able to restore it: words are represented, in anything from John's Gospel to popular horror classics like *The Evil Dead*, as raising the deceased back to life. And as we all know, language is thought to have the power to bring about a reality also in countless traditions of magic; typically, expressing wishes out loud is claimed to make them come true. Giving full articulation to what you want is treated as the key to seeing it realized. In the Jewish tradition (M *Berachot* 5.5) it is opined that if your mouth utters your prayer fluently, you can know that it will become reality; otherwise, that it is not valid.[12]

How does all this relate to individuals who get classified as being of a given nationality, or to collectivities that emerge as new nations or have a new state recognized? The instrumental role of language in such cases can be enormous. As Althusser (1970: 31) argued, if an authority hails someone as being an X, this places that person in the position of being an X. When the relevant power tells people, in multiple ways, that they are members of a particular nationality (addressing them as fellow nationals, issuing them with nation-specific ID, summoning them for military service for that nation, etc.), this gradually turns the designation placed on them into a self-evident reality which they themselves usually accept and start to confirm and reinforce. An English saying wryly quips: the third time someone tries to put a saddle on you, you should admit you're a horse. Entire communities have come to internalize and to agree with the definition of them given by others. What does your being X consist in? Consider, for instance, your ID documents – they purport to be passive reflections of independently existing facts: for example, your name is Susan; your title is Mrs; and your citizenship is British. But these statements are true primarily, if not only, inasmuch as the records state so. You are not called Susan because you are Susan; you are Susan because you have been called Susan. And yet, you normally do not distinguish the name that was assigned to you from the person that you are – we talked about this in Chapter 1. In fact, the person that you are has been shaped by others, through language, in several ways. What about any covert role of language in creating whole nations and countries? Derrida (1984: 22), in essence correctly, points out that, in the American *Declaration of Independence*, what happens is the reverse of what we read in the document. The *Declaration* tells us that the American 'people' affirms its own existence and authorizes a signed proclamation to that effect; but in truth, 'the signature invents the signer … the first signature authorizes the signer to sign'.[13] The text creates, retroactively, the author and the state of affairs that it purports to describe. By saying 'we', a 'we' is (at least tentatively) constituted, and comes to be treated as a well-established truth.

---

[11] Ps. 33:9: ‏'כִּי הוּא אָמַר וַיֶּהִי הוּא צִוָּה וַיַּעֲמֹד'‎.

[12] ‏'אם שגורה תפילתי בפי יודע אני שהוא מקובל ואם לאו יודע אני שהוא מטורף'‎.

[13] 'la signature invente le signataire … Sa première signature l'autorise à signer'.

A social category such as a nationality can emerge from a continuum of populations and then become a distinct and concrete reality. Through a similar process, a country can emerge from a continuum of lands; and a language can attain the status of 'language' rather than that of a fuzzy 'dialect' in a continuum of speech varieties. Political opponents will point out that the assertion that such nationality, country, or language exists is untrue; however, it can become familiar to all and, in time, become widely accepted as a fact. As Bourdieu (1980: 65–6), among others, argued, the very assertion that those entities are already a reality may in the end bring them into being:

> The practical representations that are most vulnerable to scientific criticism ... can contribute to produce what they seem to describe ... it is a *performative discourse* which aims to impose a new definition of the borders as legitimate ... in opposition to the dominant definition.[14]

Several factors can contribute to the acceptance of what is being claimed. For example, the sheer repetition of the assertion that something exists makes it more likely that we will accept it, both because there is a process of habituation to the idea, and because the repeated perceptual exposure to something, including to its mere verbal mention, enhances our attitude towards it (Zajonc 1968: 12, 19): we warm to, and trust, what has become well known to us. Second, in order to bolster the claim that a community constitutes a nationality in its own right, or that a speech variety is ontologically a self-standing language, another attribute that can help enormously is distinctiveness. The considerations we made previously about the correlation between mental labels (like colour terms) and perceptions of differences are pertinent here: our conceptual categories are centred on maximally distinct prototypes. That must be why, as we shall see in the next chapter, those who want to gain recognition for a nation or a language, often accentuate its unique or distinguishing features.

Finally, a key factor and attribute is power. An abstract affirmation such as 'we are a separate nation' or 'this is a separate language' can become widely accepted only if those making it have – or gain – enough clout to make their view prevail. Bourdieu (ibid.) realized this too:

> The act of social magic, which consists in trying to produce the named entity, may succeed, if he who performs it is able to get people to agree that his word has the power that it is appropriating for itself by temporary or permanent usurpation: the power to impose a new vision and a new division of the social world – *regere fines* ... to ordain a new border.[15]

---

[14] 'les représentations pratiques les plus exposées à la critique scientifique ... peuvent *contribuer* à *produire* ce qu'apparemment elles décrivent ou désignent ... / est un *discours performatif*, visant à imposer comme légitime une nouvelle définition des frontières ... contre la définition dominante'.

[15] 'L'acte de magie sociale qui consiste à tenter de produire à l'existence la chose nommée peut réussir si celui qui l'accomplit est capable de faire reconnaître à sa parole le pouvoir qu'elle s'arroge par une usurpation provisoire ou définitive, celui d'imposer une nouvelle vision et une nouvelle division du monde sociale: *regere fines* ... consacrer une nouvelle limite'.

Periodically, someone proposes the recognition of a new nationality; the process of obtaining recognition is not entirely unlike petitions to obtain recognition, for example, of a new cat breed: the breed becomes a reality only once the relevant authorities agree and declare that it exists. They do, usually, after considering the evidence (such as the distinctiveness of the new category being proposed), after being lobbied by whoever has a stake in this, and after considering their own interests.

That the invention of labels is arbitrary, and that it can be carried out successfully only by those who possess or obtain the necessary power, is not some recent post-structuralist idea. Already in Plato's *Cratylus* (388d–389a), when Socrates suggests that names are not intrinsic to objects but are given to them by normative convention (*nómos*), the question is raised of who can assign names and be name-maker (*onomatourgós*) – since, as Socrates goes on to point out, very few people have such power.[16]

Language conferring perdurance

Language is crucial also in persuading us to believe in nations as *diachronic* entities. Some modern countries and peoples bear ancient names, and this should not be taken at face value. For instance, *Britons* is, in origin, the name of the Celtic early inhabitants of Britain; despite the later Roman incursions and, above all, the overwhelming invasion, from continental Europe, of Angles, Saxons, and Jutes, followed also by the arrival of the Vikings and by the Norman conquest, the name *Britons* is now used by the current inhabitants – who, however, descend fundamentally from the latter groups. The application of names of countries has also shifted over time. For example, the region that in antiquity was called Macedonia is now split among six different countries: Bulgaria, Albania, Serbia, Greece, North Macedonia, and Kosovo. In antiquity there was a Kingdom of Macedon (inhabited by Macedonians in a different sense of the term from the one that it has today), but that too did not coincide, even approximately, with the ancient region of Macedonia. Today, that region does not coincide either with what is now the province of the state of Greece called Macedonia (inhabited mostly by Greeks) or with the state (inhabited mostly by Slavs and ethnic Albanians) that called itself Republic of Macedonia and, after a long international dispute, has accepted the name of North Macedonia. The inhabitants of both territories call themselves Macedonians, despite their different cultures, languages, likely descent, and citizenships. Both modern Greece and North Macedonia have laid claim to ancient Macedonia as their own heritage, and take deep offence at the suggestion that the Ancient Macedonians were an ethnicity unrelated to them.

Many people talk of their country as if it had always existed as such. However, in the past, the country that bore that name may have had a different culture, perhaps

---

[16] 'τίς παραδίδωσιν ἡμῖν τὰ ὀνόματα οἷς χρώμεθα; ... ἆρ' οὐχὶ ὁ νόμος δοκεῖ σοι εἶναι ὁ παραδιδοὺς αὐτά; ... νομοθέτης δέ σοι δοκεῖ πᾶς εἶναι ἀνὴρ ἢ ὁ τὴν τέχνην ἔχων; ... οὐκ ἄρα παντὸς ἀνδρός, ὦ Ἑρμόγενες, ὄνομα θέσθαι ἐστὶν ἀλλά τινος ὀνοματουργοῦ· οὗτος δ' ἐστίν, ὡς ἔοικεν, ὁ νομοθέτης, ὃς δὴ τῶν δημιουργῶν σπανιώτατος ἐν ἀνθρώποις γίγνεται'.

a different territorial extension and, of course, consisted of other individuals. The use of the same designation – applied to anything – helps to convey the notion of a timeless and unchanging entity. Giving the same ethnic or national label to two distinct populations separated by a vast time gap presents them as being biologically the same one. We can draw a comparison with national sports teams: the players of a team change often, and may even be from another country but, with an essentializing abstraction, the team is thought to be 'the same' team across time, and to 'be' always that particular country. This is also the way we are taught to conceptualize political parties, committees, and many other human groups: their members, their collective behaviour, their beliefs, their goals, and their *raisons d'être* may have changed extensively; but they are still talked about as one thing perduring across time. The constituent parts of an entity can be gradually replaced until no part of the original remains; yet, in popular thinking, the entity is confidently assumed to exist because the name continues to be applied to something, regardless of how changed it is. This is the 'Ship of Theseus' philosophical conundrum already identified by the Ancient Greeks.[17] Modern philosophers too have wrestled with this. Parfit (1987: 23) imagined the case of a group of people who constitute an association called 'The Whatever Club', which holds regular meetings somewhere, but that stops meeting after a while; years later, meetings are resumed elsewhere, perhaps with partly similar routines and goals, but some of the members have changed; is it the same club? If names were not so easily re-applicable, the designation *and therefore the perceived existence* of the object in question would come to an end when the original referent is lost. From a linguistic, rather than philosophical, point of view, the query can be dismissed as being not a question of ontology but merely one of conventional definitions: clubs are abstract concepts and so, arguably, imaginary entities; 'The Whatever Club' is just an easy and expedient, though arbitrary and imprecise, way to refer to whatever one chooses. However, the tendency to talk of nations as perduring entities is not just simplistic or sloppy. It is also well suited to a certain ideology. To take just one example: many a nation describes the process whereby it came to form an independent unit with terms that rather imply that such nation existed long before. Thus the Albanians call their struggle *Rilindja* ('rebirth'), the Estonians *Ärkamisaeg* ('awakening time'), the Italians *Risorgimento* ('rising again'), the Bulgarians възраждане ('revival'), the Indonesians *Kebangkitan* ('resurrection'), the Finns *Kansallinen herääminen* ('national awakening'), the Romanians *Renașterea națională* ('national renaissance'), etc.

In the coming chapters of the book, we will outline how the development of a standard national language has often been part of the development of the nation itself; above all, we will see that the way in which many states have dealt with – and implicitly taught their citizens to think about – language use, language change, and the very relationship between language and nationality, reflects and implicitly promotes a particular ideology.

---

[17] Plut. Thes. 23.1: 'εἰς τὸν αὐξόμενον λόγον ἀμφιδοξούμενον παράδειγμα τὸ πλοῖον εἶναι, τῶν μὲν ὡς τὸ αὐτό, τῶν δὲ ὡς οὐ τὸ αὐτὸ διαμένοι λεγόντων'.

9

Consequences of national languages

Having seen, in the last chapter, some of the practical and symbolic means by which a national identity is shaped and reinforced, in this chapter we shall refocus on language, and especially on the choice and development of a standardized national language. Part of the nationalist vision for a nation state is usually a shared idiom that can reach the whole nation and bind it together – an *Einheitssprache*, as the Germans would say. In countless countries, as we will discuss, some particular language variety has been selected, codified, expanded, officialized, and spread or sometimes imposed as the national norm, usually to the detriment of other dialects and other languages. Modern linguists, with good reason, decry such prescriptive and authoritarian policy. In Chapter 10, we will analyse the conceptual distortions and practical harm that a prescriptive language standardization has sometimes entailed; in this chapter, however, we consider possible beneficial aspects of it and point out the fallacious and ultimately prescriptive underpinning of the approach of many anti-prescriptivists and advocates of language diversity. We shall also highlight, nonetheless, the problematic motives and consequences of the choice of a particular language variety as national standard, and look at the questions of who can claim ownership or authority over an official (national or international) language. In connection with that, we will assess the validity of the concept of 'native speaker', which is nowadays contested.

Nations formed in parallel with their standard languages

The process of industrialization and urbanization that, starting in the late eighteenth century, took place in many parts of the Western world, resulted in the mixing of populations across regions and their gathering in larger concentrations. The drive to build a nation – above all, to impart it a collective identification as a nation – typically aims for amalgamation and uniformity. Such goals have frequently been further aided by the introduction of extended transport systems, a national press, a growing bureaucracy, mass military service, and compulsory schooling, all of which encourage the population of a large territory to cohere and to be on the same page, metaphorically and literally. Language standardization – the drive to create and maintain a codified and normative form of a language – has often been part of the overall endeavour to build a nation. For example, at the dawn of the nineteenth century, Czech speakers adopted an identity as a nation while Czech was worked into a language for all uses

(Thomas 2003: 37; Hroch 2010: 270–1). Among the Dutch too, the establishment of their nation co-occurred with the codification of the language, and indeed was part of the same enterprise (Rutten 2019: 25ff.). For many other nations too – Bulgarians, Norwegians, Turks, to name just a few – the formation of a distinct national state occurred in parallel with the development or the refashioning of a supra-regional, standard, written language. This, however, has not been the case in every country, especially outside Europe, which confirms that the intense preoccupation with having a single national language was not inevitable, and perhaps that a single national language was not quite as crucial and necessary as many thought.

In many European countries, nonetheless, not only has some particular form of a language been officially promoted to 'national language', but it has come to enjoy some form of state protection or even enforcement. For example, the Constitution of Portugal, among the 'Fundamental tasks of the state' includes (9f) 'to ensure forever the teaching and valorization, to defend the use, and to promote the international diffusion of the Portuguese language'.[1] The Hungarian 2011 constitution stipulates not only that Hungarian is the official language of Hungary, but that Hungary protects, or defends, the Hungarian language.[2] The Bulgarian Constitution, in Chapter 1 of its Fundamental Principles, proclaims that 'the study and use of the Bulgarian language is a right and an obligation of the Bulgarian citizens', and that the citizens whose mother tongue is not Bulgarian have the right to study and use their own language 'along with the mandatory study of the Bulgarian language'.[3] In the Spanish Constitution, among the preliminary articles, it is stated that 'Castilian is the official Spanish language of the State; all Spaniards have the duty to know it'.[4]

A state, in order to reach (and influence) the minds of the citizens and organize their lives, needs mass communication, and therefore wants its citizens schooled enough to be easily reached by its message. In this sense too, we could say that a national language and a nation can be mutually constitutive, that they help create each other: nationalist projects have often established a canonical, homogeneous, school-enforced language, and conversely such shared language has frequently contributed to fashioning a national identity and then served as an emblem of the nation it had helped to developed. The promotion (through schools, press, and books) of a standardized but often relatively vernacular language facilitated the spread not only of the language itself and of a national ideology taught through it, but also of the perception that that language is an intrinsic and defining national trait. In the process of consolidating their nation and their state, many nationalist movements, especially in Europe, have equated language with nationality.[5]

---

[1]   'Tarefas fundamentais do Estado': '(9f) Assegurar o ensino e a valorização permanente, defender o uso e promover a difusão internacional da língua portuguesa'.

[2]   '(§A.h. 1–2): Magyarországon a hivatalos nyelv a magyar. Magyarország védi a magyar nyelvet'.

[3]   'Чл. 36. (1) Изучаването и ползването на българския език е право и задължение на българските граждани. (2) Гражданите, за които българският език не е майчин, имат право наред със задължителното изучаване на българския език да изучават и ползват своя език'.

[4]   '(3.1) El castellano es la lengua española oficial del Estado. Todos los españoles tienen el deber de conocerla y el derecho a usarla'.

[5]   The equating of language with nationality will be analysed in Chapter 11.

There are also parallels between the very genesis of a national identity and that of a national standard language. Creating the latter has many a time entailed selecting and upholding a language variety as normative, and suppressing marked deviations from it that existed across the national space or that arose over time. Spreading a national identity has usually entailed selecting and upholding an idealized nationality archetype as normative, curbing its synchronic variations and downplaying its diachronic changes. In Western countries, linguistic diversity, often like ethnic diversity, has been traditionally regarded as antithetical to the very concept of nation; when not openly suppressed, it has, until recently, been unsupported and discouraged. This does not mean that regional dialects and other languages have been stamped out entirely, nor that the standard language does not evolve or include slight variants, especially in speech. The fashioning of a standard language is an ongoing process, subject to change and to resistance. Given this – and the fact that standard languages, on a world scale, are relatively uncommon – a standard language should be seen more as an ideological construct than as a tangible reality. At the same time, a campaign to create or modify a language is not, as many claim, a quixotic and doomed effort. New styles, rules, and words artificially concocted and consciously promoted have succeeded in transforming or even forming several languages, such as modern Turkish, Israeli Hebrew, Nynorsk, or Indonesian.

Merits of a national language

The merits of a standard language should be assessed with neither a deference to top-down prescriptions nor a *parti pris* opposition to conventions. There are potential benefits to a standard language, even if they come at a price, and they should be acknowledged – before we discuss the drawbacks. For a start, if we incline to the ancient philosophical cliché that only the educated are free,[6] we should accept that learning a language variety that is the conduit of a much larger, more up-to-date, and more diverse flow of information has the potential to be enriching for individual speakers and also emancipating. In addition, the establishment of a national standard language has usually come with a nation-wide campaign to generalize literacy, extending the benefits of being able to read and write to many more people – empowering them, as Americans would say.[7] A widespread and widely recognized language – as national languages typically become – is better understood by a higher number and more diverse assortment of people, and thus may also constitute a more efficient inter-regional and inter-communal medium for making one's voice heard. It may provide more access to alternative viewpoints, including yours. A standard language, moreover, is actively developed to be suited to a large range of uses; it normally has a

---

[6] Cf. Epict. Disc. 2.22: 'πιστευτέον … τοῖς φιλοσόφοις μᾶλλον, οἳ λέγουσι μόνους τοὺς παιδευθέντας ἐλευθέρους εἶναι'.

[7] Literacy is conceptualized, perceived, and used in dissimilar ways by different cultures; here, we take the term in its minimal sense of a decontextualized ability to read a written text.

gamut of registers, and is usually the main, if not the only, variety that has exhaustive abstract and technical vocabulary. As a result, it is likely to open up new educational, professional, and social opportunities. After all, many of those who are already speakers of a prestigious standard language often still seek to learn foreign languages for the same reasons; and the wish or need to communicate with a larger and more varied network of people is also one of the key factors that have given rise to pidgins and *koiné* languages. In the case of speakers of a language or dialect spoken only in a small locality, therefore, we cannot say that their learning a national language does nothing to them other than corrupting or obliterating their native speech, culture, and identity. In any event, bilingualism and bidialectalism can be additive rather than subtractive; so, in a literal sense too, knowledge of the standard language, in principle, can be a plus. Besides, some multilingual countries, especially in recent times, have supported the standardization of their multiple languages. It should also be remembered that standardizing and giving official status to (at least) one local language gives it a status that helps protect it from being ousted by powerful international languages.

Some of the specific rules of the standard language – though by no means all or even many of them – can have a point or be helpful. For one thing, a standard form, by setting up some public rules of usage, in some contexts may reduce the risk of miscommunication. This is not to suggest that we should join those who bellyache that nowadays, without old prescriptive grammatical rules, the language is going to the dogs. The main targets of the wrath of prescriptivists have usually been innovative features of the language that clash with tradition, or that are deemed low-class, or that show the influence of a disfavoured category of foreigners. Objecting to a linguistic feature for such reasons is linguistically unjustifiable. However, there may be something to be said for objecting – for example – to omitted punctuation. Some anti-prescriptivists would brand any disapprobation of other people's usage as an affront to linguistic freedom by the 'grammar police' or the 'grammar Nazis'; but punctuation – to stay with that one example – may enable you to get your point across more accurately, unambiguously, and effectively. Consider the phrase:

a) 'some Indian cities are pretty like Jaipur'
This can mean either of the following:
b) 'some Indian cities are pretty as much as Jaipur is'
c) 'some Indian cities are pretty and Jaipur is an example'

If the intended meaning is c), those who insist that you should put a comma between 'pretty' and 'like' in sentence a) are not being just fussy or dogmatic. For a starker example, take the clever title of Gyles Brandreth's book *Have You Eaten Grandma?* Arguing that you are well-advised to insert a comma before the last word (unless you are genuinely enquiring whether your interlocutors have devoured their granny) is not being dictatorial about an empty convention. After all, placing a comma there simply reports in writing a difference that all English speakers routinely choose to mark in speech with a change of intonation, and they do not consider doing so an imposition or a waste of time. That semantic difference is indicated by many languages even in their morphology or syntax, and therefore automatically also in writing. For example, in Latin, in Nepali, and in many Slavic languages, the word 'grandmother' in that sentence would have an obligatorily different form depending on whether it was the person being addressed or being eaten. Look at Icelandic:

Table 9.1 Example of the distinction between addressee and object of the action being marked morphologically

English	Icelandic
have you eaten, grandma?	hefur þú borðað, amma?
have you eaten grandma?	hefur þú borðað ömmu?

In some other languages, although all the words would be the same in both sentences, the distinction would be obligatorily made clear by a different word order. And nobody would consider this superfluous, pedantic, or oppressive. Look at German:

Table 9.2 Example of the distinction between addressee and object of the action being marked syntactically

English	German
have you eaten, grandma?	hast du gegessen, Oma?
have you eaten grandma?	hast du Oma gegessen?

Recommending punctuation is prescriptive; we can admit it, and make our peace with it. But it may be in your interest. Insisting on usage with maximum clarity can also be a defence against being deceived. There is an ancient story of unclear origin of a young man who consulted an oracle in order to know whether, if he went to war, he would survive. The oracle appeared to predict that he would not die and would come back safely. So off he went, but got killed. His family returned to the oracle to remonstrate, arguing that the hapless fellow had trusted the oracle's words:

ibis, redibis, numquam in bello peribis
literally: 'you shall go, you shall return, never in the war you will perish'

The oracle disagreed, asserting that the divination had been:

ibis, redibis numquam, in bello peribis
literally: 'you shall go, you shall return never, in the war you will perish'

The various movements and pressure groups for the use of transparent language in bureaucracy – notably the ongoing Plain English Campaign – are also undeniably prescriptive; their stated concern, nonetheless, is that the public can be confused, bamboozled, or taken advantage of through the use of obscure language. It is difficult to say that such concern has no merit. The problems with promoting a particular language variety or use over others, however, start to become evident when we consider, for example, pronunciation. On the one hand, it cannot be denied that an accent with 'standard' status is likely to be passively well-known across different social strata, regions, and even countries, and to be therefore comprehensible to a higher number and larger range of people. It is usually the accent perceived to be 'neutral' and to constitute 'speaking with no accent' – perceptions that are utterly illogical but well-entrenched. Regional accents are usually not perceived this way: they tend to have stronger specific associations. As a result, in the casting of actors, for example, a marked regional accent may raise concerns if a character is supposed to speak in a way that does not suggest or bring to mind a particular geographic or social provenance. A vampire with a (even badly faked) Romanian or Hungarian accent is likely to be construed by the audience as Transylvanian; a vampire with a standard English accent is fairly likely to be perceived by an English audience as just a vampire, with little attention to the accent; a vampire with a strong, say, Scottish accent is very likely to be perceived as Scottish. This may be somewhat jarring or spell-breaking for some viewers, or may impose changes to the storyline. It might also cause difficulties if the film is watched by international audiences who are not familiar with less standard accents in English: British films with regional accents like Scottish have occasionally had to be dubbed before release in other English-speaking countries. In other professions too, if making announcements is an important part of the job, employers may seek to hire people with a native standard accent and usage in order to ensure intelligibility to the largest audience. On the other hand, there is something clearly very problematic about asking a set category of people to falsify or conceal their accent, and all the more about penalizing them for it. We saw previously that prejudices about accent can not only be unfair, but have grievous consequences.

We already talked, in Chapters 4 and 6, about loss of vocabulary and of grammatical distinctions. Some words that are now obsolete were useful, we conceded, and did enrich the language. As John Lyons (1968: 43) remarked, 'in denying that all change in language is for the worse, we are not of course implying that it must be for the better'. To acknowledge in passing that the disuse of a particular word that expressed a meaning pithily and precisely is a regrettable loss is not the same as being doctrinal, hidebound, alarmist, or conducting a quixotic battle against change. It is perfectly reasonable to miss a handy term that was available to our ancestors or that we may know from another language – as long as we do not insist that everyone *must* adopt or restore that feature that the language lost or lacks. Besides, the doomsayers who feel that the language is just getting poor are easily disproven: languages also keep developing new words.

Language diversity within a country or region is said by many (see Poole 1969: 40–1) to impede cooperation, national unity, government efficiency, support for authority, and political participation. This description is wildly exaggerated; but we cannot say that it does not contain any truth at all: within a state, a common language makes things a bit easier for a centralized bureaucracy, simplifies mass education, spreads a homogenous culture (whether that is a plus or a minus is a separate issue), saves money, and facilitates public engagement. It may also foster collective identification (again, whether that is a positive or a negative development is another matter). For example, both before and after decolonization, the existence of Standard

Arabic in the Arab world as a supranational fixed medium, despite it being, in a sense, nobody's native language, has helped create a sense of solidarity and affinity among Arab countries, and has enabled communication among people otherwise relatively distant in dialect, location, nationality and, in a few respects, culture. Arabic is, and is felt to be, a common denominator for the people who live across seventeen independent states of which Arabic is the sole official language (Holt 1996: 11). To grant all this is not to say that multilingualism is dysfunctional or unmanageable. The belief that a single shared language will bring unity, solidarity, and harmony is also behind the invention of languages such as Esperanto, Ido, Volapük, or Interlingua, which were launched with the idea of uniting people although, in these cases, across borders.

A historical observation is also in order. The standardization of languages and the related pressure to abandon sociopolitically weaker co-territorial languages and dialects is not merely a product of modern nations and nationalism. It is true that, in modern European history, the idea of a standard language gained a political significance it never had before, and that the use of a standard language became official and mandatory as perhaps never before; after all, in the rest of the world, most languages do not have a standard form. Nonetheless, the perception that languages have a recognized variety to which users should adhere is quite old. English developed a conventionally accepted form without legislations, and did so in late Middle English. Written Arabic too acquired a virtually fixed form long before the 'Age of Nationalism', indeed before most European languages got a standardized form; among the Arab literate élite, even concerns about the 'purity' of the language date way further back than nationalism. Both the tendency to create a standard and the derogation of alternative dialects and languages (also as an effort to distinguish oneself haughtily from other nationalities or social classes) are well attested already in antiquity. Long prior to any modern nation state, Roman writers analysed Latin usage extensively, openly expressed preferences and prejudices, and voiced very little interest or sympathy for foreign languages except for Greek. A few Latin authors described the Latin of Rome with terms that suggest that it had come to be conceived as *de facto* a standard above other varieties of Latin (Adams 2003a: 191–4): local varieties of Latin were considered inferior to educated Roman Latin. Cicero asserted that there was a certain accent, characteristic of Rome, that seemed neutral, had no features that would strike one as wrong, nothing that sounded or felt foreign; and he prescriptively recommended: 'let us adopt this, and let us learn to avoid not only countryside roughness but also foreign strangeness'.[8] According to Palmer (1954:123–4), the onset of this attitude coincided with the sudden growth of the urban proletariat in Rome and with the influx into Rome of many foreigners who spoke broken Latin. The difference between Latin and official modern languages is that Latin never underwent the ideologically charged legal codification and enforcement of, say, French, or Turkish, or Indonesian. At the start of the Roman

---

[8]   Cic. De Or. 3.44: 'certa uox Romani generis urbisque propria, in qua nihil offendi, nihil displicere, nihil animaduerti possit, nihil sonare aut olere peregrinum, hanc sequamur neque solum rusticam asperitatem, sed etiam peregrinam insolentiam fugere discamus'.

conquest, the peninsula in which Rome lay was inhabited by a motley of ethnic groups differing in customs, political systems, religions, and languages. When the Roman Empire was established and held sway over these, there was no policy imposing Latin, *qua* the language of the rulers, on the conquered populations. It is true that the prestige of Latin made itself felt: there was some social pressure to learn it, and ambitious locals would learn it anyway for their own advancement. But there was no legal requirement. Despite their expansion, speakers of Latin – unlike speakers of English, French, Spanish, Italian, Russian, or Chinese in more recent centuries – did not forcibly curb the use of other languages among the populations over whom they gained ascendancy, nor did they legally demand the adoption of their own language. And after Latin spread far beyond its region of origin, the realization eventually prevailed that Latin had inevitably different forms and accents, which all counted as Roman. The Romans, furthermore, did not assume that, in order to run their Empire efficiently, it was enough for them to know Latin and that, given their imperial power, there was no need for them to learn other languages. The whole eastern part of the Roman empire used Greek, with Latin having a minimal role. When the Roman Empire spread further east, Latin, although used by officials, was not imposed on, nor adopted by, the local population to any significant degree, and Latin speakers usually learnt Greek. The oft-heard view that the position of English today is comparable to that once held by Latin is therefore mistaken in several interesting respects.

Prescriptivism and anti-prescriptivism among modern linguists

The approach of Western linguistic scholarship to languages has undergone a radical – and justified – change. For a long time, it mostly treated languages as well-defined, ideally fixed, and invariable. It focused on the standard form of each language, presenting it and promoting it as the only permissible and inherently correct form. The emphasis has since shifted to neutral, uninvolved accounts of a polyphony of localized, diverse usages. In Britain, the authority of the traditional standard language is diminishing also in public perceptions: there is now official acceptance of linguistic variations, a diversity of accents in the media, a largely uncontested adoption of Americanisms, and a higher tolerance of alternative or creative spellings. The authority and the legitimacy traditionally attributed only to one linguistic code promulgated top-down have been challenged, and academic attention has extended to multiple, subjective judgments of correctness. Linguistics has moved from prescriptive to descriptive and from linguistic absolutism to pluralism. This has been a healthy shift, but our zeal should not lead us to overlook some interesting problems and contradictions.

First, linguistics cannot ignore prescriptivism entirely, because linguistic prescriptions can alter the very objects of linguistic descriptions: the structure, use, and development of languages. The anti-prescriptivism of modern linguists, by and large, has not changed the stance of the general population, of the media, of academics in other fields, or even of language scholars in some other parts of the world. Normative and judgmental attitudes to language usage, far from being confined to old schoolbooks and conservative commentators, can be found in the average speaker, who voices them unabashedly. And this has an impact on the collective usage. Second, although many linguists sneer at the prescriptivists who urge people to speak in a particular way or in one language rather than another, they take up cudgels for obsolescent languages, decrying emotionally their demise and actively urging their use – an attitude to language that cannot be characterized as merely descriptive. Perhaps, they should just stop being coy about this. It is not surprising that linguists may be dismayed by the disappearance of smaller languages at an unprecedented rate. The existence of many languages enables linguists to ascertain what is synchronically and diachronically possible in the structure of languages, and to draw thence inferences about human cognition in general. Moreover, a growing number of linguists agree that the extinction of a language can constitute not only the loss of a repository of unattested grammatical features and of unique lexicalized knowledge, but possibly – we talked about this – of an entire frame of analysis of the world, which could turn out to be, in some respects, more useful, or insightful, or simply more interesting than that of some more familiar languages. For example, as reported by Wurm (1987: 39–41), the system of noun classes found in a number of Australian and of Papuan languages is breaking down owing to the urbanization and Westernization of the speakers; that system reportedly placed everything into grammatical categories according to features that the local culture perceives to be shared among groups of concepts. Such system therefore tells us something about the social organization, ontological beliefs, and traditional knowledge of the speakers – from the symbolic value attached to certain activities, to the role ascribed to supernatural forces, to practices for food production, to the usefulness of certain animals to native life. Loss of grammatical information here is indubitably loss of cultural information.

That said, we must also note that the notion that certain languages are invaluable because they are unique in their structure, vocabulary, and communicative power runs afoul of the tenet, to which most of those linguists subscribe, that all languages are roughly equivalent in value and in what they can do. And there are other contradictions. The suggestion that languages are not mere conduits of different cultures and world views, but that their grammar itself shows different ways of perceiving and organizing reality, smacks of the 'Sapir-Whorf' hypothesis, which is otherwise taboo for most linguists. Moreover, the argument that a population is best served by speaking its ancestral language, rather than a major Western one, presupposes that a particular language is inherently more suited to those speakers and to their civilization – a notion that, in other contexts, would probably be dismissed as essentialism, another cardinal sin in a liberal outlook. That argument also implies that native languages keep the thinking and the self-expression of indigenous populations more authentic, unadulterated, and free, characterizations that would be dismissed as naïve, unscientific, and utopic if said about something else. Besides, it presupposes that linguists, who are usually from, or educated in, a Western country, are the arbiters of authenticity (Bucholtz 2003: 407), which is hardly a humble or non-colonial viewpoint. We should also note that advocates of many small languages, including Western ones, have actively supported the creation and promotion of a standard form of those languages, often a mixed one

(Basque and Romansh are examples), as a way to aid their wide use and survival. They have either privileged one particular variety, or pretty much invented one, coining new words, purging foreign ones, and trying to discourage the use of other languages. This might be well-meaning, and may even be a good thing, but it is clearly value-loaded, artificial, and prescriptive. We may (or may not) conclude that it must be done nonetheless, for the greater linguistic good; that is fine, but then we cannot go around affirming that the approach to languages must be strictly descriptive, dispassionate, non-judgmental, non-interventionist, non-purist, and so forth.

The language that is used to talk *about* the plight of language minorities and of dying languages is, in itself, hardly descriptive and dispassionate. Consider terms like *linguicide* and *linguistic genocide*, applied to situations in which not a single life was lost. The languages that have become obsolete have only sometimes done so because of physical or political persecution. Many languages are not politically oppressed, and are even legally protected and promoted, but are economically inexpedient and socially less prized than others, and therefore get put aside by the speakers themselves – in their own country and, all the more, when they emigrate. Language teachers report that many pupils of foreign descent ('heritage students') care little for their ancestral language. A language, given its symbolic value, is said to be a *totem* for a people (Kramsch 1998: 74–5); but, again, words must be chosen with care. It is true that a language can be like a totem if we intend that term to mean the distinguishing symbol of a given clan, like a sort of flag (cf. Durkheim 1912: 294).[9] However, the expression becomes misleading if we understand the term *totem* as meaning a sort of deity, some ancestral tutelary presence that members of the group are under punitive obligation to preserve and venerate (cf. Freud 1913: 3).[10] Immigrants usually choose whether to hold on to a language simply on grounds of usefulness and relevance, with no mysticism about it, and need no overt political coercion or social stigma to drop their language. Indeed, even the idea that language is inevitably a key symbol of the group should be questioned, as we shall do in Chapter 11.

A more transparent example of prescriptivism in the contemporary discourse on language is the injunction to drop politically incorrect terminology. Consider public protests such as, for instance, the recent petition – joined also by some linguists – against the continuing inclusion of the secondary meaning 'woman' in the entry for the word *bitch* 'female dog' in English dictionaries (note that the entry, in line with the principle of being descriptively complete and accurate, usually does mark the application of the term *bitch* to a woman as offensive or not decent). Those protests do not distinguish between reporting usage and recommending it, but also illustrate the undisguised – even if perhaps sometimes appropriate – prescriptivism of a number of linguists who normally take pride in their anti-prescriptivism. Some contemporary

[9] 'le totem ... est aussi le symbole de cette société déterminée qu'on appelle le clan. C'en est le drapeau; c'est le signe par lequel chaque clan se distingue des autres'.
[10] 'Der Totem ist erstens der Stammvater der Sippe ... ihr Schutzgeist ... Die Totemgenossen stehen dafür unter der heiligen, sich selbstwirkend strafenden Verpflichtung, ihren Totem nicht zu töten (vernichten)'.

feminist philosophers too have proposed that, when dealing with politically thorny terms, rather than a descriptive approach to their usage, we should have a goal-orientated 'ameliorative' approach to their meaning (Haslanger 2005: 12–3). If, in some contexts or respects, a prescriptive approach to language use is justified, there should not be, however, a taboo on saying that this *is* prescriptivism. Several forms of linguistic normativity, after all, are routinely accepted by virtually all linguists: even the most free-thinking ones abide by conventional spelling, present papers using the expected academic registers, consult prescriptive manuals such as *Hart's Rules* while writing, and generally conform to their publishers' style guides. When they write books that report how a given language appears to be used, they may label their work 'descriptive', even denouncing 'prescriptivism', but are – or should be – aware of how their work will be used: the language learners who buy *A descriptive grammar of x* are usually seeking a kind of instruction and guidance that is fundamentally prescriptive. And ultimately, even urging people to speak their 'natural' vernacular, and encouraging them to avoid 'prescriptive' styles, entails being prescriptive.

Language normativity is definitely, in many ways, illiberal; but language is anyway based on the development and partial maintenance of rules and norms – an important point elaborated by Cameron (2012: 2–3). Language is made of socially selected rules, in its structure as much as in its pragmatics. Therefore corrections, disapproval, and value judgments of other people's (and one's own) usage are also part of language use, not just of a particular prescriptivist approach. Almost everybody has opinions as to what is linguistically 'better' – because they deem it clearer, appropriate to the occasion, or somehow more beautiful. Indeed, diachronic change in language, as we mentioned before, is partly due to social attitudes and social changes.

Imposing whose standard?

An important positive aspect of the standardization of languages that must be noted is that, in several cases, the language variety that was elevated to the role of the national standard was a variety much closer to the people's spoken language than the archaic or foreign language previously used as official and written medium. In those cases, the creation of such national standard was an altogether democratic step. However, the living language or dialect that gets elevated to national standard is sometimes not the most common among the population, and is selected for ideological reasons. For example, at the time of the foundation of the state of Pakistan in 1947, Urdu was spoken by a minority, but was chosen over languages with many more millions of speakers because Urdu fitted a distinctly Muslim identity for the new state (Simpson 2007: 8). Above all, a standard language is very commonly correlated, indeed doubly correlated, with social class. It is, recursively, both a *cause* of social hierarchies and a *consequence* of them. On the one hand, it causes them because, by being considered the only real and correct language and by being the language of the state, the judiciary, the educational system, authoritative media, and religious organizations, it inevitably increases the social prestige, political dominance, and economic power of its most proficient users. Bestowing the status of standard, official, or national to a particular language variety secures, often deliberately, higher status and advantages for a particular section of the nation. It does not create a level playing field of equal opportunities for all those who speak it to a degree. Indeed, although the standard language is prescriptively taught and promoted to everyone, those who speak it natively or (if it is only a written language) write it best may not want those beneath them in the social hierarchy to learn to talk and write in exactly the same way as they do, because that linguistic difference marks and maintains a class distinction that it is in their interests to preserve. On the other hand, the formal recognition of a given language variety as 'standard' is also, conversely, a consequence of class divisions, because the variety of language that is selected as the standard typically reflects the usage of the dominant classes, the speech of the region where finance and government are concentrated (if the centre of power ever shifts, often so does the usage that is considered 'the best'). In countless countries, the standard language has been originally developed from the speech of the region of the capital city: Standard French is based on upper-class Parisian, Standard Danish is based on usage in and around Copenhagen, Standard Romanian is based on usage in the area around Bucharest (Muntenia), Standard Hungarian is based on usage in the Budapest area, Standard Turkish is based on the variety used in Istanbul, Standard Georgian is based on the speech of the region that includes Tbilisi, Standard Thai is based on educated Bangkok speech, Filipino is based on the use of the metropolitan area of Manila. This secures the pre-existing or nascent clout and cachet of a given section of society and of its subculture.

The position of the higher classes is strengthened not only if their *native* language or dialect is enthroned as national standard, but also when the language selected as standard is a different, *non-native* language of prestige. This is because knowledge of that language, as a rule, will still be mostly confined to the top échelons of society. The written tradition, as we noted previously, frequently plays a role: texts admired for their literary worth, or attributed authority for other reasons (legal, historical, or religious, for example) sometimes have constituted the basis for a written standard, even if their language was incomprehensible to a large part of the population. High proficiency in the use of a written language like Classical Arabic in the Arab world, or of Katharevousa in pre-1976 Greece, was largely the apanage of the educated class, as were the accompanying socioeconomic advantages – even though nobody was a native speaker of that language. Similarly, in a colonial setting, the use of a living foreign language such as English or French as a medium for formal or inter-group communication has been a ticket to privilege. The use of English today in most European countries can be seen in a rather similar light, because lack of proficiency in English can now restrict access to social and professional advancement. The same applies in post-colonial contexts, where the unabated prestige of English or French, due to colonialism, means that the local languages cannot really compete. In parts of Africa, the official adoption of an old colonial language as the language of bureaucracy, media, or schooling has often been advocated with the suggestion that such language, unlike any of the many native languages, is *super partes* and constitutes a choice that gives unfair advantage to no-one; but this is not really in accordance with the facts. Giving such eminence to English or similar languages is a choice that tends to create or preserve a new ruling class consisting of the restricted élite of locals who are fluent in that language – often because previously trained by colonial rulers to work under them. This, incidentally, shows also how the socioeconomic clout of a language is not commensurate with the number of local speakers; for example, in South Africa, the decennial census (2011) shows that English, which is otherwise the top language in terms of social prestige and extent of formal use, is the 'home language' of only 8.4 per cent of the population, i.e. of fewer people than Afrikaans is (a language that some sources in South Africa declare doomed), and of far fewer people than several officially recognized African languages such as isiZulu, isiXhosa, Sepedi, and Setswana (several other African languages of South Africa do not even have official status). Most importantly, in regions of the world like Africa, retaining languages like English as mediums of education and formal discourse, and of long-distance trade and high-level social exchange, reinforces subtle ties of subordination to the erstwhile colonial powers, even though those ties are officially severed. On this point, it must be noted that, already long before the modern era, it had been realized that a language, if codified and spread internationally as an official medium, can greatly increase the ascendancy of its speakers over others. Nebrija, the Spanish scholar who, in 1492, penned a grammar of Castilian Spanish – widely thought to be the first grammar of a Romance language – was clear about this. He dedicated and formally presented his grammar as a power tool to Queen Isabel I of Castilla (Isabel the Catholic), who asked him how a grammar of a language she already knew would be useful to her; so he pointed out, in the opening of the book itself (Nebrija 1492: 1), that it is a 'very certain conclusion that language always went together with imperial ruling.'[11]

For accuracy and fairness, nonetheless, we should acknowledge also that, even in post-colonial countries, support for the use of English has not always been part of a colonial agenda, nor is the support of local languages always part of a democratic and 'progressive' strategy. To talk of 'linguistic imperialism' is broadly correct but simplistic: English and other colonial languages were arrogantly promoted as *langues de civilisation*, yes; but, on occasion, they have been appropriated by locals as a tool to advance local pluralism. Indeed, in many colonial and imperial settings, the top-down encouragement of multilingualism has sometimes been part of a *divide et impera* strategy to keep local ethnicities poorly inter-connected and out of influential positions – with less voice and less power. To continue with the example of South Africa: school teaching using African languages has, at times, been rejected by local populations, who have seen it as a ploy to limit their socioeconomic advancement, and who have requested English instead. Pluralism is not automatically an equalizer, because it can be hierarchically structured. All these considerations are not arguments against state multilingualism, but they do show that nurturing monolingualism in minority languages is not a blanket solution without potential drawbacks.

---

[11] 'conclusión mui cierta: que siempre la lengua fue compañera del imperio'.

Language as individual capital

A language like English is in a peculiar position: while the number of speakers of English as a second language has been growing exponentially, the number of native speakers of English has been declining (Graddol 2003: 157). The fluent speakers of English for whom English is the second language now far outnumber the native speakers. A question increasingly raised is, therefore, to what extent English belongs to those who are native speakers of it, or to all speakers of standard English, or both; or whether, alternatively, English belongs to all those who speak English in any form, regardless of linguistic background, nationality, or ethnic origin (Norton 1997: 422). Because the knowledge of a language deemed important is an economic, professional, and social asset, a *capital linguistique*, as Bourdieu would say, it is not surprising that there is an ongoing battle for the right to claim such language as one's own. Whether a certain language is truly your language is a linguistic question, but also a political one, as it concerns the global distribution of power and is affected by perceptions of ethnicity, race, nationality, regional provenance, and class. The customary answer to that question has been that a language is your language if you are a native speaker. Most people consider the concept of 'native speaker' to be sufficiently clear and objective. But even if we accept that it is, a number of issues remain. There are, for a start, countless undecidable cases. Some people of immigrant background did acquire first a language other than English at home, or perhaps were born in another country but moved to England very early in life. By adulthood, they have lived most of their life in England and been schooled like any English child, maybe to an advanced level; they have come to know English more than their home language and may even speak the latter rarely, falteringly, and with interferences from English. Yet, technically, English is their second language and literally not their mother tongue. Are they native speakers of English? If they were not born in an English-speaking country, they are, in a strictly literal sense, not native. Shouldn't they reasonably claim to be, nonetheless? But what if the English they speak includes subtle but detectable foreign features? Suppose they were even born in the UK, but their family and local community grew up abroad with another language, so they too have incorporated into their English some elements (e.g. accent, words, translated expressions) of their ancestral language, though they do not actually speak it at all and have never lived outside of the UK. Can they be native speakers but speak differently from those who are recognized as native speakers? Furthermore, their foreign linguistic features, as we saw in Chapter 3, may get adopted also by people in their social circle who are of other ethnic backgrounds, including a few people of exclusively local descent ('English through and through'), who grow up in the same multi-ethnic urban area or attend the same school. Are those not native speakers of English?

Intersectional factors are also at work. Some immigrants have an appearance that allows them to blend in unnoticed when they move to the UK, the United States, Australia, Canada, or Europe; for that reason, and perhaps also because they come from a similar culture, it may also be easier for them to integrate into a social circle where the standard or upper-class language variety is spoken, and to learn it well. Besides, they may be facilitated by having a first language not dramatically different from English. Others are less privileged. Experiments in the United States have found that if you are a born-and-bred local, and are a monolingual standard native speaker by the classic definition, but you are of a different race (for instance, an American of Asian descent), many people earnestly claim, even after hearing you speak, that you have a foreign accent (Cheryan and Monin 2005: 722). This odious racial prejudice is, alas, sincere: perceptual distortions induced by the racial categories that we have in our mind occur not only in the auditorial but also in the visual domain: experiments with computer-manipulated images have demonstrated that a white face is wrongly perceived to have darker skin when it has prototypical 'Black' features rather than 'Caucasian' ones, or when it is a 'racially ambiguous' face but it is presented labelled 'Black' (Levin and Banaji 2006: 510–11).

Contesting the concept of *native speaker*

The title of 'native speaker' makes quite a difference in employment and beyond, especially if the language in question has clout and prestige. In Western countries such as the UK, but also in France or Germany, whether one can claim as one's own the language variety considered national and standard has therefore become a burning issue. In the UK, for example, some non-native but very advanced English speakers seek work as copy editors, writers, translators (into English), voice coaches, radio speakers and, above all, as English teachers. The response they receive, however, is sometimes rejection on the grounds that they are not native speakers. Complaints of discrimination are voiced, with accusations of 'native speakerism' (Holliday 2006: 385). The very concepts of *native speaker* or *mother tongue speaker*, and their charisma in society and in the job market, have thus come under attack. The claim is not simply that very proficient immigrants who have learnt the language as adults should be considered as good as native speakers, or that nowadays too many people cannot be placed squarely within either the native or the non-native category; it is that there is no such thing as a native or non-native speaker, that there isn't any difference between very advanced non-natives and native speakers, and therefore that the category *native speaker* is defunct (Paikeday 1985: x). It is argued that the application of the terms *native speaker* and *mother tongue*, if any, should not be based on birth, family history, or 'heritage', but on expertise. A related claim is that all those who use daily more than one language, regardless of proficiency level, should be allowed to define themselves as bilingual (Pavlenko 2014: 22).

We must add that the majority of highly proficient non-native speakers make no such claims: they accept the view that their English, very good as it may be, cannot be called native, and reckon that it is in certain respects less authoritative than that of a prototypical educated, standard native speaker. Some of them think so even though they have been educated in English literature and linguistics to the highest levels and therefore have a deep and technical knowledge of the language. Some even teach English to speakers of foreign languages, but admit the limitations of their vast linguistic knowledge (Medgyes 1992: 334–5). They may also have lived in the UK for years, be totally integrated into a social circle where only standard English is spoken; they may be exceedingly articulate, have even a more standard-like accent and usage than most native locals, a much larger vocabulary than average, better spelling, and a greater proficiency in writing (there have been famous non-native writers, like Conrad and Nabokov). Sometimes, they are initially taken for native speakers by many of the natives who meet them. Nevertheless, because they learnt English only as adults, they do not consider themselves 'native speakers of English'.

Those who take the opposite view, the non-natives who do believe that they should be considered in the same way as native speakers, have grown in confidence, and contest the primacy long held by those traditionally recognized as mother-tongue speakers of Standard British English. The latter usually feel that the only true and fully correct English is, by definition, their own, and are taken aback that foreigners who, by that standard, still make mistakes and have an accent are trying to promote themselves to the rank of native speakers. Their doing so is a challenge not only to linguistic but also to social categorizations: for the recognized natives, what is at stake is not just the language, but their own position as owners, experts, and arbiters of a very important medium, with the sense of property, prestige, and control that has always been specific to their category – a category that largely overlapped with a nationality. The terms *mother-tongue* and *native speaker*, and the insistence on them, in this light, have unstated but important ideological underpinnings. So, of course, has the criticism of them: it is guided by an egalitarian and pluralistic spirit, but it is not usually based on psycholinguistic research and language acquisition studies (Davies 2013: 18); indeed, it sometimes includes the claim that we should give weight to people's own subjective assessment of their proficiency (Piller 2002: 180, 184). It has, overall, a postmodern flavour, as it favours prioritizing the viewpoint of the disadvantaged, postulating first-person authority on self-ascriptions, accepting self-identifications unquestioningly, interpreting social categories as arbitrary and fluid sociocultural constructions without biological basis, dismissing evidence-based epistemology as a (Western) cover-up for prejudice, rejecting universal values, and so forth.

We shall make a few observations about those two rival views on the concept of *native speaker*, because being (considered) a native speaker or a non-native speaker can also determine whether someone is or is not accepted as being of a particular nationality. On the one hand, it is true that the skills of non-native speakers should be better appreciated: those who speak a second language well should be complimented for speaking more than one language, rather than be faulted for not speaking the second quite like a native. And it is certainly absurd to regard people's first language as being always their only 'real' one.[12] A person's first language is regarded that way also because it is perceived to be associated with nationality, and both are conceived in essentialist terms: people's first nationality is, like their first language, widely considered to be forever their only real one. On the other hand, the flat denial that there is a meaningful distinction to be made between native and non-native speakers is too vulnerable to

---

[12] There is an illogical and yet widespread notion that your 'true' language is the one in which you dream; but that will normally depend on the dream's setting: its location, its characters, and the period of your life to which it refers.

counterarguments from psycholinguistics. When one learns a second language, the quality of the result, in statistical terms, depends (among other things, but markedly) on age. In the acquisition of a language, there is a particularly receptive period before puberty (according to some, before age 11–12; to others, 6–7), beyond which there cannot be effortless acquisition from untutored exposure. Children can pick up a language as if by osmosis. It's true that such blessed state does not end all of a sudden; but there is an inexorable, though gradual, transition to the (typically adult) need for laborious, conscious study, with usually imperfect results. All this is well supported by evidence (Hyltenstam and Abrahamsson 2000: 159). On average, adult learners can get started and make initial progress even faster than children; but the adults are later surpassed by children, and extremely few adult learners reach a truly comparable level. The aspiration to become truly 'native-like' may, in some respects, mean setting oneself an unreasonably high bar. Late second-language learning normally does give different and rather inferior results to native acquisition in early childhood (Hernandez and Li 2007: 642), although one can debate whether this is an absolutely unavoidable outcome (Kroll et al. 2015: 382). A few brainy, gifted, and hard-working adults can reach almost native-like proficiency, but fine-grained analysis of their use of language can detect non-native features. To describe one's knowledge of a language learnt in adulthood as 'native-like' can therefore be misleading. Different areas of the brain are employed (Dehaene et al. 1997: 3809; Kim et al. 1997: 171) in the acquisition and use of a first language (L1) and of a late-acquired second language (L2): brain areas shaped by early exposure to L1 are not necessarily activated when processing L2 (Perani et al. 1996: 2444). Native-like performance is achievable in some domains, but less in others, and extremely rarely in all. The acquisition of the lexicon receives (strangely) little attention, but it is an area in which L2 learners not unusually outperform natives. This is not surprising: people can keep learning more vocabulary also in their native language. Non-native speakers do less well, however, in grammatical structure (syntax and morphosyntax), and especially in pronunciation. Thus, many foreign students acquire a technical vocabulary and writing skills in a second language which surpass not only those of the average native but also their own skills in the 'mothertongue' of which they are 'native speakers' – but they almost never achieve also the unfaltering fluency, consistently correct grammar, and native pronunciation of those considered mothertongue speakers.

A first language can, of course, be acquired in tandem with another, making one technically a native speaker of both; but, there too, interesting differences have been posited (Osgood and Sebeok 1954: 140), for example depending on whether the two languages were learnt simultaneously but separately (one at home, one outside, as happens with the children of many immigrants) or together (both at home, in a fully bilingual household, when each parent has a different native language). This underscores that the age of acquisition is not the only important factor: so is the context of acquisition, the possession of pertinent gifts such as a good memory and a good ear, the degree of similarity between the languages one learns, the amount of explicit feedback received, motivation and interest and, crucially, the length and intensity of exposure to the language (I have met people who, though born and brought up in the UK, lived almost all their life sequestered in a different community, homeschooled, and taught not to socialize much with outsiders, and as adults spoke English only like extremely fluent foreigners, with a marked accent, unidiomatic usage, and poor writing skills).

Those who denounce 'native speakerism' as a form of discrimination in the workplace contend, for example, that there is no reason for preferring teachers who are native speakers, i.e. who learnt the language in childhood from other native speakers and maintained it fully since then. In some respects, they have a point, but this is not a simple matter. There are some advantages in having a native teacher. These include: the teacher's accent (for learning to imitate it and to understand it); response speed and self-certainty in providing grammaticality judgments (the Chomskyan 'native speaker's intuition': even linguists may require someone with 'native intuition' for certain data evaluation tests); unhesitating fluency and spontaneity of speech production; knowledge of the culture around the language, including social rules of use (i.e. pragmatic, sociolinguistic information); and sometimes range of registers. On the other hand, it must be granted that there are many native speakers who offer themselves as language teachers but whose only qualification is being native speakers. They may have no teaching training, no particular didactic or pedagogical skills, no knowledge of the language of the students (or of any foreign language), very limited *conscious* knowledge of their own language (of its syntactic, morphological, phonetic rules, let alone of its philology), a relatively meagre vocabulary, and occasionally even poor spelling. It is enough to have a quick look on YouTube to see many 'native speakers' of various languages who post language lessons having no idea of what they are discussing, explaining it chaotically, and making entirely erroneous claims. Regarding those who live, work, and teach their language in a foreign country, we must also remember that, as some long-term expats and immigrants discover, it is possible to lose proficiency in your first language – something worth underlining because the mythology of the 'mother tongue' seems reluctant to acknowledge that the 'native speaker' can cease to be the ultimate authority on the language. It is well-known that people's first language influences their use of any other language they learn as adults; however, one's second language too, if constantly used, has an influence on the first. There is such a thing as first-language attrition: reduction in fluency, inability to recall infrequent words, and structural, semantic, or phonetic interferences from the second language, such as the unwitting adoption of intonation patterns from the second language, the spontaneous production of unidiomatic phraseology, or the inadvertent use of semantic calques.

The categorization of 'native speaker of English' is denied not only to those for whom English is a language acquired much later than another. Given that by 'English' one usually refers to the standard language, the title of 'native speaker of English' is given reluctantly to natives of dialects (e.g. Yorkshire English) and often denied outright to natives of offshoot international varieties (e.g. Indian English). It is no secret that some people in England somewhat look down on other varieties of English, such as Scottish, American, Australian, South African, Nigerian, Indian, or Singaporean English. Their disdain is not quite the same for all these but has a hierarchy: while they may regard American, Australian, or Scottish English as less good than 'proper English', they may regard Nigerian, Indian, and Singaporean English as plain wrong.

A language school should not delegitimize particular varieties of English; but it may, nonetheless, feel that it cannot ignore the expressed wishes of the learners. An English language teacher who has English as first language may thus have a strong regional, international, or class-specific accent that many students – unkind and unfair as this may be – may not want to acquire. After all, the reverse can also happen: a learner who lives, say, in Australia, or South Africa, or India, or in parts of northern England, Scotland, Wales, or Ireland, may want to learn English as used and pronounced in those locations, and not wish to sound like an English aristocrat. Nonetheless, native speakers of the standard variety of a language do have native command of the variety that very many, indeed probably most, learners would like to acquire or to approximate, and some of them would feel cheated if presented with a teacher whose accent or usage diverges significantly from their target standard language. Some students would openly regard the teacher's unusual accent as being as 'bad' as their own foreign accent. Many varieties of English differ from the standard more than, say, Serbian and Croatian differ from each other; and we would not be outraged if a student who wanted to learn Serbian preferred not to have a teacher who knew only Croatian or vice versa. All this means that, even in pronunciation – the domain in which native English speakers are felt to have the most definite edge – some 'native teachers', from the viewpoint of the students, may lack that edge.

Amongst linguists, on the other hand, at least since the 1980s, there has been an increasing recognition, and ultimately an advocacy of the recognition, that several languages, including English, are pluricentric, and that they have multiple self-standing forms based in different parts of the world. Traditionalists may feel that the claim that English (or German, or French, or Portuguese) has dignity in all its international varieties, and belongs equally to all its speakers, is just current political correctness running amok. But the development of an ownerless 'world English' has solid historical parallels. In antiquity, populations who forfeited their own language and adopted Latin from their Roman conquerors later took Latin over: they appropriated it to the point that the community that had introduced Latin to them lost social ownership of it and jurisdiction over its correctness. The initially stigmatized and mixed varieties of neo-Latin that developed independently in the colonies eventually came to claim the status of independent idioms (French in France, Spanish in Spain, Portuguese in Portugal, and so forth) with a prestige of their own, outstaging the classical idiom that was once the only standard language. This process has been partly repeated, *mutatis mutandis*, also in the adoption of Spanish and of Portuguese in south America (and, more distinctly, of Dutch, now Afrikaans, in southern Africa).

In communities where the local language has no standard or no written form, linguistic variation is less judged in terms of correctness but, more simply and practically, in terms of communicative effectiveness. In Turkey, for example, there are clear preceptions of what is 'correct' Turkish, but not of what is the correct form of Turkey's local unwritten languages such as Romeyka (Bortone 2009: 81–2); variations and *ad hoc* creations in such a language do not raise eyebrows. In Papua New Guinea, the locals evaluate variants of creole differently from the way expatriates who have been exposed to standard languages do (cf. Mühlhäusler 1982: 114): the former only object to what, in their view, is unclear or rude, the latter to what they consider bad or *incorrect* pidgin.

The history of English itself, like that of French and of several other languages, suggests that an idealized standard form of a language fuels intolerance to language variations and change. Such intolerance has affected social and political relations among language users, but also determined the very way in which national languages have been described and even artificially fashioned. Moreover, how a national language has been fashioned reveals a particular conception of the nation itself. We talk about all this in the next chapter.

10

More consequences of national languages

In the last chapter, we started to consider how the standard national language has, in many cases, been developed or (re)fashioned together with the nation itself, or anyway with its nation state. We focused on the benefits and value of having a standard language – though we also flagged the inequalities that can both drive and ensue from the choice of a particular language variety for that role, notably the privileges that it bestows upon those who speak it natively or are most proficient in it. We shall now draw attention to the negative consequences of that pursuit of intra-national linguistic uniformity which became common in the nineteenth century, and to which many nationalists still incline.

It is important to review those consequences not merely in order to denounce them, but to highlight to what extent the picture we have of many languages may be artificial and misleading. The desire for one's national language to be distinct, 'pure', diachronically consistent, and homogeneously spoken has resulted not only in misrepresentations of its nature, physiognomy, development, and usage, but also in interventions in the language itself, and in actions against those who did not conform with its normative adoption. In numerous instances, the mixed origins of the national language have been denied, and false reconstructions of its history have been produced; the synchronic differences between the national language and similar languages have been overstated, and have even been artificially increased; linguistic diversity in one's country has been downplayed or airbrushed out, and even legislated against; regional varieties have been portrayed as subordinate and defective, and speakers of those varieties have been treated as socially, and even mentally, inferior; bilingualism has been pathologized and discouraged, depriving people of its social and intellectual benefits; and multilingualism has been proclaimed disruptive or seditious, thereby engendering not only contempt towards language minorities but also active hostility. Nationalist antagonism towards other languages, nevertheless, has come into effect selectively: while elements borrowed from languages associated with disfavoured or disliked communities have been rejected, elements from languages associated with admired cultures have been tolerated or even welcomed. And it is important to note that the intolerance of linguistic minorities as such appears to have been often minimal in pre-national days. Indeed, when nationalist movements – and their zeal on the national language – started gathering momentum, members of linguistic minorities were often at the forefront of their campaigns.

Overstating the language

In order to make one particular language appear to be the long-established and nation-wide accepted tongue of a sizeable country, the polyphony of dialects and perhaps of other languages that, in many cases, preceded its spread has to be erased or downplayed as much as possible. National narratives typically claim that a particular constellation of populations or regions came naturally to form a nation and to seek statehood because they had a common language; however, among regions that were later said to make up a long-united nation there has often been significant linguistic diversity and disconnection. National histories have tended to obscure the lengthy, conscious, and often only partly successful process of creating linguistic unity. The idea that humankind is everywhere divided into nations, and that each nation has a well-defined territory and a single language guided even the descriptions of aboriginal populations of remote continents. Early Western sources represented, for example, Australian native tribes as *nations*, and attributed one language (and a land) to each of them, despite the fact that such tribes were usually exogamous and multilingual (Haviland 1997: 148).

Of course, the extent to which linguistic diversity may have reigned in a given territory before the establishment of a modern nation state varies considerably; it would be misleading to suggest that linguistic diversity was extreme everywhere. Nonetheless, languages coterminous with a state are a rare exception, not the rule. It is therefore worth zooming in on cases like France or Italy, because they are well-documented and can show how different the reality was from the later rhetoric, and just how artificial linguistic homogeneity can be.

In previous centuries, Europeans who travelled within (what they considered) their own country, could find the linguistic difference insurmountable, unless they knew also other languages. The young Racine ([1661] 1810: 72), travelling from Paris across France in the seventeenth century, having arrived in the south, at Uzès, writes in a letter to la Fontaine:

> I swear to you that I have as much need of an interpreter as someone from Moscow would have in Paris. Still, I begin to notice that it is a language mixed with Spanish and Italian, and since I understand those languages quite well, I have sometimes resorted to them in order to understand people or to make myself understood.[1]

The situation was identical, if not more extreme, in the north of the country, even two centuries later. Maupassant (1884: 265), having roamed through lower Brittany in July 1882, commented:

---

[1] 'Je vous jure que j'ai autant besoin d'un interprète, qu'un Moscovite en auroit besoin dans Paris. Néanmoins je commence à m'apercevoir que c'est un langage mêlé d'espagnol et d'italien; et comme j'entends assez bien ces deux langues, j'y ai quelquefois recours pour entendre les autres et pour me faire entendre'.

Often, in the course of an entire week, while traipsing through the villages, one does not meet a [single] person who knows a word of French.[2]

According to Meillet (1918: 94), well into the twentieth century the inhabitants of northern France and those of the south were largely unable to understand each other. Across the border, in Italy, linguistic unity was even more remote. Ugo Foscolo, celebrated Italian writer and fervent supporter of Italian unification ([1824?] 1850: 149, 187), openly reported:

> We know for a fact that neither does an illiterate man from Naples understand one from Milan, nor does one from Turin understand one from Bologna; nor could four educated men, each native of those different provinces, converse without misunderstanding one another, unless they used a certain hybrid Italian which, though marked by the provincial dialect of the speaker, nonetheless adopted the forms and the grammar of the literary language of the nation ... someone from Bologna and someone from Milan would not understand each other except after several days of mutual teaching.[3]

When Italy was unified around 1862, barely 2.5 per cent of the population spoke standard Italian, and Italian speakers who travelled in the deep south were thought to be speaking English (De Mauro 1970: 43).

Increased requests for 'language' status

Nowadays, the cachet and power of 'languages', the contempt for non-standard local varieties and their speakers, and the recognition and increased autonomy that a community may attain if what it speaks is understood to be a separate language, have an additional unsurprising effect. More and more communities, albeit with some internal dissent, want their speech varieties to be considered self-standing languages. After all, the very term 'dialect', outside of linguistics, has developed dismissive connotations. Since the latter part of the twentieth century, in western Europe, not only have demands for national independence or devolution increased, but so too has the pressure, often at least partly successful, for local dialects to be recognized as languages (Trudgill 2004: 12–14). Examples abound. In France, where only French is official, some want to give language status to other *langues d'oïl* such as Picard, which has been occasionally written since the Middle Ages. In Spain, Galician is now official in its region, Aragones

---

[2] 'souvent pendant une semaine entière, en rôdant par les villages, on ne rencontre personne qui sache un mot de français'.

[3] 'Sappiamo per prova che né un Napoletano illitterato intende un Milanese, né un Torinese un Bolognese; né quattr'uomini educati, ognuno de' quali fosse nativo in una di quelle diverse provincie, potrebbero conversare senza traintendersi se non usassero fra di loro un certo italiano ibrido, che partecipando pur sempre del dialetto provinciale di chi lo parla, assume ad ogni modo le desinenze e la grammatica della lingua letteraria della nazione ... un Bolognese e un Milanese non si intenderebbero fra di loro, se non dopo parecchi giorni di mutuo insegnamento'.

is also locally recognized, Asturian has some recognition, and Valencian is striving to be recognized as distinct from Catalan – the latter being the subject of another battle. In Poland, Kashubian has been used in schools in Pomerania since 1989 and has been legally recognized as a 'regional language' (*język regionalny*) since 2005; there have been requests that the same status be conferred also to Silesian. In Sweden, Meänkieli, a form of Finnic spoken in the northeast of the country, near the Finnish border, is now locally recognized and taught. In northeast Italy, Ladin has long been recognized as a language, and is used in schools and in the media; language status is now periodically requested also for the dialects of regions with some separatist aspirations, notably Lombardy and Veneto. In Estonia, Võro, a form of south Estonian (standard Estonian is based on northern varieties) has been used in print at least since the nineteenth century and has a standardized form; other varieties of Estonian, such as Tartu, Mulgi, and Seto are also now sometimes claimed to be languages.

Stressing or fabricating differences between languages

Given the widespread notion that a nation and a language must go together, many populations feel that, in order to make a plausible claim to nationhood and bid for statehood, they have to have a distinct language. The desire to deny links with another language (and people), and perhaps to claim links with others, is what historically instigated the development of a standardized form of many languages, and the publication of their first grammars. European examples include Norwegian, Romanian, Modern Greek, Hungarian, and Finnish. It has happened repeatedly that if one group has virtually the same language as other groups from which it wants to be distinguished, it denies or downplays such linguistic similarity. Conversely, if a state wants to undermine the separatist claims of populations within its borders, it asserts or points out that the latter lack a distinct language. For Czechs and Slovaks, an increasing emphasis on their linguistic differences was a tool in their establishment as separate nations; during the Balkan conflicts of the 1990s, in the interaction between speakers of what used to be known as *Serbocroat*, politically symbolic requests for translations were advanced by Croatians in negotiations with Serbs, who responded with scorn. In a similar way, representatives of (what is now called) North Macedonia, who are seen by many Bulgarians as Bulgarian speakers, if not as Bulgarians *tout court* (just as they have been seen as Serbian speakers by some Serbs), in 1994 demanded interpreters when their president met the Bulgarian president, and Bulgaria refused (Danforth 1995: 153; Roudometof 2002: 41). The paradox is that in the late nineteenth century, when Bulgaria was becoming a separate entity, Slavic speakers of the Macedonia region advocated the creation of a common Bulgaro-Macedonian standard language close to both Bulgarian and Macedonian usage, but Bulgarians refused and opted for a markedly east-Slavic and distinctly Bulgarian written language (Friedman 1999: 19–20). This fuelled the development of a separate official Macedonian Slavic language, which many Bulgarians then claimed does not exist.

In the same way, some states have, at times, feared that the allegiance or national identification of a population under their control could gravitate towards another country because the latter had the same or a similar language as that population; the linguistic affinity between them has then been understated or refuted. The Soviet administration overplayed the differences between the Finnic languages of the Soviet Union (notably Karelian) and Finnish; it also stressed the differences among the Turkic languages of the Soviet Union (Azerbaijanian, Uzbek, Turkmen, Tartar, Kazakh, Kyrghiz, Gagauz), especially in relation to Turkish, fearing that their speakers would feel too connected amongst themselves and, above all, too closely connected to Turkey. Turkey has the opposite policy: it classifies the languages of these populations as varieties of the Turkish language, and refers to the people who speak them as Turks – for example, the language and the people of Azerbaijan, in Turkish, are usually termed, respectively, Azerbaijani Turkish (*Azeri Türkçesi*) and Azerbaijani Turks (*Azeri Türkler*). Some Moldovans, well aware that their territory (Besarabia) is by many Romanians considered Romanian, have long insisted that there is a Moldovan language distinct from Romanian; Moldova's national anthem, *Limba noastrā* 'Our Language', is a hymn to their language – which is, however, Romanian in all but name. Particular efforts to create or emphasize differences between Romanian and Moldovan usage were made under Soviet rule; Soviet linguists championed the notion that there is a Moldovan language, and called attention to parallels between Slavic and Moldovan, probably to legitimize the occupation of Bessarabia, which had seceded from Russia in 1918 and then had merged with Romania, but was occupied by the Soviets in 1940. Some Moldovans are adamant that their language is separate from Romanian and that the term *Moldovan language* is justified; in 2003, a Moldovan-Romanian dictionary was published to make the point. When I asked for that book in bookshops in Moldova, however, booksellers laughed at me and told me that such a book could not exist because the language is the same. Now it can be found online. The dictionary (Stati 2003: 6) clearly states what its concern is:

> The rejection of linguonym *Moldovan language* aims at the de-nationalisation of the Moldovans, at their transformation into Romanian masses, who tomorrow or the day after could vote for anything, including the incorporation of the homeland we inherited from our ancestors, Moldova, into a new Greater Romania. This is the final, eminently political goal of the Romanian campaign of annihilation of the Moldovan language … To deny, to forgo the linguonym *Moldovan language* means to deny, to forgo the Moldovan State.[4]

This passage itself is ostensibly in 'Moldovan' (I report the original text, as always, in the footnote), but it could be absolutely identical in Romanian except for one word.[5]

---

[4] 'Discriminarea lingvonimului limba moldovenească urmăreşte deznaţionalizarea moldovenilor, prefacerea lor în toalpă românească, care mîne-poimîne ar vota orice, inclusiv înglobarea ocinei strămoşeşti – a Moldovei în componenţa unei noi Românii Mari. Acesta este ţelul final, "eminamente politic", al campaniei româneşti de anihilare a limbii moldoveneşti … dezicerea, renunţarea de lingvonimul limba moldovenească înseamnă dezicere, renunţarea de Statul Moldovenesc'.

[5] The term *toalpă* 'mass, horde, rabble', which is Slavic (cf. Russian толпа 'crowd, throng, mob'), is not used in Standard Romanian – but it is attested regionally, for example in Bucovina.

Nationalism and language history are not only intertwined but can shape each other. The differences between barely distinguishable languages are sometimes *made* bigger artificially. In these cases, it is not a different language that marks a different people but, conversely, people that make their language different to make themselves distinct. Examples of this process abound. After Norway gained independence from Denmark in 1814, the Norwegian philologist Ivar Aasen, in the late nineteenth century, developed *Nynorsk*, a new standard language for Norway based on the dialects that differed the most from Danish and Swedish. His aim was to stress that Norwegian was distinct from Danish and Swedish and, arguably, that Norway was distinct from Denmark and Sweden, and that the Norwegians were distinct from the Danes and the Swedes. Swedish, on the other hand, adopted the letters <ä> and <ö> where Danish (and now Norwegian) had <æ> and <ø> (e.g. Swedish *bär* 'berry' and *öl* 'beer' for Danish and Norwegian *bær* and *øl*) in order to make Swedish look different and thereby to differentiate the peoples (Vikør 2000: 109). Most linguists, however, consider continental Scandinavian languages as variants of a single language. Indians and Pakistanis who speak what is largely the same language in two varieties, Hindi and Urdu, have been deliberately amplifying the lexical differences between them. Those who wanted to bring the Hindus and the Muslims of northern India together, like Gandhi and Nehru, championed instead the use of Hindustani, the shared base between Hindi and Urdu – in a fashion reminiscent of how some Norwegian linguists had hoped that the two varieties of Norwegian that are now separate standards, *Bokmål* and *Nynorsk*, could gradually merge into a single variety, *Samnorsk* – but it has not happened. The main thing that distinguishes Pakistanis from Indians is religion; Pakistanis have therefore been adding Arabic and Persian elements to Urdu, whereas Indians have been striving to make Hindi more 'pure/correct' (शुद्ध) by bringing it closer to Sanskrit. Urdu and Hindi also use different scripts that are associated with their different religions: Urdu is written in (an extended version of) the Arabic script, while Hindi is written in the Devanāgarī script, which was used for the Hindu scriptures. Many other nations have contemplated increasing the *Abstand* between their language and another language for ideological reasons: Swiss-German speakers occasionally – especially during and immediately after the First World War – considered developing *Schwyzertüütsch* into a 'language', an *Ausbausprache*, so as to be officially autonomous of High German (Germany's German). This, though unlikely to happen, should not be dismissed as unfeasible: Dutch used to be considered a German dialect, and Norwegian used to be considered a Danish one. And, in this game of language differentiation, English is no exception. At the start of the nineteenth century, American lexicographer and nationalist Noah Webster, wanting the United States to be culturally and symbolically more detached from Britain, advocated a distinct orthography for American English, and studiously chose or invented American spellings that would differ from British ones. He turned (to this day) *colour* into *color*, *defence* into *defense*, and *theatre* into *theater*. And the efforts to affirm a distinct national identity through language differentiation, in many countries, continue. Linguistic interventions in modern Croatian, after the 1990s, have been mainly aimed at underscoring differences from Serbian (G. Thomas 1991: 54) and in some cases from Russian (Kordić 2006: 341). Small differences between languages are, on the other hand, happily ignored when they are processed in a way that does not load them with symbolic significance and the attitude, instead of defensive, is friendly. Having previously learnt a bit of Croatian on a short trip to Zagreb, when I used it during my first visit to Serbia I was kindly complimented on my Serbian – just as I was complimented on my Norwegian on my only visit to Norway, when I spoke Swedish, and I was complimented on my Moldovan when, on my only visit to Moldova, I spoke Romanian.

Purism

The most symbolically rich form of language alteration is perhaps the one that goes by the telling name of *purism*: the removal of (perceived) foreign elements, especially from the lexicon. The notion of language 'purity' is based on a conceptualization of languages as autonomous and distinct from one another – and of 'foreign' elements as contaminants. But concerns about purity imply also a correspondence between languages and peoples. The presence of many visibly foreign words in one's language can be experienced as a taint not only in the sense of being defiling but also of being dishonouring, as it usually reflects the (current or past) political ascendancy of a disliked outgroup. In the interaction between two language communities, the one that adopts more words from the other is the one lower in prestige (Myers-Scotton 2006: 209). In our efforts to be non-prescriptive, we should not deny that the eagerness to adopt many foreign terms, even for objects and concepts for which a common native word already exists, often reflects a feeling and a posture of inferiority towards another culture and perhaps state. The identified presence of a strong foreign influence in one's own language is felt by some people to be an affront to their dignity because they see it as a symptom of their collective cultural, social, and perhaps political subordination. This should be borne in mind in order to understand linguistic purism and the zeal of purists.

We do not even need to describe purism at length here, as it is very common. There have been efforts to 'cleanse' one's language of foreign terms and replace them with 'native' words (or seemingly so) in French, German, Welsh, Swedish, Icelandic, Lithuanian, Hungarian, Hebrew, Finnish, Persian, Armenian, Italian, Japanese, Greek, Croatian, Turkish, Tamil, Korean, and – in the nineteenth century – also in English: William Barnes (1878: 55, 61, 76) advocated that English words of French, Latin, or Greek origin be replaced with terms derived from Anglo-Saxon – for example *fragile* with *breaksome*, *democracy* with *folkdom*, *religion* with *faith-law*. To be clear, there was nothing linguistically wrong with the terms that purists of all these languages objected to. The words that Modern Greek purists wanted to expunge because they were Turkish (and which they therefore deemed an embarrassing mark left by centuries of foreign rule), were often the same words that Turkish purists wanted to expunge because they were *not* Turkish, but were from Arabic or Persian: Greeks objected, for example, to *derti* (ντέρτι) 'heartache' because it is from Turkish *dert* 'suffering', and Turks objected to *dert* because it is from Persian *dard* (درد) 'pain' (the purging efforts failed: that word is still used in all three languages).

The other proof that purism was primarily symbolic is that, very often, purists accepted words and phrases as long as they *looked* native, and even created many native-looking words after the model of foreign ones. For instance, Modern Greek *sidiródromos* (σιδηρόδρομος) 'railway', is a term created by combining the Ancient Greek words for *iron* and *road* – but is a calque on foreign terms like German *Eisenbahn* and French *chemin de fer*.[6] Some Modern Greek nationalists have also often boasted that Greek has given so many words to foreign languages, especially technical or medical terms, like *photography, cardiology, telepathy, dermatitis, homeopathy, tracheotomy*, and so forth. The truth is the opposite: these words are, yes, based on *Ancient* Greek roots, but they were made up, usually in the nineteenth century, by German, or French, or English, or Italian scholars with classical training, and later were adopted by Modern Greek in imitation of western European languages. But because they seemed perfectly Greek, they were welcome.

For the same reason, there has also been more tolerance, given their relative inconspicuousness, of semantic borrowings: the meaning of pre-existing native words gets extended to include new meanings found in a foreign word of the same basic meaning. For example, owing to the influence of English in computing, Turkish *uygulama* 'applying, appliance, implementation' and the unrelated Arabic *taṭbīq* (تَطْبِيق), of the same meaning, now also mean 'software application'; Italian *salvare* and Greek *sózo* (σώζω), both meaning 'rescue, salvage', now also mean 'save' in the sense of 'store away electronic data'; Indonesian *jendela* and Hungarian *ablak*, both meaning 'window (in a building)', now also mean 'framed section appearing on a computer screen'; and the word for 'mouse' – the little animal – in many languages (cf. French *souris*, Portuguese *rato*, Russian мышь, Finnish *hiiri*, Hungarian *egér*, Arabic فَأْرَة, Hebrew עַכְבָּר, Vietnamese *chuột*) now also indicates a computer mouse.

There are also many cases of camouflaged borrowing (Zuckermann 2003: 2). For example, Turkish purists resolved to eliminate, among many others, the Ottoman word for 'school', *mektep*, because of its Arabic provenance, and to replace it with a 'pure Turkish' (*öztürkçe*) neologism; what they came up with, apparently starting from the Turkish verbal root *oku-* 'read, study', was *okul*, a word that gained complete acceptance, replacing the older term. But in truth, although the native root *oku-* did play an important role in the deliberate coining of *okul*, the word that was already ringing in the neologizers' ears and that guided their choice was French *école* (English *school*). This does not mean that the latter etymology is correct and true while the other is mistaken and false: the word *okul* derives from two words (cf. Lewis 1999: 44, 117–9).

All these creative modifications and innovative interventions may belie the widespread idea that nationalist and, more generally, prescriptive approaches to language are, by their nature, linguistically conservative and afraid of language change. However, the nationalist approach to language is conservative in a different sense: it usually aims to preserve, restore, or confer a monoethnic timbre to the language, to

---

[6] So also Swedish *järnväg*, Italian *ferrovia*, Hungarian *vasúti*, Irish *iarnród*, Latvian *dzelzceļš*, Georgian რკინიგზა, Finnish *rautatie*, Armenian երկաթուղի, Persian راه آهن, Turkish *demiryolu*, Albanian *hekurudha*, and many others.

safeguard or establish a link with a certain lineage of speakers and writers, and to claim a continuity in national traditions and identity.

Insisting on language boundaries

Divisions between languages, in some interesting respects, are not as real as they may seem. For a start, related languages are often not separated. Many nations insist that their national languages are totally distinct, but the speech of a village can shade into the speech of the next even if there is a border between them. So the Turkic languages form a continuum across countries, as Germanic languages form a continuum, and so do Romance languages, and so do varieties of Arabic, and varieties of Chinese, and branches of Slavic languages. A speaker of standard Italian may, without previous exposure or study, understand Spanish better than Piedmontese or Sicilian, which are ostensibly dialects of Italian. Even if we look only at the standard form of languages, the differences between Turkish and Azerbaijani, Kyrgyz and Kazakh, Hindi and Urdu, Indonesian and Malay, or isiXhosa and isiZulu, let alone between Romanian and Moldovan or Serbian and Croatian, are not bigger than those among the so-called 'dialects' of spoken Chinese, or among the dialects of Ancient Greece, which both ancient scholars and the Ancient Greeks themselves regarded as the same 'language'. The high degree of similarity between Serbian and Croatian is comparable to that between Dutch and Flemish but, as Blommaert and Verschueren (1992: 367) noted, in the former case, the small differences have been touted as a solid reason for separating of the peoples, and in the latter case for uniting them. Two speech varieties such as, say, a Swahili dialect and a Korean dialect may be readily perceived as distinct languages, regardless of whether they are the standard form and have official status, because of the inherent differences between them, which make them mutually unintelligible. They are *Abstandsprachen*, different languages by virtue of their structural and lexical distance from each other. But two other speech varieties – say, Swedish and Norwegian – may be very similar to each other and be bestowed the status of 'languages' because they have been cultivated into fully fledged 'languages' by expanding their vocabulary, multiplying their registers, extending their functions, and standardizing their use: they are *Ausbausprachen*, languages labelled as such owing to that process of development.

An eagerness to keep languages separate is also clear in traditional attitudes to code-switching, the blending of two languages in the same exchange or even sentence. This is a widespread feature of the speaking style of many bilingual communities, notably of many linguistic minorities within a state, but it has been particularly condemned as ignorant and dysfunctional, as it has been taken to indicate defective mastery of both languages. And for a long time, an advanced, though perhaps not perfect, command of two languages was pathologized as intellectually and emotionally impoverishing 'semilingualism' (*halvspråkighet* – cf. Hansegård 1968: 58). Code-switching has only in recent decades come to be recognized as exceptionally nuanced, pragmatically rule-governed, and as serving well a number of sociolinguistic and metalinguistic functions. For example, it used to be thought that code-switching was random and without norms or constraints, but both general and community-specific constraints have been identified. Speakers know when to switch and which switch is permissible and indeed appropriate, although they can transgress for effect.

And intrasentential switching usually presupposes mastery of the languages involved. Above all, the main function of code-switching is not to compensate for inadequate proficiency or for lexical gaps; it is to add to the linguistic meaning, a bit like prosody and gestures do. Switching language is a deft shift in discursive gear and can serve many purposes, such as marking a change in topic or tone or register, hinting at one's attitude towards what is being said, adding intimacy, or distance, or authority, or humour. It enables the speaker to target distinct interlocutors (singling out some and perhaps excluding others), or to address the same interlocutor but in a different role, or to signal solidarity and group membership – for instance, asserting one's identity as, say, not only British, not only Indian, but as British Indian. Many 'mixed-heritage' individuals often report that their being bilingual is essential for them to claim a dual national identity that otherwise would be contested or denied (Pao, Wong, and Teuben-Rowe 1997: 626). In that light, the linguistic behaviour of bilinguals, as can be seen in many linguistic minorities, is not just an amalgam of two strands, not the mix-up of two 'real' languages, but the creation of a new code, a distinct *novum* emerging from that amalgam, which can then become the unstated norm in their social circle, and therefore become a mark of group membership. Indeed, bilinguals are known to code-switch primarily in informal conversations with interlocutors who share their background more than at a linguistic level (Hoffmann 1991: 113). A number of academics describe this as 'translanguaging', because those who speak in this way disregard the standard boundaries between different languages not out of laziness, carelessness, or inability to express themselves well in either language but, on the contrary, 'to maximize communicative potential' (García 2009: 140); they draw deftly, *ad hoc*, from their whole communicative repertoire (cf. Creese et al. 2018: 842). The fact that, to them, the two language systems are not separate and watertight, highlights that the concept of 'a language' as a discrete entity can be, at least to a degree, an abstraction and a (political and) cultural construction. Some researchers who studied the use of multiple languages in practice have abandoned the view of languages as distinct and bounded entities (cf. Blackledge and Creese 2016: 273–4). But the apparent fusion of two languages, the blurring of their distinctions, is considered by many others to be utter linguistic chaos.

There is also a disinclination to recognize the mixed nature of individual languages, a disinclination that is reflected in the way languages are classified. English is routinely classified as a Germanic language although it has lost a large part of its distinctly Germanic syntax and morphology, and well over half of its vocabulary is of Latin and French derivation. Especially in the 'higher' registers, the Latin/French component of English is more than double the Germanic. The classification of English as Germanic does not stem from political aims but simply from a traditional approach to language study focused on history; however, the classification of languages does have political ramifications. To focus on one example: the main language of today's Israel is normally described as 'Hebrew' or, at most, as 'Modern Hebrew', as if it were the same language as Ancient Hebrew or had descended from it through an unbroken chain of living speakers, in the way that Modern Arabic, Modern Greek, Modern Armenian, or Modern Tamil have gradually developed from their ancient counterparts. But Hebrew died out as a living spoken language in the third century CE, although a passive reading knowledge of it remained widespread among Jewish men. Hebrew was revived and expanded (revernacularized) into a living modern language owing to a movement that started in the 1880s. The link between Ancient Hebrew and 'Modern Hebrew', besides being artificial, has at least two complications. One is that there is uncertainty about what Ancient Hebrew was really like: the ancient texts that we read have a slightly checkered genealogy (they underwent an extensive selective editorial process), and they originally comprised only consonants: diacritics indicating the vowels and some suprasegmental features were added only starting in the seventh century BCE. The second, more important, issue is that the revivers of Hebrew inevitably infused the new language with the structure and usage of their native languages. Only few daring voices have called attention to this: Wexler (1990: 99) propounded, in essence, that 'Modern Hebrew' is a translation (a relexification) of Yiddish (and that Yiddish was Slavic relexified as German), and concluded that 'Modern Hebrew' cannot be classified as a Semitic language. More recently, it has been also suggested that it should be called 'Israeli' rather than Hebrew (Zuckermann 2008: *passim*), to reflect more accurately its nature. The furore caused by these suggestions was certainly not confined to the ivory towers of academia, because their implications are not just philological: the use of 'Hebrew' by (Jewish) Israelis unifies them and, above all, helps them legitimize their contested presence and power in Palestine by indicating a link betweem them and the ancient Israelites. Supporters of Zionism often point out that the Jewishness of the land of Israel is proven by the coin, seals, and texts written in Hebrew spanning three and a half millennia, which crop up all over the country; to resuscitate (ostensibly, to continue) the use of spoken Hebrew has huge symbolic significance. Yiddish could have been (and, in the opinion of many, was) an obvious choice for a national language of Israeli Jews: it was, as the name implies, a distinctly Jewish language, was widespread, and had a literary tradition. Non-Yiddish speaking Jews deported to Nazi concentration camps found that Ashkenazi Jews did not see them as Jews because they did not know Yiddish (Levi [1962] 1997: I: 102; Levi [1982] 1997: II: 378).[7] Nevertheless, the cachet of Hebrew both among Jews and internationally did not seem to be commensurable to the status of Yiddish, which many did not even regard as a language, and which was appraised by Jews themselves with a mixture of familial affection and embarrassed denigration. Hebrew eventually became a Jewish *lingua franca* in Palestine, but in the early stages, at the end of the nineteenth century, Hebrew was revitalized in towns that were solidly and uniformly Yiddish-speaking (Spolsky 1996: 186) and certainly not in need of a new language; the motivation was ideological. Today, the primacy of 'Modern Hebrew' among Israeli Jews is uncontestable, even if – naturally and inevitably – the language is increasingly different from the idiom of the Torah: Modern Hebrew differs

---

[7]   In Primo Levi's orthography: 'Ihr sprecht keyn Jiddisch: ihr seyd ja keyne Jiden!' and 'Redest keyn yiddish, bist nit keyn yid'.

from Biblical Hebrew in pronunciation, vocabulary, orthography, syntax, word order, the use of verbal forms, idioms, and more besides.

Intolerance towards minority languages

The very presence of a minority language in one's nation state has been described as a problem. Quite a few countries of western and eastern Europe, as well as the United States, have regarded complete linguistic uniformity as important for national cohesion, strength, and peaceful coexistence. Even minor linguistic differences across the country, in a nationalist perspective, are perceived as disagreeable: tests have found that individuals scoring high on ethno-nationalism have less favourable perceptions also of fellow citizens with regional accents (Giles 1972: 168–70). This is in line with a political (and psychological) stance that, more generally, regards a society without intergroup differences as ideal – Blommaert and Verschueren (1992: 362) have termed this attitude *homogeneism*.

After the end of the eighteenth century, in the 'Age of Nationalism', the promotion of a single, standardized, national language both rested on and reinforced a conceptual equation between nation and language (an equation that we will discuss in the next chapter). Many concomitant developments and consequences of this were deplorable. The worst one, arguably, has been that the other languages spoken on the national territory, even those indigenous to the country, often became the object of repressive legislation, and their speakers became the target of hostility. In France, all local languages were declared a threat to national unity; the Abbé Grégoire in 1794 produced a 'Report on the necessity and the means to wipe out *patois* and to universalize the use of the French language'. By *patois*, he meant not only the 'dialects' of French but also other 'languages' – anything from Catalan, Occitan, and Corsican to Breton, Flemish, Basque, and Alsatian. Although the French Revolution was meant to be a victory for the people and for liberal democracy, the truth is that, linguistically, there was more freedom in pre-revolutionary France than after. In Spain, successive governments from the eighteenth century onwards suppressed and vilified any indigenous languages other than Castilian (what is, quite significantly, usually simply known as Spanish); they attacked Basque, Galician, and especially Catalan, numerically the most substantial minority language. Persecution was particularly fierce under the long dictatorship of General Franco, who reportedly referred to Catalan as *la lengua de perros*, 'dogs' language'; but even today the friction between Spanish and Catalan speakers continues. In Britain, Welsh was forbidden in schools in 1870; it was only as late as 1993 that Welsh and English obtained fully equal legal recognition and public services were instructed to treat the two languages on the same footing. Britain strove also to eradicate Irish Gaelic, as several strongly worded laws attest. In the territory that is now Italy, after an Italian state was created in the late nineteenth century, books began to appear advocating the abolition of languages other than Italian as necessary for the making of the nation. The Italian Constitution (Art. 6) did pledge the safeguard of linguistic minorities with apposite laws, but the state started forcefully promoting Italian over the *dialetti*, a term which usually included also varieties of Romance regarded by their speakers and by many linguists as separate languages, such as Sardinian and Ladin. In the Fascist era, the state's attitude hardened; all questions about languages were removed from the census, indigenous languages other than Italian (e.g. French, Croatian, German, Albanian, Romany, Slovene, Occitan, Catalan, Provençal, Greek) were banned from schools, the press, and tombstones, and Italian speakers were settled in non-Italian speaking areas. Pseudo-scientific 'research' was produced that aimed at proving that people who spoke languages other than Italian were originally Italian, or at least that the territory where they now lived was originally Italian (Salvi 1975: 72). In Nordic countries such as Norway and Finland, by the end of the nineteenth century, the Sámi language ('Lappish') started being suppressed; there were improvements only in the second half of the nineteenth century, and significant legislation protecting the Sámi language came only in the early 1990s. By then, most Sámi speakers had switched to the national language of the country that they inhabited.

The United States, among developed countries, is a case worth lingering on, because almost the entire population of the country either descends from or consists of immigrants. It is a nation born multiethnic, and originally multilingual; and yet, in keeping with the language=nationality equation, Americanness came to be equated with monolingualism, and largely continues to be. Native American languages were suppressed early on, with particular ferocity – despite the fact that they were, in a sense, more truly American than English is. European languages – some of which were once widely spoken in the United States – were initially allowed to prosper. When Ronald Reagan, in his 1981 address to the Congressional City Conference of the National League of Cities, stated that bilingual education programmes aiming at preserving the native language of immigrants are 'absolutely wrong and against the American concept', he was not just being narrow-minded but also historically inaccurate: in the United States, large-scale rejection of bilingualism has been a late development. In the eighteenth and nineteenth centuries, multilingualism was accepted in the United States as a national reality, and bilingual education, notably in German, had flourished. Only in the late nineteenth century did overt opposition to the multilingualism of immigrants start in earnest. The least multilingual century in US history has been the twentieth, and not by chance. From the 1880s on, there was a massive immigration of speakers of a variety of other languages to the United States; an Immigration Commission formed by Congress explicitly concluded, in 1911, that immigration from southern and eastern Europe threatened US culture and needed to be curbed, and that language tests should be introduced. President Theodore Roosevelt in 1919 stated:

[W]e have room for but one language here ... we have room for but one loyalty ... we have but one flag. We must learn one language and that language is English.

From 1924, a series of US Immigration Acts, over forty years, favoured immigration from the British isles and northern Europe, blocking most immigration from southern and eastern Europe, and forbidding altogether immigration from East Asia and India. This strengthened the primacy of English in the United States. The drive against other languages peaked after the First World War: German was the second largest language in the United States but, during that war, anti-German sentiment soared; after the war, the teaching of foreign languages was drastically restricted in most US states (Pavlenko 2002: 178–9). Becoming part of the American nation meant conforming to a single typology; homogeneity was deemed good, and was expected at all levels; a well-known American sociologist of the time, Pratt Fairchild (1926: 141, 144, 154), saw this clearly and totally approved:

> [T]he elements or qualities of nationality ... are – language, religion, political ideas, moral standards, economic abilities, dress, recreation, food, ornamentation, family customs, all sorts of habits, traditions, beliefs, and loyalties. In all of these particulars the immigrant must be transformed into the type of the receiving nationality ... Can languages be mixed? ... in the sense that the mixing of languages may be a device for group harmonization under modern conditions the answer is emphatically no! ... [the immigrant] must undergo the entire transformation; the true member of the American nationality is not called upon to change in the least. The traits of foreign nationality which the immigrant brings with him are not to be mixed or interwoven. They are to be *abandoned*.

Even in the late twentieth century, a number of US states held referenda on giving primacy or official status to the English language, or on restricting bilingual education; and, in most cases, the measures were ratified. In the twenty-first century, campaigns to make the United States monolingual are continuing. In Washington, there are powerful and active lobbies such as *ProEnglish* and *US-English*, which champion the exclusive official use of English in the United States. The US Immigration and Nationality Act already stipulates that knowledge of English is a pre-requisite for US naturalization.[8] Similar language requirements exist also in Britain, Switzerland, the Netherlands, and many other countries of immigration.

The expectation that, barring unusual circumstances, one should learn, at least to a functional degree, *also* the most common language of the country in which one comes to live long-term is not unreasonable. This has not been the whole message, however. In the twentieth century, the insistence on proficiency in the main national language was often fused with a pathologization of bilingualism. Despite the fact that bilinguals are the majority of the world's population, which makes bilingualism statistically the norm, parents used to be advised that a second language would confuse and hold back their children. As late as 1998, an advert by *US-English* (quoted by Davis 2001: 139) described bilingual education as 'child abuse', proclaiming that it is bound to 'deprive', 'handicap', and 'restrict' children. There are indications that, on the contrary, it is this attitude that causes pupils from minority-language homes to underachieve at school, with repercussions in their self-image and career prospects (even pupils who speak a non-standard version of the national language have often been classified as intellectually deficient). Some evidence

---

[8] Title III, Act 312. [8 U.S.C. 1423]: '(a) No person except as otherwise provided in this title shall hereafter be naturalized as a citizen of the United States upon his own application who cannot demonstrate: (1) an understanding of the English language, including an ability to read, write, and speak words in ordinary usage in the English language'.

leads linguists to recommend that the home language be used in schools at least in the first years, while introducing the country's main language as a second language; pupils in schools with such a system reportedly learn both languages better than pupils with a minority home language who are sent to schools where only the national language is used (Appel and Muysken 1987: 61–3). But, across the world, schools very rarely use a minority language as language of instruction, even as a means to introduce the national language. The expectation is that pupils should adapt to the school system and not the other way round, and this does not surprise any of us, given our own prescriptivist schooling (Bortone 2009: 75).

The fears underlying the opposition to alloglossy

Several considerations confirm that antipathy to minority languages is likely to be a proxy for a different worry or prejudice. If members of the dominant, mainstream ethno-linguistic group learn also another language as part of their adult education, their knowledge and occasional use of that language is usually not considered a problem. Indeed, it is normally seen as skilful, handy, cool, and professionally qualifying. If, however, an ethnic community who may even have learnt also the national language of its adoptive country to a sufficient degree (so that there are, in the main, no communication problems), retains and uses extensively its 'ethnic' language – as Mexicans in the United States do, for example – some people find this kind of bilingualism unacceptable and unsettling. It is taken to signal that such community, which is settled and expanding in the new country, is preserving and perhaps spreading its different way of being. Only if one dreads the thought that ethnic minorities may gradually achieve some political and social power can the spread of their languages seem so threatening (cf. Padilla and Borsato 2010: 13). At the root of the opposition to bilingualism, besides misinformation and ethnocentrism, is a feeling of weakness, and therefore an anxiety about disempowerment, diminishment, and gradual erasure. One concern often expressed in the United States is that English will be overwhelmed by Spanish; but fearing for the future of English in the United States is irrational. Spanish in the United States appears growing and resistant, but this is because it is currently reinforced by additional immigrants. It might not last across generations: where Spanish speakers have settled for generations, English appears to win. Practically all immigrant minorities in the United States lose their language by the third generation (Fishman 1989: 644–5). Indeed, speakers of other languages in the United States are jettisoning their original language faster than ever (Wiley 2001: 99). In Canada or Australia too (Cavallaro 2005: 561), English has been expanding at the expense of the other languages: both aboriginal and immigrants' languages show a steep decline. In small communities under pressure, a hyper-protective attitude to one's language would not be surprising; for instance, in Switzerland, the Rumantsch speakers nowadays are only about 44,000, and the motto of their organization *Uniun dals Grischs* is 'among Rumantschs, only Rumantsch (should be spoken)'.[9] But in the United States there is no need to protect English from any other languages.

Why are apprehension and wariness triggered specifically by bilingualism? The multilingualism of many Jews, for example, prompted disapproval and suspicion; Hitler noted in his *Mein Kampf* (1925: I: 172) that Jews were the ones who spoke the highest number of languages[10] – an ability that he clearly found irritating and suspect. Bilinguals, given their ability to have exchanges unintelligible to others, to function well in an alien community, and to signal another group allegiance if they so choose, have often been thought to be likely turncoats, double agents, and plotters. An attitude of antipathy or diffidence towards bilinguals, we should note, is not just a product of modern nationalism: the Ancient Greeks appear to have considered bilinguals and interpreters untrustworthy and shady: they thought it was unclear where their political loyalties lay and which moral code they followed. Among the Romans too, bilinguals and their environment were often perceived as inherently duplicitous and traitorous.[11] Foreigners known for their multilingual skills, such as the Carthaginians, were considered dodgy (Adams 2003b: 755). The etymon of the term *bilingual* itself, the Latin word *bilinguis*, had negative connotations: it could mean 'two-faced, deceitful, treacherous'. And there are other ancient cultures that saw bilinguals in the same suspicious light (cf. Asheri 1983: 22).

There is another belief that leads people to feel that, while it is a good thing if their nation has a language of its own, it is a bad thing if the minorities who live in the same country have a language of their own too. A shared language in a group is frequently believed to give to it cohesion, strength, autonomy, and the ability to challenge the powerful. This belief is adumbrated already in the Biblical story of Babel (Genesis 11: 6–7): a united population in the kingdom of Nimrod (a name popularly reinterpreted as deriving from the Hebrew root *m-r-d* indicating insurrection) sets out to build a tower as high as Heaven; God notes that they are linguistically united and surmises that their daring act is therefore only a beginning with no end; he then punishes and weakens them by making them linguistically mixed:

> And said the Lord: 'Behold, [the] people [is] one, and a single language [is] to all of them; and this they begin to do: and now will not be impeded from them all that they have thought to do. Right, let's-descend, and confound there their language, that won't man understand the language of another'.[12]

The Biblical story of Babel thus describes multilingualism as a scourge and a handicap that hampers coordinated collective activity. It implies that a single shared

---

[9] 'Tanter Rumanschs, be rumansch!'.
[10] 'die Juden ... die meisten Sprachen sprechen'.
[11] Cf. e.g. in Verg. Aen. 1.661: 'domum timet ambiguam Tyriosque bilinguis'.
[12] וַיֹּאמֶר יְהוָה הֵן עַם אֶחָד וְשָׂפָה אַחַת לְכֻלָּם וְזֶה הַחִלָּם לַעֲשׂוֹת וְעַתָּה לֹא־יִבָּצֵר מֵהֶם כֹּל אֲשֶׁר יָזְמוּ לַעֲשׂוֹת הָבָה נֵרְדָה וְנָבְלָה שָׁם שְׂפָתָם אֲשֶׁר לֹא יִשְׁמְעוּ אִישׁ שְׂפַת רֵעֵהוּ

language would foster unity and common purposes, and that God made humanity multilingual to avoid his power being challenged. In human history, it is certainly true that language differences have often been exploited, or encouraged, in order to limit the cohesion and strength of populations that one wanted to control or subdue. For instance, the nationalist government in South Africa used to support the use of the many local 'Black' languages; this may have seemed surprisingly democratic, but the aim was to prevent the consolidation of large blocks of non-White populations. It was a linguistic *divide-and-rule* policy. In the meantime, Afrikaans (the language grown out of the speech of the white Dutch colonists) was being promoted as the national language of South Africa. In a similar vein, enslaved Africans in the United States were mixed with speakers of other languages to forestall collective resistance or rebellion (Wiley 2010: 305). When the United States seized new territories on the southwest, in the nineteenth century, the government specifically set state borders in a way that would split Spanish-speaking communities and create an English-speaking majority (Nieto 2009: 62). The perception that multilingualism is only a sociopolitical weakness still has currency in the United States. Bob Dole, Senate majority leader, addressing the 77th National Convention of the American Legion in 1995, said:

> With all the divisive forces tearing at our country, we need the glue of language to help hold us together. We must stop the practise of multilingual education as a means of instilling ethnic pride.

The idea that multilingualism naturally prevents unity and leads to conflict has a long history in Western thought; as Kant (AA VIII 367) opined:

> Nature ... uses two means to stop peoples from mixing and to isolate them: the dissimilarity of languages and of religions, which do carry with themselves a propensity for mutual hatred and a pretext for war.[13]

The US Ambassador to Denmark, Edward Elton, declared in 1997 that 'the most serious problem for the European Union is that it has so many languages, this preventing real integration and development of the Union' (Phillipson 2003: 1). Underneath that sentiment, there is not only the assumption that monolingualism is how things were meant to be, but also – most importantly – the assumption that the language that should prevail over the others, and would be the natural and most suited medium for everyone, is *our* language, whatever that happens to be. Voltaire, in his satirical story *L'ingénu* (1767: 9) portrayed the French upper-class as musing on multilingualism and on the Babel story over dinner:

---

[13] 'die Natur ... bedient sich zweier Mittel, um Völker von der Vermischung abzuhalten und sie abzusondern, der Verschiedenheit der S p r a c h e n und der R e l i g i o n e n, die zwar den Hang zum wechselseitigen Hasse, und Vorwand zum Kriege bei sich führt'.

They discussed about the multiplicity of languages a little, and they concurred that, had it not been for that muddle with the Tower of Babel, the whole earth would have spoken French.[14]

Rejecting the language of the 'other' – but not always

If a language is perceived as expressing the identity and power of a disliked 'other', its adoption, even just in part, is likely to be opposed or resisted, especially if that 'other' is judged to be already too close or too strong for comfort. In the early 2000s, several Romanians explained to me, totally unprompted and with pride, that they did not know any Russian whatsoever – though, at the same time, they were pleased to show their proficiency in English. Many Greek-Cypriots, when the possible terms of a reunited Cyprus have been discussed, have been aghast at the idea that their offspring might be taught also some Turkish at school. Children of immigrants, not infrequently, avoid using or downplay their knowledge of their family's language, either to resist the implicit pressure from their parents to identify with their ancestral background, or to forestall intimations from their peers that they are too 'foreign' to be part of their in-group.

However, a very different response to foreign languages is possible. A foreign language is sometimes recognized as the vehicle of a high culture, and its unmatched prestige is accepted. In ancient Rome, such language was Greek: the Romans, despite their high view of themselves, vied to hire Greek instructors, and in a few authors we find instances of code-switching between Latin and Greek (cf. Chahoud 2004: 9–29). For Medieval western Europeans, the higher language was Latin, and intellectuals even liked to give a Latin form to their names, as we noted in Chapter 1. In eighteenth-century Europe, the language of prestige was French: at the German, Danish, or Russian courts, French was *the* language, and the élite of many Western countries used to code-switch between French and their national language, in speech as in writing; some of the best Russian authors, like Tolstoy or Pushkin, interspersed French in their works. The pundits who pathologized bilinguals, as in twentieth-century America, besides being misguided and unfair, were therefore also myopic: they associated the (intermixed) use of another language only with foreign immigration, and therefore with economic poverty, social subordination, and with cultures, nationalities, and ethnicities that they deemed second-class. They did not consider the 'horizontal' communities of highly educated, socially dominant aristocracies in other parts of the world, whose enviable position was partly symbolized and maintained through the use of multiple (usually prestigious) languages.

---

[14] 'On disputa un peu sur la multiplicité des langues, & on convint que, sans l'aventure de la Tour de Babel, toute la terre aurait parlé Français'.

In other words, speaking with code-switches and interjecting a profusion of loanwords, if it involves a language highly rated, does not elicit opprobrium – at least not by all those who have some admiration for such a language, and at times even a lurking sense of inferiority for their own native tongue. It all depends on how the use of a different language is interpreted by them. In some countries, in my experience, the locals who have xenophobic attitudes often respond more positively to you if you address them in English – a foreign language to them – than in their own language: this is because, if you only speak to them in good English, they think that you are an educated tourist on a brief visit from some country they respect, who cannot be expected to know their language; but if you speak to them in their language, though imperfectly, they think that you are a resident immigrant from some poor country they look down on, and this may dispose them far less favourably towards you, even though it spares them the inconvenience of having to answer, perhaps with difficulty, in a foreign language.

More tolerance in pre-national times

Objections to the use of foreign languages were sporadically raised also in the distant past: the Roman Emperor Tiberius (who reigned 14–37 AD) once objected to a Greek word used in a senate decree, and affirmed that instead of a foreign term, a native should be sought.[15] Emperor Claudius (who reigned 41–54 AD) once put a question, in the Senate, to a Lycian man who had long become a Roman citizen; seeing that this man did not understand him and did not know Latin, he stripped him of Roman citizenship, saying that someone who could not understand what was being said could not be a Roman.[16] Code-switching between Latin and Greek was not rare, but those who chastised it were finding it pretentious rather than ignorant or slovenly (cf. Adams 2003b: 19–20). Indeed, Claudius himself, on another occasion, referred to both Latin and Greek as 'our languages'.[17] Whatever the meaning of these isolated episodes, there was no set policy and no laws about language use. As we noted before, in the Roman Empire, the language was not legally imposed on the conquered populations. In ancient Rome and Greece, furthermore, despite all the attention given to language by grammarians, rhetoricians, writers, and philosophers, there were no state-sponsored academies systematically inventing 'native' words to replace foreign ones. Such academies, on the other hand, have been established, for example, in France, Sweden, Italy, Canada, Iran, Croatia, Turkey, the Philippines, India, and Korea; and their

---

[15] Suet. Tib. 71: 'commutandam censuit uocem et pro peregrina nostratem requirendam ... militem quoque Graece testimonium interrogatum nisi Latine respondere uetuit'.

[16] Suet. Cl. 16:4: 'splendidum uirum Graeciaeque prouinciae principem, uerum Latini sermonis ignarum, non modo albo iudicum erasit, sed in peregrinitatem redegit'. So also in D.C.60.17.4: 'ἐν τῷ βουλευτηρίῳ ἐπύθετο τῇ Λατίνων γλώσσῃ τῶν πρεσβευτῶν τινος, Λυκίου μὲν τὸ ἀρχαῖον ὄντος Ῥωμαίου δὲ γεγονότος· καὶ αὐτόν, ἐπειδὴ μὴ συνῆκε τὸ λεχθέν, τὴν πολιτείαν ἀφείλετο, εἰπὼν μὴ δεῖν Ῥωμαῖον εἶναι τὸν μὴ καὶ τὴν διάλεξιν σφων ἐπιστάμενον'.

[17] Suet. ibid. 42.2: 'cuidam barbaro Graece ac Latine disserenti: «cum utroque» inquit «sermone nostro sis paratus»'.

underlying concern is not just linguistic: the English slogan of the *National Institute of the Korean Language* is 'people make words, and words make the people'. In pre-modern times, there was, broadly speaking, usually no formal expectation that you should know the language of the state you were in. In the Ottoman Empire too, the authorities were quite relaxed about the linguistic heterogeneity of the population. They rewarded those with multilingual skills with prominent jobs and positions; the Ottoman language itself was a mixture of Turkish, Arabic, and Persian, and this was not a source of concern. The Austro-Hungarian Empire too had no problem with the native use of other languages in its territory; only in its final stages did it become more oppressive. The early years of the Soviet Union were also fairly tolerant. There too, hostility towards languages other than Russian (and to alphabets other than Cyrillic) was a relatively late development.

Campaigners for the national language

There is another fascinating paradox in the nationalist promotion of the national language. As we saw, being a speaker of the national language came to be treated as the pre-requisite for the required identification with the nation, and being a speaker of another language was considered evidence of different loyalties and traitorous views. But campaigners for the national language were themselves often the tacit demonstration that this was not true. A case that shows this particularly well is that of Swedish in Finland. Finnish nationals (in Swedish called *finländare*) are broadly divided into two groups: the overwhelming majority, the Finnish-speaking Finns (in Swedish called *finnar*) and a minority of Swedish-speaking Finns (in Swedish called *Finlandssvenskar*). Their Swedish is different but mutually intelligible with the standard Swedish of Sweden (*Rikssvenska*); Finnish, on the other hand, is unrelated and radically dissimilar from Swedish. Finland was annexed to the Kingdom of Sweden in the thirteenth century, and remained part of Sweden for six centuries. Swedish, being the language of the rulers, the administration, and the educated class, became also the language of education. Swedish in Finland was therefore not only the prestige language of the ruling minority, but the only official language of the country, even after Finland ceased to be under the Swedish crown; Finland was then conquered by Russia in 1809, and gained independence only in 1917, at the time when nationalist ideology was spreading across Europe. Already under Russian sovereignty, the use of Finnish had been actively encouraged by the Russian authorities so as to weaken the previous long-standing cultural connection with Sweden. The trend towards emphasizing the difference between Finns and Swedes grew stronger after independence, since Swedes had come to be seen as despots. Only in 1902, after a lively struggle, did Finnish begin to be accepted as one of the national languages of Finland (note that the name of the Finnish language, *suomi*, is also the name of the country); and it was fully recognized by the country's Constitution only in 1919. What is especially noteworthy is that Finnish nationalism and the successful promotion of Finnish as the national language at the expense of Swedish were spearheaded by the cultured élite that was primarily Swedish-speaking and usually of Swedish origin. Its members, when Finnish nationalism took off, switched to Finnish not only in their writing but also in their daily usage. Among the ethnically Swedish aristocracy, several families also changed their Swedish family names to Finnish ones. This nominal change of ethnicity has a further complicating twist, in that some of the families that jettisoned their Swedish surname for a Finnish one had had a Finnish surname originally, generations before, which they had sloughed off in order to be upwardly mobile. With the advent of nationalism in Finland, very many Swedish-speaking Finns passionately espoused the national(ist) cause to the point of being known as *fennomaner* 'Finno-maniacs'. To start with one of the most famous Finns: Jean Sibelius, still known today internationally for his patriotic musical compositions, spoke exclusively Swedish at home; he only started to learn Finnish late in school, and remained more proficient in Swedish all his life. The painter Akseli Gallén-Kallela, who painted scenes from the Kalevala (a visual parallel to Sibelius) and is reckoned to have been pivotal in Finnish nationalism, was also a native Swedish speaker. Johan Ludvig Runeberg, the man traditionally considered the national poet of Finland (much admired by Sibelius), wrote most of his work in Swedish, his native language, including what became the Finnish national anthem – once it was translated into Finnish. That hymn was set to music by 'the father of Finnish music', Fredrik Pacius, who was also part of Swedish-speaking circles, and was German-born. Johan Vilhelm Snellman, the main campaigner for the Swedish-speaking Finnish *intelligentsia* to learn Finnish, and for Finnish to be given official recognition on a par with Swedish, was not only a Swedish-speaker but also Swedish-born. The key figures of Finnish nationalism were thus not ethnic Finns; in some cases they were even foreign-born. Parallels in other countries are easily found. Eliezer Ben Yehuda, the main proponent of the re-vernacularization of Hebrew, is known as the father of Modern Hebrew; the mother tongue of Ben Yehuda, however, and of many other supporters of the adoption of Hebrew in Israel, was Yiddish – the main rival language. Several national leaders have been speakers of another language. Napoleon, who became French Emperor and fought for France's expansion, was a native speaker of Corsican and Italian, not French. Stalin was a native speaker of Georgian, not Russian; he spoke the latter with a thick accent, but promoted Russian resolutely, and even defined the concept of 'nation' putting language first (Hobsbawm 1992: 5 n11).

Linguistic differences, therefore, are often not *per se* what matters; the meaning attributed to those differences is what matters. This takes us to the last chapter, on the link between language and nationality.

11

Language and nationality, a hasty equation

Equating language and nationality

We have talked about the twin development of nations and their languages, and about the practical and symbolic role given to languages in a national framework (often in contrast with pre-national days). Languages have frequently been used as a principle for the ethnic classification of people – and not only by nationalist movements. Language doubtlessly *can* be a marker of nationality and ethnicity; but the evidence that this need not be the case, and that it is essential for all to bear this in mind, is compelling. It is time, in this final chapter, to discuss more broadly the link, customarily posited, between language and nationality, and its merits, problems, and consequences.

There is nothing new in the presumption that language usage identifies an ethnicity or, at any rate, a human group that has, reputedly, a common ancestry and perhaps a common culture – which is the most basic understanding of the term *ethnicity*. Nor is there anything new in the fact that, alas, people may treat you either favourably or unfavourably depending on the ethnicity that your use of language is thought to indicate. Another Biblical story (Judges 12: 6) illustrates both points. The Gileadites, in order to identify and kill the Ephraimites – the members of another tribe – relied on the fact that the latter had a different dialect; the Gileadites would therefore stop any man they thought might be an Ephraimite and ask him to pronounce the word *shibboleth* (שִׁבֹּלֶת); if he appeared unable to pronounce /ʃ/, and instead of saying *shibboleth*, said *sibboleth* (סִבֹּלֶת), the Gileadites would identify him as an Ephraimite and slay him.

As regards the idea that each language uniquely identifies a nation, rather than an ethnicity, the earliest expressions of it are routinely traced back (cf. Minogue 1967: 57) to eighteenth-century German romantics, notably Herder, with some possible antecedents in France. Such an idea has, nonetheless, much older roots. For instance, in the Biblical outlook illustrated by the tale of the Tower of Babel, which we discussed in the last chapter, languages take precedence over nations; that story suggests, as Isidore noted in the seventh century AD, that 'peoples have arisen from languages, not languages from peoples'.[1]

Still, there is no question that the idea that a language reflects and pinpoints a nation received unprecedented elaboration, affirmation, and political meaning in the

---

[1] Isid. Orig. 9.1.14: 'prius de linguis, ac deinde de gentibus posuimus, quia ex linguis gentes, non ex gentibus linguae exhortae sunt'.

eighteenth and nineteenth centuries. Condillac not only spoke unhesitatingly about 'the character of a nation', but kept asserting (1746: 197–8, 200, 213, 221):

> The character of peoples influences that of languages ... each language expresses the character of the people that speaks it ... the genius of languages begins to take shape according to that of the peoples ... the character of languages takes shape gradually and in conformity with that of the peoples ... languages, for someone who knew them well, would be a portrayal of the character and the genius of each people.[2]

Even among Germans intellectuals, references to language as a principle for defining oneself as a nation predate Herder. But it is true that, as many sources say, Herder inspired nationalists to focus on language. However, while nationalist movements have often been derogatory of other languages and cultures, and eager to impose their own tongue and way of life on other nations, we should note that Herder's vision was more regardful and nuanced. He was fascinated by ethnography and by the world's diversity of civilizations, outlooks, and languages; and his notion that languages expressed the true nature and creativity of each nation also meant, in his perception, that different languages were owed respect. His conclusion (Herder [1769] 1840: 484–5) was

> that every nation has its riches and peculiarities of spirit, of character, as well as of land; these are to be sought after, to be cultivated ... if another nation is taken blindly as a model, then everything is stifled.[3]

The basic tenet that a language reflects a nation was repeated throughout the nineteenth century. Humboldt (1836: 198–200) stated:

> Every language assumes a certain uniqueness through that of the nation ... Since the development of human nature in people depends on that of the language, it is directly through language that the concept itself of the nation is constituted as that of a cluster of people who configure language in a particular way ... From each language it is thus possible to infer the national character.[4]

---

[2] 'le caractère des Peuples influe sur celui des Langues ... chaque langue exprime le caractère du Peuple qui la parle ... Si le génie des Langues commence à se former d'après celui des Peuples ... le caractère des Langues ... se forme peu à peu & conformément à celui des Peuples ... les Langues, pour quelqu'un qui les connoîtroit bien, seroient une peinture du caractère & du génie de chaque peuple'.

[3] 'daß jede Nation ihre Reichthümer und Eigenheiten des Geistes, des Charakters, wie des Landes hat. Diese sind aufzusuchen, und zu cultiviren ... Wird dies nicht gesucht, wird blindlings eine andre Nation zum Muster genommen, so Alles erstickt'.

[4] 'Jede Sprache empfängt eine bestimmte Eigenthümlichkeit durch die der Nation ... Da die Entwicklung seiner menschlichen Natur im Menschen vor der der Sprache abhängt, so ist durch diese unmittelbar selbst der Begriff der Nation als der eines auf bestimmte Weise sprachbildenden Menschenhaufens gegeben ... Aus jeder Sprache lässt sich daher auf den Nationalcharakter zurück-schliessen ... '

Many nineteenth-century sources make analogous assertions. Böckh (1866: 261–66 et passim) wrote a whole treatise titled *The Statistical Significance of the Language of the People as Indicator of Nationality*, arguing that it is language, rather than citizenship, or lifestyle, or physical features, that shows nationality.

One needs to understand the cultural context of this: at that time, it was even claimed that a language is so specific and intrinsic to an ethnicity that people of one ethnicity are inherently, physically unable to learn the language of another. Some pundits did realize and concede that acquiring the language of another ethnicity was possible, but considered it unnatural. Several nationalists propounded not only that each language is specifically suited to a particular ethnicity or nation, but also that to adopt another language is a distortion of one's world, a violence to one's mind, and a misuse of one's anatomy. The Irish writer Thomas O. Davis (1846: 173–4, 176–8) was adamant:

> The language, which grows up with a people, is conformed to their organs, descriptive of their climate, constitution, and manners, mingled inseparably with their history and their soil … To impose another language on such a people is to … corrupt their very organs, and abridge their power of expression … How unnatural – how corrupting 'tis for us, three-fourths of whom are of Celtic blood, to speak a medley of Teutonic dialects [i.e. English] … Nothing can make us believe that it is natural or honourable for the Irish to speak the speech of the alien, the invader.

Even Schleicher (1865: 12–13, 16), a renowned philologist acquainted with several languages, did not believe that full bilingualism or the native acquisition of the language of another 'race' was possible:

> Above all, the question is whether a foreign language is ever at all acquired [natively] fully. I doubt this … For a start, show me the person who thinks and speaks completely equally in German and Chinese … I do not think that one such exists … A German … he will never speak a Negro language by birth.[5]

Such an essentialist view is often expressed by small children, who assume that babies adopted at birth will nevertheless speak the language of their biological parents. And yet, Schleicher was not the only linguist misled by the assumptions of his time.

The equation in philology

The conceptual equation between language and ethnicity or nationality was paradoxically strengthened by the development of comparative philology. In the late

---

[5] 'Vor allem fragt es sich, ob überhaupt jemals eine fremde Sprache vollkommen angeeignet wird. Ich bezweifele dies … Man zeige mir aber erst den Menschen, der vollkommen gleich im Deutschen und in Chinesischen … denkt und spricht. Ich glaube nicht, dass es einen solchen gibt … Ein Deutscher … eine Negersprache wird er aber von Hause aus niemals reden'.

eighteenth century, it became common knowledge that most European languages stem from the one single prehistorical language. As all British philologists learn, Sir William Jones ([1786] 1807: 34), in a public lecture, called attention to the fact that, among Greek, Latin, and Sanskrit, there was a theretofore little noticed

> stronger affinity, both in the roots of verbs and the forms of grammar, than could possibly have been produced by accident; so strong indeed, that no philologer could examine them all three without believing them to have sprung from some common source, which, perhaps, no longer exists.

To the same source from which Greek, Latin, and Sanskrit sprang, Jones traced also, somewhat more tentatively but correctly, Celtic, Gothic, and Persian. Although Jones's words have been traditionally cited as the revelation that created comparative linguistics, parallels among (what we now call) Indo-European languages had been incidentally spotted long before him, indeed repeatedly; but nobody had had the impact that Jones was going to have. The methods that were eventually developed as a result of his remarks helped scholars trace links of historical derivation among languages – even though, by reading his lectures more extensively, and with the unfair advantage of hindsight, one can see at once that his approach was actually far from the rigorous comparative method of modern philology, that some of his groupings were mistaken, and that inter-lingual influences (horizontal rather than vertical ones, one could say) were underestimated.

Jones's 'discovery', given the particular era in which it occurred, influenced also other areas of scholarship. His goal was not only the classification of languages: the origins and grouping of 'nations' was a topic that exercised him at length. His assumption, then shared by many, was that comparative linguistics provided direct information about the history of 'races', a subject in which the philologists of his time were very interested. Such interest, to them, probably seemed merely descriptive and politically inert; but it could not be either. Jones believed that a connection between two languages indicated a racial link between the populations that spoke them and that, conversely, the lack of a linguistic connection proved a racial distinction. For example, the following year, after comparing Arabic with his beloved Sanskrit, and noticing compelling differences, Jones concluded ([1787] 1807: 52–3) that 'they seem totally distinct, and must have been invented by two different races of men'.

His remark, it should be noted, did not imply any disparagement of Arabic, a language which, he proclaimed, 'yields to none ever spoken by mortals in the number of its words and the precision of its phrases'. There are good reasons for criticizing Jones (cf. Said 1979: 76–8) because he was in India as part of the British colonial enterprise; by pointing out that Sanskrit was related to European languages, he also enabled a reinterpretation of the presence of the British in India 'not as colonialist adventurers pillaging the riches of the East, but as restoring a far-flung, ancient outpost of Aryan civilization' (Harris 2006: 58). Yet the very fact that, in his famous lecture, Jones had described Sanskrit (until then considered merely an exotic language of the alien and inferior Orient) as 'more perfect than the Greek, more copious than the Latin, and more exquisitely refined than either' was altogether daring. Above all, so was Jones' correct suggestion, at a time when language equalled race, that most languages of Europe, of India, and of parts of the Middle East (i.e. Persian and Kurdish) were all members of one family. By his implications, so were the speakers. Today's defenders of Jones argue that he 'radically adjusted pre-conceptions of Western cultural superiority, introducing disconcerting notions of familial relationship between the rulers and their "black" subjects' (Franklin 2011: 37). That might be an overstatement, but it is certain that Jones' admiration for India was not limited to grammar but encompassed many aspects of the Indian intellectual, social, and political tradition; in this too, Jones' stance contrasted with that of many of his contemporaries, who mocked him for it (Momma 1999: 174–5).

The view of the connection between languages and human groups that was developed at that time had misleading effects. The notion that related languages had derived from what was described as an *Ursprache*, a single initial language (e.g. Welsh, Irish, Gaelic, and Cornish had derived from 'Celtic'; Russian, Polish, Czech, and Slovenian from 'Proto-Slavic') fed the perception that such initial languages had been spoken by respective *Urvölker*, distinctive 'initial populations' – what Mühlmann (1985: 15–16) wryly called 'the pseudopeoples of linguistics'. This presupposed that such populations only later, when splitting and dispersing, had mixed with other peoples, and thereby given rise to different daughter languages. However, the posited initial populations, such as 'the Celts' or 'the Slavs', in truth, originally had likewise formed through mergers with others (Ramat 2009: 24). Moreover, as Franz Boas (1911: 11) realized, the notion that 'a certain definite people whose members have always been related by blood must have been the carriers of [a] language through history' is a 'purely arbitrary' assumption. To talk – as it is commonly done – of, for example, the Arab, Vietnamese, or Latvian language and of the Arab, Vietnamese, or Latvian people as matching entities that always, completely, and exclusively co-occurred presupposes that populations did not move, inter-breed, and fuse, and that languages and peoples remained in a neat one-to-one correspondence. This is unlikely to have been the case.

The idea of a common origin for most European languages (though with related languages in India) thus contributed to the development of particular European racial self-concepts. Jones' observation implicitly linked, for instance, Ancient Greek and Latin with German but not with Hebrew – whereas many scholars had, for centuries, grouped Greek and Latin with Hebrew because all three are associated with the Christian Bible, and so had long been deemed the three 'sacred languages'.[6] Franz Bopp (1833: v–vi), in his monumental description of the Indo-European languages, stressed the 'close kinship' of his native Germanic to the prestigious Classical languages, i.e. Greek and Latin, a kinship which had 'gone almost entirely unnoticed' until the appearance of Sanskrit. He also asserted that 'the Semitic languages are of a coarser nature'.[7] Connecting German (philologically) with Latin and Greek, and seeing

---

[6] Cf. e.g. Isid. Orig. 9.1.3: 'Tres sunt autem linguae sacrae: Hebraea, Graeca, Latina'.

[7] 'Die Semitischen Sprachen sind von einer derberen Natur … Die enge Verwandtschaft der klassischen mit den germanischen Sprachen ist … vor Erscheinung des asiatischen Vermittelungsgliedes fast ganz übersehen worden'.

Hebrew as genetically unrelated, was correct; but some extra-linguistic conclusions that were drawn from this were not, and ranged from the innocently fanciful to the odious. Given the existence of an Indo-European 'family' of languages, at that time also called Aryan languages, it was surmised that a distinct and united Indo-European people once existed, from which a distinct Aryan race descended. Europeans were, in that vision, relatives of the glorious Classical Greeks and Romans and heirs of their unparalleled achievements, unlike Jews and others who were identified as racially different – and not in a good way. A cultural critic such as Matthew Arnold (1869: 162), while stressing the 'essential unity of man' and the elements that connect the English (and Americans) with the Jews, felt justified in saying that

> Science has now made visible to everybody the great and pregnant elements of difference which lie in race … Hellenism is of Indo-European growth, Hebraism of Semitic growth; and we English, a nation of Indo-European stock, seem to belong naturally to the movement of Hellenism.

This kind of discourse arguably helped to pave the way for baseless and baleful claims about the genetically-inherited brilliance of Europeans and the need to protect it from racial defilement. At the same time, a truthful and salutary lesson that could have been drawn from historical linguistics was not heeded: languages inevitably change, and this is a normal, eternal, and inevitable process that cannot be seen as overall deterioration. What many regard as the 'proper' form of a language, and strive to preserve on that account, is already the altered version of an earlier form. If we deplore new features appearing, say, in modern French and we consider them 'corruption' of the language of Molière, we should also consider French a corruption of Latin, and Latin a corruption of Indo-European, which would be absurd.

The rise of the equation

As concerns the *political* implications of equating languages with nationalities, it must be noted that, in the so-called 'Age of Nationalism', these were clear from the outset. Fichte (1808: 395), a philosopher influential also in politics, declared:

> It is without doubt true that everywhere where a separate language is found, a separate nation also exists, which has the right to take care of its one's affairs independently, and to govern itself.[8]

This is a rather explosive idea, and it is still with us. That each language group is, by definition, a nation and, as such, ought to have its own government is also a key tenet of modern militant nationalism. As summed up by Kedourie (1993: 62):

---

[8] 'Wie es ohne Zweifel wahr ist, daß allenthalben wo eine besondere Sprache angetroffen wird, auch eine besondere Nation vorhanden ist, die das Recht hat, selbstständig ihre Angelegenheiten zu besorgen und sich selber zu regieren'.

The test, then, by which a nation is known to exist is that of language. A group speaking the same language is known as a nation, and a nation ought to constitute a state.

In the nineteenth century, as new states were being established and developed, language scholars routinely equated language and nation, and the struggle for a population to have its language officially accepted was felt to coincide with the struggle to have its political sovereignty recognized. In the words of Jean Psycharis ([1888] 1971: 23):

Language and fatherland are the same thing. Whether somebody fights for his fatherland or for the national language, the struggle is one.[9]

By the twentieth century, the equation between language and nationality was well-established. Among linguists as much as among sociologists, on both sides of the Atlantic, the same view continued to be affirmed by many. There is no point in listing countless quotations, but let us note that Otto Jespersen (1912: 1, 17), in a book on language still read today, wrote about the 'relation of language to national character', concluding that 'As the language is, so is also the nation'[10]; Max Weber (1922: 224) concurred that a national group is a linguistic community, a *Sprachgemeinschaft*[11]; Pratt Fairchild (1926: 144) insisted that, of the elements that constitute and indicate nationality, 'at the top stands language'.

In nineteenth and twentieth centuries, as many new countries emerged from the crumbling of empires, the importance of languages and, above all, their role as social markers thus increased dramatically. As more peoples embraced the nationalist principles that, in essence, human beings naturally constitute nations and that a nation should have an independent state all to itself, languages were turned into a nationality symbol and a key political reference. The idea was that ethnicities and states should coincide, but also that languages and nations should coincide. As we remarked in the last chapter, modern nations have demanded both ethnic homogeneity and linguistic homogeneity in a way medieval states usually did not, and this played a role in shaping modern nations as we know them.

Western observers often think that the antagonism towards linguistic minorities seen in some non-Western countries proves that these countries are less civilized and modern than 'we' are. But the evidence shows not only that in western Europe there has been, until relatively recently, very little tolerance for minority languages, but also that a specific type of intolerant nationalism has mostly come to those non-Western countries

---

[9] Γλώσσα καὶ πατρίδα εἶναι τὸ ἴδιο. Νὰ πολεμᾷ κανεὶς γιὰ τὴν πατρίδα του ἤ γιὰ τὴν ἐθνικὴ τὴ γλῶσσα, ἕνας εἶναι ὁ ἀγώνας.

[10] It may seem ironic that Sapir (1921: 232–4), contrary to his reputation as the wild champion of the notion that languages dictate a distinct cast of mind, thought that 'It is impossible to show that the form of a language has the slightest connection with national temperament'.

[11] 'Die realen Gründe des Glaubens an den Bestand einer »nationalen« Gemeinsamkeit und des darauf sich aufbauenden Gemeinschaftshandelns sind sehr verschieden. Heute gilt vor allem »Sprachgemeinschaft«, im Zeitalter der Sprachenkämpfe, als ihre normale Basis'.

from Europe. The very idea that the division of humankind that really matters is the one into nations, that each nation has one language intrinsic to it, that each nation should have its own state, and that each state should have a prescriptive language, is primarily a set of western European ideas that came, belatedly, into cultures that – though perhaps illiberal in other ways – often had conceived society and the state differently.

Semantic changes that one can spot in the languages of countries that became nation states sometimes testify to this. Just a couple of examples: in Turkey, in the Ottoman era, the state was an empire, and the population was officially divided into many a *millet*, a term that indicated a community – one of several – defined by religion, whose members could vary in language; now Turkey is a republic, and the term *millet*, which is used to describe the population of Turkey as a singular entity, means 'nation', and indicates a community of people who speak the same language. In Indonesia, pupils are taught the old dictum *bahasa menunjukkan bangsa* 'language indicates nation(ality)'; but the modern understanding of that phrase (indicated in that translation) obscures the fact that both the term *bahasa* and the term *bangsa* have undergone a shift in meaning with the advent of nationalism (Heryanto 2007: 45–8): before, the phrase would have meant something closer to '(good) manners reveal (noble) descent'.

Today, the assumption remains that linguistic groups correspond to self-identified communities with language-based 'identities', allegiances, and political interests. Many modern researchers simply state that language is 'an identifying feature of members of a national ... group' (Lambert et al. 1960: 44), 'a defining characteristic of a nationality' (Fishman 1973: 44), and the 'most plausible' criterion for nationhood (Miller 1995: 22). It has been concluded (Opeibi 2012: 272) that

> There appears to be a general consensus among language scholars all over the world that among symbols and badges of national identity, language remains the most profound, most unique, and the most treasured.

In parallel – and this is relevant to the question of linguistic minorities within a nation – it is said that ethnicity is 'in large part established and maintained through language' (Gumperz and Cook-Gumperz 1982: 7), that language is a 'crucial element' of ethnic identification, a 'critical element' in the meaning of ethnicity, and gives 'meaning' and 'distinctiveness' to an ethnic group (Padilla and Borsato 2010: 12). A position of this kind is taken also by a number of cultural theorists who are themselves from ethnic minorities: 'Ethnic identity is twin skin to linguistic identity' (Anzaldúa 1987: 59). In other fields too, for example economics, language is the most commonly-used ethnicity marker (Grin 2010: 71). It is now indeed common to talk of 'ethnolinguistic identity'. Even academics who study the past, such as classicists, archaeologists and historians, use languages as a criterion of ethnic classification also for ancient civilizations: for example, regardless of other cultural differences or similarities, they classify the Mycenaeans as Greeks, but the Minoans as not Greeks, because of their language. Many other scholars, more broadly, declare language to be *the* criterion for identity in general. David Crystal (2003: 20) stated that the language of a people 'is their identity', indeed (2000: 40) that 'Language is the primary index, or symbol, or register of identity'.

The effects of the equation

Since, in the nation-based outlook, languages are an ethnic or national category, language can be the criterion by which people are informally classified even irrespective of actual ethnicity and nationality. In Canada, Francophone Canadians call English-speaking Canadians simply *les Anglais*, regardless of their appearance, origin, or ethnic background. In South Africa, white individuals are generally classified as either *Afrikaners* or as *English* depending on whether they speak Afrikaans or English – although both groups include people of French, German, or other European extraction. In the United States, peoples of a variety of nationalities are all now called *Hispanics* because of the language that they (are assumed to) speak. The term has even been adopted by some of them as a self-description, although it is a category label that does not exist in most other languages. *Hispanic* is, essentially, a white generalization which lumps together distinct national groups such as Mexicans, Cubans, or Puerto Ricans, and distinct ethnic backgrounds: those classified as 'Hispanic' may have European, Native-American, or African ancestry. For the same reason, some populations in the United States now identify themselves by their language ignoring the racial categorization assigned to them. The Dominicans of the US state of Rhode Island think of themselves as Hispanic because they speak Spanish, although they descend from Africans and are therefore phenotypically like Black or African Americans and are so classified by other Americans (Bailey 2000: 556). Notably, many people that in the United States are classified as 'Hispanics' do not even know Spanish: *Hispanic* is literally a language label that has become a race label.

In curious ways, language is now sometimes treated as having a stronger association with nationality than nationality itself. In March 2008, German Chancellor Angela Merkel, already known as a vocal champion of Israel, was welcomed in Jerusalem on an official visit; this included Merkel addressing the Knesset, the Israeli Parliament. The fact that she was German was not deemed a problem but, even before her speech, language became a hotly contested issue. Some members of the Knesset protested vehemently at the idea that she would use German. When she spoke, Merkel first said a few sentences in Hebrew, to loud applause; but when she switched to her mother tongue – to profess her unflagging support for Israel and to express Germany's contrition for the Holocaust ('die Shoah erfüllt uns Deutsche mit Scham') – some of the Members of the Knesset walked out, angry, as they explained, that Merkel had spoken to them in the language of the Nazis. In Germany itself, where a particular ethnic pedigree, less than a century ago, was deemed absolutely necessary in order to belong at all, there has been a marked shift in perspective: according to recent research (Foroutan et al. 2014: 26), the question 'what is important in order to be German?' was answered with 'being able to speak German' by 96.8% of the respondents, and only 37% said that in order to be German it is important to have German ancestry.

Nowadays, the friction – in some cases over separatist demands – between different ethnic or national groups in various European countries is symbolized by, and often focused on, language: between the Flemings and the Walloons, between the Südtiroler and the Italians, the Corsicans and the French, the Romanians and the Hungarians, the Welsh and the English, the Basques and the Spaniards. This is also true of the frictions between the Québécois and the Anglo-Canadians, the Abkhazians and the Georgians, the Kurds and the Turks. The mere presence of other languages is considered by academics to be a 'key variable' that predicts whether a consolidated state will find itself threatened by separatist demands from one of its regions (Laitin 1988: 289). Anthony Smith (1976: 18), one of the best-known scholars of nationalism, claimed that 'With regard to nationalist movements, language differences have been the chief source of ethnic tensions since the eighteenth century, and every secession movement is fundamentally a linguistic movement'. This axiom, in a nationalist mindset, is also applied backwards: minorities demanding more language rights are typically perceived as secessionist. The ideology that language signals a national allegiance and a national identity is thus doubly hostile to linguistic minorities: not only does it object to them because it would prefer a monolingual community and state, but it also presumes that linguistic minorities think in the same way, and therefore imagines them to be disloyal to the larger community and keen to break up the state and proclaim political independence.

When there is a conflict between national groups, the idea that it might not be an issue of language differences seems hard to grasp for many Western reporters. For example, in the clash between Russia and Ukraine in 2014, some commentators claimed that there was a language communication problem, although Ukrainians understand Russian well, and Russian speakers, even on Ukrainian TV, use their own language without translations. Conversely, frictions between linguistic groups are automatically reported by the Western media as 'inter-ethnic' conflicts (Blommaert and Verschueren 1992: 360). It is true that, in a number of cases, languages have been used as an ethnic/national indicator and therefore as an exclusionary criterion: we have seen examples of this before. To highlight linguistic differences can be a way to suggest that another nationality does not belong in your midst, and to justify its exclusion. The erstwhile French President Valery Giscard d'Estaing referred, albeit very incidentally, to the fact that Turkish is not an Indo-European language when he listed reasons, in an article in *Le Monde*, why Turks, in his view, would not fit in the European Union.[12] In truth, the European Union, already in 1995, had accepted the Finns as members, although their national language is not Indo-European – not to mention indigenous European groups who speak non-Indo-European languages but have no state of their own, such as the Basques and the Sámi. And within two years of Giscard d'Estaing making his remark, three more states whose language is not Indo-European were accepted into the EU without fuss: Estonia (Finnic), Hungary (Ugric), and Malta (Semitic). At the same time, EU membership applications from countries that speak languages that do descend from Indo-European, such as Iran or Pakistan, would probably not have been met favourably – by Giscard d'Estaing or by the EU. One can therefore argue that, in Giscard d'Estaing's argument mentioning language as an indication of an irreconcilable difference was disingenuous, and that the reason for his disquiet at the idea of Turkey joining the EU was to be sought elsewhere. Even so, he apparently felt that his mention

[12] A. Leparmentier and L. Zecchini: 'Pour ou contre l'adhésion de la Turquie à l'Union européenne'. *Le Monde*, 9 November 2002.

of the language could appear sensible and persuasive. We also need to consider that expressing intolerance to other languages appears more socially and politically acceptable than expressing intolerance to other ethnicities, and may also be a way to do so indirectly. Discredited racial categories can return as language categories. Besides, treating language, biological descent, appearance, history, and culture as naturally and inevitably co-occurring traits, and nationality as a whole cluster of such necessary features, helps xenophobic nationalist discourse (Blommaert and Verschueren 1992: 363) because immigrants can never fit the bill entirely and therefore can never, in that view, qualify for acceptance.

There are other ways in which the language=nationality equation encourages distortions of facts for political ends. If a language is treated as intrinsic to a nationality, those eager to claim a separate nationality are under pressure to claim that they have a separate language. Almost two-thirds of Ukrainians declare Ukrainian to be their native language, but less than half of them speak it by preference (Kulyk 2011: 663). The language claimed as mother tongue in a census may therefore be an affirmation of allegiance, rather than a reflection of daily practice. Language, as we have seen time and again, can have a symbolic 'identity' value besides its more content-based communicative function – typically, that of professing loyalty to an ethnic, social, or kin group. In the case of those who speak, or at least constantly hear, a different language at home from the one used outside, it is often *not* the language they know best but the language used at home that is associated with their professed 'identity'– the Hungarians of the Ukraine (Huszti 2009: 61) being an example.

The language=nationality equation is also sometimes used, though turned on its head, by nations alarmed that a particular population asserts a separate ethnic or national identity. If that population does not have a distinct language, this is said to prove that there are no grounds for it to claim to be a different ethnicity or nation. As a Welsh motto asserts: 'no language, no nation'.[13] To stay with the example of Ukraine: the right of the Ukrainians to be a distinct nation is sometimes dismissed by pointing out that, before the start of the Russo-Ukrainian war in 2014, most TV programmes, newspapers, and books in Ukraine were in Russian. Similarly, many people in Turkey adduce the lack of a unified, standardized Kurdish language as proof that there is no Kurdish ethnicity; many Kurds, conversely, feel that the fact that they do have a different language from Turkish is a key proof of their different ethnicity – for which some of them demand a separate state.

An important corollary of the language=nationality equation has often been the argument that regions should be assigned to (or could be legitimately conquered by) the main country that speaks the same language. As Kedourie (1993: 62) summarized it: 'if a nation is a group of people speaking the same language, then if political frontiers separate the members of such a group, these frontiers are arbitrary, unnatural, unjust'. Although the argument that speakers of x should be under the rule of country x long predates nationalism, in the 'Age of Nationalism' it started to be treated as self-evidently

---

[13] 'Heb iaith, heb genedl', also known as 'cenedl heb iaith, cenedl heb galon' 'nation without a language, nation without a heart', and 'gwlad heb iaith, gwlad heb genedl' 'land without language, a land without a nation'.

logical and to be put into practice more forcefully. In the nineteenth century, to quote but one instance, the spearhead of the movement for Italian unification, Mazzini (1860: 59) was exhorting people to 'have no joy or rest as long as a fraction of the territory upon which your language is spoken is dirempt from the nation'.[14] Many nationalists who advocate the annexation of regions of other countries where their language is spoken choose to overlook the (sometimes vast) cultural and material dissimilarities between the two territories in question – dissimilarities that may be important to the inhabitants of those regions, and valuable in themselves. A few nationalist leaders did realize that forcibly appropriating a land because of its language entails bulldozing differences that are worth respecting and preserving: Carlo Cattaneo, a leader in the 1848 insurrection of northern Italy against Austrian rule, an insurrection that was part of the push for Italian unification, used to say that annexing the Italian-speaking Swiss Canton of Ticino to Italy, on a nationalist (linguistic) principle, 'would have been like killing a nightingale for the sake of adding an ounce of meat to a goose' (Dossi [1912] 1964: II: 581).[15]

The merits of the equation

As we saw in Chapters 2 and 3, our use of language, whether we want it to or not, can suggest – often correctly but not always – that we are of a given class, age, gender, and other variables. Those other variables can include also ethnicity and nationality. But are there good grounds for equating the use of a particular language with either an ethnicity or a nationality? Let us start with ethnicity. As we previously noted, the concept of *ethnicity* (much more than that of *nationality*) denotes a group that, though perhaps also culturally distinct, is thought to be defined by descent, by a common ancestry. It is a concept akin to what scholars of Jones' time meant by the term *race*. Do ethnicities (in that sense of the term) and languages coincide? This conjecture is already adumbrated by Darwin (1859: 319):

> If we possessed a perfect pedigree of mankind, a genealogical arrangement of the races of man would afford the best classification of the various languages now spoken throughout the world.

Is it reasonable to link language with ancestry? To put it differently: do languages match identifiable DNA profiles – do they correspond to the incidence of certain gene variants (alleles) in a given population? In recent years, there have been efforts to combine language data with genetic data, and to draw conclusions about the migratory paths and histories of populations – in essence, to check the degree of overlap of linguistic, geographical, and genetic information. Cavalli-Sforza et al. (1988: 6003) compared the

---

[14] 'non abbiate gioia e riposo finché una frazione del territorio sul quale si parla la vostra lingua è divelta dalla Nazione'.
[15] 'sarebbe stato come uccidere un usignolo per aggiungere un' oncia di carne ad un' oca'.

likely genetic tree diagrams (the allele frequency) of forty-two human populations with similar tree diagrams of the phylogeny of the world's languages, and found extensive correlations. A few questions were raised about some of the methodologies and sources used in that study, but more works have since appeared (cf. e.g. Poloni et al. 1997: 1019) that corroborate the overall view that languages and ancestry groups can show important overlaps and shared borders, though such congruences are stronger in some regions and less so in others. We can leave aside more daring conjectures that have been advanced, such as that, among genetically similar individuals, a particular genetic predisposition may favour the development of particular structural features in their language (Dediu and Ladd 2007: 10947), but we cannot dismiss outright the evidence that a sudden difference in the genetic profiles of neighbouring population does tend to correspond to either a language border or a landmark barrier (Barbujani and Sokal 1990: 1817–8; Baker, Rotimi, Shriner 2017: 7). This is taken to mean that languages tend to match genetically-identifiable human groups.

Of course, there are key differences between languages and genes: language transmission, unlike gene transmission, is not exclusively, nor inevitably, nor unidirectionally from parents to offspring; a population can also adopt a language from another. In those cases, while the population genetically lives on, the language disappears. Indeed, about a quarter of the distinct language families of the world have died out (Campbell 2015: 204) and, in most cases, they have died because the speakers, across generations, have changed language, not because they have not reproduced. It is true that language differences can act as a sociocultural barrier to gene flow, but such a barrier is surmountable and its strength is culturally variable. Language differences still allow genetic exchanges, and tests have shown that genes spread across populations less than linguistic features. Contiguous populations, in other words, can mix their genes more than their languages. For example, analyses of the mitochondrial gene pool of Finnish speakers and of the adjacent speakers of Sámi, a related language (Sajantila et al. 1995: 47), shows that Finns are now genetically close to speakers of the (unrelated) Indo-European languages, and even to Basque speakers, and genetically unlike the Sámi. In like manner, structural linguistic influences between neighbouring Oceanic and Papuan languages have been minimal, but Oceanic-speaking and Papuan-speaking populations have grown genetically very much alike (Hunley et al. 2008: 10). A group can, and often does, maintain its language and its collective (national or ethnic) denomination, while it modifies its gene pool. We tend to imagine a strong continuity in nations, but the name of a nationality may be applied to a population that slowly but radically changes. Even when we find a significant degree of genetic uniformity in a language community, we must remember that such a population may be the result of a mixture of different human groups which, through extensive but local interbreeding, has become more uniform over time. Linguistic and genetic exchanges can blur the earlier history of a population.

Traditional comparative linguistics strove to identify separate language 'families' and to build a picture of the unattested 'parent' languages from which known languages descended. In looking for traits shared by attested languages, it therefore focused on putative 'sister languages', on what these had inherited from earlier stages, on what could confirm genetic links. It had less interest in the history of innovative traits due to recent inputs. The description of many languages thus typically foregrounded their continuity with the past, rather than their imports from neighbouring languages. However, in many parts of the world there has been widespread (though often downplayed) multilingualism and therefore large-scale linguistic borrowing. Languages unrelated by descent but geographically contiguous can thus develop parallel linguistic features extensively. In some regions – for example the Balkans, the Indian subcontinent, or mainland Southeast Asia – such linguistic convergence among neighbours is rather evident, and involves several languages; these have come to constitute localized language ensembles (*Sprachbunden*) though they have, historically, quite distinct lineages. The under-reported horizontal transmission of linguistic traits that many languages show may well have entailed also an under-reported or covert horizontal transmission of genes between the communities of the speakers: there have been more intermarriages, infidelities and, alas, forced relocations and sexual assaults than records report. And when it comes to nationalities, rather than ethnicities, we need to remember that what we call nationalities are even more likely to encompass or to have absorbed multiple ethnicities, even though the extent of this is variable, and endogamy (the tendency to marry within the community) in a nation may, in the long run, slightly re-homogenize its genetic profile. As we saw, where the members of a nation were multi-ethnic, the adoption of a shared, and perhaps single, language throughout the nation was in many cases forcefully encouraged or even imposed. The resulting community, in time, may appear fairly homogeneous and therefore perhaps distinctive – linguistically, culturally, and to a degree even phenotypically, and be eager to see itself that way – while its history may have been much more complex than it may seem. Besides, even where its distinguishing traits, such as nationality and language, now appear to match one another – to carry the same label – they may diverge in the future.

Problems with the equation

The problem with the language=nationality equation is, at one level, simple: the people who speak a language, the language itself, and other characteristics of the people's mental and social life (what is broadly labelled their 'culture') are potentially independent. They most certainly *can* be aligned in the way conventionally expected, but they do not need to be. And regardless of whether, upon inspection, they appear aligned or not, their relationship can change over time. Already more than a century ago, Franz Boas (1911: 11) was observing:

> It [is] fairly clear ... that a people may remain constant in type and language and change in culture; that they may remain constant in type, but change in language; or that they may remain constant in language and change in type and culture.

Concerning language and nationality, there is a popular view that nations exist only so long as they preserve a distinct language; as a traditional Czech proverb asserts: 'a nation is not extinguished so long as the language lives'.[16] Irish nationalists, in the nineteenth century, expected that their ethnic or national identity could not survive a shift to another language. Thomas O. Davis (1846: 174–5) affirmed:

> A people without a language of its own is only half a nation ... when the language of its cradle goes, [the nation] itself craves a tomb ... To have lost entirely the national language is death.

But this is not so. In Ireland, ethnic identification is still very strong, but only some 3% of the population still has Irish as their main language. Among the Basque too, although nationalism is very strong and is even language-based, only about a quarter of the population actually knows Basque (Euskara). In Scotland, similarly, there is a popular movement for independence essentially aiming at affirming a different identity from England (45% of voters endorsed breaking away from the UK in a 2014 referendum), and there is also a distinct language, Scots Gaelic; but that is moribund, and is not stressed as a marker of Scottishness. Scots who are passionate about being Scottish, and even those who are anti-English, do not usually consider switching to Gaelic and abandoning English to make the point. They accept that English is now a more effective medium for communicating and promoting their *different* identity. After all, one can choose to adopt a more widespread language for convenience, and use it to put across a message of *non*-identification: Kateb Yacine, who was born in French-colonized Algeria and wrote both in French and in Algerian Arabic, was unequivocal ([1966] 1994: 132):

> What people call 'Francophony' is a neo-colonial political machine that only perpetuates our alienation ... but the use of French does not mean that one is the agent of a foreign power ... I write in French to tell the French that I am not French.[17]

The example of Jewish communities, among others, shows that a single ethnic group can speak several languages, and that, conversely, an older identification can continue while and after the community becomes linguistically assimilated into another and even monolingual. A compromise is also possible: the dominant or mainstream language can be fully adopted, but marked with optional features that signal a certain ethnic background. As we noted in Chapter 3, in order to indicate national or ethnic membership by linguistic markers, minor signals such as accent or just occasional words and expressions from the ancestral language can suffice. Or they can be substituted by other symbols such as distinctive ceremonies, music, clothing, jewellery, hairstyles, and so forth. Even nationalism itself has not always needed

---

[16] 'Národy nehasnou, dokud jazyk žije'.
[17] 'Ce qu'on appelle ≪francophonie≫ est une machine politique néo-coloniale qui ne fait que perpétuer notre aliénation ... Mais l'usage de la langue française ne signifie pas qu'on soit l'agent d'une puissance étrangère ... j'écris en français pour dire aux Français que je ne suis pas français'.

language: some national movements – for instance, the Polish one – were not based on language (Hobsbawn 1992: 103).

We should also add, incidentally, that statehood alone does not preserve languages: Irish is more endangered than Welsh, although it has, so to speak, its own republic. Nor is it necessarily true that, if a language has no official recognition in the country in which it is used, this reflects or causes social oppression or a lower status for its speakers. Switzerland recognizes four national languages but not Swiss-German (*Schwyzertüütsch*), which is the mother tongue of most Swiss, and the language of the most influential part of Switzerland, spoken by all social classes up to the highest; foreigners seeking citizenship in places such as Zürich are expected to demonstrate an adequate knowledge of Swiss-German. And yet, Switzerland affords only 'dialect' status to Swiss-German, while it gives official status to Germany's German (*Hochdeutsch*) although the latter is used only in specific contexts and with some reluctance, both because it is not usually natively mastered by the Swiss except as a written medium, and because it is the language of a powerful and bigger neighbouring country. Many languages have survived without receiving, for a long time, state support or recognition, and even while finding themselves under considerable political and social oppression: Welsh, Basque, Yiddish, Romany, Sámi, Kurdish, to name but a few. The recognition of a second or third language at official level, though symbolically a very good thing, does not automatically cause that language to spread: bilingual countries can have fewer bilingual inhabitants than monolingual countries have, precisely because in a bilingual country any citizen can function fully by using just one of the recognized languages. People and communities are bilingual if they need to be, and they need to be if others are not (cf. Mackey 1962: 51–2).

It is enough to look at numbers to realize that the equation between language and nationality is untrue for much of humankind. In the world, there are more multilingual than monolingual peoples, including in Europe, and languages coterminous with one state are a rare exception, not the rule. Many Westerners think that Switzerland, with its four languages, is an unusual case; but Papua New Guinea alone is reputed to have between 750 and 850 languages, and is considered a single nation. There are anyway at least thirty times more languages than countries in the world (e.g. the *Ethnologue* database, in 2021, indicates 7,117).[18]

Plenty of countries with essentially the same language have rather different cultures and allegiances. The many English-speaking countries of today, despite a common language, have distinct national identities. So do the many Spanish-speaking countries, notwithstanding the fact that, in the main, they have also the same religion. Overemphasizing the language can thus generate mistaken assumptions about someone's professed identity. Swiss-Italians, for example, have been fighting to preserve their language and cultural affiliation in the face of the growing hegemony of Swiss-Germans; but they have been simultaneously fighting to be distinguished from the Italians across the border, who have a considerably larger country and much better-known culture. The very fact that, if you are Swiss and your language is Italian, you

[18] Cf. https://www.ethnologue.com/guides/how-many-languages (last accessed February 2021).

are termed 'Swiss-Italian' (just as, if you are Swiss and your language is French, you are called 'Swiss-French', and so forth) shows the inordinate weight given to language in ethnic identifications: in Britain, one would never call an English-speaking Welsh person in Wales 'Welsh-English'. But the very region in which Swiss-Italians live is officially called *Svizzera italiana* (so also in German: *italienische Schweiz*, French: *Suisse italienne*, and Rumantsch: *Svizra taliana*).[19] This is misleading, as the region is not a piece of Switzerland that belongs to Italy, as the name could seem to suggest, but a part of Switzerland that is Italian-speaking.

Several countries or nations have a national language that they adopted from groups now considered separate nationalities, or with whom they chose to sever ties. A common language has not led them to a single collective identification, and has not inspired formal unity amongst the speakers, nor prevented secessionism. In a number of cases, the language still bears the name of the other group: north Americans call their (main) language English and not American; Austrians call their (main) language German; not Austrian; and most south American countries call their language Spanish, not just 'Mexican', 'Cuban', and so on.

We should admit that, in any population, a background of shared beliefs, values, and behavioural conventions (a 'culture') facilitates understanding and bolsters a sense of common purpose. The association of a language with a culture, however, while true in a few subtle ways, as we saw in Chapters 5 and 6, should not be considered automatic nor be given an excessive symbolic value. Language is not a complete or inflexible determinant of someone's outlook. In Québec (Handler 1988: 160), it was said that the very use of French, instead of English, encouraged thinking and living in a Catholic way ('la langue gardienne de la foi', as leader Henri Bourassa summarized it), but most Catholics in the world do not know any French. Hitler spoke of 'thinking German, behaving German' ('deutsch denken, deutsch handeln'), but German – and many other languages, including Russian, Greek, Latin, and Persian – have been, at different points in their histories, vehicles of very different outlooks, religions, philosophies, and political creeds.

A single national language may appear desirable because it facilitates communication. Since a language lays down rules as to how one conveys one's perception of reality, it is generally true that language does create, through the sharing of the same *forms* (grammar and lexicon), a basic mutual understanding that excludes to a large degree those who speak only another language. However, the use of the 'same' language does not ensure that the mutual understanding will extend to the *contents*, i.e. that there will be collective agreement that a given perception of reality is correct. It is therefore unclear how a language can be the reflection, the *imago animi*, of a whole nation. The idea that people of the same language think alike is both trivially true and glaringly untrue, and the evidence for this is neither new nor esoteric. A banal and yet important point to make is that plenty of individuals sharing a language do not see eye-to-eye, and therefore plenty of countries with, in principle, the same

---

[19] It is more accurately designated in Chinese as 'Swiss Italian-speaking area' (瑞士意大利语) and in Modern Greek as 'Italophone Switzerland' (Ιταλόφωνη Ελβετία).

language have significantly different cultural, social, and political orientations – suffice it to think of West and East Germany before 1989. Whorf, when arguing that each language makes the speakers think in a distinct way, described this idea ([1940] 1956: 214) as 'a new principle of relativity'; the term 'relativity' makes one think of Einstein – and not wrongly: Einstein himself ([1941] 1954: 336), around the same time, stated:

> The mental development of the individual and his way of forming concepts depend to a high degree upon language. This makes us realize to what extent the same language means the same mentality.

Before we surmise that this must be correct because it was believed by no less than Einstein, we must spot the paradox: it is truly puzzling that Einstein held such a view, considering that he was a Jewish refugee from Nazism: he was a native speaker of German, like the Nazis, but certainly did not share their outlook. His own life disproves his remark.

Speakers of 'the same language' can also miscommunicate or give each other the wrong impression. As many learners of foreign languages are well-aware, even if you attain perfect grammar, a flawless accent, and have an appearance that allows you to 'pass' as native, you may be instantly outed as foreign by your manners or cultural conventions. The concept of 'same language' is too imprecise and nebulous; there are subtle but instantly detected linguistic variations in what use of language is deemed socially and culturally appropriate, as we discussed in Chapter 5: differences in phonetics, syntax, or semantics, but also in the rules of linguistic interaction. This is clear if one observes the use of what is ostensibly 'the same language' in different countries. To go back to an earlier example: the use of Italian in southern Switzerland and in southern Italy, even when speakers aim for the standard form, not only differs somewhat in accent and marginally in vocabulary, but may vary in choice of register, level of formality, amount of information exchanged, rules of turn-taking, volume, gestural accompaniment, and more besides. Similar considerations could be made for British and American English, or for European and Brazilian Portuguese, and other pairs of countries where the 'same language' is said to be spoken.

The idea that having the same language brings unity and a shared identity is also a sweeping generalization. The inhabitants of Alsace (Hoffmann 1991: 200), which lies within France but borders with Germany, were presumed by the Germans to have a German identity because they spoke a variety of German. Germany got control of the area repeatedly, and expected that the language would determine the national preferences of the Alsatians; but the Alsatians, then largely Germanic-speaking, felt more allegiance to France. Conversely, there are populations outside the borders of France who speak French, notably the Swiss-French and the Walloons of Belgium, but – despite the same language – the three harbour a strong sense of difference and are known for their playful but savage jokes about one another (e.g. an old French quip says: 'if you meet a Swiss who is particularly stupid, watch out, he is a Belgian'[20]). There

---

[20] 'Si vous rencontrez un Suisse particulièrement stupide, méfiez vous, il est belge'.

are many cases in which language, even among populations who coexisted in the same state, has not secured a collective ethnic identification. Czechs and Slovaks, who speak two similar, mutually intelligible languages that shade into each other, and who used to be one nation state, decided to split in 1992. Croats, Serbs, and Bosnians, who speak roughly the same language (many linguists still call it just Serbocroat), warred against each other and ended with independent states. The clear wish of many Slavs to identify only with a specific nationality rather that with a pan-Slavic community has led an eminent Slavist (Seton-Watson 1988: 5) to conclude that, although there are still Slavic languages and Slavic philology, when talking of people, '[t]oday ... the category Slav has lost virtually all meaning'. In Northern Ireland too, despite a common language between communities, there were years of bloodshed. The warring sides in Somalia too had very considerable linguistic and cultural affinity. And in Rwanda, the Tutsis and the Hutus too had a common language and largely a common religion, but their conflict left 800,000 people dead.

The local leaders, and at times the founders, of several countries spoke another language from the one now considered the national and natural language of that country. Haakon VII, the Norwegian King after Independence in 1905, spoke Danish – whereas many Danish rulers spoke German. The educated élite of Bohemia, in the eighteenth century, also used German, and was largely German-identified. Although Israelis speak a revived form of Hebrew, Theodor Herzl, who is widely described as the founding father of Israel, and who believed that Jews constitute a nation and therefore should have a country of their own, did not speak Hebrew and was totally dismissive of the idea that the Jews could start speaking Hebrew as a modern language (Herzl 1896: 75).[21] The ruling classes and the monarchy in England spoke French at least until the thirteenth century; no other language was permitted in the English courts until 1362, and English was considered a lowly and inadequate patois. Many other European courts used French as late as the eighteenth century. Count Cavour, the creator of Italy, also spoke French, including when he announced to the newly-created country its own existence. As we saw in the last chapter, even some of the nationalist figureheads who specifically championed a particular language as the sole national tongue, spoke a different language at home.

In the light of all this, the presence of other languages in a country should not, in itself, be considered a serious problem, as it sometimes still is. There is, nonetheless, a performative factor: if the presence of those languages is proclaimed to be a serious problem, serious problems may indeed begin.

---

[21] 'Wir können doch nicht Hebräisch miteinander reden. Wer von uns weiss genug Hebräisch, um in dieser Sprache ein Bahnbillet zu verlangen? Das gibt es nicht'.

Epilogue

The theme of language and nationality, and of the link between them, is pertinent and sometimes central to a range of questions currently being raised – usually with strong views – by campaigners of various persuasions, by media commentators, by policy makers, and by ordinary citizens. Such questions include, for example: what makes a nation; how old nations are; whether national histories make sense; when a given territory should be considered part of another; when a given community should be considered part of another; what determines an individual's nationality; what someone's real name is; who is best qualified to teach a language; whether foreign-language lessons are worthwhile; what the rights and obligations of linguistic minorities should be; which variety of a language is the 'correct' one; whether the spread of English constitutes progress or tyranny; whether language diversity is valuable or problematic; whether different languages are just equivalent alternatives for saying the same things; whether each particular language determines how its users think; whether the gradual disappearance of dialects and 'small' languages should be opposed; how to detect covert forms of social exclusion; what constitutes offensive language; whether stereotypes are justified; what people's linguistic peculiarities prove about them; whether your language (however defined) reveals your national identification and loyalties; whether your language qualifies you, or disqualifies you, for a given nationality. Most discussions one hears on such questions are guided by understandings that, even when they are not erroneous, are rather superficial and, above all else, narrow. A key aim of this book, therefore, has been to sketch out, within the constraints of the space available, a broader picture: to provide some contextualizations, observations, and reflections that may amplify, enrich, or nuance the views that readers form on such questions, or at least to alert them to the existence of additional facets to issues that many non-academic sources, owing either to partisanship or to insufficient knowledge, all too frequently treat as straightforward.

In the last chapter, we have also discussed the merits and faults of the common wisdom that the use of a given language bespeaks a certain nationality, national identification, or national allegiance – and, conversely, that rightful membership of a given nation entails, among other things, one particular language. That discussion has been the point of arrival of the book, but not its sole or overriding concern. The many facts that have been collected and presented in all the preceding chapters, and the analysis and commentary that have been provided, have not been just ancillary to that goal. They have been included so as to elucidate, more generally, why people conceive language and nationality in the way they do.

Rightly or wrongly, the people you meet feel able to infer many things about you from your language, as also from your nationality. In order to explain why they feel that way, the book has first illustrated how language puts on people not only overt labels, but also covert ones. Chapter 1 has looked at names because these, despite being the most obvious badges of 'identity', are commonly considered meaningless and aleatory; and yet they can say a lot about their bearers, even unbeknownst to them. Chapter 2 then has observed how, when we speak or write, not only is information about us provided overtly in the content of what we say, but the manner in which we say it leads others to infer – often correctly but also incorrectly – covert information such as our age, sex, family background, place of origin, native language, level of education, ideology, intellectual ability, occupation, character, physical and emotional state, or looks. Our linguistic peculiarities get us quickly placed into various categories like 'upper class', 'male', 'northerner', 'elderly', 'foreign', 'extrovert', 'ignoramus', 'drunkard', 'flirt', 'whiner', and so forth. It is important to realize how people of all walks of life – and, therefore, we too – respond to the language use of others according to preconceptions and social preferences, and how this has concrete repercussions. Inferences from language use are not infallible, and are frequently value-laden. In Chapter 3, it has been remarked that since accent, vocabulary, syntax, or whole languages act as markers of social categories, they create several intersecting 'us'/'them' divides, and become principles for social acceptance or rejection, inclusion or exclusion. However, while some linguistic cues that get a person classified in this or that category are rooted in biology, a large part of those cues are something we learn. Precisely because language can identify groups, its use is constantly adapted, challenged, and transformed; and the versatility of language in shaping group relationships and in designating social categories confers elasticity to those relationships and categories themselves. Many social categories or groups that are identified by language have borders that are arbitrary and mutable, and that may be penetrable through negotiation, subconscious self-adjustments, or conscious mimicry. Most people modify their language or style at times, even unwittingly, so as to blend in or to stand out, to assert that they belong or that they are different, to claim membership of a category or to position themselves socially in another way. And, as the book has repeatedly underscored, it is not just a matter of creating an impression in others. Since different uses of language have associations with class, education, ethnicity, profession, gender, and other categories, including nationality, they elicit a variable social response, and they can make the speakers experience themselves in variable ways. Switching to another of the languages we know, or adopting a new language, can alter both our public image and our self-perception. Many bilinguals and immigrants apprehend this clearly. A language, furthermore – because of its emotional associations to individuals, social milieus, places, and times – can be connected, in a person's mind, with a certain behavioural package. Attaining high proficiency in a new language can thus be eye-opening and possibly emancipating, because it can facilitate the exploration, development, and expression of slightly different modes of being; some people, as we have mentioned, subconsciously resist learning a foreign language well because they fear that something in its use might violate their cultural norms or misrepresent their ethnicity or nationality. In this connection, it was logical for the book to ask also whether languages, despite having different social associations, are not merely different codes for saying the same things. The answer, as it has been illustrated in Chapter 4 and later, is that they are not: languages can differ significantly among themselves in their grammar, vocabulary, and pragmatic norms. This means that exact translations from one language into another are much harder to achieve than they seem. It also means that the learning of an additional language can increase a person's repertoire of terms, concepts, and styles. More importantly, it may enable one to notice, through contrast, the expressive limitations – and the social and cultural connotations – of different languages. The words and modes of speaking or writing that are part of different languages can sometimes contain dissimilar undertones and a specific evaluative stance. These may reveal something about the mentality, beliefs, and values of a collectivity, as well as about its history or its material environment – which shows that language can be a group marker more than just symbolically. We have examined, in Chapter 5, how words used by different language communities can carry hidden connotations and implicit judgments, which may say something about the speakers' culture. This does not apply only to words: the manner in which something is phrased, the tone in which it is said, and whether it is said at all, are also, as we have seen, cross-linguistically variable; they reflect, and arguably reinforce, a certain style of interaction and perhaps an outlook. A question that therefore arises – and has been discussed in Chapter 6 – is whether our language (whichever that be), through its particular structure and lexicon, inescapably determines our thinking. Since it is common to impart a language to children, to pupils, and sometimes to entire countries, the issue is not just one of culture and psychology but also of equity and power. If that question is put in deterministic terms – whether having this or that language as your native tongue blocks you from thinking in an alternative fashion – the answer, we argued, is no. Language is not an inescapable cognitive prison. It has a prominent position in most people's social interactions, private cogitations, cultural symbolism, and professed identifications; but it is possible to communicate and connect with others by means other than language, to process reality and think without language, and to share a language without agreeing with a culture. Nevertheless, language does have a weak ability to draw routinely our attention to one detail rather than to another, or possibly to suggest certain mental associations. Furthermore, the connotations, the use, or even the sheer presence of certain words can have an unstated ideological tinge, carry a given attitude, and present it as undisputed.

All this is not a reason for suppressing multilingualism as divisive and seditious, but for promoting it across all communities, so that more of us get access to more people and perspectives; it is, indeed, a reason for studying language in general: to become a little bit more alert to the ideology and attitude that may be embedded in some elements of a language. A keener sense of language may help one become more cognizant of how language is deployed on all of us and affects us. Similar considerations can be made about becoming totally immersed and conversant in a second culture, and thereby becoming better equipped to deconstruct some of the cultural package that we originally received as part of our own upbringing, schooling, and nationality.

In the latter part of the book, the topic of nationality has come more into focus. First, in Chapter 7, we have made a few brief remarks on when and how nations arose, on the repercussions of their establishment and, above all, on the consequences of thinking of humankind as being naturally divided into distinct nationalities. The very arrangement of most of the world into nation states, and the perception that this is an inevitable state of affairs, is largely the product of a certain history. We have also observed, in Chapter 8, how forging and maintaining a nation is an active process, and that several cultural artefacts and symbols – language prominently included – are pressed into service in the making and teaching of a national identity. Nationality is, among other things, a label that we come to internalize, and is a way of looking at the world that we learn. It is a particular perspective, which can provide a sense of distinctiveness, belonging, community, self-esteem, direction, history, perdurance, transcendence, and meaning. Just as a language puts various category labels on people and leads them to talk about themselves (including to themselves) in particular terms, so also nationality is a normative interpretive framework, a mode of understanding oneself and others. Such a framework can be invigorating, comforting, and occasionally even illuminating. But it is oftentimes limiting, misleading, and detrimental. Nonetheless, nationality, like language, does not constitute an inescapable cognitive prison, but only a common default thinking mode that can be profitably used and also profitably questioned – in truth, easily so, because it is not as natural, well-defined, and constantly relevant as it is sometimes made out to be. The book, at various points, has talked about the way such a thinking mode is inculcated into us, and about the capacity that language has to establish, legitimize, teach, and uphold social divisions like nationality. Language has a reifying power, not only psychologically but also practically. It formulates concepts, magnifies the contrast between them, and presents them implicitly as a solid and lasting truth; moreover, it can also help turn them into a tangible sociopolitical reality. It does this also with nationalities. In Chapter 9, we have therefore discussed how a sociopolitical entity such as a nation state becomes established as such with the help of language: language enables the decision and assertion that a nation does or is to exist; it provides the idiom and the medium needed to promote that assertion and thereby to turn it into a fact; and then stands as a symbol and seeming proof that such assertion is independently true. The fashioning of a nation and that of its language have frequently mirrored each other, as we have remarked, and they have done so in ways that were deliberate and are quite telling. We have acknowledged the usefulness and collective benefits of having a standardized national language, and indeed the democratic intentions that, in many cases, have lead to its creation. But we have also pointed out the agenda behind the choice of a particular language variety as the standard form, and the unfair prestige, privileges, and powers that such choice bestows upon those who speak that variety natively or are most proficient in it. Furthermore, as Chapter 10 has elaborated, the standard language employed and prescriptively taught as the national medium has, in countless cases, been subjected to artificial interventions, so that it would fit and corroborate a certain national ideology and would reflect the desired image of the nation itself: for instance, as distinctive, homogeneous across the country, embodying a given ethnicity (or religion), unsullied by foreigners (or, on the contrary, nourished by some prestigious ones), ancient and unchanging (or, on the contrary, modern and unshackled by the past). The interventions in pursuit of that effect have frequently included fabrications about the history and the lineage of the language, and forced alterations to its structure, its vocabulary, and its usage. All this has distorted also the public understanding of the ontology, the nature, the form, the origin, and the development of languages in general: many lay folks mistakenly assume that languages are concrete entities, rather than codes in our minds, that they are neatly distinct from one another, that they have one true and correct form, that they are timeless, that they each come from a single strand, and that they are merely a product of nature. And these misconceptions are not even the most deplorable side of the efforts to establish a national language. Many times, there has been a more troubling side: a requirement that the national language, like the national identity, be mandatorily adopted by the whole population of the country in question, and be given undivided loyalty. This has typically involved the suppression of minority languages and the vilification of dialects – and of their speakers. While a prescriptive approach to language is not limited to one side of the political spectrum, as we have stressed, it does have a special connection to nationalism. In pre-national days, as the book has underscored, linguistic intolerance in many countries was not so widespread, and definitely not official state practice. The demand, and the belief, that nationality determines language, and that language determines nationality, although it has had occasional antecedents in other eras, has otherwise been a typical feature of late modern history. Both language and nationality have been said, by many sources, to give a distinctive and inescapable shape to a person's mindset. Indeed, both have been claimed to be reflecting 'racial', biological, innate distinctions. A common perception has been that, as William Barnes (1854: 259) asserted, 'Mankind live on the earth in sundry tribes or nations, each of them composed of men of one stock and language'. In this light, it is perhaps unsurprising that language and nationality have been treated as inherent in each other, and as inferable from each other.

Analysing the relationship between language and nationality can be informative in several respects. It makes us aware that, for example, nations have often artificially fashioned languages, and languages, in turn, nations; and it highlights that the nature of both languages and nationalities may not be quite what it seems or what we have been traditionally taught. It also enables us to comprehend why many people implicitly conceptualize both language and nationality in unrealistic ways and, as a result, have misguided responses to some issues surrounding them. The presumed automatic correspondence between language and nationality affects public perceptions and has numerous consequences. As Chapter 11 has pointed out, the national or ethnic identification of many individuals is contested when their language is felt to be at odds with their nationality or ethnicity; frictions between language groups are described as inter-ethnic conflicts; territories where a given language is spoken are claimed to belong manifestly to the country with which that language is associated (thus linguistic similarity, and not only linguistic difference, is a source of trouble); language minorities who advance requests for more language rights are wrongly assumed by their governments to be harbouring separatist aspirations – and the same baseless inference is made, though with glee, by nearby nation states where that minority language is the main or national idiom; requests for admission into supranational entities are informally evaluated with references to language; bids for independence made by a community that speaks the same language are dismissed as self-evidently groundless; the ethnic or racial labels that people apply to themselves and to others have sometimes been changed on the basis of the language they speak; clashes between nations due to economic or political factors are now routinely blamed on language differences; some linguistic minorities wholly devoted to their country are told that they are speaking the 'wrong' language, that they are being unpatriotic, or that they do not belong there – assertions that were not made to them before their country became a nation state.

This book has shown and emphasized that the manners in which we speak (and write) can say a lot about us and justify certain inferences by others; and that languages can differ considerably among themselves, including in ways that reflect peculiarities of the groups that speak them. However, the book has also maintained that whether a given language and a given nationality should imply each other is, to an important degree, a rather different question. The link between languages and national affiliations, identifications, or loyalties, it has argued, is not simple and not to be assumed. The use of language as a signal of group belonging and allegiance, while undeniable, is highly flexible; and so is the construction of a nation and the criteria for its membership. As we have illustrated, both language and nationality are, ultimately, abstract concepts, and the realities to which those two concepts refer change over time and vary across space. And so does, therefore, also the relationship between them – and its social and political meaning.

Bibliography

Adams, J. N. (2003). '"Romanitas" and the Latin language'. *The Classical Quarterly* 53(1), 184–205.

Adams, J. N. (2003b). *Bilingualism and the Latin language*. Cambridge: Cambridge University Press.

Addi, L. (1997). 'The failure of Third World nationalism'. *Journal of Democracy* 8(4), 110–24.

Agirdag, O. (2014). 'The long-term effects of bilingualism on children of immigration: student bilingualism and future earnings'. *International Journal of Bilingual Education and Bilingualism* 17(4), 449–64.

Akmajian, A., Farmer, A. K., Bickmore, L., Demers, R. A., and Harnish, R. M. (2017). *Linguistics: An introduction to language and communication*. Cambridge MA: MIT Press.

Alford, D. K. H. (1978). 'The demise of the Whorf Hypothesis (a major revision in the history of linguistics)'. *Proceedings of the 4th Annual Meeting of the Berkeley Linguistics Society*, 485–99.

Allport, G. W. (1954). *The nature of prejudice*. Cambridge MA: Addison-Wesley.

Althusser, L. (1970). 'Idéologie et appareils idéologiques d'État (Notes pour une recherche)'. *La pensée* 151, 3–38.

Ameel, E., Storms, G., Malt, B.C., and Sloman, S. A. (2005). 'How bilinguals solve the naming problem'. *Journal of Memory and Language* 53, 60–80.

Anderson, B. (1991). *Imagined Communities – reflections on the origin and spread of nationalism*. London/NY: Verso.

Anzaldúa, G. (1987). *Borderlands/La frontera*. San Francisco: Spinsters/Aunt Lute.

Appel, R. and Muysken, P. (1987). *Language contact and bilingualism*. London: Edward Arnold.

Aragno, A. and Schlachet, P. J. (1996). 'Accessibility of early experience through the language of origin: a theoretical integration'. *Psychoanalytic Psychology* 13(1), 23–34.

Arnold, M. (1869). *Culture and anarchy – an essay in political and social criticism*. London: Smith, Elder, and Co.

Asheri, D. (1983). *Fra ellenismo e iranismo – studi sulla società e cultura di Xanthos nella età achemenide*. Bologna: Pàtron.

Austin, J. L. (1975). *How to do things with words*. Oxford: Oxford University Press.

Bailey, B. (2000). 'Language and negotiation of ethnic/racial identity among Dominican Americans'. *Language in Society* 29, 555–82.

Bak, T. H., Nissan, J. J., Allerhand, M. M., and Deary, I. J. (2014). 'Does bilingualism influence cognitive aging?'. *Annals of Neurology* 75, 959–63.

Baker, J. L., Rotimi, C. N., and Shriner, D. (2017). 'Human ancestry correlates with language and reveals that race is not an objective genomic classifier'. *Scientific Reports* 7(1), 1–10.

Barbujani, G. and Sokal, R. R. (1990). 'Zones of sharp genetic change in Europe are also linguistic boundaries'. *Proceedings of the Natural Academy of Sciences* 87 (5), 1816–19.

Barnes, W. (1854). *A philological grammar grounded upon English, and formed from a comparison of more than sixty languages*. London: J.R. Smith.

Barnes, W. (1878). *An outline of English speech-craft.* London: C. Kegan Paul.

Barrington, L. W. (1997). '"Nation" and "Nationalism": the misuse of key concepts in political science and politics'. *Political Science and Politics* 30(4), 712–16.

Barry, H. and Harper, A.S. (1995). 'Increased choice of female phonetic attributes in first names'. *Sex Roles* 32, 809–19.

Barth, F. (1969). *Introduction.* In Barth, F. (ed.) *Ethnic groups and boundaries.* Bergen: Universitetsforlaget, 9–38.

Bauman, Z. (2004). *Identity – conversations with Benedetto Vecchi.* Cambridge: Polity Press.

Bergel, K. (ed.) (1956). *Georg Brandes und Arthur Schnitzler – ein Briefwechsel.* Bern: Francke Verlag.

Berlin, B. and Kay, P. (1969). *Basic color terms.* Berkeley: University of California Press.

Bertrand, M. and Mullainathan, S. (2004). 'Are Emily and Greg more employable than Lakisha and Jamal? A field experiment on labor market discrimination'. *American Economic Review,* 94(4), 991–1013.

Bialystok, E. (2007). 'Cognitive effects of bilingualism: how linguistic experience leads to cognitive change'. *International Journal of Bilingual Education and Bilingualism* 10(3), 210–23.

Biber, D. (1994). 'An analytical framework for register studies'. In Biber, D. and Finegan, E. (eds.) *Sociolinguistic perspectives on register,* Oxford: Oxford University Press, 31–56.

Billig, M. (1995). *Banal nationalism.* London: Sage publications.

Björk, I. (2008). *Relativizing linguistic relativity: investigating underlying assumptions about language in the neo-Whorfian literature.* Uppsala: Acta Universitatis Upsaliensis.

Blackledge, A. and Creese, A. (2016). 'A linguistic ethnography of identity – adopting a heteroglossic frame'. In Preece, S. (ed.) *The Routledge Handbook of Language and Identity.* Abingdon: Routledge, 272–88.

Block, D. (2009). *Second language identities.* New York: Continuum.

Blommaert, J. and Verschueren, J. (1992). 'The role of language in European nationalist ideologies'. *Pragmatics* 2(3), 355–75.

Boas, F. (1911). *Handbook of American Indian languages – Part 1.* Washington: Government Printing Office.

Böckh, R. (1866). 'Die statistische *Bedeutung* der *Volksprache als Kennzeichen* der Nationalität'. In Lazarus, M. and Steinthal, H. (eds.) *Zeitschrift für Völkerpsychologie und Sprachwissenschaft* 4. Berlin: Dümmler, 259–402.

Bopp, F. (1833). *Vergleichende Grammatik des Sanskrit, Zend, Armenischen, Griechischen, Lateinischen, Litthauischen, Gothischen, und Deutschen. Erste Abtheilung.* Berlin: Dümmler.

Boroditsky, L., Schmidt, L. A., and Phillips, W. (2003). 'Sex, syntax, and semantics'. In Gentner, D. and Goldin-Meadow, S. (eds.) *Language in mind: advances in the study of language and thought.* Cambridge, MA: MIT Press, 61–79.

Bortone, P. (2009). 'Greek with no history, no standard, no models'. A. Georgakopoulou and M. Silk (eds.) *Standard languages and language standards: Greek, past and present.* London: Ashgate, 67–89.

Bortone, P. (2010). *Greek prepositions from antiquity to the present.* Oxford: Oxford University Press.

Bourdieu, P. (1980). 'L'identité et la représentation'. *Actes de la recherche en sciences sociales* 35(1), 63–72.

Bourdieu, P. (1986). 'L'illusion biographique'. *Actes de la recherche en sciences sociales* 62–63, 69–72.

Bradac, J. J., Bowers, J. W., and Courtright, J. A. (1979). 'Three language variables in communication research: intensity, immediacy, and diversity'. *Human Communication Research* 5(3), 257–69.

Brandreth, G. (2018). *Have you eaten grandma? Or, the life-saving importance of correct punctuation, grammar, and good English.* London: Michael Joseph.

Bronkhorst, J. A. (2011). *Language and reality – on an episode in Indian thought.* Boston: Brill.

Broom, L., Beem, H. P., and Harris, V. (1955). 'Characteristics of 1,107 petitioners for change of name'. *American Sociological Review* 20(1), 33–9.

Brown, P. and Levinson, S. C. (1987). *Politeness: some universals in language usage.* Cambridge: Cambridge University Press.

Bucholtz, M. (2003). 'Sociolinguistic nostalgia and the authentication of identity'. *Journal of Sociolinguistics* 7(3), 398–416.

Bucholtz, M. and Hall, K. (2004). 'Language and identity'. In Duranti, A. (ed.) *A companion to linguistic anthropology.* Oxford: Blackwell's, 369–94.

Bulgakov Булгаков, M.A. [1925] (2012). *Собачье сердце.* Санкт-Петербург: Азбука.

Burck, C. (2005). *Multilingual living – explorations of language and subjectivity.* Houndmills, Basingstoke: Palgrave Macmillan.

Burke, P. (2013). 'Nationalisms and vernaculars, 1500–1800'. In Breuilly, J. (ed.) *The Oxford handbook of the history of nationalism.* Oxford: Oxford University Press.

Butler, J. (1990). *Gender trouble: feminism and the subversion of identity.* New York: Routledge.

Butler, J. (1991). 'Imitation and gender insubordination'. In Fuss, D. (ed.) *Inside/Out: Lesbian theories, Gay theories.* New York: Routledge, 13–31.

Butler, J. (1997). *The psychic life of power – theories in subjection.* Stanford: Stanford University Press.

Cameron, D. (2012). *Verbal hygiene.* London: Routledge.

Campbell, L. (2015). 'Do languages and genes correlate? Some methodological issues'. *Language Dynamics and Change* 5(2), 202–26.

Carmichael, L, Hogan, H. P., Walter, A. A. (1932). 'An experimental study of the effect of language on the reproduction of visually perceived form'. *Journal of Experimental Psychology* 15, 73–86.

Carney, D. R., Cuddy, A. J. C., and Yap, A. J. (2010). 'Power posing: brief nonverbal displays affect neuroendocrine levels and risk tolerance'. *Psychological Science* 21(10), 1363–8.

Cassidy, K. W., Kelly, M. H., and Sharoni, L. J. (1999). 'Inferring gender from name phonology'. *Journal of Experimental Psychology: General* 128(3), 362–81.

Cavallaro, F. (2005). 'Language maintenance revisited: an Australian perspective'. *Bilingual Research Journal,* 29(3), 561–82.

Cavalli-Sforza, L. L., Piazza, A., Menozzi, P., and Mountain, J. (1988). 'Reconstruction of human evolution: bringing together genetic, archaeological, and linguistic data'. *Proceedings of the National Academy of Sciences,* 85, 6002–6.

Chahoud, A. (2004). 'The Roman satirist speaks Greek'. *Classics Ireland* 11, 1–46.

Cheryan, S. and Monin, B. (2005). '"Where are you *really* from?" Asian Americans and identity denial'. *Journal of Personality and Social Psychology* 89(5), 717–30.

Cialdini, R. B., Borden, R. J., Thorne, A., Walker, M. R., Freeman, S., and Sloan, L. R. (1976). 'Basking in reflected glory: three (football) field studies'. *Journal of Personality and Social Psychology,* 34(3), 366–75.

Clackson, J. and Horrocks, G. (2007). *The Blackwell history of the Latin language.* Malden, MA: Blackwell.

Coates, J. (2003). *Men talk.* Oxford: Blackwell.

Connor, W. (1990). 'When is a nation?'. *Ethnic and Racial Studies* 13(1), 92–103.

Connor, W. (2004). 'The timelessness of nations'. *Nations and Nationalism* 10(1/2), 35–47.

Coupland, N. and Bishop, H. (2007). 'Ideologised values for British accents'. *Journal of Sociolinguistics* 11(1), 74–93.

Creese, A., Blackledge, A., and Hu, R. (2018). 'Translanguaging and translation: the construction of social difference across city spaces'. *International Journal of Bilingual Education and Bilingualism* 21(7), 841–52.

CRIHL (2013). *Victims of our own narratives? Portrayal of the Other in Palestinian and Israeli school books*. Jerusalem: Council of Religious Institutions of the Holy Land in Jerusalem.

Crystal, D. (2000). *Language death*. Cambridge: Cambridge University Press.

Crystal, D. (2003). *English as a global language*. 2nd edition. Cambridge: Cambridge University Press.

Danforth, L. M. (1995). *The Macedonian conflict: ethnic nationalism in a transnational world*. Princeton: Princeton University Press.

Darwin, C. R. (1859). *On the origin of species*. 1st edition. London: John Murray.

Davies, A. (2013). 'Is the native speaker dead?'. *Histoire, Épistémologie, Language* 35(2), 17–28.

Davis, M. (2001). *Magical urbanism: Latinos reinvent the US city*. London/NewYork: Verso.

Davis, T. (1846). 'Our national language'. In Gavan Duffy, C. (ed.), *Literary and historical essays*. Dublin: Duffy, 173–82.

De Condillac, E. B. (1746). *Essai sur l'origine des connoissances humaines*. Amsterdam: Pierre Mortier.

De Klerk, V. (1992). 'How taboo are taboo words for girls?'. *Language in Society* 21, 277–89.

De Mauro, T. (1970). *Storia linguistica dell'Italia unita*. Bari: Laterza.

Dediu, D. and Ladd, D. R. (2007). 'Linguistic tone is related to the population frequency of the adaptive haplogroups of two brain size genes, ASPM and Microcephalin'. *Proceedings of the National Academy of Sciences* 104(26), 10944–9.

Dehaene, S., Dupoux, E., Mehler, J., Cohen, L., Paulesu, E., Perani, D., van de Moortele, P.F., Lehéricy, S., and Le Bihan, D., (1997). 'Anatomical variability in the cortical representation of first and second language'. *Neuroreport* 8(17), 3809–15.

Derrida, J. (1967). *De la grammatologie*. Paris: Éditions de Minuit.

Derrida, J. (1984). *Otobiographies: l'enseignement de Nietzsche et la politique du nom propre*. Paris: Galilée.

Derrida, J. (1996). *Le monolinguisme de l'autre – ou la prothèse d'origine*. Paris: Galilée.

Deutsch, E. (1966). 'The self in Advaita Vedānta'. *International Philosophical Quarterly* 6(1), 5–21.

Dixon, J. A., Mahoney, B., and Cocks, R. (2002). 'Accents of guilt effects of regional accent, race, and crime type on attributions of guilt'. *Journal of Language and Social Psychology* 21(2), 162–8.

Donner, J. P. H. (2011). 'Integratiebeleid – brief van de Minister van Binnenlandse Zaken en Koninkrijksrelaties aan de Voorzitter van de Tweede Kamer der Staten-Generaal Den Haag, 16 juni 2011'. *Tweede Kamer, vergaderjaar 2010–2011*, 32 824, nr. 1.

Dorian, N. (2010). 'Linguistic and ethnographic fieldwork'. In Fishman, J. and García, O. (eds.) *Handbook of language and ethnic identity. Vol. 1: disciplinary and regional perspectives*. 2nd edition. Oxford: Oxford University Press, 89–106.

Dörnyei, Z. (2009). 'The L2 motivational system'. In Dörnyei, Z. and Ushioda, E. (eds.) *Motivation, language identity, and the L2 self*, Bristol: Multilingual Matters, 9–42.

Dossi, C. [1912] (1964). *Note azzurre*. Milan: Adelphi.

Durkheim, É. (1912). *Les formes élémentaires de la vie religieuse – le système totémique en Australie*. Paris: Presse Universitaire de France.

Edwards, D. and Middleton, D. (1988). 'Conversational remembering and family relationships: how children learn to remember'. *Journal of Social and Personal Relationships* 5(1), 3–25.

Edwards, J. (2009). *Language and identity.* Cambridge: Cambridge University Press.

Einstein, A. [1941] (1954). 'The common language of science'. In Seelig, C. (ed.) *Ideas and opinions by Albert Einstein.* NY: Bonanza Books.

Ellis, D. G. and Maoz, I. (2002). Cross-cultural argument interactions between Israeli-Jews and Palestinians. *Journal of Applied Communication Research* 30(3), 181–94.

Enfield, N. J. (2002). 'Ethnosyntax: introduction'. In Enfield, N. J. (ed.) *Ethnosyntax: explorations in culture and grammar.* Oxford: Oxford University Press, 1–30.

Eriksen, T. H. (2004). 'Place, kinship and the case for non-ethnic nations'. *Nations and Nationalism,* 10(1–2), 49–62.

Ervin-Tripp, S. (1964). 'An analysis of the interaction of language, topic and listener'. *American Anthropologist* 66(6):part 2, 86–102.

Etaugh, C. E., Bridges, J. S., Cummings-Hill, M., and Cohen, J. (1999). '"Names can never hurt me?" The effects of surname use on perceptions of married women'. *Psychology of Women Quarterly* 23(4), 819–23.

Fanon, F. [1952] (1971). *Peau noire, masques blancs.* Paris: Éditions du Seuil.

Farkas, T. (2003). 'A magyar családnévanyag két nagy típusáról'. *Magyar Nyelv* 9, 144–63.

Farkas, T. (2012). 'Jewish name magyarization in Hungary'. *AHEA: E-journal of the American Hungarian Educators Association* 5, 1–19.

Fast, L. A. and Funder, D. C. (2008). Personality as manifest in word use: correlations with self-report, acquaintance report, and behavior. *Journal of Personality and Social Psychology* 94(2), 334.

Fêng, Y. (1952). *A history of Chinese philosophy – Volume 1: the period of the philosophers.* Princeton: Princeton University Press.

Ferguson, C. A. (1994), 'Dialect, register, and genre: working assumptions about conventionalization'. In Biber, D. and Finegan, E. (eds.) *Sociolinguistic perspectives on register.* Oxford: Oxford University Press, 15–30.

Fichte, J. G. 1808. *Reden an die deutsche nation.* Berlin.

Fischer, R. and Schwartz, S. H. (2011). 'Whence differences in value priorities? Individual, cultural, or artifactual sources'. *Journal of Cross-Cultural Psychology* 42, 1127–44.

Fishman, J. A. (1973). *Language and nationalism: two integrative essays.* Rowley, MA: Newbury House Publishers.

Fishman, J. A. (1972). 'The sociology of language'. In Fishman, J. A. (ed.) *The sociology of language: an interdisciplinary social science approach to language in society.* Rowley, MA: Newbury House Publishers, 1–7.

Fishman, J. A. (1989). 'Bias and anti-intellectualism: the frenzied fiction of "English Only"'. In Fishman, J. (ed.) *Language and ethnicity in minority sociolinguistics perspective.* Clevedon: Multilingual Matters, 638–54.

Fishman, J.A. [1977] (1989). 'Language and ethnicity'. In Fishman, J. (1989). *Language and ethnicity in minority sociolinguistics perspective.* Clevedon: Multilingual Matters, 23–65.

Foroutan, N., Canan, C., Arnold, S., Schwarze, B., Beigang, S., and Kalkum, D. (2014). *Deutschland postmigrantisch I: Gesellschaft, Religion, Identität.* Berlin: Berliner Institut für empirische Integrations- und Migrationsforschung.

Forrester, M. A. (2001). 'The embedding of the self in early interaction'. *Infant and Child Development* 10, 189–202.

Forston, B. W. (2010). *Indo-European language and culture: an introduction.* 2nd edition. Malden, MA/Oxford: Blackwell.

Foscolo, U. (1850). 'Sulla lingua italiana – discorsi sei'. In *Opere edite e postume IV.* Florence: Le Monnier, 107–260.

Foucault, M. (1969). *L'archéologie du savoir,* Paris: Gallimard.

Foucault, M. (1982). 'Le sujet et le pouvoir'. *Dits et écrits IV,* text 306.

Fowler, H. W. and Fowler, F. G. [1930] (1962). *The King's english.* 3rd edition. Oxford: The Clarendon Press.

Francis, E. K. (1976). *Interethnic relations – an essay in sociological theory.* New York: Elsevier.

Franklin, M. J. (2011). *Orientalist Jones – sir William Jones, poet, lawyer, and linguist, 1746-1794.* Oxford: Oxford University Press.

Franzos, K. E. [1897] (2012). *Namensstudien/Étude de noms.* Ansull, O. (ed.) Hannover: Hohesufer.com.

Frege, G. (1892). 'Über Sinn und Bedeutung'. *Zeitschrift für Philosophie und philosophische Kritik* 100(1), 25–50.

Freud, S. (1913). *Totem und Tabu – einige Übereinstimmungen im Seelenleben der Wilden und der Neurotiker.* Leipzig and Vienna: Hugo Heller.

Friedman, V. A. (1999). *Linguistic emblems and emblematic languages: on language as flag in the Balkans.* Columbus: Ohio State University.

Friedman, V. A. (2003). 'Evidentiality in the Balkans with special attention to Macedonian and Albanian'. In Aikhenvald, A. Y. and Dixon, R. M. W. (eds.) *Studies in evidentiality.* Amsterdam/Philadelphia: John Benjamins, 189–218.

Gal, S. (1995). 'Language, gender, and power – an anthropological review'. *Gender Articulated: Language and the Socially Constructed Self,* 169–82.

Galilei, G. (1632). *Dialogo di Galileo Galilei Linceo matematico sopraordinario dello studio di Pisa. E filosofo, e matematico primario del serenissimo Gr. Duca di Toscana. Doue ne i congressi di quattro giornate si discorre sopre i due massimi sistemi del mondo Tolemaico, e Copernicano; proponendo indeterminatamente le ragioni filosofiche, e naturali tanto per l'vna, quanto per l'altra parte.* Florence: Landini.

García, O. (2009). 'Education, multilingualism and translanguaging in the 21st century'. In Mohanty, A., Panda, M., Phillipson, R., and Skutnabb-Kangas, T. (eds.) *Multilingual education for social justice: globalising the local.* New Delhi: Orient Blackswan, 128–45.

Garrett, P., Coupland, N., and Williams, A. (eds.) (2003). *Investigating language attitudes: Social meanings of dialect, ethnicity and performance.* Cardiff: University of Wales Press.

Gat, A. (2013). *Nations: the long history and deep roots of political ethnicity and nationalism.* Cambridge: Cambridge University Press.

Geertz, C. (1973). *The Interpretation of Cultures.* New York: Basic.

Gellner, E. (1997). *Nationalism.* London: Phoenix.

Gellner, E. (1983). *Nations and Nationalism.* Ithaca, NY: Cornell University Press.

Giles, H. (1972). 'Evaluation of personality content from accented speech as a function of listeners' social attitudes'. *Perceptual and Motor Skills* 34(1), 168–70.

Giles, H. and Billings, A. C. (2004). 'Assessing language attitudes: speaker evaluation studies'. In Davies, A. and Elder, C. (eds.) *The handbook of applied linguistics.* Oxford: Blackwell, 187–209.

Giles, H., Henwood, K., Coupland, N., Harriman, J., Coupland, J. (1992). 'Language attitudes and cognitive mediation'. *Human Communication Research* 18(4), 500–27.

Giles, H., and Ogay, T. (2007). 'Communication accommodation theory'. In B. B. Whaley and W. Samter (eds.), *Explaining communication: contemporary theories and exemplars.* Mahwah, NJ: Lawrence Erlbaum, 293–310.

Giles, H. and Powesland, P. F. (1975). *Speech style and social evaluation*. London and New York: Academic Press.

Giles, H., Coupland, J., and Coupland, N. (1991). 'Accommodation theory: communication, context, and consequence'. In Giles, H., Coupland, J., Coupland, N. (eds.) *Contexts of accommodation*. New York, NY: Cambridge University Press, 1–68.

Giles, H., Taylor, D. M., and Bourhis, R. (1973). 'Towards a theory of interpersonal accommodation through language: Some Canadian data'. *Language in Society* 2(2), 177–192.

Gioberti, V. (1843). *Del primato morale e civile degli italiani 1*. Brussels: Meline, Cans, et co.

Gladkova, A. (2015). 'Ethnosyntax'. In Sharifian, F. (ed.) *The Routledge handbook of language and culture*. Abingdon: Routledge, 33–50.

Gladstone, W. E. (1858). *Studies on Homer and the Homeric age*. Oxford: Oxford University Press.

Goddard, C. and Wierzbicka, A. (2013). *Words and meanings: lexical semantics across domains, languages, and cultures*. Oxford: Oxford University Press.

Goddard, Cliff. (2010). 'The natural semantic metalanguage approach'. In Heine, B. and Narrog, H. (eds.) *The Oxford handbook of linguistic analysis*. Oxford: Oxford University Press, 459–84.

Goethe, W. (1833). 'Maximen und Reflexionen'. Werke 49. Stuttgart und Tübingen: J.G. Cotta.

Gombocz, Z. [1926] (1997). *Jelentéstan és nyelvtörténet – válogatott tanulmányok*. Budapest: Akadémiai Kiadó.

Gordon, P. (2004). 'Numerical cognition without words: evidence from Amazonia'. *Science* 306, 496–9.

Gordon, S. A. (1984). *Hitler, Germans, and the 'Jewish question'*. Princeton: Princeton University Press.

Grace, G. W. (1987). *The linguistic construction of reality*. London/New York/Sydney: Croon Helm.

Graddol, D. (2003). 'The decline of the native speaker'. In Anderman, G. and Rogers, M. (eds.) *Translation today: Trends and perspectives*. Clevedon: Multilingual matters, 152–67.

Greenfeld, L. (1992). *Nationalism – five roads to modernity*. Cambridge, MA: Harvard University Press.

Greenfeld, L. (1996). 'Nationalism and modernity'. *Social Research* 63(1), 3–40.

Greenfeld, L. (2005). 'Nationalism and the mind'. *Nations and Nationalism* 11(3), 325–41.

Grégoire, H. B. (1794). *Rapport sur la nécessité et les moyens d'anéantir les patois et d'universaliser la langue française*. Available at www.quellehistoire.com/docu/rapport%20gregoire.pdf

Grice, H. P. (1975). 'Logic and conversation'. In Cole, P. and Morgan, J. L. (eds.) *Syntax and semantics – 3: Speech acts*. London: Academic Press, 41–58.

Grimm, J. (1822). *Deutsche Grammatik – 1*. 2nd edition. Göttingen: Dieterich.

Grin, F. (2010). 'Economics'. In Fishman, J. and García, O. (eds.). *Handbook of language and ethnic identity. Vol. 1: disciplinary and regional perspectives*. 2nd edition. Oxford: Oxford University Press, 70–88.

Gumperz, J. J. and Cook-Gumperz, J. (1982). 'Introduction'. In Gumperz, J. J. (ed.) *Language and social identity*. Cambridge: Cambridge University Press, 1–22.

Haas, E. B. (1986). 'Review: what is nationalism and why should we study it?'. *International Organization* 40(3), 707–44.

Hamermesh, D. S. and Biddle, J. E. (1994). 'Beauty and the labor market'. *American Economic Review* 84, 1174–94.

Handler, R. (1988). *Nationalism and the politics of culture in Quebec*. Madison WI: University of Wisconsin Press.

Hann, C. (1995). 'Intellectuals, ethnic groups, and nations: two late-twentieth-century cases'. In Periwal, S. (ed.) *Notions of nationalism*. Budapest: Central European University Press, 106–28.

Hansegård, N. E. (1968). *Tvåspråkighet eller halvspråkighet?* Stockholm: Bonniers förlag.

Harari, H. and McDavid, J. W. (1973). 'Name stereotypes and teachers' expectations'. *Journal of Educational Psychology* 65(2), 222–5.

Haraway, D. (1988). 'Situated knowledges: the science question in Feminism and the privilege of partial perspective'. *Feminist Studies* 14(3), 575–99.

Harris, R. (2006). 'History and comparative philology'. In Love, N. (ed.) *Language and history – integrationist perspectives*. London: Routledge, 41–59.

Haslanger, S. (2005). 'What are we talking about? The semantics and politics of social kinds'. *Hypatia* 20(4), 10–26.

Hastings, H. (1997). *The construction of nationhood: ethnicity, religion, and nationalism*. Cambridge: Cambridge University Press.

Haviland, J. B. (1997). 'Owners versus Bubu Gujin: land rights and getting the language right in Guugu Yimithirr country'. *Journal of Linguistic Anthropology* 6(2), 145–60.

Heilbrun, C. G. (1988). *Writing a woman's life*. New York and London: W. W. Norton & Company.

Henton, C. (1992). 'The abnormality of male speech'. In Wolf, G. (ed.) *New departures in linguistics*. New York and London: Garland Publishing, 27–58.

Herder, J. G. (1769). 'Ueber die Bildung der Völker'. In Herder, J. G. (ed.) 1840. *Herder's Lebensbild: sein chronologisch-geordneter Briefwechsel*. Band 2. Erlangen: Biasing, 478–85.

Hernandez, A. E. and Li, P. (2007). 'Age of acquisition: its neural and computational mechanisms'. *Psychological Bulletin* 133(4), 638.

Heryanto, A. (2007). 'Then there were languages: Bahasa Indonesia was one among many'. In Makoni, S. and Pennycook, A. (eds.) *Disinventing and reconstituting languages*. Clevedon: Multilingual Matters, 42–61.

Herzl, T. (1896). *Der Judenstaat. Versuch einer modernen Lösung der Judenfrage*. Berlin & Vienna: Breitenstein.

Hitler, A. (1925). *Mein Kampf*. Vol. I. Munich: Franz Eher Nachfolger GmbH.

Hobsbawm, E. J. (1992). *Nations and nationalism since 1780 – programme, myth, and reality*. 2nd edition. Cambridge: Cambridge University Press.

Hockett, C. F. (1958). *A course in modern linguistics*. New York: Macmillan.

Hoerr Charles, L. (1951). 'Drama in first-naming ceremonies'. *The Journal of American Folklore* 64(251), 11–35.

Hoffmann, C. (1991). *An Introduction to Bilingualism*. London: Longman.

Hoffman, C., Lau, I., and Johnson, D. R. (1986). 'The linguistic relativity of person cognition: an English-Chinese comparison'. *Journal of Personality and Social Psychology* 51(6), 1097–105.

Hogg, M. A. (2001). 'Social categorization, depersonalisation, and group behavior'. In Hogg, M.A. and Tindale, R. S. (eds.) *Blackwell handbook of social psychology: group processes*. Oxford: Malden (Mass): Blackwell, 56–85.

Holliday, A. (2006). 'Native-speakerism'. *ELT Journal* 60(4), 385–7.

Holt, M. (1996). 'Divided loyalties: language and ethnic identity in the Arab world'.
  In Suleiman, Y. (ed.) *Language and identity in the Middle East and North Africa*.
  Richmond: Curzon, 11–24.
Horobin, S. (2013). *Does spelling matter?* Oxford: Oxford University Press.
Hourani, A. (1980). *Europe and the middle east*. Berkeley: University of California Press.
Hroch, M. (2010). 'The Slavic world'. In Fishman, J. and Garcia, O. (eds.) *Handbook of
  language and ethnic identity. Vol. 1*. Oxford: Oxford University Press, 269–85.
Humboldt, von W. [1820] (1843). *Gesammelte Werke*. Dritter Band. Berlin: G. Reimer.
Hunley, K., Dunn, M., Lindström, E., Reesink, G., Terrill, A., Healy, M. E., Koki, G.,
  Friedlaender, F. R., and Friedlaender, J. S. (2008). 'Genetic and linguistic coevolution in
  Northern Island Melanesia'. *PLoS Genetics* 4(10), 1–14.
Huszti, I. (2009). 'Beregszászi magyar tannyelvű iskolába járó ötödikesek identitástudata
  és a nyelvtanulás közötti összefüggések'. In Karmacsi Z. and Márku A. (eds.) *Nyelv,
  identitás és anyanyelvi nevelés a XXI. században – nemzetközi tudományos konferencia
  előadásainak gyűjteménye*. Ungvár: PoliPrint, 54–63.
Hutton, C. (1992). 'Arbitrariness and rational signs'. In Wolf, G. (ed.) *New departures in
  linguistics*. New York and London: Garland Publishing, 250–9.
Hylland Eriksen, T. (2004). 'Place, kinship and the case for non-ethnic nations'. *Nations
  and Nationalism* 10(1/2), 49–62.
Hyltenstam, K. and Abrahamsson, N. (2000). 'Who can become native-like in a second
  language? All, some, or none?' *Studia Linguistica* 54(2), 150–66.
Hymes, D. (1972) 'On communicative competence'. In Pride, J. and Holmes, J. (eds.)
  Sociolinguistics. Harmondsworth: Penguin Books, 269–93.
Jackendoff, R. (1994). *Patterns in the mind*. New York: Basic Books.
Jackendoff, R. (2011). 'What is the human language faculty?: Two views'. *Language* 87(3),
  586–624.
Jespersen, O. (1912). *Growth and structure of the English language*. 2nd edition. Leipzig: B.
  G. Teubner.
Jones, W. [1786] (1807). 'The third anniversary discourse, on the Hindus'. In Lord Teignmouth
  (ed.) *The works of Sir William Jones – vol. 3*. London: Stockdale and Walker, 24–46.
Joseph, J. E. (2004). *Language and identity: national, ethnic, religious*. Basingstoke: Palgrave
  Macmillan.
Joubert, C. E. (1991). 'Relationship of liking of one's given names to self-esteem and social
  desirability'. *Psychological Reports* 69(3), 821–2.
Kalist, D. E and Lee, D. Y. (2009). 'First names and crime: does unpopularity spell
  trouble?'. *Social Science Quarterly*, 90(1), 39–49.
Kalmár, I. (1985). 'Are there really no primitive language?'. In Olson, D. R., Torrance, N.,
  and Hildyard, A. (eds.) *Literacy, language and learning: the nature and consequences of
  reading and writing*. Cambridge: Cambridge University Press, 148–66.
Kant, I. (1796). 'Zum ewigen Frieden – ein philosophischer Entwurf'. In Reimer, G. (ed.)
  (1912). *Kants gesammelte Schriften VIII*. Berlin: Königlich Preußische Akademie der
  Wissenschaften, 341–86.
Kay, P. and Kempton, W. (1984). 'What is the Sapir-Whorf hypothesis?' *American
  Anthropologist* 65–79.
Kedourie, E. (1993). *Nationalism*. 4th expanded edition. Oxford: Blackwell.
Kim, K. H., Relkin, N. R., Lee, K. M., and Hirsch, J. (1997). 'Distinct cortical areas
  associated with native and second languages'. *Nature* 388(6638), 171–4.
Kinzler, K. D., Shutts, K., and Spelke, E. S. (2012). 'Language-based social preferences
  among children in South Africa'. *Language Learning and Development* 8(3), 215–32.

Kinzler, K., Dupoux, E., and Spelke, E. (2007). 'The native language of social cognition'. *Proceedings of the National Academy of Sciences of the United States of America* 104(30), 12577–80.

Kitchin, R., Perkins, C., and Dodge, M. (2009). 'Thinking about maps'. In Dodge, M., Kitchin, R., and Perkins, C. (eds.) *Rethinking maps. New frontiers in cartographic theory*. London: Routledge, 1–25.

Klemperer, V. (1947). *LTI – Lingua Tertii Imperii: Notizbuch eines Philologen*. Berlin: Aufbau-Verlag.

Klofstad, C. A., Anderson, R. C., and Peters, S. (2012). 'Sounds like a winner: voice pitch influences perception of leadership capacity in both men and women'. *Proceedings of the Royal Society B* 279(1738), 2698–704.

Kordić, S. (2006). 'Sprache und Nationalismus in Kroatien'. In Symanzik, B. (ed.) *Studia Philologica Slavica: Festschrift für Gerhard Birkfellner zum 65. Geburtstag* Vol. 1, Berlin: LIT Verlag, 337–48.

Kortmann, B. and Szmrecsanyi, B. (2009). 'World Englishes between simplification and complexification'. In Hoffmann, T. and Siebers, L. (eds.) *World Englishes: problems, properties, and prospects*. Amsterdam: John Benjamins, 265–85.

Kosztolányi, S. [1924] (1985). *Pacsirta*. Budapest: Szépirodalmi Könyvkiadó.

Kramer, C. (1974). 'Women's speech: separate but unequal?'. *Quarterly Journal of Speech* 60(1), 14–24.

Kramsch, C. (1998). *Language and culture*. Oxford: Oxford University Press.

Kripke, S. (1980). *Naming and necessity*. Revised and enlarged edition. Oxford: Basil Blackwell.

Kroll, J. F., Dussias, P. E., Bice, K., and Perrotti, L. (2015). 'Bilingualism, mind, and brain'. *Annual Review of Linguistics* 1, 377–94.

Kulyk, V. (2011). 'Language identity, linguistic diversity and political cleavages: evidence from Ukraine'. *Nations and Nationalism* 17(3), 627–48.

Kupchan, C. A. (1995). 'Introduction: nationalism resurgent'. In Kupchan, C. A. (ed.) *Nationalism and nationalities in the new Europe*. Ithaca, NY: Cornell University Press, 1–14.

Labov, W. (1972). *Sociolinguistic patterns*. Philadelphia: University of Pennsylvania Press.

Laham, S. M., Koval, P., and Alter, A. L. (2012). 'The name-pronunciation effect: why people like Mr. Smith more than Mr. Colquhoun'. *Journal of Experimental Social Psychology* 48(3), 752–6.

Laitin, D. D. (1988). 'Language games'. *Comparative Politics* 20(3), 289–302.

Lakoff, G. and Johnson, M. (1980). *Metaphors we live by*. Chicago: University of Chicago Press.

Lakoff, R. (1973). 'Language and woman's place'. *Language in Society* 2(1), 45–80.

Lambert, W. E., Hodgson, R. C., Gardner, R. C., and Fillenbaum, S. (1960). 'Evaluational reactions to spoken languages'. *Journal of Abnormal and Social Psychology* 60(1), 44–51.

Laskowski, K. A. (2010) 'Women's post-marital mame retention and the communication of identity'. *Names – A Journal of Onomastics* 58(2), 75–89.

Lauterbach, J. Z. (1949). *Mekilta de-Rabbi Ishmael – Vol. 1*. Philadelphia, PA: The Jewish Publication Society of America.

Lave, J. (1991). 'Situating learning in communities of practice'. In Resnick, L. B., Levine, J. M., and Teasley, S. D. (eds.) *Perspectives on socially shared cognition*. Washington, DC: American Psychological Association, pp. 63–82

Lawson-Sako, S. and Sachdev, I. (1996). 'Ethnolinguistic communication in Tunisian streets: convergence and divergence'. In Suleiman, Y. (ed.) *Language and identity in the Middle East and North Africa*. Richmond: Curzon, 61–79.

Le Page, R. B. and Tabouret-Keller, A. (1985). *Acts of identity: creole-based approaches to language and ethnicity*. Cambridge: Cambridge University Press.

Lev-Ari, S. and Keysar, B. (2010). 'Why don't we believe non-native speakers? The influence of accent on credibility'. *Journal of Experimental Social Psychology* 46(10).

Leventhal, G. and Krate, R. (1977). 'Physical attractiveness and severity of sentencing'. *Psychological Reports* 40, 315–18.

Lévi-Strauss, C. (1971). 'Race et histoire'. *Revue internationale des sciences sociales*, 23(4), 647–66.

Levi, P. (1962). 'La tregua'. In Levi, P. 1997. *Opere I*. Turin: Einaudi, 202–397.

Levi, P. (1982). 'Se non ora, quando?'. In Levi, P. 1997. *Opere II*. Turin: Einaudi, 207–513.

Levin, D. T. and Banaji, M. R. (2006). 'Distortions in the perceived lightness of faces: the role of race categories'. *Journal of Experimental Psychology* 135(4), 501–12.

Levin, H., Giles, H., and Garrett, P. (1994). 'The effects of lexical formality and accent on trait attributions'. *Language & Communication*, 14(3), 265–74.

Levinson, S. C. (2003). 'Language and mind: Let's get the issues straight!'. In Gentner D. and Goldin-Meadow, S. (eds.) *Language in mind: advances in the study of language and cognition*. Cambridge, MA: MIT Press, 25–46.

Levisen, C. (2012). *Cultural semantics and social cognition: a case study on the Danish universe of meaning*. Berlin: De Gruyter Mouton.

Levitt, S. and Dubner, S. J. (2005). *Freakonomics – a rogue economist explores the hidden side of everything*. New York: William Morrow & Co.

Lewis, G. (1999). *The Turkish language reform: a catastrophic success*. Oxford: Oxford University Press.

Lewis, M. B. (1917). *Teach yourself Malay*. London: English Universities Press.

Ling, T. (1968). *A history of religion East and West – an introduction and interpretation*. London: Palgrave Macmillan.

Linnet, J. T. (2011). 'Money can't buy me hygge: Danish middle-class consumption, egalitarianism and the sanctity of inner space'. *Social Analysis* 55(2), 21–44.

Loftus, E. F. and Palmer, J. C. (1974). 'Reconstruction of automobile destruction: an example of the interaction between language and memory'. *Journal of Verbal Learning and Verbal Behavior* 13(5), 585–9.

Lucy, J. A. (1997). 'The linguistics of "color"'. In Hardin, C. L. and Maffi.L. (eds.) *Color categories in thought and language*. Cambridge: Cambridge University Press.

Lupyan, G. (2006). 'Labels facilitate learning of novel categories'. In Cangelosi, A., Smith, A. D. M., and Smith, K. (eds.) *The evolution of language – Proceedings of the 6th International Conference on the Evolution of Language*. Singapore: World Scientific, 190–7.

Lyons, J. (1968). *Introduction to theoretical linguistics*. Cambridge: Cambridge University Press.

Mackey, W.F. (1962) 'The description of bilingualism'. *Canadian Journal of Linguistics* 7, 51–85.

Mackridge, P. (1985). *The Modern Greek language: a descriptive analysis of standard Modern Greek*. Oxford: Oxford University Press.

Magun, V., Rudnev, M., and Schmidt, P. (2016). 'Within- and between-country value diversity in Europe: a typological approach'. *European Sociological Review* 32, 189–202.

Mahmood Arai, M. and Skogman Thoursie, P. (2009). 'Renouncing personal names: an empirical examination of surname change and earnings'. *Journal of Labor Economics* 27(1), 127–47.

Majid, A. (2002). 'Frames of reference and language concepts'. *Trends in Cognitive Sciences* 6(12), 503–4.

Malt, B. C., Sloman, S. A., Gennari, S., Shi, M., and Wang, Y. (1999). 'Knowing versus naming: similarity and the linguistic categorization of artifacts'. *Journal of Memory and Language* 40, 230–62.

Marx, A. W. (2003). *Faith in nation: exclusionary origins of nationalism*. Oxford: Oxford University Press.

Marx, N. (2002). 'Never quite a "native speaker": accent and identity in the L2 and the L1'. *Canadian Modern Language Review* 59(2), 264–81.

Matthew, A. (1869). *Culture and anarchy – an essay in political and social criticism*. London: Smith, Elder, and Co.

Maupassant, G. de (1884). *Au soleil*. Paris: Victor. Havard.

Mazzini, G. (1860). *Doveri dell'uomo*. London [s.n.].

McEnery, T. 2006. *Swearing in English – bad language, purity and power from 1586 to the present*. London: Routledge.

Mechelli, A., Crinion, J. T., Noppeney, U., O'Doherty, J., Ashburner, J., Frackowiak, R. S., Price, C. J. (2004). 'Neurolinguistics: structural plasticity in the bilingual brain'. *Nature* 431, 757.

Medgyes, P. (1992). 'Native or non-native: who's worth more?'. *ELT Journal* 46(4), 340–9.

Medgyes, P. (2001). 'When the teacher is a non-native speaker'. *Teaching English as a Second or Foreign Language* 3, 429–42.

Meillet, A. (1918). *Les langues dans l'Europe nouvelle*. Paris: Payot.

Mikes, G. [1946] (1952). *How to be an alien – a book for beginners and more advanced pupils*. London: Wingate.

Mill, J. S. (1843). *A system of logic, ratiocinative and inductive: being a connected view of the principles of evidence, and the methods of scientific investigation*. London: John W. Parker.

Miller, D. (1995). *On nationality*. Oxford: Clarendon Press.

Milroy, J. and Milroy, L. (2012). *Authority in language – investigating standard English*. London: Taylor & Francis.

Minogue, K. R. (1967). *Nationalism*. London: Methuen.

Mizel, O. (2016). 'The language of musāyara in Arab-Moslem culture'. *Journal of Modern Education Review* 6(4), 271–8.

Moerk, E. L. (1970). 'Quantitative analysis of writing styles's'. *Journal of Linguistics* 6(2), 223–30.

Momma, H. (1999). 'A man on the cusp: Sir William Jones's "Philology" and "Oriental Studies"'. *Texas Studies in Literature and Language*, 41(2), 160–79.

Mosse, G. L. (1985). *German Jews beyond Judaism*. Cincinnati: Hebrew Union College Press/Bloomington: Indiana University Press.

Mühlhäusler, P. (1982). 'Language and communicational efficiency: the case of Tok Pisin'. *Language & Communication* 2(2), 105–21.

Mühlmann, W. E. (1985). 'Ethnogonie und Ethnogenese. Theoretisch-ethnologische und ideokritische Studie'. *Studien zur Ethnogenese*. Opladen: Westdeutscher Verlag, 9–27.

Müller, H. (2003). *Der König verneigt sich und tötet*. München: Hanser.

Myers-Scotton, C. (2006). *Multiple voices – an introduction to bilingualism*. Malden, MA: Blackwells.

Namier, L. B. (1944). *1848: the revolution of the intellectuals*. London: Geoffrey Cumberlege.

Namlagen (1982), at https://www.riksdagen.se/sv/dokument-lagar/dokument/svensk-forfattningssamling/namnlag-1982670_sfs-1982-670

Nebrija De, A. (1492). *Gramática castellana*. Salamanca [s.n.].

Needham, R. (1954). 'The system of teknonyms and death-names of the Penan'. *Southwestern Journal of Anthropology* 10(4), 416–31.

Nettle, D. (2012). 'Social scale and structural complexity in human languages'. *Philosophical Transactions of the Royal Society B: Biological Sciences*, 367(1597), 1829–36.

Newman, E. J., Sanson, M., Miller, E. K., Quigley-mcbride, A., Foster, J. L., Bernstein, D. M., and Garry, M. (2014). 'People with easier to pronounce names promote truthiness of claims'. *PloS One* 9(2), e88671.

Nichols, J. (2009). 'Linguistic complexity: a comprehensive definition and survey'. In Sampson, G., Gil, D., and Trudgill, P. (eds.) *Language complexity as an evolving variable*. Oxford: Oxford University Press, 110–125.

Nieto, D. (2009). 'A brief history of bilingual education in the United States'. *Perspectives on Urban Education* 6(1), 61–72.

Nietzsche, F. (1930). *Der Wille zur Macht – Versuch einer Umwertung aller Werte*. Leipzig: Alfred Kröner.

Nimilaki/Namnlag (1991). The Finnish version is at https://finlex.fi/fi/laki/ajantasa/kumotut/1985/19850694. The Swedish version is at https://www.finlex.fi/sv/laki/ajantasa/kumotut/1985/19850694

Nisbett, R. E. and Wilson, T. D. (1977). 'Telling more than we can know: verbal reports on mental processes'. *Psychological Review* 84, 231–59.

Norton, B. (1997). 'Language, identity, and the ownership of English'. *TESOL Quarterly* 31(3), 409–29.

Ogunnaike, O., Dunham, Y., and Banaji, M. R. (2010). 'The language of implicit preferences'. *Journal of Experimental Social Psychology* 46(6), 999–1003.

Opeibi, T. O. (2012). 'Investigating the language situation in Africa'. In Tiersma, P.M. and Solan, L. (eds.) *The Oxford handbook of language and law*. Oxford: Oxford University Press, 272–85.

Osgood, C. E. and Sebeok, T. A. (1954). *Psycholinguistics: a survey of theory and research problems*. Baltimore: Waverly Press.

Östling, J. (2008). *Nazismens sensmoral – Svenska erfarenheter i andra världskrigets efterdyning*. Stockholm: Atlantis.

Padilla, A. M. and Borsato, G. N. (2010). 'Psychology'. In Fishman, J. and Garcia, O. (eds.) *Handbook of language and ethnic identity. Vol. 1: disciplinary and regional perspectives*. 2nd edition. Oxford: Oxford University Press, 5–17.

Paikeday, T. (1985). *The native speaker is dead!* Toronto: Paikeday Publishing Inc.

Palmer, L. R. (1954). *The Latin language*. London: Faber and Faber.

Pao, D. L., Wong, S. D., and Teuben-Rowe, S. (1997). 'Identity formation for mixed-heritage adults and implications for educators'. *Tesol Quarterly* 31(3), 622–31.

Parfit, D. (1987). 'Divided minds and the nature of persons'. In Blakemore, C., and Greenfield, S. (eds.) *Mindwaves: thoughts on intelligence, identity and consciousness*. Oxford: Blackwell, p. 19–28.

Parker, D. (2004). 'Global English, culture and western modernity'. In Tam, K. and T. Weiss, T. (eds.) *English and globalization: perspectives from Hong Kong and mainland China*. Hong Kong: The Chinese University Press, 23–42.

Parker, R. (2001). 'Greek religion'. In J. Boardman, J. Griffin, and O. Murray (eds.) *The Oxford history of Greece and the Hellenistic world*. Oxford: Oxford University Press, 306–29.

Pavlenko, A. (2002). 'Language and national identity in the US at the turn of the 20th century'. *Multilingua* 21, 163–96.

Pavlenko, A. (2014). *The bilingual mind – and what it tells us about language and thought.* Cambridge: Cambridge University Press.

Pennebaker, J. W. and King, L. A. (1999). 'Linguistic styles: language use as an individual difference'. *Journal of Personality and Social Psychology,* 77(6), 1296–312.

Perani, D., Dehaene, S., Grassi, F., Cohen, L., Cappa, S.F., Dupoux, E., Fazio, F., and Mehler, J., (1996). 'Brain processing of native and foreign languages'. *NeuroReport-International Journal for Rapid Communications of Research in Neuroscience* 7(15), 2439–44.

Phillipson, R. (2003). *English-only Europe? Challenging language policy.* London and New York: Routledge.

Piaget, J. [1947] (1926). *La représentation du monde chez l'enfant.* Paris: Presses Universitaires de France.

Piller, I. (2002). 'Passing for a native speaker: identity and success in second language learning'. *Journal of Sociolinguistics* 6(2), 179–206.

Pinker, S. (1994). *The language instinct – how the mind creates language.* New York: W. Morrow and Co.

Poloni, E. S., Semino, O., Passarino, G., Santachiara-Benerecetti, A. S., Dupanloup, I., Langaney, A., and Excoffier, L. (1997). 'Human genetic affinities for Y-chromosome P49a,f/*Taq*I haplotypes show strong correspondence with linguistics'. *The American Journal of Human Genetics* 61(5), 1015–35.

Poole, J. (1969). 'National development and language diversity'. *La monda lingvo-problemo* 1(3), 140–56.

Pound, E. (1931). *How to read.* London: D. Harmsworth.

Pratt Fairchild, H. (1926). *The melting-pot mistake.* Boston: Little, Brown, and Company.

Psycharis > Ψυχάρης, Γ. [1888] (1971). *Τὸ ταξίδι μου.* Αθήνα· Ερμής.

Purnell, T., Idsardi, W., and Baugh, J. (1999). 'Perceptual and phonetic experiments on American English dialect identification'. *Journal of Language and Social Psychology,* 18(1), 10–30.

Racine, J. (1661). 'Lettre VIII a m. de la Fontaine, 11 novembre 1661'. In Racine, J. (ed.) 1810. *Œuvres* 4. Paris: Le Normant, 70–4.

Ramat, P. (2009). 'Uno sguardo d'insieme'. In Cotticelli Kurras, P. and Graffi, G. (eds.) *Lingue, ethnos e popolazioni: evidenze linguistiche, biologiche e culturali.* Rome: Il Calamo, 11–31.

Riach, P. A. and Rich, J. (2002). 'Field experiments of discrimination in the market place'. *The Economic Journal* 122, F480–518.

Rich, A. (1977). 'Conditions for work: the common world of women'. *Heresies* 3, 53–4.

Roberson, D. (2005). 'Color categories are culturally diverse in cognition as well as in language'. *Cross-Cultural Research* 39(1), 56–71.

Roberson, D. and Hanley, J. R. (2007). 'Color categories vary with language after all'. *Current Biology* 17(15), 605–6.

Roberson, D., Davidoff, J., Davies, I. R., and Shapiro, L. R. (2006). 'Colour categories and category acquisition in Himba and English'. In Pitchford, N. and Biggam, C. P. (eds.) *Progress in colour studies 2 – psychological aspects,* 159–72.

Rodenburg, P. 2002. *The actor speaks.* Basingstoke: Palgrave Macmillan.

Romaine, S. (2000). *Language in society: an introduction to sociolinguistics.* Oxford: Oxford University Press.

Ross, M., Xun, W. Q. E., and Wilson, A. E. (2002). 'Language and the bicultural self'. *Personality and Social Psychology Bulletin* 28, 1040–50.

Rottenberg, D. (1977). *Finding our fathers: a guidebook to Jewish genealogy.* New York: Random House.

Roudometof, V. (2002). *Collective memory, national identity, and ethnic conflict: Greece, Bulgaria, and the Macedonian question.* Westport/London: Praeger.

Rousseau, J.-J. (1782). 'Considérations sur le gouvernement de Pologne'. In Rousseau, J.-J. (ed.) *Collection complète des œuvres de J. J. Rousseau 1.* [s.n.], 415–540.

Rowe, D. (1991). *The depression handbook.* London: Collins.

Russell, B. [1928] (2004). 'On the value of Skepticism'. In *Sceptical essays.* London: Routledge, 1–13.

Rutten, G. (2019). *Language Planning as Nation Building Ideology, policy and implementation in the Netherlands,* 1750–1850. Amsterdam/Philadelphia: John Benjamins.

Saïd, E. (1979). *Orientalism.* New York: Vintage.

Sajantila, A., Lahermo, P., Anttinen, T., Lukka, M., Sistonen, P., Savontaus, M.L., Aula, P., Beckman, L., Tranebjaerg, L., Gedde-Dahl, T. and Issel-Tarver, L., DiRienzo, A., Pääbo, S. (1995). 'Genes and languages in Europe: an analysis of mitochondrial lineages'. *Genome Research* 5(1), 42–52.

Salvi, S. (1975). *Le lingue tagliate – Storia delle minoranze linguistiche in Italia.* Milan: Rizzoli.

Sampson, G. (2009) 'A linguistic axiom challenged'. In Sampson, G., Gil, D., and Trudgill, P. (eds.) *Language complexity as an evolving variable.* Oxford: Oxford University Press, 1–18.

Sapir, E. (1921). *Language: an introduction to the study of speech.* New York: Harcourt, Brace and Company.

Sapir, E. (1929). 'The status of linguistics as a science'. *Language* 5(4), 207–14.

Schleicher, A. (1865). *Über die Bedeutung der Sprache für die Naturgeschichte des Menschen.* Weimar: Böhlau.

Schooler, J. W. and Engstler-Schooler, T. Y. (1990). 'Verbal overshadowing of visual memories: some things are better left unsaid'. *Cognitive Psychology* 22, 36–71.

Schopenhauer, A. (1851). *Parerga und Paralipomena – kleine philosophische Schriften II.* Berlin: A. W. Hayn.

Schroeder, S. R. and Marian, V. (2012). 'A bilingual advantage for episodic memory in older adults'. *Journal of Cognitive Psychology* 24(5), 591–601.

Searles, E. (2008). 'Inuit identity in the Canadian Arctic'. *Ethnology* 47(4), 239–55.

Seton-Watson, H. (1988). 'On trying to be a historian of Eastern Europe'. In Deletant, D. and Hanak, H. (eds.) *Historians as nation-builders – Central and South-East Europe.* London: MacMillan, 1–14.

Sharifian, F. (2017). *Cultural linguistics: cultural conceptualisations and language.* Amsterdam/Philadelphia: John Benjamins.

Shaw, B. (1916). *Androcles and the lion – Overruled – Pygmalion.* London: Constable and Company Ldt.

Silverstein, M. (2003). 'The whens and wheres—as well as hows—of ethnolinguistic recognition'. *Public Culture* 15(3), 531–57.

Simpson, A. (ed.) (2007). 'Language and national identity in Asia: a thematic introduction'. In *Language and national identity in Asia.* Oxford: Oxford University Press, 1–30.

Slater, A. S., and Feinman, S. (1985). 'Gender and the phonology of north American first names'. *Sex Roles* 13(7–8), 429–40.

Slobin, D. I. (1996). 'From "thought and language" to "thinking for speaking"'. In J. Gumperz and S. Levinson (eds.) *Rethinking linguistic relativity.* Cambridge: Cambridge University Press, 70–96.

Slobin, D. I. (1977). 'Language change in childhood and in history'. In Macnamara, J. (ed.) *Language learning and thought.* New York: Academic Press, 185–214.

Smith, A. D. (1976). 'Introduction: the formation of nationalist movements'. In *Nationalist movements*. London: Macmillan, 1–30.

Smith, A. D. (1998). *Nationalism and modernism: a critical survey of recent theories of nations*. London: Routledge.

Song, H. and Schwarz, N. (2009). 'If it's difficult to pronounce, it must be risky – fluency, familiarity, and risk perception'. *Psychological Science* 20(2), 135–8.

Spark, M. (1961). *The prime of Miss Jean Brodie*. London: MacMillan.

Spolsky, B. (1996). 'Hebrew and Israeli identity'. In Suleiman, Y. (ed.) *Language and identity in the Middle East and North Africa*. Richmond: Curzon, 181–92.

Spolsky, B. (2009). *Language management*. Cambridge: Cambridge University Press.

Stapleton, K. (2010). 'Swearing'. In Locher, M. A., Sage, L. G. (eds.) *Interpersonal pragmatics*. Berlin/New York: Mouton De Gruyter, 289–306.

Stati, V. (2003). *Dicţionar Moldovenesc – Românesc*. Chişinău: Tipografia Centrală.

Steiner, G. (1975). *After Babel – aspects of language and translation*. Oxford: Oxford University Press.

Strunk, O. (1958). 'Attitudes toward one's name and one's self'. *Journal of Individual Psychology* 14, 64–7.

Sussman, N. M. and Rosenfeld, H. M. (1982). 'Influence of culture, language, and sex on conversational distance'. *Journal of Personality and Social Psychology*, 42, 66–74.

Suzuki, N., Takeuchi, Y., Ishii, K., and Okada, M. (2003). 'Effects of echoic mimicry using hummed sounds on human–computer interaction'. *Speech Communication* 40(4), 559–73.

Taylor, A. R. (1982). '"Male" and "female" speech in Gros Ventre'. *Anthropological Linguistics* 24(3), 301–7.

Templeton, A. R. (2001). 'The genetic and evolutionary significance or human races'. In Fish, J. M. (ed.) *Race and intelligence: separating science from myth*. Mahwah, NJ/London: Erlbaum, 31–56.

Thierry, G., Athanasopoulos, P., Wiggett, A., Dering, B., and Kuipers, J. (2009). 'Unconscious effects of language-specific terminology on preattentive color perception'. *Proceedings of the National Academy of Science of the United States of America* 106(11), 4567–70.

Thomas, A. (2003). 'Forging Czechs – the reinvention of national identity in the Bohemian lands'. In Ryan, J. and Thomas, A. (eds.) *Cultures of forgery: Making nations, making selves*. New York: Routledge, 29–51.

Thomas, G. (1991). *Linguistic purism*. London & New York: Longman.

Tosun, S., Vaid, J., and Geraci, L. (2013). 'Does obligatory linguistic marking of source of evidence affect source memory? A Turkish/English investigation'. *Journal of Memory and Language* 69, 121–34.

Trudgill, P. (1972). 'Sex, covert prestige and linguistic change in the urban British English of Norwich'. *Language in Society* 1(2),179–95.

Trudgill, P. (1974). *The social differentiation of English in Norwich*. New York, NY: Cambridge University Press.

Trudgill, P. (2004). 'Glocalisation and the Ausbau sociolinguistics of modern Europe'. In Duszak, A. and Okulska, U. (eds.) *Speaking from the margin: global English from a European perspective*. Frankfurt: Peter Lang, 35–49.

Trudgill. P. (2009). 'Sociolinguistic typology and complexification'. In Sampson, G., Gil, D., and Trudgill, P. (eds.) *Language complexity as an evolving variable*. Oxford: Oxford University Press, 97–108.

Twain, M. (1880). 'The awful German language'. In *A tramp abroad - vol II*. London: Chatto and Windus, 262–87.

Vandermeeren, S. (1996). 'Language attitudes on either side of the linguistic frontier: a sociolinguistic survey in the Voeren/Fouron area and in Old Belgium north'. In Hellinger, M., and Ammon, U. (eds.) *Contrastive sociolinguistics*. Berlin/New York: Mouton De Gruyter.

Vignoles, V. L., Smith, P. B., Becker, M., and Easterbrook, M. J. (2018). 'In search of a pan-European culture: European values, beliefs, and models of selfhood in global perspective'. *Journal of Cross-Cultural Psychology* 49(6), 868–7.

Vikør, L. S. (2000). 'Northern Europe: languages as prime markers of ethnic and national identity'. In Barbour, S. and Carmichael, C. (eds.) *Language and nationalism in Europe*. Oxford: Oxford University Press, 104–29.

Vincent, A. (1997). 'Liberal nationalism: an irresponsible compound?'. *Political Studies* 45, 275–95.

Vingerhoets, A. J., Bylsma, L. M., and De Vlam, C. (2013). 'Swearing: a biopsychosocial perspective'. *Psihologijske teme* 22(2), 287–304.

Voltaire, F. M. A. de (1767). *L'ingénu - histoire veritable*. Geneva [s.n.].

Walton, G. M. and Banaji, M. (2004). 'Being what you say: the effect of essentialist linguistic labels on preferences'. *Social Cognition* 22(2), 193–213.

Waters, M. C. (1990). *Ethnic options: choosing identities in America*. Berkeley: University of California Press.

Weber, E. (1976). *Peasants into Frenchmen: the modernization of rural France 1870–1914*. Stanford: Stanford University Press.

Weber, M. (1922). *Grundriss der Sozialökonomik - III Abteilung: Wirtschaft und Gesellschaft*. Tübingen: J.C.B. Mohr.

Wells, J. C. (1982). *Accents of English - 1: an introduction*. Cambridge: Cambridge University Press.

Wexler, P. (1990). *The schizoid nature of modern Hebrew: a Slavic language in search of a Semitic past*. Wiesbaden: Otto Harrassowitz.

Whorf, B. L. (1940). 'Science and Linguistics'. Reprinted in Carroll, J. B. (ed.) 1956. *Language, thought, and reality: selected writings of Benjamin Lee Whorf*. Cambridge, MA: MIT Press, 207–19.

Wierzbicka, A. (2004). ' "Happiness" in cross-linguistic & cross-cultural perspective'. *Daedalus* 133(2), 34–43.

Wierzbicka, A. (2005). 'There are no "color universals" but there are universals of visual semantics'. *Anthropological Linguistics* 47(2), 217–44.

Wierzbicka, A. (2006). *English - meaning and culture*. Oxford: Oxford University Press.

Wilde, O. (1890). 'The picture of Dorian Gray'. In *Lippincott's monthly magazine*. London: Ward Lock & co./1891: 29 London: Simpkin, Marshall, Hamilton, Kent, & Co.

Wiley, T. G. (2001). 'Policy formation and implementation'. In Peyton, J. K., Ranard, D. A, McGinnis, S. (eds.) *Heritage languages in America: preserving a national resource*. McHenry IL, Delta Systems, 99–108.

Wiley, T. G. (2010). 'The United States'. In Fishman, J. and Garcia, O. (eds.) *Handbook of language and ethnic identity. Vol. 1*. Oxford: Oxford University Press, 302–22.

Winawer, J. Witthoft, N., Frank, M.C., Wu, L., Wade, A. R., and Lera Boroditsky, L. (2007). 'Russian blues reveal effects of language on color discrimination'. *Proceedings of the National Academy of Sciences of the United States of America* 104(19), 7780–5.

Wurm, S.A. (1987). 'Change of languages as a result of decay and change of culture'. *Diogenes* 35, 39–51.

Xenidou-Dervou, I., Gilmore, C., van der Schoot, M., and van Lieshout, E. C. (2015). 'The developmental onset of symbolic approximation: beyond nonsymbolic representations, the language of numbers matters'. *Frontiers in Psychology* 6, 487.

Xu, F. (2002). 'The role of language in acquiring object kind concepts in infancy'. *Cognition* 85, 223–50.

Yacine, K. (1994). *Le poète comme un boxeur – Entretiens 1958–1989*. Paris: Éditions du Seuil.

Yzerbyt, V. and Rocher, S. (2002). 'Subjective essentialism and the emergence of stereotypes'. In McGarthy, C., Yzerbyt, V. Y., and Spears, R. (eds.) *Stereotypes as explanations – the formation of meaningful beliefs about social groups*. Cambridge: Cambridge University Press, 38–66.

Zajonc, R. B. (1968). 'Attitudinal effects of mere exposure'. *Journal of Personality and Social Psychology* 9 (2, 2), 1–27.

Zuckermann, G. (2003). *Language contact and lexical enrichment in Israeli Hebrew*. New York: Palgrave Macmillan.

Zuckermann, G. (2008) < עם עובד :תל אביב. ישראלית שפה יפה .ג ,צוקרמן

Index

Printed in the USA
CPSIA information can be obtained
at www.ICGtesting.com
LVHW020159131023
761007LV00008B/230